Practical Methods of Financial Engineering and Risk Management

The Stevens Series in Quantitative Finance

George Calhoun & Khaldoun Khashanah, Series Editors

Practical Methods of Financial Engineering and Risk Management

Tools for Modern Financial Professionals

Rupak Chatterjee

Apress®

Practical Methods of Financial Engineering and Risk Management: Tools for Modern Financial Professionals

Copyright © 2014 by Rupak Chatterjee

This work is subject to copyright. All rights are reserved by the Publisher, whether the whole or part of the material is concerned, specifically the rights of translation, reprinting, reuse of illustrations, recitation, broadcasting, reproduction on microfilms or in any other physical way, and transmission or information storage and retrieval, electronic adaptation, computer software, or by similar or dissimilar methodology now known or hereafter developed. Exempted from this legal reservation are brief excerpts in connection with reviews or scholarly analysis or material supplied specifically for the purpose of being entered and executed on a computer system, for exclusive use by the purchaser of the work. Duplication of this publication or parts thereof is permitted only under the provisions of the Copyright Law of the Publisher's location, in its current version, and permission for use must always be obtained from Springer. Permissions for use may be obtained through RightsLink at the Copyright Clearance Center. Violations are liable to prosecution under the respective Copyright Law.

ISBN-13 (pbk): 978-1-4302-6133-9

ISBN-13 (electronic): 978-1-4302-6134-6

Bloomberg screens are used with permission of Bloomberg L.P. Copyright© 2014.

Trademarked names, logos, and images may appear in this book. Rather than use a trademark symbol with every occurrence of a trademarked name, logo, or image we use the names, logos, and images only in an editorial fashion and to the benefit of the trademark owner, with no intention of infringement of the trademark.

The use in this publication of trade names, trademarks, service marks, and similar terms, even if they are not identified as such, is not to be taken as an expression of opinion as to whether or not they are subject to proprietary rights.

While the advice and information in this book are believed to be true and accurate at the date of publication, neither the authors nor the editors nor the publisher can accept any legal responsibility for any errors or omissions that may be made. The publisher makes no warranty, express or implied, with respect to the material contained herein.

Publisher: Heinz Weinheimer
Acquisitions Editor: Robert Hutchinson
Technical Reviewer: Neville O'Reilly
Editorial Board: Steve Anglin, Mark Beckner, Ewan Buckingham, Gary Cornell, Louise Corrigan, James DeWolf, Jonathan Gennick, Robert Hutchinson, Michelle Lowman, James Markham, Matthew Moodie, Jeff Olson, Jeffrey Pepper, Douglas Pundick, Ben Renow-Clarke, Dominic Shakeshaft, Gwenan Spearing, Matt Wade, Steve Weiss
Coordinating Editor: Rita Fernando
Copy Editor: Laura Poole
Compositor: SPi Global
Indexer: SPi Global
Cover Designer: Anna Ishchenko

Distributed to the book trade worldwide by Springer Science+Business Media New York, 233 Spring Street, 6th Floor, New York, NY 10013. Phone 1-800-SPRINGER, fax (201) 348-4505, e-mail orders-ny@springer-sbm.com, or visit www.springeronline.com. Apress Media, LLC is a California LLC and the sole member (owner) is Springer Science + Business Media Finance Inc (SSBM Finance Inc). SSBM Finance Inc is a **Delaware** corporation.

For information on translations, please e-mail rights@apress.com, or visit www.apress.com.

Apress and friends of ED books may be purchased in bulk for academic, corporate, or promotional use. eBook versions and licenses are also available for most titles. For more information, reference our Special Bulk Sales–eBook Licensing web page at www.apress.com/bulk-sales.

Any source code or other supplementary material referenced by the author in this text is available to readers at www.apress.com. For detailed information about how to locate your book's source code, go to www.apress.com/source-code/.

To my parents with love and gratitude

Contents at a Glance

Series Editors' Foreword xix

About the Author xxi

About the Technical Reviewer xxiii

Acknowledgments xxv

Introduction xxvii

■Chapter 1: Financial Instruments 1

■Chapter 2: Building a Yield Curve 53

■Chapter 3: Statistical Analysis of Financial Data 65

■Chapter 4: Stochastic Processes 143

■Chapter 5: Optimal Hedging Monte Carlo Methods 195

■Chapter 6: Introduction to Credit Derivatives 237

■Chapter 7: Risk Types, CVA, Basel III, and OIS Discounting 283

■Chapter 8: Power Laws and Extreme Value Theory 315

■Chapter 9: Hedge Fund Replication 333

Index 349

Contents

Series Editors' Foreword xix

About the Author xxi

About the Technical Reviewer xxiii

Acknowledgments xxv

Introduction xxvii

■Chapter 1: Financial Instruments 1

Bloomberg Market Data Screens 3

Cash Instruments 6

    Fed Funds 6

    Eurodollar Deposits 7

    US Treasury Bills, Notes, and Bonds 7

    Repo and Reverse Repo 9

    Equity Indices 10

    Commercial Paper 13

    LIBOR 14

    Spot Forex 14

    Key Rates 15

    Gold 16

Futures and Swaps 17

    Crude Oil 18

    Fed Funds Futures 19

    90-Day Eurodollar Futures 20

ix

10-Year Treasury Note Futures 21
Swaps 23
Swap Valuation 24
Swap Spreads 26
Swap Futures 27

Derivatives and Structured Products 29
Dynamic Hedging and Replication 36
Implied Volatility 38
Caps and Floors 39
Market Implied Volatility Quotes for Caps and Floors 40
Swaptions 43
Mortgage-Backed Securities 47

Appendix: Daycount Conventions 49
Problems 50
Further Reading 52

Chapter 2: Building a Yield Curve 53
Overview of Yield Curve Construction 54
Cash LIBOR Rates 55
90D Eurodollar Futures 56
Swaps 58
Generic Discount Factors 60
Problems 61
Problem 2.1: Build a Simple Yield Curve 61
Further Reading 63

Chapter 3: Statistical Analysis of Financial Data 65

Tools in Probability Theory 65
Moments of a Distribution 72

Creating Random Variables and Distributions 77
The Inverse Transform Method 77
Creating a Density Function: Histograms and Frequencies 79
Mixture of Gaussians: Creating a Distribution with High Kurtosis 84
Skew Normal Distribution: Creating a Distribution with Skewness 90

Calibrating Distributions through Moment Matching 92
Calibrating a Mixed Gaussian Distribution to Equity Returns 92
Calibrating a Generalized Student's-t Distribution to Equity Returns 95
Calibrating a Beta Distribution to Recovery Rates of Defaulted Bonds ... 98

Basic Risk Measures 101
Calculating VaR and CVaR from Financial Return Data 104

The Term Structure of Statistics 106
The Term Structure of the Mean 106
The Term Structure of Skew 107
The Term Structure of Kurtosis 108
The Term Structure of Volatility 110
The Term Structure of "Up" Volatility 110
The Term Structure of "Down" Volatility 110
Autocorrelation 112

Dynamic Portfolio Allocation 114
Modern Portfolio Theory 114
Generic Rules to Dynamic Portfolio Allocation with Volatility Targets ... 119

Appendix. Joint Distributions and Correlation 126
Joint Distribution Function 126
Joint Density Function 126
Marginal Distribution Function 127

Independence 128

Covariance and Correlation 129

Cauchy-Schwarz Inequality 129

Conditional Distribution and Density Functions 131

Conditional Expectation 132

Convolution 133

Problems 134

Problem 3-1. Create a Gaussian Random Number Generator in Excel 134

Problem 3-2. Create a Mixture of Gaussians in Excel 134

Problem 3-3. Calibrate S&P 500 Returns to a Mixed Normal in Excel 135

Problem 3-4. Calibrate SX5E Returns to a Student's-t distribution in Excel 136

Problem 3-5. Create a Skew Normal Distribution in Excel 137

Problem 3-6. VaR and CVaR 138

Problem 3-7. Term Structure of Statistics 139

References 141

Chapter 4: Stochastic Processes 143

Stochastic Calculus 143

Wiener Stochastic Process 145

Quadratic Variation 147

Stochastic Integrals 148

Geometric Brownian Motion and Monte Carlo Simulations 155

Creating Random Stock Paths in Excel 159

GARCH Process for Stock Returns 163

GARCH(1,1) 163

The GARCH(1,1) Model for the "Traditional" Term Structure of Volatility 169

Statistical Modeling of Trading Strategies 170

Pairs Trading 172

Models for Residuals: Mean Reverting Ornstein-Uhlenbeck Process 174

Equilibrium Statistics 175

ETF Factor-Neutral Calibration and Trading Strategy 175
Including the Drift Term 178
Hints for Constructing Market-Neutral Portfolios 179
The Rolling NAV Equation 180

Appendix A. Black-Scholes with Holes 186

Appendix B. Moment Matching and Binomial Trees 188

Problems 192

Problem 4-1. Create a Brownian Motion Process for Stock Returns Using Monte Carlo Simulations in Excel 192

Problem 4-2. Ito's Lemma 193

Problem 4-3. Calibrate a GARCH(1,1) Process for SX5E 193

Problem 4-4. Create a GARCH(1,1) Simulator in Excel 193

Problem 4-5. Volume Adjustment for Pairs Trading for MCD versus XLY 194

References 194

■ Chapter 5: Optimal Hedging Monte Carlo Methods 195

Dynamic Hedging and Replication 196

Wealth Change Equations: Spot, Forwards, and Options 199

Forward Contracts 200

European Options 203

The OHMC Optimization Problem and Solution Methodology 204

The OHMC Optimization Problem 205

The OHMC Technique 206

Basis Function Expansions and the Lagrange Multiplier Technique 207

Risk Capital 214

OHMC Examples 215

Hedge Fund Index: GARCH Calibration to Daily Returns 215

Option Pricing: Hedge Fund Index: 1.20Yr 110% Strike Call, 2 Day Liquidity 216

Option Pricing: Hedge Fund Index: 1.20Yr 99% Strike Put, 2 Day Liquidity 220

Dynamic Portfolio Allocation Index: GARCH Calibration to Daily Returns.... 222

Option Pricing: Dynamic Portfolio Allocation: 2.00Yr 110% Strike Call, 5 Day Liquidity 223

Option Pricing: Dynamic Portfolio Allocation: 2.00Yr 95% Strike Put, 5 Day Liquidity 225

Hedge Fund Index: GARCH Calibration to Monthly Returns 227

Option Pricing: Hedge Fund Index: 3.00Yr 100% Strike Put, 3-Month Liquidity 228

Option Pricing: Hedge Fund Index: 3.00-Yr 110% Strike Call, 3-Month Liquidity 230

Cliquet Contracts 232

Knockout Cliquet Sellers Wealth Change Equation 233

Problems 235

Problem 5-1. *Linear Basis Function Expansion* 235

Problem 5-2. *Hermite Cubic Basis Function Expansion* 235

Problem 5-3. *One-Time-Step OHMC Problem* 236

References and Further Reading 236

Chapter 6: Introduction to Credit Derivatives 237

The CDS Contract: Overview 238

The CDS Contract: Pricing 242

Intensity-Based Reduced-Form Default Models 245

Bootstrapping a Survival Curve with Piecewise Constant Hazard Rates 247

Credit Triangle 249

Quotation Conventions for Standard Contracts 250

Par Asset Swaps 252

Collateralization 255

CDO^2 257

Standard CDS Indices and Tranches 258

Correlation and Copulas 260

Density Method 260

Variable Method 261

    Factor Models 262

    Copulas 263

    Large Homogeneous Portfolio Approximation 264

    One-Factor Gaussian Model 266

    Implied Compound and Base Correlations 270

Stochastic Hazard Rates 271

    Case 1: Risky Zero Coupon Discount Bond $B(t)$ Maturing at T with No Recovery 273

    Case 2: Continuous Coupon Payment C_t until Default 273

    Case 3: Recovery Payment R_t at Default 273

OHMC and the Static Hedging of a Risky Bond with a CDS 274

OHMC and CDS Swaptions 276

Appendix. Bloomberg Functionality 279

Problems 279

    Problem 6-1. Calculate Hazard Rates from Par CDS Spreads 279

    Problem 6-2. Standard Convention Upfront Payment 280

    Problem 6-3. Generating Correlated Bivariate Normal Variables 280

References 280

Chapter 7: Risk Types, CVA, Basel III, and OIS Discounting 283

Risk Types 283

    Market Risk 283

    Credit Risk 284

    Operational Risk 284

    Liquidity Risk 285

    Systemic Risk 285

Coherent Risk Measures 286

Regulation and Its Effects 287

Accounting Credit Valuation Adjustment (CVA) 288

    Wrong-Way Risk 291

CONTENTS

Basel I 292

Basel II 294

    CCR RWA 295

    Market Risk RWA 297

    Operational Risk RWA 298

Basel III 300

    Capital Requirements under Basel III 302

EAD and EPE Profiles 304

Portfolio CCR Aggregation, Netting Sets, and Collateral Margin 307

    Initial Margin 307

    Variation Margin 307

    Margin Period of Risk 308

    Margin Threshold 308

    Minimum Transfer Amount 308

OIS Discounting 309

    Calculating "Adjusted" Forward LIBOR Rates from OIS Curves
and Basis Swaps 312

References 314

Chapter 8: Power Laws and Extreme Value Theory 315

Power Laws and Scaling 315

    Moments 318

    Extrapolation 319

    Power-Law Monte Carlo Simulation 321

    Maximum Likelihood Calibration 322

Extreme Value Theory 324

    Maximum Likelihood Calibration for the GPD 327

    The Power-Law Equivalence of the GPD 328

VaR and CVaR 329
Problems 330
    Problem 8-1. Power-Law MC Simulation in Excel 330
    Problem 8-2. The Power-Law Nature of the GPD.................................. 331
References 331

Chapter 9: Hedge Fund Replication 333

Overview of Hedge Fund Styles 334
Replicating Methodologies 336
A Heuristic Example 337
Replication through Kalman Filtering 341
    Process Model 341
    Measurement Model 342
    Kalman Filter 342
    Time Update with an Initial Prediction 343
    Measurement (Observation) Update with Kalman Filter Correction 343
References 348

Index 349

Series Editors' Foreword

Rupak Chatterjee's book, *Practical Methods of Financial Engineering and Risk Management*, inaugurates an important and innovative series of books targeting the concrete needs of participants in the 21st-century financial industry—The Stevens Series in Quantitative Finance.

Finance today is an industry in the throes of a technological and regulatory revolution which is transforming the capital markets, upending traditional business models, and rewriting the academic curriculum. It is an industry characterized by an expanding spectrum of risk, driven by technological changes that are engendering more dangerous "unknown unknowns" than ever before. It is an industry confronting the emergence of systemic phenomena—especially intensified network effects or "contagions"—that are the result of vastly increased levels of interconnectedness among automated agents in fully globalized electronic markets. It is an industry where everything is suddenly speeding up. The old manual markets and the old relationship-based networks have been displaced by high-tech, high-speed systems that threaten to outstrip our governance structures and management capabilities. Finance is an industry where up-to-date technical knowledge is more critical than ever. It is an industry in need of a new syllabus.

The aim of this series is to supply our industry that new syllabus. For more than a decade, we at the Stevens Institute of Technology have been developing new academic programs to address the needs of the rapidly evolving field of quantitative finance. We have benefited from our location in the New York/New Jersey financial center, which has given us access to practitioners who are grappling directly with these changes and can help orient our curriculum to the real needs of the industry. We are convinced that this is one of those periods in history in which practice is leading theory. That is why the perspective of Professor Chatterjee, who spent fifteen years working at some of the leading financial firms before joining our faculty, is so valuable.

Working with Springer and Apress, we are designing this series to project to the widest possible audience the curriculum and knowledge assets underlying the "New Finance." The series' audience includes practitioners working in the finance industry today and students and faculty involved in undergraduate and graduate finance programs. The audience also includes researchers, policymakers, analysts, consultants, and legal and accounting professionals engaged in developing and implementing new regulatory frameworks for the industry. It is an audience that is pragmatic in its motivation and that prizes clarity and accessibility in the treatment of potentially complex topics.

Our goal in this series is to bring the complexities of the financial system and its supporting technologies into focus in a way that our audience will find practical, useful, and appealingly presented. The titles forthcoming in this series will range from highly specific "skill set"-oriented books aimed at mastering particular tools, techniques, or problems, to more comprehensive surveys of major fields, such as Professor Chatterjee provides in the present work for the field of financial risk engineering. Some titles will meet

SERIES EDITORS' FOREWORD

the criteria for standard classroom textbooks. Others will be better suited as supplemental readings, foregoing the textbook paraphernalia of axioms, exercises, and problem sets in favor of a more efficient exposition of important practical issues. Some of these will focus on the messy interstices between different perspectives or disciplines within finance. Others will address broad trends, such as the rise of "analytics," data science, and "large p, large n" statistics for dealing with "high-dimensional data" (all right, yes, Big Data for financial applications). We also plan policy-oriented primers to translate complex topics into suitable guidance for regulators (and regulatees).

In short, we plan to be opportunistically versatile with respect to both topic and format, but always with the goal of publishing books that are accurate, accessible, high-quality, up-to-date, and useful for all the various segments of our industry audience.

A fertile dimension of our partnership with Springer/Apress is the program for full electronic distribution of all titles through the industry-leading SpringerLink channel as well as all the major commercial ebook formats. In addition, some of the series titles will be coming out under the open-access model known as ApressOpen and will be available to everybody free of charge for unlimited ebook downloads. Like the finance industry, the publishing industry is undergoing its own tech-driven revolution, as traditional hardcopy print forms yield increasingly to digital media and open-source models. It is our joint intention with Springer/Apress to respond vigorously and imaginatively to opportunities for innovative content distribution and for the widest dissemination enabled by the new technologies.

The Stevens Series in Quantitative Finance aspires to serve as a uniquely valuable resource for current and future practitioners of modern finance. To that end, we cordially invite you to send your comments, suggestions, and proposals to us at gcalhoun@stevens.edu and kkhashan@stevens.edu, and we thank you in advance for your interest and support.

—George Calhoun
Program Director, Quantitative Finance
Stevens Institute of Technology

—Khaldoun Khashanah
Program Director, Financial Engineering
Stevens Institute of Technology

About the Author

Rupak Chatterjee, PhD, is an Industry Professor and the Deputy Director of the Financial Engineering Division at the Stevens Institute of Technology. He is also the Program Manager for the Accenture-Stevens Financial Services Analytics graduate program. Dr. Chatterjee has over fifteen years of experience as a quantitative analyst working for various Wall Street firms. His last role before returning to academia was as the Director of the Multi-Asset Hybrid Derivatives Quantitative Research group at Citi in New York. He was also the global Basel III coordinator for all the modeling efforts needed to satisfy the new regulatory risk requirements. Previously, he was a quantitative analyst at Barclays Capital, a vice president at Credit Suisse, and a senior vice president at HSBC. His educational background is in theoretical physics, which he studied at the University of Waterloo, Stony Brook University, and the University of Chicago. His research interests have included discrete time hedging problems using the Optimal Hedging Monte Carlo (OHMC) method and the design and execution of systematic trading strategies that embody the hallmarks of capital preservation and measured risk-taking.

About the Technical Reviewer

Dr. Neville O'Reilly is the Associate Director of the Financial Statistics and Risk Management Program at Rutgers University and a Research Professor in the Department of Statistics. His academic interests are in risk management education and in doing research in the application of statistical methods to risk management and finance. He has held senior management positions in finance and operations in the insurance, credit card processing and private equity industries prior to returning in 2012 to an academic career at Rutgers University. Dr. O'Reilly holds a PhD in Mathematical Statistics from Columbia University.

Acknowledgments

Throughout my many years working as a quantitative analyst, I have learned many things from my colleagues. I would like to thank Jess Saypoff and Sean Reed (at Barclays), Raj Kumar and Victor Hong (at CSFB), Paul Romanelli, Juan Eroles and Julian Manzano (at HSBC), L. Sankar, Yann Coatanlem, Igor Tydniouk, Alvin Wang, and especially Vivek Kapoor (at Citi). Without their help and encouragement, I wouldn't have lasted long on Wall Street.

A special thanks goes out to Dr. Neville O'Reilly, my technical editor and the Associate Director of the Financial Statistics and Risk Management Program at Rutgers University and a Research Professor in the Department of Statistics. His mathematical assistance is greatly appreciated.

I would also like to acknowledge the people at Apress-Springer, including Rita Fernando and Robert Hutchinson, and the series editors at the Stevens Institute of Technology, Dr. George Calhoun and Dr. Khaldoun Khashanah.

Introduction

The two fields featured in the title of this book—*Practical Methods of Financial Engineering and Risk Management*—are intertwined. The practical methods I teach in this book focus on the interplay and overlap of financial engineering and risk management in the real world.

My goal is to take you beyond the artificial assumptions still relied on by too many financial practitioners who prefer to treat financial engineering and risk management as separate specialties. These assumptions don't just distort reality—they can be dangerous. Performing either financial engineering or risk management without due regard for the other has led with increasing frequency to disastrous results.

The dual purpose of risk management is pricing and hedging. *Pricing* provides a valuation of financial instruments. *Hedging* provides various measures of risk together with methods to offset those risks as best as possible. These tasks are performed not only by risk managers but also by traders who price and hedge their respective trading books on a daily basis. Successful trading over extended periods of time comes down to successful risk management. And successful risk management comes down to robust valuation, which is the main prerogative of financial engineering.

Pricing begins with an analysis of possible future events, such as stock price changes, interest rate shifts, and credit default events. Dealing with the future involves the mathematics of statistics and probability. The first step is to find a probability distribution that is suitable for the financial instrument at hand. The next step is to calibrate this distribution. The third step is to generate future events using the calibrated distribution and, based on this, provide the necessary valuation and risk measures for the financial contract at hand. Failure in any of these steps can lead to incorrect valuation and therefore an incorrect assessment of the risks of the financial instrument under consideration.

Hedging market risk and managing credit risk cannot be adequately executed simply by monitoring the financial markets. Leveraging the analytic tools used by the traders is also inadequate for risk management purposes because their front office (trading floor) models tend to look at risk measures over very short time scales (today's value of a financial instrument), in regular market environments (as opposed to stressful conditions under which large losses are common), and under largely unrealistic assumptions (risk-neutral probabilities).

To offset traditional front-office myopia and assess all potential future risks that may occur, proper financial engineering is needed. Risk management through prudent financial engineering and risk control—these have become the watchwords of all financial firms in the twenty-first century. Yet as many events, such as the mortgage crisis of 2008, have shown, commonly used statistical and probabilistic tools have failed to either measure or predict large moves in the financial markets. Many of the standard models seen on Wall Street are based on simplified assumptions and can lead to systematic and sometimes catastrophic underestimation of real risks. Starting from a detailed analysis of market data, traders and risk managers can take into account more faithfully the implications of the real

INTRODUCTION

behavior of financial markets—particularly in response to rare events and exceedingly rare events of large magnitude (often called *black swan events*). Including such scenarios can have significant impacts on asset allocation, derivative pricing and hedging, and general risk control.

Like financial engineering and risk management, market risk and credit risk are tightly interrelated. Large, sudden negative returns in the market can lead to the credit deterioration of many small and large financial firms, leading in turn to unstable counterparties (such as Lehman Brothers and Bear Stearns during their 2008 collapse) and eventually to unstable countries (such as the sovereign debt crisis in Greece beginning in 2009). The concept of credit risk management therefore goes beyond the simple valuation and risk of financial instruments and includes topics such as *counterparty credit risk* (CCR), wrong way risk, and *credit valuation adjustments* (CVAs)—all of which are considered at length in this book.

The 2008 struggles of Wall Street have given regulators such as the Federal Reserve System (Fed) and the Securities and Exchange Commission (SEC) a broad mandate to create various regulations that they feel will induce banks to be more prudent in taking risks. A large amount of regulation modeling is currently under way in all the bulge-bracket firms to satisfy such regulatory requirements as those of Basel III, CVA, and Dodd-Frank. A working knowledge of these regulatory analytic requirements is essential for a complete understanding of Wall Street risk management.

All these risks and regulations can lead to increased levels of risk capital that firms must keep against their positions. After the events of 2008, the cost of risk capital has gone up substantially, even while interest rates have reached an all-time low. Capital optimization has in consequence become a major task for banks. Large financial firms are requiring that their specific businesses meet minimum target returns on risk capital—that is, minimum levels of profits versus the amount of risk capital that the firms must hold). Beginning in 2012, firms report their returns on Basel III risk capital in their 10Q and 10K regulatory filings.

The goal of this book is to introduce those concepts that will best enable modern practitioners to address all of these issues.

Audience

This book is intended for readers with basic knowledge of finance and first-year college math. The mathematical prerequisites are kept to a minimum: two-variable calculus and some exposure to probability and statistics. A familiarity with basic financial instruments such as stocks and bonds is assumed in Chapter 1, which reviews this material from a trader's perspective. Financial engineering is the purview of quantitative analysts ("quants") on Wall Street (taken in the generic nongeographic sense of bulge-bracket banks, brokerage firms, and hedge funds). The mathematical models described in this book are usually implemented in C++, Python, or Java at Wall Street firms, as I know firsthand from having spent more than fifteen years creating them for Citigroup, HSBC, Credit Suisse, and Barclays. Nonetheless, to make this book more accessible to practitioners and students in all areas of finance and at all levels of programming proficiency, I have designed the end-of-chapter problems to be solvable using Microsoft Excel. One should understand the concepts first and test their application in a simple format such as Excel before moving on to more advanced applications requiring a coding language. Many of the end-of-chapter problems are mini-projects. They take time and involve all the standard steps in quantitative analysis: get data, clean data, calibrate to a model, get a result, make a trading decision, and make a risk management decision. It is important to note that doing the problems in this book is an integral part of understanding the material. The problems are designed to be representative of real-world problems that working quantitative professionals solve on a regular basis. They should all be done because there is a codependence on later topics.

Chapter Descriptions

Chapter 1 ("Financial Instruments") describes several basic U.S. financial instruments that drive all asset classes in one way or another. I present these instruments in the universal form in which Wall Street traders interact with them: Bloomberg Terminal screens. The ability to read quotes from these screens is a matter of basic literacy on any Wall Street trading floor.

Chapter 2 ("Building a Yield Curve") describes the generic algorithm for building LIBOR-based yield curves from cash instruments, futures, and swaps. Yield curve construction is often described as simply "getting zero coupon rates." In reality, this is far from true. On Wall Street, a yield curve is a set of discount factors, not rates. All firms need the ability to calculate the *present value* (PV) of future cash flows using discount factors in various currencies. The techniques described in this chapter are widely used in the industry for all major currencies. The increasingly important OIS discounting curve is described in Chapter 7.

Chapter 3 ("Statistical Analysis of Financial Data") introduces various fundamental tools in probability theory that are used to analyze financial data. The chapter deals with calibrating distributions to real financial data. A thorough understanding of this material is needed to fully appreciate the remaining chapters. I have trained many new analysts at various Wall Street firms. All these fresh analysts knew probability theory very well, but almost none of them knew how to use it. Chapter 3 introduces key risk concepts such as fat-tailed distributions, the term structure of statistics, and volatility clustering. A discussion of dynamic portfolio theory is used to demonstrate many of the key concepts developed in the chapter. This chapter is of great importance to implementing risk management in terms of the probabilities that are typically used in real-world risk valuation systems—*value at risk* (VaR), *conditional value at risk* (CVaR), and Basel II/III—as opposed to the risk-neutral probabilities used in traditional front-office systems.

Chapter 4 ("Stochastic Processes") discusses stochastic processes, paying close attention to the GARCH(1,1) fat-tailed processes that are often used for VaR and CVaR calculations. Further examples are discussed in the realm of systematic trading strategies. Here a simple statistical arbitrage strategy is explained to demonstrate the power of modeling pairs trading via a mean-reverting stochastic process. The Monte Carlo techniques explained in this chapter are used throughout Wall Street for risk management purposes and for regulatory use such as in Basel II and III.

Chapter 5 ("Optimal Hedging Monte Carlo Methods") introduces a very modern research area in derivatives pricing: the *optimal hedging Monte Carlo* (OHMC) method. This is an advanced derivative pricing methodology that deals with all the real-life trading problems often ignored by both Wall Street and academic researchers: discrete time

INTRODUCTION

hedging, quantification of hedging errors, hedge slippage, rare events, gap risk, transaction costs, liquidity costs, risk capital, and so on. It is a realistic framework that takes into account real-world financial conditions, as opposed to hiding behind the fictitious assumptions of the risk-neutral Black-Scholes world.

Chapter 6 ("Introduction to Credit Derivatives") introduces credit derivatives, paying special attention to the models needed for the Basel II and III calculations presented in Chapter 7. All the standard contract methodologies for *credit default swaps* (CDS) are described with a view to elucidating their market quotes for pricing and hedging. Asset swaps, collateralization, and the OHMC method applied to CDS contracts are also discussed.

Chapter 7 ("Risk Types, CVA, Basel III, and OIS Discounting") is a very timely and pertinent chapter on the various new financial regulations that have affected and will continue to affect Wall Street for the foreseeable future. Every Wall Street firm is scrambling to understand and implement the requirements of Basel II and III and CVA. Knowledge of these topics is essential for working within the risk management division of a bank. The effect of counterparty credit risk on discounting and the increasingly important use of OIS discounting to address these issues is also presented.

Chapter 8 ("Power Laws and Extreme Value Theory") describes power-law techniques for pinpointing rare and extreme moves. Power-law distributions are often used to better represent the statistical tail properties of financial data that are not described by standard distributions. This chapter describes how power laws can be used to capture rare events and incorporate them into VaR and CVaR calculations.

Chapter 9 ("Hedge Fund Replication") deals with the concept of asset replication through Kalman filtering. The *Kalman filter* is a mathematical method used to estimate the true value of a hidden state given only a sequence of noisy observations. Many prestigious financial indices and hedge funds erect high barriers to market participants or charge exorbitant fees. The idea here is to replicate the returns of these assets with a portfolio that provides a lower fee structure, easier access, and better liquidity.

The first six chapters are precisely and coherently related and constitute the solid core of valuation and risk management, consisting of the following basic operations:

1. Understand the nature of the financial instrument in question (Chapters 1 and 2).
2. Provide a description of the statistical properties of the instrument by calibrating a realistic distribution to real time series data (Chapter 3).
3. Perform a Monte Carlo simulation of this instrument using the calibrated distribution for the purposes of risk assessment, recognizing that all risk is from the perspective of future events (Chapter 4).
4. Evaluate the pricing, hedging, and market risk analysis of derivatives on this instrument (Chapter 5).
5. Evaluate the pricing, hedging, and risk analysis of credit derivatives (Chapter 6).

CHAPTER 1

■ ■ ■

Financial Instruments

Traditionally, Wall Street has categorized financial instruments using the following classification:

- Fixed income
- Credit
- Emerging markets
- Mortgage-backed securities (MBS)
- Equities
- Commodities
- Foreign exchange (FX)

These categories are often referred to as *asset classes*. *Fixed-income* assets include all sorts of high-quality government bonds and interest-rate products from the G7 countries. The main source of risk here is interest-rate uncertainty. Bonds issued from emerging market countries such as the BRIC (Brazil, Russia, India, China) counties fall under *emerging markets*. Corporate bonds are classified under *credit* because they pose some credit risk to the buyer in terms of potentially defaulting on coupon payments or principal. They are often further separated into *investment-grade* and *high-yield* categories. Asset classes clearly overlap: a high-yield bond is obviously a fixed-income instrument. This classification is based more on the nature of how Wall Street views the trading, selling, and risk management of these assets. High-yield trading desks certainly must deal with interest-rate risk, but they also have credit risk. Therefore, they are divided off from *fixed income*. Note that emerging-market bonds also have substantial credit risk (as governments can also default). The nature of their credit risk can be different than corporate bonds—for instance, corporations tend not to have military coups. To complicate matters further, there also exist emerging-market corporate bonds. *Mortgage-backed securities* (MBS) are fixed-income instruments backed by the interest and principal payments of mortgage loans for real estate (residential and commercial). Since many vanilla mortgages can be paid off early or refinanced (refinancing involves the prepayment of the original mortgage loan for a new one with lower interest rate payments), MBS instruments have this specialized prepayment risk on top of interest-rate risk and therefore earn their own category.

Equities are the best-known asset class. They include both single-name equities (such as Apple and Citi) and indices (such as the S&P 500 and NASDAQ). Equities can also encompass mutual funds, hedge fund shares, and private equity interests. *Commodities* are another well-known asset class that includes oil, natural gas, gold and other precious metals such as silver, platinum, and palladium, coffee, corn, sugar, live cattle, and so on. *Foreign exchange* (FX) is another well-known asset class. Anyone who has exchanged money from one currency to another realizes that the currency exchange made a profit from their FX transaction. FX is split into G7 currencies and others (such as emerging market FX).

Each of these asset classes has three generic types of products:

- **Cash instruments**
- **Futures and swaps**
- **Derivatives and structured products**

Cash instruments (sometimes known as *spot instruments*) are the standard instruments described above: stocks, bonds, corn, and so forth. These are instruments that you pay cash for upfront and receive the instrument immediately (or within one to three days thereafter as opposed to sometime further in the future). People who trade these instruments are called *cash traders* as opposed to *futures traders* or *derivatives traders*. Futures on a financial instrument lock in the price of the underlying instrument at a prespecified future date and a fixed price. Both the delivery and payment (of the fixed price) of the underlying asset is made at this future date—with the proviso that physical delivery is not necessary when one can cash-settle the futures contract. *Swaps* are instruments whereby different types of payments (*cash flows*) are exchanged (*swapped*) between two counterparties at a series of prespecified dates. A swap can be seen as a series of future contracts. *Derivatives* are contracts on an underlying asset whereby the payoff of the derivative is based on (*derived* from) the price movement of the asset. Strictly speaking, a futures contract is a type of derivative. Neither futures nor derivatives can exist without their respective reference asset. Derivatives can become very complicated, and these complexities may lead to perilous difficulties in pricing and hedging these instruments (Warren Buffet calls derivatives "financial weapons of mass destruction"). In general, the valuation and risk management of financial assets become progressively harder as one moves from cash instruments to derivatives.

Since the late 1990s, asset classes have become progressively more correlated to each other, especially in downward-turning markets. For instance, the default of Russian local currency bonds (GKOs) in 1998 sent most financial markets crashing while producing a massive rally in the G7 government bond market. The dot-com equity buildup that pushed the NASDAQ above 5,000 in 2000 had an effect on the US dollar FX rate because foreign investors needed US currency to buy all the new US dot-com stocks, thereby making the dollar stronger. The 2008 residential mortgage crash sent the S&P 500 spiraling down to 700. It also led to higher prices in gold and other commodities. Therefore, traders of various asset classes have had to become more aware of the markets outside their respective areas. This is why this chapter covers a wide array of asset classes that tend to affect the market as a whole. A useful way to achieve this is to analyze the method in which these instruments are quoted in the way familiar to Wall Street traders. These quotes typically come to traders from two well-known market data providers to Wall Street: *Thomson Reuters* and *Bloomberg*.

(His creation of the latter platform is how Michael Bloomberg, former mayor of New York City, became a multibillionaire). Cash instruments are discussed first, followed by futures and swaps and ending with derivatives. The next section presents two Bloomberg market data pages that most traders across assets classes tend to monitor.

Bloomberg Market Data Screens

The goal of this chapter is to study the majority of assets displayed on the two Bloomberg market data screens captured in Figures 1-1 and 1-2. Figure 1-1 displays many of the liquid instruments found in the US Treasury and money markets sector. <BTMM> is the Bloomberg keyboard command associated with this page. (Note that the country of interest can be changed using the scroll-down menu displayed on the top left corner of Figure 1-1). Figure 1-2 is a similar page with more emphasis on instruments from the US futures, swaps, and options sector. <USSW> is the Bloomberg keyboard command associated with this page.

In the remainder of this chapter, these two Bloomberg screens are denoted *BTMM* (Bloomberg Treasury and Money Markets Monitor) and *USSW* (US Swaps). All the interest rates quoted on these screens are in percentage points—so a quote of "0.1500" means 0.15% (not "15.0%"). In the financial community, 0.15% is referred to as 15 basis points. A *basis point* (bp) is one hundredth of a percentage point (that is, one part per ten thousand).

The financial products displayed on these two Bloomberg screens are successively described in this chapter under their three generic types: cash instruments, futures and swaps, and derivatives and structured products.

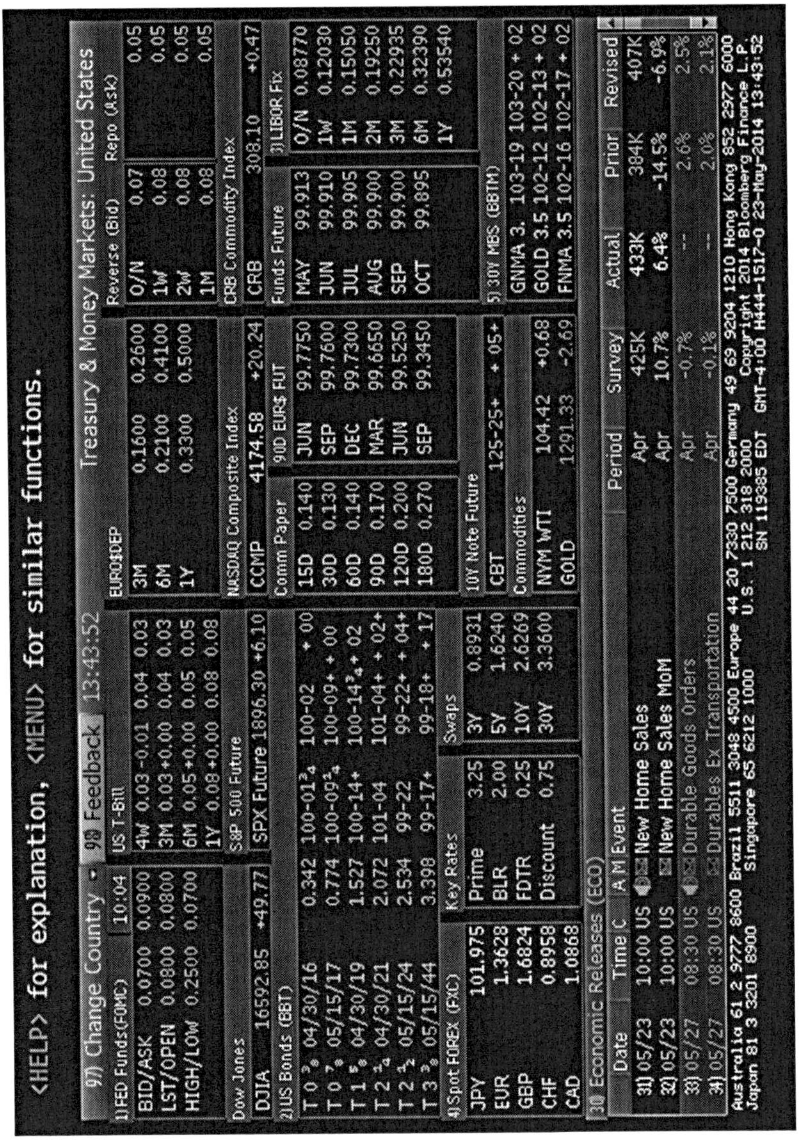

Figure 1-1. <BTMM> Bloomberg screen, monitoring US Treasury and money market rates and bond prices. *Used with permission of Bloomberg L.P. Copyright © 2014.*

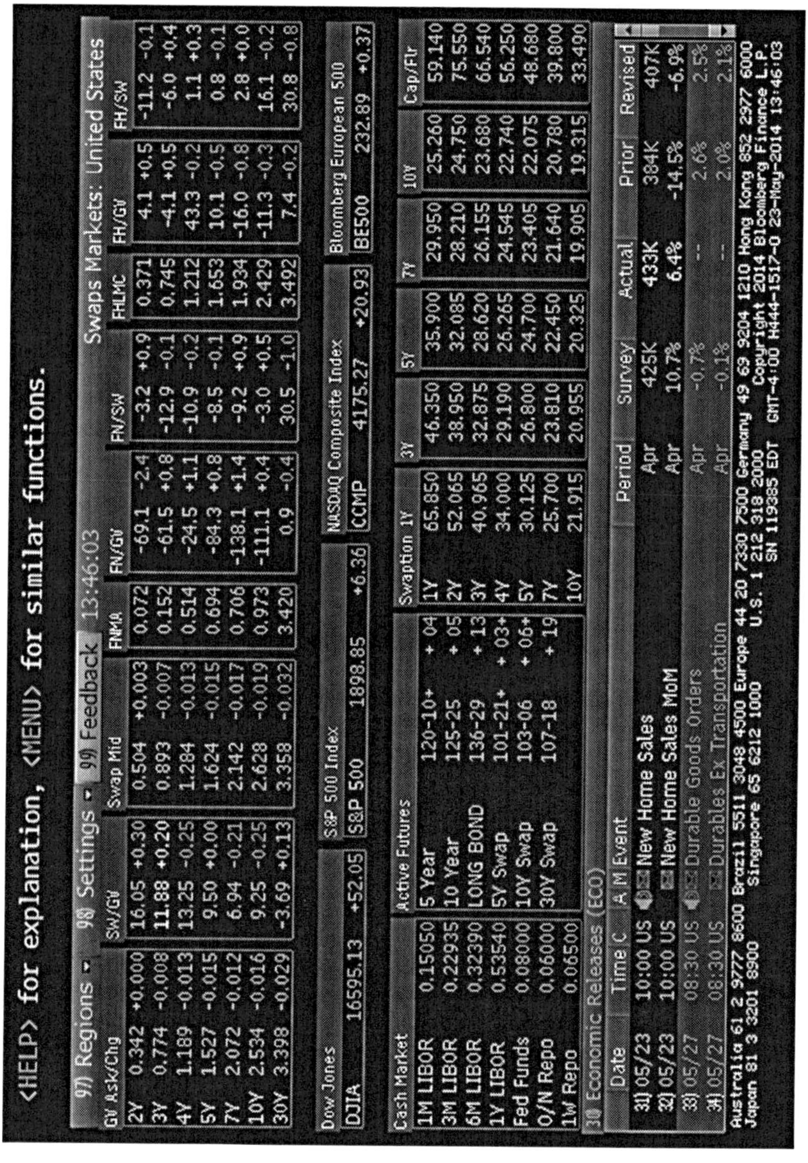

CHAPTER 1 ■ FINANCIAL INSTRUMENTS

Figure 1-2. <USSW> *Bloomberg screen, monitoring a composite of US government and agency rates, interest rate swaps, and option volatilities.* Used with permission of Bloomberg L.P. Copyright© 2014. All rights reserved.

Cash Instruments

The cash instruments discussed in this section are fed funds, eurodollar deposits, US Treasury bills, notes, and bonds, repo and reverse repo, equity indices, commercial paper, LIBOR, spot forex, key rates, and gold. All allusions to "Bloomberg screen" in this section are to the BTMM screen (Figure 1-1) and exploded views of certain sections of this screen.

Fed Funds

"FED Funds" found at the top left corner of BTMM are interest rates (see Figure 1-3). "FOMC" stands for the Federal Open Market Committee. US banks are obligated to maintain certain levels of cash reserves with the Federal Reserve (the Fed). The amount that a depository institution must place depends on the amount of bank's assets and the composition of its liabilities. The total amount placed with the Fed is usually in the neighborhood of 10% of the bank's demand accounts (*deposit base*). Whenever a US bank provides a loan, the ratio of the bank's reserves decreases. If this reserve ratio drops below a minimum amount, the bank must increase its reserves to the Fed's minimum levels. The bank can increase these levels by several means, such as selling assets.

Figure 1-3. *Fed Funds Overnight Rate.* Used with permission of Bloomberg L.P. Copyright© 2014. All rights reserved.

Another method is for the bank to borrow the required extra funds from another bank that has an account with the Fed. The interest rate paid from the borrowing bank to the lending bank goes through the mechanism of *bid and offer* (or ask). The first row in the fed funds section of Bloomberg shows the bid rate (second column) and the ask rate (third column). These rates are valid for only one day, that is "overnight". A transaction is executed when either the offer side brings its rate down to the bid level (*hits the bid*) or the bid side brings its rate up to the offer level (*lifts the offer*). This transaction mechanism is also the primary mechanism of trading for all instruments on Wall Street. The second row shows the last-traded rate and opening rate of the day. The third row shows the high and low transacted fed fund rates of the day. The weighted average of all transacted rates during the day is the *federal funds effective rate*. This rate hovers around the *federal funds target rate* (FDTR—listed under "Key Rates") which is set by the governors of the Federal Reserve. On December 16, 2008, the Federal Open Market Committee established a very low target range for the fed funds rate of 0.00% to 0.25% in order to provide liquidity for the 2008 mortgage crisis. As of 2014, this was still the target range. These rates are quoted on a daycount convention (or basis) of act/360 (see this chapter's appendix, "Daycount Conventions").

Participants in the federal funds market include commercial banks, savings and loan associations, government-sponsored entities (such as Fannie Mae and Freddie Mac), branches of foreign banks in the United States, and securities firms.

Eurodollar Deposits

Many governments hold cash reserves in foreign currencies. During the Cold War, Soviet-bloc nations often had to pay for imports with US dollars (or receive US dollars for their exports). They were hesitant to leave their dollar deposits with banks in the United States due to the risks of those deposits being frozen for political reasons. Instead, they placed their US dollars in European banks. These funds became known as *eurodollars*, and the interest they received on their deposits were based on eurodollar rates. These dollar accounts are not under the jurisdiction of the Federal Reserve. In time, these European banks (many of which were in London) started to lend these dollars out, which precipitated the eurodollar market (see the subsequent section, "LIBOR"). Do not confuse eurodollars with the euro currency. Eurodollars are still dollars. Note that the euro is the second most popular reserve currency in the world after the US dollar. The Bloomberg quotes list the tenor of the deposit in the first column and the bid and offer rates in the second and third columns, respectively (see Figure 1-4). The tenor of the deposit is either in months ("3M" is three months) or years ("1Y" is one year).

EURO$DEP		
3M	0.1600	0.2600
6M	0.2100	0.4100
1Y	0.3300	0.5000

Figure 1-4. Eurodollar Deposit Rates. Used with permission of Bloomberg L.P. Copyright© 2014. All rights reserved.

US Treasury Bills, Notes, and Bonds

Governments are very much like corporations inasmuch as they need to raise capital to run their entities. Corporations tend to raise capital by issuing stock (selling a part of themselves) or issuing bonds (borrowing money). Governments raise capital by taxation or issuing bonds. Bonds are often called *debt instruments* because the issuer owes a debt to the buyer of the bond. The US government issues several different kinds of bonds through the Bureau of the Public Debt, an agency of the Department of the Treasury. Treasury debt securities are classified according to their maturities:

1. *Treasury bills* have maturities of one year or less.
2. *Treasury notes* have maturities of two to ten years.
3. *Treasury bonds* have maturities greater than ten years.

Treasury bills, notes, and bonds are all issued in face values of $1,000, though there are different purchase minimums for each type of security. All notes and bonds pay interest (*coupons*) twice a year. The daycount basis used for coupon payments is act/act. All coupon payments are exempt from local and state taxes (but not from federal income taxes). One can buy Treasury bonds directly from the government via Treasury Direct online. The main attraction of Treasury Direct is that there are no brokerage fees or other transaction charges when you buy through this program.

US Treasury bills (*T-bills*) are *discount bonds* that do not pay coupons but pay the face value at maturity—that is, the price is discounted to less than 100% of the face value (aka *notional*) of the bond. If one pays 99% of face and receives 100% at maturity, the interest payment is implicit in the 1% gain. T-bills are quoted on a discount yield basis (act/360). The invoice price in percent of a T-bill is given by

$$P = 100 \cdot \left[1 - \frac{(actual\ days\ to\ maturity)(quoted\ discount\ rate)}{360}\right]. \quad (1.1)$$

The Bloomberg quote for T-bills ("US T-Bill" at the top of BTMM and Figure 1-5) comes in five columns according to the following order: Term, Last Traded Discount Yield, Yield Change, Bid Discount Yield, and Offer Discount Yield. The terms start at weeks ("4W" means four weeks) and end with one year (1Y). The Bloomberg quote for Treasury notes and bonds ("US BONDS (BBT)") has seven columns in this order: T for Treasury, Coupon Rate, Maturity Date, Yield, Bid Price, Offer Price, Last Change in Price (see Figure 1-5). The price quotes here follow a traditional convention that predates the use of computers and calculators: fractional *ticks* are used instead of decimal places. The standard tick size is equal to **1/32**. The number following the dash in the price is the number of ticks, as in the following examples:

$$"99-22" = 99 + \frac{22}{32} \quad (1.2)$$

or

$$"100-01\frac{3}{4}" = 100 + \frac{1}{32} + \left(\frac{3}{4}\right)\frac{1}{32}. \quad (1.3)$$

"+" after the tick size signifies half a tick, **1/64**. For instance,

$$"100-14+" = 100 + \frac{14}{32} + \frac{1}{64}. \quad (1.4)$$

US T-Bill					2) US Bonds (BBT)				
4W	0.03	-0.01	0.04	0.03	T 0 ³⁄₈ 04/30/16	0.342	100-01³⁄₄	100-02	+ 00
3M	0.03	+0.00	0.04	0.03	T 0 ⅞ 05/15/17	0.774	100-09¼	100-09+	+ 00
6M	0.05	+0.00	0.05	0.05	T 1 ⅝ 04/30/19	1.527	100-14+	100-14³⁄₄	+ 02
1Y	0.08	+0.00	0.08	0.08	T 2 ¼ 04/30/21	2.072	101-04	101-04+	+ 02+
					T 2 ½ 05/15/24	2.534	99-22	99-22+	+ 04+
					T 3 ³⁄₈ 05/15/44	3.398	99-17+	99-18+	+ 17

Figure 1-5. *US Treasury Bills, Notes, and Bonds.* Used with permission of Bloomberg L.P. Copyright© 2014. All rights reserved.

Repo and Reverse Repo

A *repurchase* (repo) agreement is a form of a secured loan between two counterparties. It is also the standard way to "go short" securities. The secured loan transaction process is as follows. The *repo side* is the counterparty who wishes to borrow money and pay the implied interest rate. The *reverse repo side* is willing to lend money but needs collateral against the loan to protect against the possibility of the repo side's defaulting on the loan. The repo side sells securities to the reverse repo side, thereby receiving a cash payment (which is the loan). The repo side agrees to buy back (repurchase) these securities at a predetermined future date and price. This is equivalent to a spot transaction and a forward contract (explained in the next section). The repurchase forward price (which is almost always higher than the initial spot price) implies the borrowing interest rate paid by the repo side. Because of this fixed future price, the reverse repo side does not have any market risk to this security. This borrowing interest rate is the repo rate quoted in Bloomberg. Since the repo side wishes to borrow money, they are the *bid side*, whereas the reverse repo side is the *offer side*. The Bloomberg screen has three columns: Term, Reverse (Bid), and Repo (Ask) (see Figure 1-6). On this screen, the "Bid" reference to the reverse repo side is with respect to the purchase of the collateral (the reverse repo side initially buys the collateral securities, see Figure 1-7), *not* to the repo rate. The same holds true to the "Ask" reference with respect to the repo column. Clearly, the offer rate is higher than the bid. "O/N" stands for *overnight*. These rates are valid for riskless (from a default perspective), liquid instruments such as Treasury bills, notes, and bonds. Risky instruments and stocks have their own repo rates.

Term	Reverse (Bid)	Repo (Ask)
O/N	0.07	0.05
1W	0.08	0.05
2W	0.08	0.05
1M	0.08	0.05

Figure 1-6. Repo Rates. *Used with permission of Bloomberg L.P. Copyright© 2014. All rights reserved.*

	Repo	Reverse Repo
Financial Purpose	Borrowing Cash	Secured Lender
Initial Transaction	Sells Securities	Buys Securities
Intermediate Transaction (optional)		Short Transaction (sells and buys back)
Final Transaction	Repurchases Securities	Sells Securities

Figure 1-7. Repurchase agreement mechanics

During the interim time between the initial repo transaction and the final buyback of the collateral by the repo side, the reverse repo side can actually sell the collateral in the open market and buy it back before the maturity of the repo contract. The goal here is to sell the security at a high price and buy it back at a lower price. This is what it means to *go short* a security (short selling). This is not the same as owning a security, selling it, and buying it back. The reverse repo side did not originally buy the security as an investment but obtained it as collateral against a loan. The reverse repo side will sell it back to the repo side at a predetermined (non-open market) future price and therefore does not take the price risk of this security with respect to the repo transaction (whereas he does take price risk if he executes a short sale on top of the repo transaction). The reverse repo transaction is often associated with "borrowing a security" to go short, in the language of short sellers. For many securities, the short-selling aspect of this transaction drives the market (the repo rate), rather than the loan side (Figure 1-7).

The Fed uses the repo mechanism to enforce the fed funds target rate when the traded fed funds rate departs from the target rate. If the traded rate becomes higher than the target rate, the Fed provides liquidity to the banking system by acting as the reverse repo side. If the traded rate gets much lower that the target rate, the Fed attempts to remove liquidity by acting as the repo side.

Equity Indices

An *index* is a pool of assets that have been grouped together because of similar characteristics. The purpose of the index is to reflect that portion of the financial market with these characteristics. Such characteristics might be as general as being a global equity stock (as opposed to, say, a commodity) or as specific as being a US healthcare stock with small-market capitalization. The level of the index can be determined in many different ways, but the two most popular methods are *price weighting* and *market capitalization weighting*. A price-weighted index simply weights the underlying by its price. An underlying trading at $20 will have 10 times the weight of one trading at $2. Clearly, changes in higher-priced assets have a greater effect on the price weighted index than lower-priced assets. Note that the absolute level of an asset does not necessarily indicate the financial importance of the underlying company. A $200 stock could be from a start-up firm, whereas a $20 stock could be from a multinational corporation. A better indicator of the size of a company is the market *capitalization* (cap) of that company, which is simply its stock price multiplied by the number of outstanding shares. Also, the financial health of large-cap companies is usually a better indicator of a specific sector, and therefore market cap indices are also very popular. Finally, another type of financial index is a *total return index*, in which each underlying has an equal weight. The index follows the total percentage return of each underlying (price return plus dividend return) rather than absolute changes in price or market cap. It should be noted that many index providers simply provide financial data for their respective index. Unlike financial trading companies, they do not provide investments in their indices, which are simply synthetic instruments based on mathematical calculations that track a pool of assets based upon strict rules. The providers of two popular indices described below—the Dow Jones and the S&P 500—do not provide investment access to their respective indices. Financial companies such as banks and mutual funds provide investments that closely *track* these indices.

Dow Jones

The *Dow Jones Industrial Average* (DJIA) is a price-weighted average of thirty blue chip US stocks that are considered leaders in their industries. The Bloomberg index quote and the change from the previous day can be found on the left hand side of BTMM under the heading "Dow Jones". It is considered a barometer of the US economy. It was initiated in its current form on October 1, 1928. Initially, the value of the index was generated by adding the prices of the thirty stocks in the index and dividing them by 30. To take into account stock splits, spin-offs, changing underlyings, and other structural changes in a way that does not change the level of the index, a new divisor is used each time such an event happens. The present divisor is actually less than 1, meaning the index is larger than the sum of its component prices. The index is calculated as

$$\text{DJIA} = \frac{\sum_{i=1}^{30} Px_i}{\text{Divisor}} \qquad (1.5)$$

where Px_i is the price of each stock in the index.

To avoid discontinuities in the level of the index after events such as stock splits or changes in the list of underlying companies, the divisor is updated to preserve identity immediately before and after the event:

$$\text{DJIA} = \frac{\sum_{i=1}^{30} Px_i^{old}}{\text{Divisor}_{old}} = \frac{\sum_{i=1}^{30} Px_i^{new}}{\text{Divisor}_{new}} \qquad (1.6)$$

Figure 1-8 is a sample of recent divisors.

DATE	NEW DIVISOR	OLD DIVISOR	REASON For CHANGE
9/23/13	0.15571590501117	0.130216081	The Goldman Sachs Group Inc. replaced Bank of America Corp., Visa Inc. replaced Hewlett-Packard Co., and Nike Inc. replaced Alcoa Inc.
9/24/12	0.130216081	0.129146820	UnitedHealth Group Inc. replaced Kraft Foods Incorporated Cl A.
8/13/12	0.129146820	0.132129493	Coca-Cola Co. stock split 2 for 1.
7/2/10	0.132129493	0.132319125	Verizon Communications Incorporated spun off New Communications Holdings Inc. (Spinco). Immediately following the spin off, Frontier Communications Corp. acquired Spinco.
6/8/09	0.132319125	0.125552709	Cisco Systems Inc. replaced General Motors Corp. and Travelers Companies Inc. replaced Citigroup Inc.
MANY MORE	MANY MORE	MANY MORE	MANY MORE
11/5/28	16.02	16.67	Atlantic Refining stock split 4 for 1.

Figure 1-8. *DJIA historical divisor changes*

Dow Jones and Company started out as a news and publishing company. In 2010, the CME Group bought the Dow Jones Indexes (DJI) from News Corporation.

S&P 500

The Standard & Poor's 500 Index (S&P 500) is a market capitalization weighted index of 500 large-cap common stocks. The Bloomberg quote on BTMM (Figure 1-1) is actually the futures price (discussed in the next section). The spot quote and the change from the previous day is on USSW (Figure 1-2). A committee at Standard and Poor's determines the components of this index based on several criteria, including market capitalization, financial viability, and length of time publicly traded. The large majority of the components are US entities; as of 2014, 27 components are non-US companies. The chosen companies are meant to represent all the large industries of the US economy. It is far more diverse than the DJIA and is considered the general measure of stock prices in the US market. The index is calculated as

$$\text{S\&P 500} = \frac{\sum_{i=1}^{500} Px_i \cdot \text{Shares}_i}{\text{Divisor}} \quad (1.7)$$

where Px_i is the price of each stock in the index, Shares_i is the number of outstanding publicly traded shares of that stock, and the divisor is used in a similar manner as that of the DJIA. This divisor adjustment is made to take into account changes in the constituent stocks and corporate actions such as spin-offs and special cash dividends. Unlike the DJIA, it does not take into account stock splits, because the effect is usually small for a pool of 500 assets. The divisor is proprietary to Standard and Poor's and therefore can only be approximated from historical data.

The index is updated every 15 seconds during the course of a trading day and disseminated by Thomson Reuters. The first provider of an investment tracking the S&P 500 was the Vanguard Group's mutual fund Vanguard 500 in 1976.

Standard and Poor's is a financial research and credit rating firm. They are one of the best-known credit rating agencies in the world (along with Moody's). In February 2013, the Department of Justice sued Standard & Poor's for fraudulently inflating its ratings of risky mortgage investments and thus helping trigger the 2008 financial crisis.

NASDAQ Composite Index

The NASDAQ Composite Index is a capitalization-weighted stock market index of over 3,000 common stocks, ADRs (American Depository Receipts), limited partnerships, and other securities. It is not exclusive to US companies. All the underlying stocks trade on the NASDAQ Stock Market. It is usually seen as an indicator of technology and growth stocks. Another popular index is the NASDAQ 100, composed of the largest nonfinancial companies by market cap listed on the NASDAQ exchange. NASDAQ is the largest electronic stock exchange in the world by trading volume.

The National Association of Securities Dealers (NASD) founded the National Association of Securities Dealers Automated Quotations (NASDAQ) stock exchange in 1971—the first electronic exchange using a computerized trading system without a physical trading floor.

(It is generally conceded that physical trading floors will disappear in the not-so-distant future.) The NASDAQ became popular during the infancy of the computer revolution. Many technology companies (such as Apple, Microsoft, and Cisco) traded on the NASDAQ rather than the New York Stock Exchange (NYSE). The NASDAQ index peaked during the dot-com bubble at an all-time high of 5,048 on March 10, 2000, and hit the bottom of the post-burst decline at an intra-day low of 1,108 on October 10, 2002. As of early 2014, it recovered to above 4,000 (whereas both the DJIA and the S&P 500 recovered to their all-time highs).

Commercial Paper

Just as the US Treasury issues short-dated T-bills, large banks and corporations issue similar short-dated unsecured discount bonds for which the quoted interest rates imply the discount price of the bond. These types of bonds are called *commercial paper* (CP)—as opposed to *government paper*. Those coming specifically from financial firms are called *dealer CP*. The Bloomberg "Comm Paper" quotes (Figure 1-1) are in two columns: the term (in days) and the implied interest rate (discount yield) (Figure 1-9). CP is a form of unsecured promissory notes with a fixed maturity under 270 days. They are issued to meet short-term cash flow issues. Like T-bills, they are discount bonds whose face value is paid at the maturity date. The discount yields quoted on BTMM are a composite of offered levels for highly-rated (A1/P1-rated) short-term debt. A1 is the highest short-term rating assigned by S&P; P1 is the highest rating assigned by Moody's. Most large US banks have CP conduits to issue dealer CP. The discount rates of CP are almost always higher than T-bills owing to the differential credit risk of the issuer compared to the US government. During the financial crisis of 2008, many dealers could not raise money through their CP conduits and therefore had to go to the Fed for liquid cash (through the fed funds window and the *Discount Window*, discussed in the "Discount Rate" section). The term *paper* originates from the original "bearer bonds," whereby the bearer of the physical paper describing the bond is the owner (the paper having no owner's name attached to it). They were used by investors who wished to remain anonymous. Bearer bonds are no longer used but the term *paper* has remained.

Comm Paper	
15D	0.140
30D	0.130
60D	0.140
90D	0.170
120D	0.200
180D	0.270

Figure 1-9. Commercial Paper Discount Rates. Used with permission of Bloomberg L.P. Copyright© 2014. All rights reserved.

LIBOR

Recall that eurodollar deposits were created to hold US dollars outside the United States, primarily by British banks headquartered in London. In general, foreign banks cannot go to the Federal Reserve to borrow dollars. Instead, they go to these London banks to borrow dollars (and other currencies), and the interest rates they are charged are called the *London Interbank Offered Rate* (LIBOR). This is the hub of a very large interbank market of unsecured funds. Currencies now having LIBOR rates include the US dollar (USD), British pound sterling, Japanese yen, and Canadian dollars. The LIBOR market is (very) loosely regulated by the British Bankers Association (BBA). The June 2012 LIBOR scandal revealed significant fraud and collusion among member banks and serious lack of oversight by the BBA. Member banks of the BBA now come from more than 60 nations.

LIBOR has developed into one of the most important interest rate for US dollars in spite of being a largely foreign-controlled rate. In 2012, 45% of prime adjustable-rate mortgages (ARMs) and 80% of subprime mortgages in the US were indexed to LIBOR. The majority of US interest rate swaps (discussed in the "Futures and Swaps" section) are based on USD LIBOR. Almost all standard *yield curves* used by large US banks for discounting purposes are based on LIBOR rates, eurodollar futures, and LIBOR swaps. As of 2013, there has been a strong trend towards OIS discounting discussed in Chapter 7. Over $400 trillion of derivatives are linked to LIBOR. The Bloomberg "LIBOR Fix" rate quotes (Figure 1-1) are the average of all rates transacted during the day between member banks. Note that USD LIBOR is calculated on an act/360 daycount basis convention. These quotes (Figure 1-10) are in two columns: the term and the LIBOR fixing rate.

3) LIBOR Fix	
O/N	0.08770
1W	0.12030
1M	0.15050
2M	0.19250
3M	0.22935
6M	0.32390
1Y	0.53540

Figure 1-10. LIBOR Fix rate quote. Used with permission of Bloomberg L.P. Copyright© 2014. All rights reserved.

Spot Forex

The foreign exchange (forex, FX) market is very large and is one of the first markets to trade 24 hours a day. It is also one of the first markets to embrace electronic trading. The first high-frequency electronic trading algorithms were initiated in the FX market. The FX market for G7 countries is very liquid. These countries have *free-floating* currencies. Other countries such as India and China limit the volume of FX transactions in their countries and are not free-floating. The FX market is driven by many factors, both economic and geopolitical.

It is one of the few markets that must deal with external manipulation when countries try to control their exchange rates by buying or selling their currencies appropriately. For instance, Japan, as a traditional net exporter, wants a relatively weak yen compared to the dollar. When the yen reaches levels considered too strong for the Japanese economy, the Bank of Japan sells yen and buys dollars, creating a downward pressure on the yen in the open market. From this point of view, the yen is not completely free-floating.

This Bloomberg section has the most common spot forex rates with respect to the US dollar (see Figure 1-11). Each FX rate has its own quotation convention, as follows:

> JPY = yen/US dollars
>
> EUR = US dollars/euro
>
> GBP = US dollars/pound
>
> CHF = Swiss francs/US dollars
>
> CAD = Canadian dollars/US dollars

The reverse conventions to the ones just here are occasionally used, so one must be wary.

Figure 1-11. *Popular Foreign Exchange Rates with respect to the US Dollar.*
Used with permission of Bloomberg L.P. Copyright© 2014. All rights reserved.

Key Rates

Three domestic interest rates important to all financial institutions in the United States are the prime rate, the federal funds target rate, and the discount rate (see Figure 1-12).

Figure 1-12. *Key US Dollar Interest Rates.* Used with permission of Bloomberg L.P. Copyright© 2014. All rights reserved.

Prime Rate

Historically, this has been the interest rate at which banks lent to their favored (least risky) customers (as opposed to subprime lending). The method of determining the credit risk of a customer often comes down to the customer's credit score (from three well-known consumer credit agencies). Consumer credit scores are very much analogous to the credit ratings of bonds by credit rating agencies such as Moody's and S&P.

The prime rate is an average rate calculated from about 30 banks. The Bloomberg quote is updated when 13 out of the top 25 banks (based on assets) change their prime rate. Many variables rates, such as those used for ARMs and home equity loans, are indexed off the prime rate (i.e., prime + fixed spread).

Federal Funds Target Rate

As discussed in the "Federal Funds" section, the federal funds target rate (Bloomberg symbol, FDTR) is set in a target range (0.00%–0.25% between 2008 and 2014). The Fed monitors the actual fed funds rate transacted between banks and executes repo and reverse repo transactions to keep the transacted rate in line with the target rate.

Discount Rate

On the rare occasion that a bank cannot borrow money from another bank in the fed funds market, it can go directly to the Fed, which charges the *discount rate*. This rate is set higher than the FDTR because the Fed wants to discourage the use of this mechanism, called the *Discount Window*. The term is usually overnight. During the 2008 financial crisis, many large banks used the Discount Window but kept that fact quiet so as not to create a larger panic. The Fed also did not release this information until after the initial phase of the crisis had subsided.

Gold

The Bloomberg GOLD quote is listed on BTMM under "Commodities" in two columns: the last traded price for 1 troy ounce of gold (~31.1 grams); and the change from the previous day's price. Gold has a long history as a form of currency and as a tool in the management of national and international financial and economic systems. It is still used as a standard hedge against poor economic times. The price of gold broke the $1,800 barrier in 2011 in response to the recession following the 2008 financial crisis, tripling its value from pre-crisis levels. Until 1971, the United States had a *gold standard*, by which the US dollar was pegged to one troy ounce of gold at $35. This was the rate at which foreign governments could exchange US dollars for gold, thereby implying an FX rate with their own local currency. At that time, the United States had very large reserves of gold. Other currencies have had gold standards, with the Swiss franc being the last one to divorce itself from this practice in 2000. Although gold has only relatively minor industrial use apart from jewelry, it is the most popular precious metal investment for financial reasons of hedging, harbor, and speculation. When the price of gold shot up in the Great Recession, people started buying silver as "the poor man's gold."

CHAPTER 1 ■ FINANCIAL INSTRUMENTS

Futures and Swaps

A *futures contract* is a financial agreement to buy or sell a prespecified quality and quantity of an asset (physical or financial) at a fixed date in the future (*maturity date* or *delivery date*) for a prespecified price (the *futures price* or the *strike price*). Physical assets include commodities such as oil, corn, wheat, and gold. Any financial asset—such as equity indices, bonds, or currencies—can serve as the underlying asset of a futures contract. The first futures ever traded were on commodities. The original rationale for buying a futures contract was to lock in the price of an asset in the future, thereby eliminating any price risk at the delivery date. For instance, cattle ranchers sell cattle futures and deliver the cattle on the delivery date at the fixed futures price. If they had not sold futures contracts, they would have taken the price risk of cattle on the delivery day making either more or less than by the futures transaction. By selling futures contracts, these ranchers guarantee a fixed price (and, they hope, an assured profit).

A *long position* in the futures contract commits the holder to purchase the asset at the maturity date at the futures price. The holder is said to be *long* the underlying asset. The *short seller* of the futures contract must deliver the asset to the long holder at the maturity date. Certain futures contracts are cash-settled without an actual delivery of the underlying asset. In these cases, the cash exchange is based on the difference between the futures price and the spot price of the asset at the maturity date.

Futures trade on a *futures exchange* that acts as an intermediary between the buyer and seller of the futures contract. Famous exchanges are the Chicago Board of Trade (CBOT) and the Chicago Mercantile Exchange (CME). The exchange creates the standardization of futures contracts by setting the types and qualities of the underlying assets, the various delivery dates, and other details. This standardization process makes futures very liquid, because all investors have a common set of assets to trade. Cash-settled futures can have a greater volume than their underlying assets because the futures contracts are completely synthetic. Futures provide access to all popular financial indices such as the S&P 500 and the DJIA (which are themselves synthetic constructs). The futures exchange also acts as a mechanism to reduce *counterparty credit risk* (CCR) (discussed in Chapter 7). CCR is the risk to either counterparty of a futures contract from failing to execute their contractual obligation (*defaulting*). A futures exchange minimizes CCR through the use of a *clearing house*. First, the exchange distributes buyers and sellers of futures between all participating investors, thereby reducing the exposure to any one counterparty. Second, the exchange requires all participants to have a *margin account* of cash or very liquid securities such as T-bills. For every transaction, traders must *post margin* of between 5% and 15% of a future contracts value. This margin account is held at the clearing house.

The clearing house deals with all post-trading issues such as the clearing of payments between the two counterparties and settlements of contracts at maturity. Their largest role is to guarantee the futures contract by effectively becoming seller to each buyer and buyer to each seller of the contract. If the original buyer or seller defaults, the clearing house assumes the defaulted counterparty's role and responsibilities. The margin account is designed to minimize this credit risk to the clearing house. There are two main types of margin: initial margin and variation margin. *Initial margin* is the initial amount of cash needed to transact a futures contract. This amount is determined by the exchange and is based on the typical daily price changes of a specific futures contract. More volatile futures have higher initial margins. Once a trade is initiated, its end-of-day profit and loss

17

(P&L) statement is calculated. This is known as daily *marking to market* (which may be performed for intraday periods as well). This daily P&L will be taken from the margin account of the loss side and given to the profit side's margin account. This daily settlement of margin accounts is what is referred to as *variation margin*. If a margin account does not have the requisite amount, a margin call is made to the account holder, who must deposit the necessary funds within a day to meet the margin requirement. If the account holder does not meet the margin call, the clearing house may close profitable positions of the account holder to satisfy the margin requirement.

Trading in futures involves "leverage". Other than the margin, there is no other cost to purchase a futures contract. One simply enters a futures contract as a buyer or seller. For example, the S&P 500 futures contract quoted in BTMM is for front month delivery (March, June, September, and Dec). The contract size is $250 * S&P500 index level. Suppose the margin requirement for one contract is 10% (at most). This implies a leverage of 10 times as compared to a pure cash position since one needs to put down only 10% to get a 100% exposure of the notional amount $250 * S&P500 index.

Not all futures like contracts are traded on the exchange. *Forward* contracts, which are almost identical to futures, are traded directly between counterparties. This type of transaction is called a *over-the-counter* (OTC) trade. Forwards have no margin requirements or settlement of daily P&L and have no credit risk mitigants. The OTC forward market is not large (unlike the OTC derivatives market discussed in the "Derivatives and Structured Products" section). Note that the forward price and the future price of an asset need not be the same.

Crude Oil

Under "Commodities" BTMM quotes the prices of two physical assets (see Figure 1-13): gold and a specific quality and quantity of crude oil called the New York Mercantile West Texas Intermediate (NYM WTI) light sweet crude oil, as specified in a front-month-delivery futures contract. Light crude oil is liquid petroleum that has a low density, allowing it to flow freely at room temperature. It is worth more than heavy crude because it produces a higher percentage of gasoline and diesel fuel. Sweet crude oil is also a type of petroleum that contains less than 0.5% of sulfur and actually has a mildly sweet taste. Light sweet crude oil is the most sought-after version of crude oil for producing gasoline, kerosene, diesel fuel, heating oil, and jet fuel. The specific light sweet crude oil for delivery underlying this futures contract is West Texas Intermediate (WTI). It is the basic benchmark for all oil pricing. The other standard light sweet oil is Brent Crude from the North Sea. NYM WTI future contracts trade in units of 1,000 barrels, and the delivery point is Cushing, Oklahoma, which is accessible to the international market via pipelines. The characteristics of this futures contract are as follow:

>*Trading units*: 1,000 barrels (42,000 gallons)

>*Trading month*: The front-month contract (there exist several other maturities, this one being the first of 30 consecutive months plus 36, 48, 60, 72, and 84 months to delivery)

>*Last trading day*: Third business day prior to the 25th calendar day of the month

Futures price quote: US dollars per barrel

Delivery location: Cushing, Oklahoma

Delivery period: Starts on the first calendar day and ends on the last calendar day

These futures trade on the New York Mercantile Exchange (NYME). The Bloomberg BTMM quote consists of the last traded price and the change from the previous day's price.

```
Commodities
NYM WTI      104.42    +0.68
GOLD        1291.33    -2.69
```

Figure 1-13. *Crude Oil Quote. Used with permission of Bloomberg L.P. Copyright© 2014. All rights reserved.*

Fed Funds Futures

The underlying asset of fed funds futures is the effective fed funds interest rate. The underlying unit (that is, the futures' standardized quantity) is the interest earned on fed funds having a face value of $5,000,000 for one month calculated on a 30-day basis at a rate equal to the average overnight fed funds rate for the contract month indicated in the first column under "Funds Future" on BTMM (see Figure 1-14). The price quote in the second column is 100 minus the futures fed fund rate. For instance, a quote of 99.9 implies a futures fed fund rate of 10 basis points. The settlement price at expiration is $\left[100 - \bar{r}_{\textit{effective}}\right]$ where it is cash settled as follows. Suppose the January futures contract is trading at 95. Then the initial *contract* price is

$$\text{Price} = \$5,000,000\left(1 - 0.05\frac{30}{360}\right) = \$4,979,167 \quad . \tag{1.8}$$

Suppose that the settlement price the end of January is 96. Then the contract settles at

$$\text{Price} = \$5,000,000\left(1 - 0.04\frac{30}{360}\right) = \$4,983,333 \quad , \tag{1.9}$$

leaving a profit of $4,167. Because of the $\left[100 - \bar{r}_{\textit{effective}}\right]$ quotation convention, going long the futures is equivalent to going short the fed funds rate.

Funds Future	
MAY	99.913
JUN	99.910
JUL	99.905
AUG	99.900
SEP	99.900
OCT	99.895

Figure 1-14. Fed Funds Futures Contracts. Used with permission of Bloomberg L.P. Copyright© 2014. All rights reserved.

90-Day Eurodollar Futures

LIBOR is the most commonly used US dollar interest rate, and 3-month (3M) LIBOR is the most popular of the LIBOR rates. 90-day eurodollar futures are futures on 3M LIBOR. These futures contracts trade with delivery months of March, June, September, and December up to 10 years in the future. The Bloomberg quote indicates the term and the futures price quote (see Figure 1-15). The 3M LIBOR rate is applicable to a 90-day period beginning on the third Wednesday of the delivery month. The futures contract is settled in cash on the second London business day before the third Wednesday of the month. These futures *imply* a series of forward-starting 3M LIBOR rates. The implied rate (*in percent*) is derived from the futures quote by the relation

$$\text{forward implied 3M LIBOR} = 100 - \textit{futures price} \quad \cdot \quad (1.10)$$

90D EUR$ FUT	
JUN	99.7750
SEP	99.7600
DEC	99.7300
MAR	99.6650
JUN	99.5250
SEP	99.3450

Figure 1-15. 3M LIBOR Futures Contracts. Used with permission of Bloomberg L.P. Copyright© 2014. All rights reserved.

For instance, a futures price of 99.6 implies an interest rate of 0.40%. The relationship between the quoted futures price and the contract price (contract size 1 mm) is

$$Contract = 1,000,000\left[1 - \frac{90}{360}\frac{(100 - futures\ price)}{100}\right]$$
$$= 1,000,000\left[1 - \frac{90}{360}\frac{(forward\ implied\ 3M\ LIBOR)}{100}\right] \quad (1.11)$$

Consider, for example, a futures quote of 99.6. The futures contract price is

$$1,000,000\left[1 - .25\frac{(100 - 99.6000)}{100}\right] = \$999,000.00 \quad (1.12)$$

This contract will be settled in cash at the 3M LIBOR rate setting on the settlement date of the futures delivery month. Assume this rate settled at 0.35%. Then the final contract value is

$$1,000,000[1 - .25(0.0035)] = \$999,125.00 \quad (1.13)$$

As with fed funds futures, going long the 90-day eurodollar futures is equivalent to going short 3M LIBOR. Note that a 3M LIBOR spot rate is not exactly applicable over 90 days as the basis convention is act/360, making the actual days between 88 and 92. The futures contract ignores this discrepancy, but market participants who use this contract to hedge their interest rate exposures must take this into account.

10-Year Treasury Note Futures

The Bloomberg BTMM quote under "10Y Note Future" is for the CBOT 10-year Treasury note futures (see Figure 1-16). The price quote uses the *tick* convention of Treasury notes and bonds. The underlying bond for delivery for this futures contract can be any US government bond (on-the-run or off-the-run) with a maturity between 6.5 to 10 years. There is no prespecified coupon for the delivered bond. To deal with these varying characteristics, such as coupon and maturity, the Treasury uses a *conversion factor* invoicing system to reflect the value of the delivered security with respect to a standardized reference 6% bond. In particular, the *principal invoice amount* paid from the long position holder to the short position holder on delivery is given by

principal invoice price = futures settlement price · conversion factor · 1000 (1.14)

Figure 1-16. *T-Note Futures. Used with permission of Bloomberg L.P. Copyright© 2014. All rights reserved.*

The factor of a 1,000 reflects the contract size of $100,000. The *total invoice amount* includes accrued interest (as typical of all bond calculations):

$$\text{total invoice price} = \text{principal invoice price} + \text{accrued interest} \qquad (1.15)$$

Figure 1-17 displays conversion factors for commonly delivered bonds. Treasury note futures have quarterly contract months (March, June, September, December). The Bloomberg quote is for the nearest-month delivery.

Coupon	Issue Date	Maturity Date	Jun. 2014	Sep. 2014	Dec. 2014	Mar. 2015	Jun. 2015
2 3/8	12/31/13	12/31/20	0.8072	-----	-----	-----	-----
2 1/8	01/31/14	01/31/21	0.7939	-----	-----	-----	-----
3 5/8	02/15/11	02/15/21	0.8737	-----	-----	-----	-----
2	02/28/14	02/28/21	0.7873	-----	-----	-----	-----
2 1/4	03/31/14	03/31/21	0.7943	0.8006	-----	-----	-----
2 1/4	04/30/14	04/30/21	0.7943	0.8006	-----	-----	-----
3 1/8	05/16/11	05/15/21	0.8423	0.8471	-----	-----	-----
2 1/8	08/15/11	08/15/21	0.7811	0.7875	0.7939	-----	-----
2	11/15/11	11/15/21	0.7676	0.7741	0.7806	0.7873	-----
2	02/15/12	02/15/22	0.7612	0.7676	0.7741	0.7806	0.7873
1 3/4	05/15/12	05/15/22	0.7396	0.7463	0.7531	0.7600	0.7669
1 5/8	08/15/12	08/15/22	0.7252	0.7320	0.7389	0.7458	0.7529
1 5/8	11/15/12	11/15/22	0.7185	0.7252	0.7320	0.7389	0.7458
2	02/15/13	02/15/23	0.7367	0.7426	0.7488	0.7549	0.7612
1 3/4	05/15/13	05/15/23	0.7139	0.7202	0.7266	0.7331	0.7396
2 1/2	08/15/13	08/15/23	0.7593	0.7644	0.7696	0.7748	0.7802
2 3/4	11/15/13	11/15/23	0.7718	0.7765	0.7812	0.7861	0.7909
2 3/4	02/18/14	02/15/24	0.7672	0.7718	0.7765	0.7812	0.7861
2 1/2	05/15/14	05/15/24	0.7444	0.7493	0.7542	0.7593	0.7644

Figure 1-17. 10-year Treasury note futures contract conversion factors for nineteen listed Treasury notes

These conversion factors may be thought of as standardizing the prices of the delivered securities as though they were yielding 6%. Clearly, high-coupon securities tend to have high conversion factors and low-coupon securities tend to have low conversion factors. In particular, bonds with coupons lower than the 6% contract standard have factors that are less than 1.0 (factors greater than one do not exist due to the low interest rate environment circa 2014).

Say, or example, one delivers the first bond listed in Figure 1-17 for a futures price of 125-25+. Upon delivery, the cash exchanged (excluding accrued interest) is

$$\begin{aligned}\text{principal invoice price} &= (125-25+) \cdot (0.8072) \cdot 1000 \\ &= (125.796875)(0.8072)(1000) = \$101{,}543.24\end{aligned} \qquad (1.16)$$

There exists a *cheapest-to-deliver* option embedded into the Treasury note futures, whereby the short holder of a futures contact has an option to deliver a variety of different bonds. The short seller will go through every allowable bond to find what appears to be the cheapest to deliver using live bond prices. This has become so common that Treasury note futures trade with an implied cheapest-to-deliver bond, such that most sellers converge to the same bond.

Swaps

A *swap* is a generic term for a financial contract between two parties to exchange cash flows at periodic times in the future. These cash flows are linked to some underlying financial instrument in a manner similar to futures. The five most common types of swaps are *interest rate* swaps, *cross currency* swaps, *credit default* swaps, *total return* swaps, and *equity* swaps. Recall that a futures contract is a contractual agreement to exchange cash (the futures price) for delivery of the underlying instrument at the maturity date or a cash settlement at a maturity date. A cash-settled futures contract can be seen as a one-period swap, and therefore a swap may be seen as series of forward-starting cash-settled futures contracts. The majority of swaps are OTC, as opposed to futures, which trade on an exchange.

A *vanilla interest rate swap* is a contractual agreement between two parties to exchange a fixed interest rate cash flow (the swap rate) for a floating interest rate cash flow (3M LIBOR) based on a predefined principal amount (the notional) for a fixed period of time (the tenor or maturity) (see Figure 1-18). For standard interest rate swaps, the notional is not exchanged at the end. The US dollar swap rates quoted on BTMM are for swaps with semiannual fixed swap rate payments (the *fixed leg*), as opposed to quarterly 3M LIBOR floating rate payments (the *floating leg*). The swap rate is fixed for the life of the deal, whereas the floating rate 3M LIBOR payments are set in the future. The Bloomberg quote lists the appropriate swap tenor and the corresponding fixed swap rate (see Figure 1-19). Note that this is a mid-market estimate, and standard bid–offer mechanisms come into play. Also note that this market has become so tight and liquid that many live quotes have four decimal places.

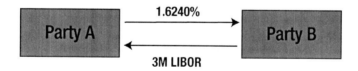

Figure 1-18. A Vanilla Interest Rate Swap.

CHAPTER 1 ■ FINANCIAL INSTRUMENTS

Swaps	
3Y	0.8931
5Y	1.6240
10Y	2.6269
30Y	3.3600

Figure 1-19. USD 3M LIBOR Swap Rates. *Used with permission of Bloomberg L.P. Copyright© 2014. All rights reserved.*

The characteristics of the payment legs arise from the original use of these swaps, which was to turn fixed-rate bonds into floating-rate bonds. Historically, a large majority of fixed-rate bonds pay semiannually on a 30/360 basis (this is no longer the case). The most popular US interest rate is 3M LIBOR, which pays quarterly on an act/360 basis.

Swap Valuation

Swap valuation comes down to the notion that the ability to calculate the *present value* (PV) of future cash flows is the most basic technique needed in financial valuation. All large financial institutions use *yield curves* (often called *discount curves*) to calculate the PV of all future cash flows (positive or negative) coming from the financial instruments held on the balance sheet of the firm. Many yield curves are created from LIBOR rates, LIBOR futures, and swap rates. The interdependency is clear. One needs swap rate quotes to create yield curves, and one needs a yield curve to value a swap. What order should one follow? This section gives an abbreviated description of the role in swap valuation of *discount factors*—the factors by which future cash flows must be multiplied to return present values. Chapter 2 gives a full description of yield curve construction.

Even though pure LIBOR based discounting has been used for years on Wall Street, the financial crisis of 2008 has led to technical nuances such that one needs to take into account the counterparty and collaralization of swaps that materially affect the discounting methodology of swaps. These issues are further explored in Chapter 7 ("OIS Discounting").

Suppose one invests $1 for three months earning 3M LIBOR. The final value of the investment at the end of three months will be

$$\text{Final Value} = \$1 \cdot (1 + \delta L)$$
$$\text{where } \delta = \frac{\text{actual days in three month period}}{360} \,. \quad (1.17)$$
$$L = \text{3M LIBOR}$$

If you want to receive exactly $1 in three months, you invest $[1/(1+\delta L)]$ today. A LIBOR-based discount factor is defined as the price today ($t = 0$, where t denotes time) of a *zero coupon* bond whereby one receives $1 at maturity $t = T$. This discount factor is denoted $df(0, T)$. If $T = 3M$,

$$df(0,3M) = \frac{1}{1+\delta L} \qquad (1.18)$$

Other tenors need a combination of LIBOR rates and cannot be written like the foregoing expression (see Chapter 2). Nonetheless, to calculate the present value of a cash flow at some future time T, multiply it by the discount factor $df(0, T)$. Discount factors need not start at time $t = 0$. Forward-starting discount factors are given by $(0 < t < T)$

$$df(t,T) = \frac{df(0,T)}{df(0,t)} \qquad (1.19)$$

Clearly, $df(t, t) = 1$.

Let $t_1^{fxd}, t_2^{fxd}, t_3^{fxd}, \ldots t_{n_{fixed}}^{fxd} = T$ denote the semiannual coupon dates of the semiannual fixed leg of a vanilla interest rate swap with maturity T. The *PV of the fixed leg of the swap* is the sum of present values of all the coupon payments,

$$PV_{fixed} = \sum_{i=1}^{n_{fixed}} S\Delta_i df(0,t_i^{fxd}) \qquad (1.20)$$

S = swap rate

$\Delta_i = 30/360$ daycount fraction from t_{i-1}^{fxd} to t_i^{fxd}

Since the swap rate is fixed, it can be moved out of the sum. The sum without the swap rate is called the *dollar value of a basis point* (DV01),

$$DV01 = \sum_{i=1}^{n_{fixed}} \Delta_i df(0,t_i^{fxd}) \qquad (1.21)$$

The fixed-leg PV is then given by

$$PV_{fixed} = S \cdot DV01 \qquad (1.22)$$

Let $t_1^{flt}, t_2^{flt}, t_3^{flt}, \ldots, T$ denote the coupon dates of the quarterly-paying floating LIBOR leg. The PV of the floating leg of the swap is

$$PV_{floating} = \sum_{j=1}^{n_{flt}} L_j \delta_j df(0,t_j^{flt}) \qquad (1.23)$$

L_j = 3M foward LIBOR set at t_{j-1}^{flt}

δ_j = Act/360 daycount fraction from t_{j-1}^{flt} to t_j^{flt}

The forward-starting LIBOR rates L_j are related to the LIBOR discount factors as

$$df(0,t_j) = \frac{df(0,t_{j-1}^{flt})}{1+\delta_j L_j} \qquad (1.24)$$

or

$$L_j = \left[\frac{df(0,t_{j-1}^{flt})}{df(0,t_j^{flt})} - 1\right]\frac{1}{\delta_j} \quad . \quad (1.25)$$

Substituting this expression into $PV_{floating}$ leaves one with ($t_0 = 0$)

$$\begin{aligned} PV_{floating} &= df(0,t_0) - df(0,T) = 1 - df(0,T) \\ PV_{floating} &+ df(0,T) = 1 \\ PV_{floating} &= 1 - df(0,T) \end{aligned} \quad (1.26)$$

Equation 1.26 simply states that at $t = 0$, a series of LIBOR floating rate payments discounted at LIBOR plus a par payment at maturity is worth par today. Note that once the first LIBOR rate has been set ($t > 0$), this is no longer true.

One of the purposes of swap valuation is to find an expression for the swap rate, S. The swap rate is the single most important characteristic of an interest rate swap. It is the swap rate that is quoted market pricing. The LIBOR rates, other than the first one, are unknown (that is why they are called "floating"). At the initiation of a swap, $t = 0$, both parties wish to have the same PV for their future cash flows (or else someone is getting the better deal). Therefore at $t = 0$, set the two swap legs equal to each other and solve for the fair value swap rate,

$$PV_{fixed} = PV_{floating} \quad (1.27)$$

$$S \cdot DV01 = 1 - df(0,T) \quad (1.28)$$

$$S = \frac{1 - df(0,T)}{DV01} \quad . \quad (1.29)$$

As time evolves ($t > 0$), the PV of each leg changes as LIBOR rates change and coupon payments are made. Either leg could be more valuable than the other at any time in the future depending on the level of interest rates. For instance, if one is paying fixed and receiving float, the value of their swap after initiation is $PV_{swap} = PV_{floating} - PV_{fixed}$. If is is the other way around, one has $PV_{swap} = PV_{floating} - PV_{fixed}$. The receiver of the swap rate is short interest rates, whereas the receiver of the floating payments is long.

Swap Spreads

As there are many different kinds of interest rates, it is often useful to compare them with each other. A *swap spread* is the difference between a LIBOR-based swap rate and the yield of the equivalent on-the-run US Treasury bond of the same maturity as the term of the swap. They are derived from the traded swap rates. The 2-, 3-, 5-, 10-, and 30-year swap spreads are over the actual benchmarks. Other maturities are interpolated. The top left corner of Bloomberg screen USSW (Figure 1-2) has three columns of US Treasury yields in percent: terms, ask side yields, and their changes from the previous close (GV ASK/CHG). Next to this section are the corresponding swap spreads in basis points (SW/GV). The adjacent section (SWAP MID) lists the mid-market swap rates by tenor (see Figure 1-20).

CHAPTER 1 ■ FINANCIAL INSTRUMENTS

GV Ask/Chg			SW/GV		Swap Mid	
2Y	0.342	+0.000	16.05 +0.30		0.504	+0.003
3Y	0.774	-0.008	11.88 +0.20		0.893	-0.007
4Y	1.189	-0.013	13.25 -0.25		1.284	-0.013
5Y	1.527	-0.015	9.50 +0.00		1.624	-0.015
7Y	2.072	-0.012	6.94 -0.21		2.142	-0.017
10Y	2.534	-0.016	9.25 -0.25		2.628	-0.019
30Y	3.398	-0.029	-3.69 +0.13		3.358	-0.032

Figure 1-20. USD Swap Spreads. Used with permission of Bloomberg L.P. Copyright© 2014. All rights reserved.

Swap spreads can be decomposed into three components:

- There exists a convenience yield for holding US Treasuries, because they are very liquid and are often seen as equivalent to cash. Therefore, their yields are almost always tighter (smaller) than LIBOR leading to positive swap spreads.

- The inherent credit risk of LIBOR used to be AA. (Prior to the 2008 crisis, the majority of large banks dealing in LIBOR were rated AA.) US Treasuries are seen as virtually riskless compared to any other investment such as swaps, and therefore swap rates are wider than Treasury yields.

- There are swap-specific factors driven by market conditions, such as periods of strong refinancing in the MBS market (described in the "30-Year MBS" section) and large fixed-rate bond issuance.

Since 2008, owing to the budget and political problems in the United States, long-dated swap spreads such as the 30-year swap spread occasionally became negative.

Swap Futures

The creation of swap futures was the first attempt to bring the OTC interest rate swap market into the exchange environment. It has not been that successful: most interest rate swaps are still traded OTC. Bloomberg-listed swap futures are exchange-traded and cleared on the CME, largely eliminating counterparty credit risk. Unlike the OTC market, swap futures have standardized terms and constant maturity, are marked-to-market daily, and do not require International Swaps and Derivatives Association (ISDA) agreements. These futures are either deliverable or cash settled, with delivery months of March, June, September, and December.

Swap futures are futures on a prespecified fixed leg of an interest rate swap (the swap rate via the fixed leg is the traded component of a swap). For instance, the 5-year swap future is based on the notional price of a 5-year fixed leg with notional $100,000 that has a swap rate of 2% and receives 3M LIBOR. These are the standardized characteristics needed for listing on the CME (see Figure 1-21). Rather than quoting a future 5-year swap rate, the convention is to represent the contract in PV terms. The implied future swap rate is used as the one interest rate to discount all future cash flows of the standardized fixed leg (using simple discounting), such that

27

CHAPTER 1 ■ FINANCIAL INSTRUMENTS

$$PV_{fixed} = 100\sum_{i=1}^{10} S\Delta_i df(0,t_i^{fxd}) + 100 \cdot df(0,t_{10}^{fxd})$$

$$S = 2\%$$

$$\Delta_i = 1/2 \text{(semi-annual)} \qquad (1.30)$$

$$df(0,t_i^{fxd}) = \frac{1}{\left(1+\frac{R_5}{2}\right)^i}$$

$$R_5 = \text{Implied 5 yr Swap Rate}$$

Reference Swap Tenor	Jun 2014	Sept 2014
5 YR	2.00%	2.25%
10 YR	3.00%	3.25%
30 YR	3.75%	4.00%

Figure 1-21. *Swap Future Coupon Rates*

This expression can be simplified to

$$PV_{fixed} = \frac{(100)(0.02)}{2}\sum_{i=1}^{10}\left(1+\frac{R_5}{2}\right)^{-i} + 100\cdot\left(1+\frac{R_5}{2}\right)^{-10} \qquad (1.31)$$

A geometric series formula may be used to explicitly sum the (1.31) expression

$$\sum_{i=1}^{n} x^i = \frac{x(1-x^n)}{1-x}, x = \left(1+\frac{R_5}{2}\right)^{-1} \qquad (1.32)$$

$$\sum_{i=1}^{10}\left(1+\frac{R_5}{2}\right)^{-i} = \frac{\left(1+\frac{R_5}{2}\right)^{-1}\left[1-\left(1+\frac{R_5}{2}\right)^{-10}\right]}{1-\left(1+\frac{R_5}{2}\right)^{-1}} = \frac{2}{R_5}\left[1-\left(1+\frac{R_5}{2}\right)^{-10}\right] \qquad (1.33)$$

Finally,

$$PV_{fixed} = 100\left[\frac{0.02}{R_5} + \left(1-\frac{0.02}{R_5}\right)\left(1+\frac{R_5}{2}\right)^{-10}\right] \qquad (1.34)$$

From this formula, it is easy to see that if the swap rate is precisely 2%, PV_{fixed} is par. Swap rates higher than 2% make the PV less than par and conversely. Going long the futures means going short the swap rate. The final settlement price of each contract is the PV of the standard fixed leg (with notional payment) discounted at a yield equal to the ISDA benchmark 5-year swap rate set on the expiry date.

Similarly, the formula for a 10-year swap futures is

$$PV_{fixed} = 100\left[\frac{0.03}{R_{10}} + \left(1-\frac{0.03}{R_{10}}\right)\left(1+\frac{R_{10}}{2}\right)^{-20}\right] \qquad (1.35)$$

Examples:

1. 5-year implied futures swap quote: 1.6503%

   5-year swap futures formula gives = 101.6719, which is quoted as 101-21+.

2. 10-year implied futures swap quote: 2.6353%

   10-year swap futures formula gives = 103.1875, which is quoted as 103-06.

Swap futures mature quarterly on the third Wednesday of March, June, September, and December. The Bloomberg quote on the USSW screen under "Active Futures" lists the 5-year, 10-year, and 30-year nearest-month swap futures price according to the given convention (see Figure 1-22) where the first three rows are the Treasury Bond Futures discussed previously.

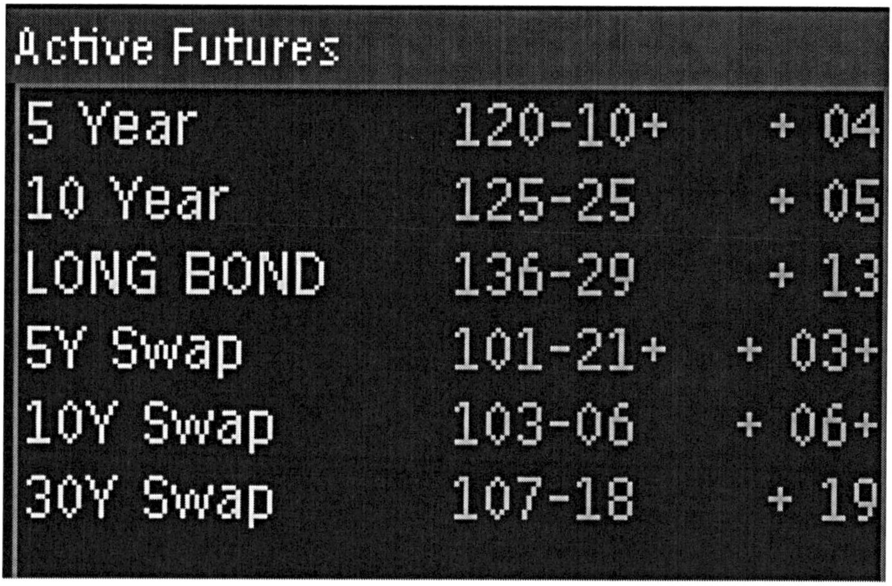

Active Futures		
5 Year	120-10+	+ 04
10 Year	125-25	+ 05
LONG BOND	136-29	+ 13
5Y Swap	101-21+	+ 03+
10Y Swap	103-06	+ 06+
30Y Swap	107-18	+ 19

Figure 1-22. *Swap and Treasury Bond Futures.* *Used with permission of Bloomberg L.P. Copyright© 2014. All rights reserved.*

Derivatives and Structured Products

This section deals with more complex forms of financial products relative to both spot and futures instruments. The derivatives world is very large and diverse. A *derivative* is any financial instrument that derives its value from a separate underlying security. A derivative cannot exist by itself and is purely a synthetic product. Technically speaking, both futures and swaps are derivatives ("only spot instruments are real"). True derivatives have some form of optionality for the holder of the derivative product, giving him a choice at some point (or points) in the future to execute or not execute a particular type of transaction.

The holder of a long futures contract must purchase the underlying security at maturity (or cash settle). The comparable derivative—a *call option*, to be discussed in this section—gives the long holder the option to purchase the underlying security at maturity. The holder can always walk away without executing any transaction. This optionality is what makes the valuation of such products difficult.

Structured products are a category of financial instruments that involve a certain amount of complexity. They include all securitized financial instruments, where pools of assets are brought together to make one or more other assets with different characteristics. Structured products can also include derivative-style features (optionality) as well. This type of investments is briefly touched upon at the end this section with respect to mortgage-backed securities and discussed further with respect to credit derivatives in Chapter 6.

Between them, the BTMM and USSW Bloomberg screens list all three possible types of financial contracts on interest rates (mostly 3M LIBOR): spot, futures, and options. Spot instruments lock in an interest rate today. Futures and swaps lock in an interest rate in the future. Options give one the ability potentially to lock in an interest rate in the future. Before discussing interest-rate derivatives (caps, floors, and swaptions), I introduce some basic options terminology.

There are two basic types of options. A *call option* (Figure 1-23) is the option to buy the underlying asset at a specific price, called the *strike price*, within the *maturity* time of the option. If the purchase can only happen on the maturity date, the option is called *European*. If it can happen anytime until and including the maturity date, it is called an *American* option. A *put option* (Figure 1-24) is the option to sell the underlying asset. Therefore, the main characteristics for options are the following:

- *Type*: call or put
- *Maturity date*: length of optionality
- *Exercise horizon*: European or American
- *Strike price*: price at which the security can be either bought or sold

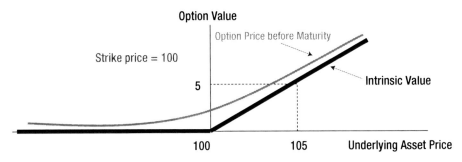

Figure 1-23. Call option

An option is a function of the underlying spot value and time to maturity. In Figures 1-23 and 1-24, both the option value at expiry (*intrinsic value*) and the option value before expiry are shown as functions of the underlying asset value for a call option struck at 100. The fact that the option value before maturity has curvature is the reason options are

CHAPTER 1 ■ FINANCIAL INSTRUMENTS

called *nonlinear instruments*. Their value is not a linear function of the underlying asset value, such as a futures payoff. For call options, when the underlying spot value is greater than the strike, the option is *in-the-money* (ITM). If it is less than the strike, the call is *out-of-the-money* (OTM). An analogous nomenclature is used for put options. In general, OTM options are more liquid than ITM options. The curvature of options comes from the fact that OTM options still have value, because there is a possibility of their being ITM at maturity on account of the price movement of the underlying asset. The option value before maturity is the up-front premium one must pay to enter into this option.

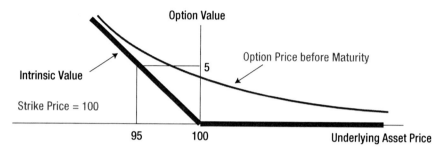

Figure 1-24. Put option

Figures 1-23 and 1-24 do not include the option premium that one must pay to hold the option. Both call and put intrinsic value graphs must be lowered vertically to take into account the option premium. The resulting graph is a *payoff* (or profit) function at maturity. Figure 1-25 shows the payoff functions for [A] long futures, [B] long call option, [C] long put option, [D] short call option, [E] short futures, and [F] short put option.

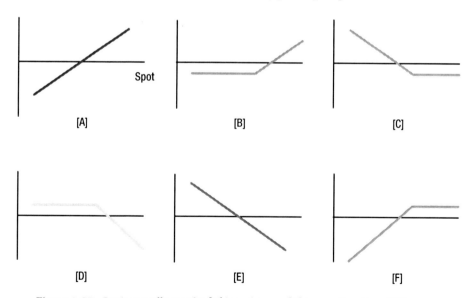

Figure 1-25. Basic payoff types for [A] long futures, [B] long call option, [C] long put option, [D] short call option, [E] short futures, and [F] short put option

A brief description of the risk management of options follows. This complex topic is treated in more detail in Chapter 5. Risk managing options is often called *hedging*. Hedging is sometimes called *replication* because the hedge tries to replicate the payoff of the option using either spot or derivative instruments. The seller of a call option (short position) goes long the underlying either through a long position of the underlying asset or futures contract (linear instruments). One can also simply go long a similar call option—although it is rarely done because this can lose money in the bid-offer spread). The seller of a put option (short position) goes short the underlying through a short position of either the underlying asset or futures contract. One could also buy an offsetting put. The real question here is how much does one go long or short when hedging an option position with a linear instrument? It is not simply one unit of an option matched with one unit of hedge. For instance, for a *way OTM option*, the *hedge ratio* is close to zero. For a *way ITM option*, the hedge ratio is close to one. As the underlying spot price moves, both the option value and hedge ratios move in a nonlinear fashion. Hedging derivatives often comes down to attempting to replicate non-linear instruments with linear ones. To get a sense of the offsetting feature of a hedge, Figure 1-26 shows an option payoff along with a linear hedge and the combined payoff at maturity. The strike is denoted as K and the underlying asset price at maturity T is denoted as S_T. For instance, Figure 1-26 (a) shows a short call along with a spot or futures position. When $S_T > K$, the two positions offset each other leaving the flat part of the combined payoff (the thicker line).

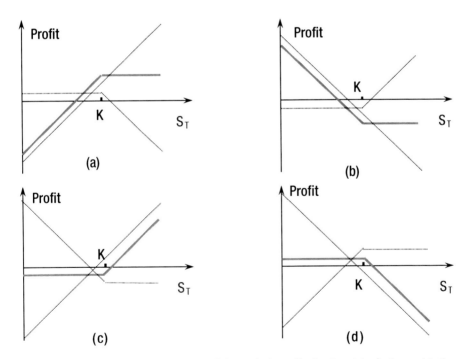

Figure 1-26. Positions in an option and the underlying (hedged position) along with the combined (thicker line) position

Basic strategies for combining options include the following:

- *Covered (hedged) strategies*: Take a position in the option and the underlying asset, as described in the preceding paragraph.
- *Spread strategies*: Take a position in two or more options of the same type, thereby creating a "spread" among them.
- *Combination strategies*: Take a position in a mixture of calls and puts.

Figures 1-27 through 1-33 illustrate several standard option strategies along with their payoff graphs. The combined payoff is once again illustrated by the thicker line.

- *Bull spread using calls*: This strategy (Figure 1-27) involves buying a call struck at K_1 and selling a call struck at K_2. The combined strategy is cheaper than buying the K_1 call outright, as can be seen from the y-axis intercept of the combined strategy versus the call. An investor who purchases this strategy is moderately bullish but gives up some of the upside profit for a cheaper premium than a pure call option at K_1.

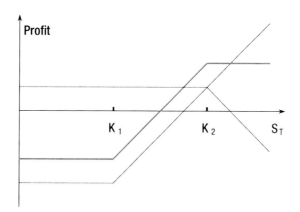

Figure 1-27. Bull spread (thick line) using calls

- *Bull spread using puts*: This strategy (Figure 1-28) is the same payoff as above except it is created using put options, whereby one buys a put at K_1 and sells a put at K_2.

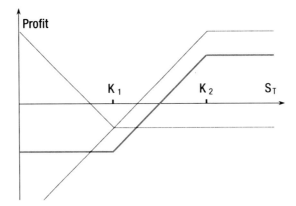

Figure 1-28. Bull spread using puts

- *Bear spread using puts*: This strategy (Figure 1-29) involves buying a put struck at K_2 and selling a put struck at K_1. The combined strategy is cheaper than buying the K_2 put outright, as can be seen from the y-axis intercept of the combined strategy versus the put. An investor who purchases this strategy is moderately bearish but gives up some of the upside profit for a cheaper premium than a pure put option at K_2.

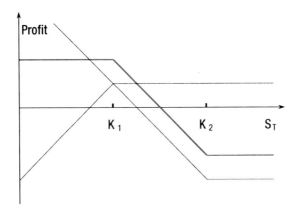

Figure 1-29. Bear spread using puts

- *Bear spread using calls*: This strategy (Figure 1-30) is the same payoff as above except it is created using call options, where one buys a call at K_2 and sells a call at K_1.

CHAPTER 1 ■ FINANCIAL INSTRUMENTS

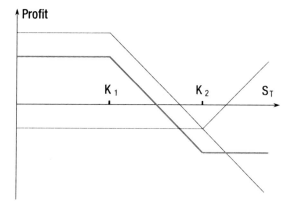

Figure 1-30. Bear spread using calls

- *Butterfly spread using four calls* (two short calls at K_2): This strategy (Figure 1-31) consists of two long calls at K_1 and K_3 and two short calls at K_2. An investor of this strategy has no directional view but believes the underlying asset will not move far from K_2. This is also considered a low-volatility strategy.

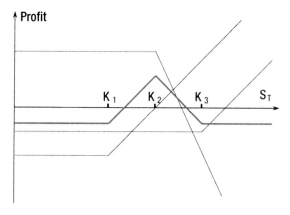

Figure 1-31. Butterfly spread using four calls (two short calls at K_2)

- *Butterfly spread using four puts* (two short puts at K_2): This strategy (Figure 1-32) is the same payoff as above except it was created using put options. Note that a seller of a butterfly spread has the reverse payoff (mirror image along x-axis) and has the reverse view that the asset will have a large move in either direction.

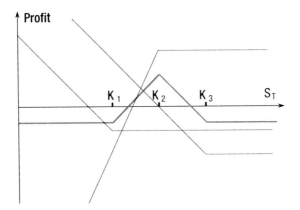

Figure 1-32. *Butterfly spread using four puts (two short puts at K_2)*

- *Straddle*: This strategy (Figure 1-33) is a combination of a long call and put option at the same strike. It is similar to a short butterfly spread. The investor has no directional view but believes a large move in the underlying asset is possible. This is a popular strategy for stocks of two corporations that are about to merge when one is uncertain whether the merger will be successful. The holder of this strategy is long volatility (see the next two sections).

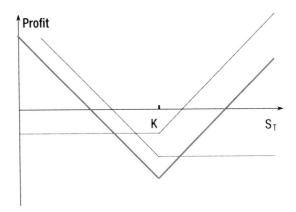

Figure 1-33. *Straddle market quotation convention for options*

Dynamic Hedging and Replication

Dynamic hedging is the hedging of a nonlinear payoff (option) with linear instruments like cash and futures. The hedge amounts of linear instruments, called *deltas*, of the nonlinear position are meant to offset the nonlinear payoff risk, yielding an instantaneous zero risk position overall. However, as the underlying asset value moves up or down, the delta of the nonlinear position changes while that of the linear hedge does not. The risk is no longer offset, so the linear hedge amount has to be adjusted (increased or decreased) to restore the delta hedge. This continual adjusting of the linear position to maintain a delta hedge is called *dynamic hedging*. Standard option pricing methodologies, known as risk-neutral pricing, assume that dynamic hedging works almost perfectly and therefore the hedger has effectively replicated the option payoff with linear instruments. They make assumptions—which never hold—of instantaneous delta hedging with no friction costs (no bid-offer spread, no transaction cost, and no liquidity premium) and no residual risks (no hedge slippage). The common use of this methodology has unfortunately evolved into a market convention of quoting a specific parameter, called the *implied volatility*, used in the standard pricing model for options rather than quoting the option price itself. Therefore, some familiarity with these standard formulas, called *Black's formula*, is useful and is succinctly presented as follows:

European call options: ***Black's formula***

Call Option Payoff at Maturity (T) = Max$\{S_T-K, 0\}$ (see Figure 1-23)

S_T = Underlying Price (Stock, LIBOR, FX, etc) at Maturity (T)

$S_T \rightarrow$ unknown price in the future

$\rightarrow$ Black's Formula makes an assumption on the distribution of S_T (1.36)

Call Price = $df(0,T)E[Max\{S_T - K, 0\}]$

$E \rightarrow$ Expectation using Black's Distribution Assumption (log-normal distribution)

■ **Note** Chapters 3 and 4 describe distributions that are more realistic than the one used in Black's model, including the log-normal distribution and the related stochastic process of geometric Brownian motion. Only the last-mentioned option pricing formula is needed here for the discussion of implied volatilities and the market quotation convention for option prices.

Black's Call Option Price = $df(0,T)[F_T N(d_1) - KN(d_2)]$

$df(0,T)$ = discount factor to time T

F_T = foward of underlying at time T

K = Strike

$$d_1 = \frac{\ln(F_T/K) + \sigma^2 T/2}{\sigma\sqrt{T}}$$ (1.37)

$$d_2 = d_1 - \sigma\sqrt{T}$$

$$N(d) = \int_{-\infty}^{d} \frac{1}{\sqrt{2\pi}} e^{-\frac{x^2}{2}} dx$$

σ = Volatility of underlying

European put options: **Black's formula**

Put Option Payoff at Maturity $(T) = Max\{K-S_T, 0\}$ (see Figure 1-30)

Black's Put Option Price $= df(0,T)[KN(-d_2) - F_T N(-d_1)]$

$df(0,T) =$ discount factor to time T

$F_T =$ foward of underlying at time T

$K =$ Strike

$$d_1 = \frac{\ln(F_T/K) + \sigma^2 T/2}{\sigma\sqrt{T}} \quad (1.38)$$

$$d_2 = d_1 - \sigma\sqrt{T}$$

$$N(d) = \int_{-\infty}^{d} \frac{1}{\sqrt{2\pi}} e^{-\frac{x^2}{2}} dx$$

$\sigma =$ Volatility of underlying

To calculate $N(d)$, one can use the following approximation

$$N(d) = \int_{-\infty}^{d} \frac{1}{\sqrt{2\pi}} e^{-\frac{x^2}{2}} dx$$

Let $N'(d) = \frac{1}{\sqrt{2\pi}} e^{-\frac{d^2}{2}}$

$$N(d) = \begin{cases} 1 - N'(d)[a_1 k + a_2 k^2 + a_3 k^3 + a_4 k^4 + a_5 k^5] & d \geq 0 \\ 1 - N(-d) & d < 0 \end{cases} \quad (1.39)$$

$$k = \frac{1}{1+\gamma d}$$

$\gamma = 0.2316419 \quad a_1 = 0.319381530 \quad a_2 = -0.356563782$
$a_3 = 1.781477937 \quad a_4 = -1.821255978 \quad a_5 = 1.330274429$

$N(d)$ is a standard function also found in many applications such as Microsoft Excel.

Implied Volatility

The implied volatility of a specific option contract is the volatility one uses in Black's formula that reproduces the market-quoted price for that option. The market can quote either the implied volatility or the option price. Suppose one has a market-quoted implied volatility σ_{imp} for a 90-day call option on the S&P 500 struck at the current spot value. Then

$$\sigma_{imp} = 18.14\%$$

$\rightarrow$ Market Call Option Price $= 44.89 = df(0,T)[F_T N(d_1) - KN(d_2)]$

$F_T =$ foward of underlying at time $T = 0.25 = 1313.00$ \quad (1.40)

$K =$ ATM (at the money) Spot $= 1318.40$

$df(0,0.25) = 0.9986$

Such calculations found in many books (see [Hull, 2012]). Problem 1.1 will further help the reader in calculating implied volatilities. Our purpose here is to demonstrate in the following sections how this formula is adapted for interest rate options and their corresponding implied volatility quotes found on USSW.

Caps and Floors

An interest rate *caplet* is an interest rate derivative whereby the writer of the option has the obligation to pay the holder of the option cash if a particular interest rate exceeds a predefined level at some future date. If one envisions this interest rate as the "underlying asset", and the predefined level as the "strike", the caplet payoff is a call option. The standard caplet is on 3M LIBOR. The payoff of this derivative is

$$\text{Payoff} = \delta_j \, Max[L_j - K, 0]$$
$$L_j = \text{3M foward LIBOR set at } t_{j-1} \tag{1.41}$$
$$\delta_j = \text{Act} / 360 \text{ daycount fraction from } t_{j-1} \text{ to } t_j$$
$$K = \text{Strike of Caplet}$$

Note the use of the daycount fraction δ_j that is always needed when dealing with interest rates.

Similarly, an interest rate *floorlet* is an interest rate derivative whereby the writer of the option has the obligation to pay the holder of the option cash if a particular interest rate goes below a predefined level at some future date. A floorlet has a put like payoff given by

$$\text{Payoff} = \delta_j \, Max[K - L_j, 0] \tag{1.42}$$

Clearly, caplets and floorlets are call and put options, respectively, on forward 3M LIBOR rates. Therefore, the market uses a Black type formula to quote the implied volatility of these 3M LIBOR interest rate derivatives. Analogous to (1.37), a caplet has a market standard European option formula given by

Caplet Option: **Black's formula**

$$\text{Call options (caplet): Caplet}_j = \delta_j df(0, t_j)[L_j N(d_1) - K N(d_2)]$$

$$L_j = \text{3M foward LIBOR set at } t_{j-1} = \left[\frac{df(0, t_{j-1})}{df(0, t_j)} - 1\right]\frac{1}{\delta_j}$$

$$\delta_j = \text{Act}/360 \text{ daycount fraction from } t_{j-1} \text{ to } t_j$$

$$K = \text{Strike of Caplet} \tag{1.43}$$

$$d_1 = \frac{\ln(L_j / K) + \sigma_j^2 t_{j-1}/2}{\sigma_j \sqrt{t_{j-1}}}$$

$$d_2 = d_1 - \sigma_j \sqrt{t_{j-1}}$$

$$N(d) = \int_{-\infty}^{d} \frac{1}{\sqrt{2\pi}} e^{-\frac{x^2}{2}} dx$$

$$\sigma_j = \text{Implied Volatility}$$

Analogous to (1.38), the market floorlet formula is given by:
Floorlet Option: **Black's Formula**

$$\delta_j df(0,t_j)[KN(-d_2) - L_j N(-d_1)] \quad (1.44)$$

The discount factors used above go to the end of the accrual period t_j even though the LIBOR rate L_j is set at the beginning of the accrual period t_{j-1}. This is because the actual payment is made at the end of the accrual period similar to the floating leg payments of a swap. A caplet can clearly be used to hedge the risk of a LIBOR payment in the future going up. Yet, most floating rate payments are associated with a series of payments in the future, not just one. For instance, a 10 year floating rate loan indexed to 3M LIBOR (plus a spread) will have 40 future 3M LIBOR payments. How can one hedge this? If they are sure LIBOR is going up imminently, they can enter into a standard floating for fixed rate swap where they receive float and pay fixed as discussed earlier. If they are unsure if LIBOR is going up, but still wish to hedge their interest rate risk, they need to but a series of caplets, known as a "cap".

A *cap* is a strip of caplets starting at periodic forward dates all having the same strike.

$$\text{Cap} = \sum_{j=1}^{n} \text{Caplet}_j = \sum_{j=1}^{n} \delta_j df(0,t_j)[L_j N(d_1) - KN(d_2)] \quad (1.45)$$

For example, a 10-year cap on 3M LIBOR is composed of 39 caplets (each lasting for 3 months). Note that the first 3M period is not included because LIBOR is set at the beginning of the period so there is no optionality left. This cap could be used to hedge the 10 year floating rate loan as the max coupon one must pay on the loan will be "capped" at K.

Similarly, a *floor* is a strip of floorlets starting at periodic forward dates all having the same strike,

$$\text{Floor} = \sum_{j=1}^{n} \text{Floorlet}_j = \sum_{j=1}^{n} \delta_j df(0,t_j)\left[KN(-d_2) - L_j N(-d_1)\right] \quad (1.46)$$

A floor can be used by a loan provider who is receiving 3M LIBOR in order to hedge the risk of falling interest rates as the minimum coupon payment will be "floored" at K.

Market Implied Volatility Quotes for Caps and Floors

The market uses the simple Black model described in the preceding section to have a common methodology to quote cap and floor prices. No market participant believes that this model is an accurate representation of the dynamics of LIBOR interest rates. It is merely a convenient tool to quote tradable prices, whereas market participants have their own interest rate models to determine for themselves the price of these options.

Market-implied volatilities are organized by:

- Option maturity
- Tenor of the underlying instrument
- Strike of the option

CHAPTER 1 ■ FINANCIAL INSTRUMENTS

For simplicity, the market quotes cap and floor prices in terms of the *flat volatilities* implicit in Black's formula, whereby the same volatility is applied to all implied volatility caplets forming a cap or all and floorlets forming a floor, such that $\sigma_j = \sigma$. The Bloomberg quotes on USSW under "CAP/FL" are listed for option tenors (1 yr, 2 yr, 3 yr, 4 yr, 5 yr, 7 yr, 10 yr) for 3M LIBOR *at-the-money* (ATM) *strike* caps/floors (see Figure 1-34). The ATM strike for a cap or floor is given in the next section.

Swaption	1Y	3Y	5Y	7Y	10Y	Cap/Flr
1Y	65.850	46.350	35.900	29.950	25.260	59.140
2Y	52.065	38.950	32.085	28.210	24.750	75.550
3Y	40.965	32.875	28.620	26.155	23.680	66.540
4Y	34.000	29.190	26.265	24.545	22.740	56.250
5Y	30.125	26.800	24.700	23.405	22.075	48.680
7Y	25.700	23.810	22.450	21.640	20.780	39.800
10Y	21.915	20.955	20.325	19.905	19.315	33.490

Figure 1-34. *Cap and Swaption ATM Implied Volatilities.* Used with permission of Bloomberg L.P. Copyright© 2014. All rights reserved.

ATM Strike strike

The characteristic of ATM options is that both call and put options struck ATM have the same value. The relationship between ATM caps and floors with the same strike K is

$$\text{Floor} - \text{Cap} = \sum_j \delta_j \, df(0, t_j) \{ Max[K - L_j, 0] - Max[L_j - K, 0] \}$$
$$\text{Floor} - \text{Cap} = \sum_j \delta_j \, df(0, t_j) [K - L_j] = K \cdot DV01 - \sum_j \delta_j L_j \, df(0, t_j) \quad (1.47)$$
$$\text{Floor} - \text{Cap} = PV_{fixed} - PV_{floating} = PV_{swap}$$

Note that the fixed leg of this swap is different from the standard swap in that it pays quarterly using a basis of act/360.

The ATM strike for a cap or floor is the strike K that makes the present value of this swap equal to zero (break-even swap rate or fair value swap rate), i.e., $PV_{swap} = 0$. This fair value swap rate will be close (but not identical) to the standard fair value swap rate. There is also a separate Bloomberg screen VCUB (volatility cube) that lists the ATM implied volatilities as well as volatilities for other strikes and tenors (see Figure 1-35).

41

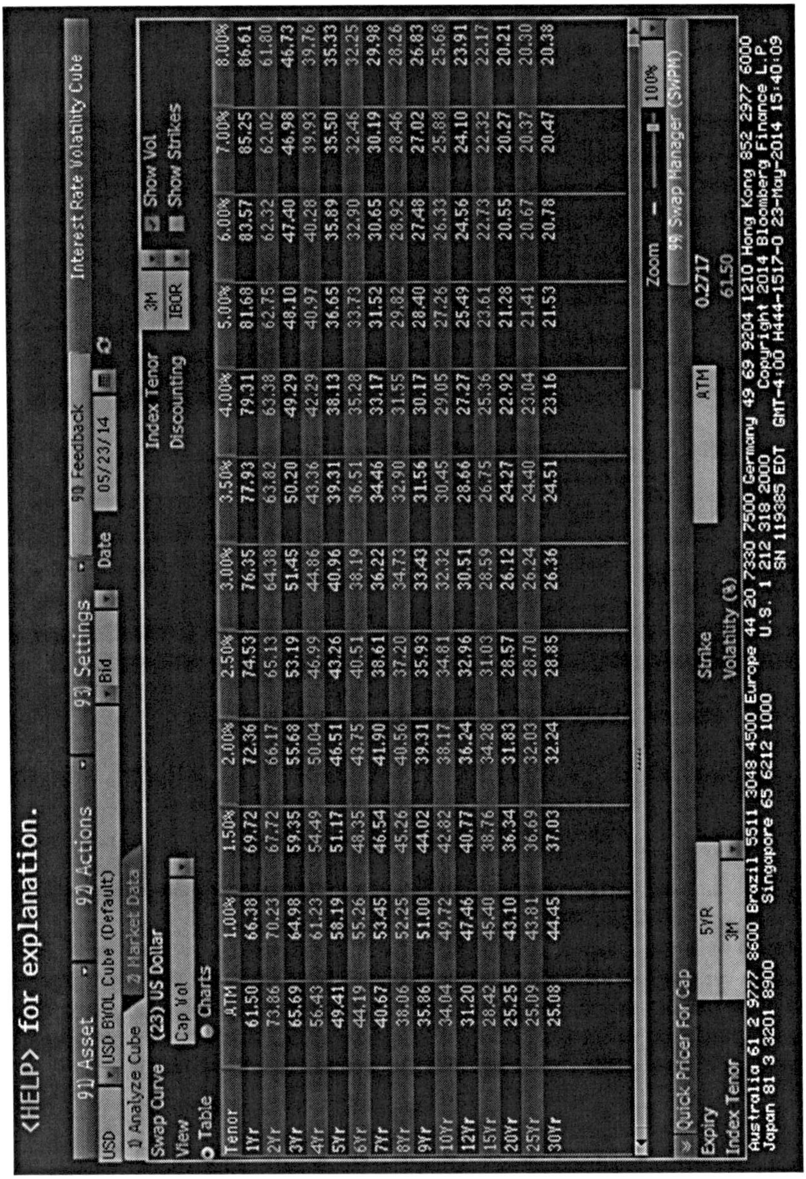

Figure 1-35. <VCUB> *Bloomberg Screen with Tenors versus Strike of Cap Implied Volatilities.* Used with permission of Bloomberg L.P. Copyright© 2014. All rights reserved.

Swaptions

European swaptions are essentially European calls and puts on a forward swap rate. It is the option to enter into a swap. A *receiver* swaption is the option to receive the fixed side of a swap and pay the floating leg starting at the swaption maturity. A *payer* swaption is the option to enter into a swap that pays the fixed side of a swap and receives the floating leg. For example, a "1 yr into 5 yr" receiver swaption struck at 1.5% gives the holder the right to begin a 5-year maturity swap starting in 1 year where the holder receives 1.5% (semiannual, 30/360, 5-year maturity) and pays 3M LIBOR (quarterly, act/360, 5-year maturity). If the actual 5-year spot swap rate in 1 year is less than the strike of 1.5%, the holder makes money. Therefore, a receiver swaption is analogous to a put option because the holder exercises when the underlying swap rate is below the strike level. A payer swaption is analogous to a call option on the swap rate. The market quotes for swaptions are similar to caps and floors in that they are quoted as implied volatilities via Black's formula. To use this formula, you first need an expression for a forward starting swap. Recall that the PV of a floating leg starting at $(t_0 = 0)$ is

$$PV_{floating} = 1 - df(0,T) \quad . \tag{1.48}$$

The PV of a floating leg starting at $t_0 = t_s > 0$ is

$$PV_{floating} = df(0,t_s) - df(0,T) \quad . \tag{1.49}$$

The break-even forward starting swap rate is $(t_0 = t_s > 0)$

$$S(0,t_s,T) = \frac{df(0,t_s) - df(0,T)}{DV01}$$
$$DV01 = \sum_{i=1}^{n_{fixed}} \Delta_i df(0,t_i^{fxd}) \tag{1.50}$$

Defining a forward DV01

$$DV01_{forward}(t_s) = \sum_{i=1}^{n_{fixed}} \Delta_i df(t_s,t_i^{fxd}) \quad , \tag{1.51}$$

one can rewrite the forward starting swap rate by dividing throughout by $df(0,t_s)$

$$S(0,t_s,T) = \frac{1 - df(t_s,T)}{DV01_{forward}(t_s)} \quad , \tag{1.52}$$

which is analogous to the spot starting swap rate formula.

The market convention pricing of a receiver swaption uses Black's formula for a put option on the swap rate,

$$\text{Swaption}_{receiver} = DV01 \cdot [KN(-d_2) - S(0,t_s,T)N(-d_1)]$$
$$d_1 = \frac{\ln(S(0,t_s,T)/K) + \sigma^2 t_s / 2}{\sigma \sqrt{t_s}} \tag{1.53}$$
$$d_2 = d_1 - \sigma \sqrt{t_s}$$

whereas a payer swaption is given by

$$\text{Swaption}_{payer} = DV01 \cdot [S(0,t_s,T)N(d_1) - KN(d_2)]$$

$$d_1 = \frac{\ln(S(0,t_s,T)/K) + \sigma^2 t_s / 2}{\sigma \sqrt{t_s}} \quad (1.54)$$

$$d_2 = d_1 - \sigma \sqrt{t_s}$$

The DV01 is used here as there are a series of fixed payments made during the life of a swap, not just one. Recall that the DV01 encompasses the correct series of daycounts and discount factors.

For example, a "1 yr into 5 yr" receiver swaption struck at 1.5% has t_s = 1 year, T = 6 years, and K = 1.5%. Analogous to the caps and floors, the ATM strike formula is found by equating payer and receiver swaptions such that

$$\text{Swaption}_{receiver} - \text{Swaption}_{payer} = DV01\{Max[K - S(0,t_s,T),0] - Max[S(0,t_s,T) - K,0]\}$$

$$\text{Swaption}_{receiver} - \text{Swaption}_{payer} = DV01 \cdot K - DV01 \cdot S(0,t_s,T) \quad (1.55)$$

$$= PV_{fixed} - [df(0,t_s) - df(0,T)] = PV_{fixed} - PV_{floating}$$

$$\text{Swaption}_{receiver} - \text{Swaption}_{payer} = PV_{forward\ starting\ swap} \text{ at } t_s$$

The fixed leg of this forward starting swap is the standard swap that pays semiannually using a basis of 30/360.

The ATM strike K for a swaption is the strike that makes the present value of this forward starting swap equal to zero (the break-even forward swap rate or fair-value forward swap rate) i.e. $PV_{forward\ starting\ swap}$ = 0. For simplicity, the market quotes swaption prices (both payer and receiver) as the one flat volatility of Black's formula, which reproduces the market price. The implied volatility quotes on the Bloomberg screen USSW listed under "Swaptions" are listed for each ATM option in matrix form as $t_s \times T$ (row, column) (see Figure 1-30). For example, a "1 yr into 5 yr" ATM receiver swaption has an implied volatility in the first row and third column of the swaption volatility matrix in USSW. One can find more interest rate volatility information on the Bloomberg page VCUB. Figure 1-36 shows ATM swaption volatilities. One can also find ATM strikes for caps, floors, and swaptions by navigating this page as well as an ATM swaption volatility surface as depicted in Figure 1-37.

CHAPTER 1 ■ FINANCIAL INSTRUMENTS

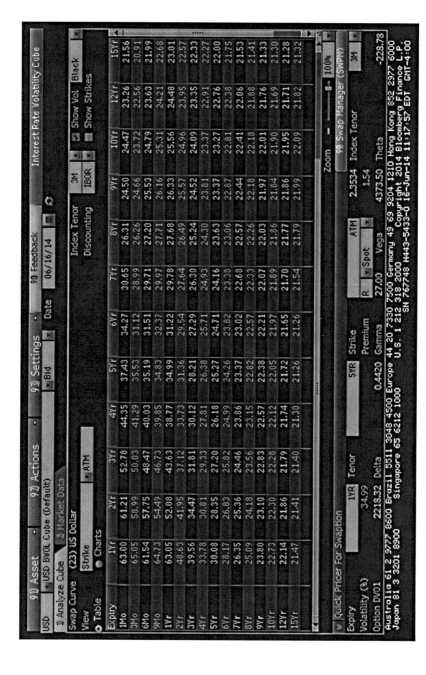

Figure 1-36. *<VCUB> Bloomberg Screen of Swaption ATM Implied Volatilities.* Used with permission of Bloomberg L.P. Copyright© 2014. All rights reserved.

CHAPTER 1 ■ FINANCIAL INSTRUMENTS

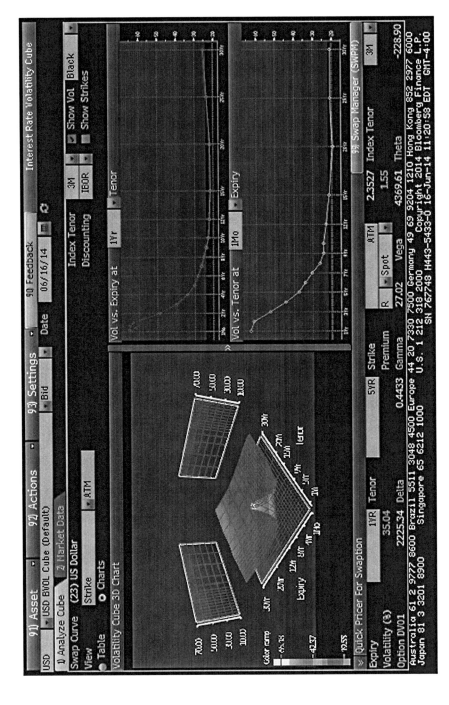

Figure 1-37. ATM Swaption Volatility Surface. Used with permission of Bloomberg L.P. Copyright© 2014. All rights reserved.

As discussed above, both a swap and a cap can be used to hedge the interest rate risk of a floating rate loan linked to 3M LIBOR. A payer swaption can also be used as a hedge but its choice depends upon the interest rate outlook of the loan holder. Suppose again the loan is for 10 years. If the holder is convinced that LIBOR will go imminently, he enters into a 10yr swap where he pays fixed. If he is unsure, he can buy a cap. Now, if he is sure LIBOR will not go up for at least two years, but could thereafter, he enters into a 2 into 8 year payer swaption. This allows him to go unhedged for the first two years (as he perceives little risk here) but has the option on hedging the last eight years of his loan at the 2 year exercise date. That is, in 2 years, he has the option to enter into a 8 year swap where he pays fixed (the strike K) and receives 3m LIBOR to hedge his floating rate loan payments.

Mortgage-Backed Securities

Mortgage-backed securities (MBS) are investments in a pool of mortgage loans that are the underlying assets providing the cash flow for the securities. MBS are commonly referred to as *pass-through* securities because the principal and interest of the underlying mortgage loans passes through to the investor. All bondholders receive a monthly pro-rata distribution of principal and interest over the life of the security. MBS are issued with maturities of up to 30 years, although most mature earlier, driven by the *prepayment* characteristics of the underlying loans. Each MBS has an *average life*, an estimate of the time remaining until the final principal payment. These average life estimates vary based on changes in principal payments, which are driven by interest rates and the speed by which mortgage holders prepay their loans. Therefore, one of the primary risks on these assets is prepayment risk.

MBS can be considered structured products because they involve the securitization of either residential or commercial mortgages to create *residential mortgage-backed securities* (RMBS) or *commercial mortgage-backed securities* (CMBS). The process of *mortgage securitization* is broadly defined as follows:

1. Mortgage loans are purchased from banks and other lenders and assigned to a trust.
2. The trust assembles these loans into collections (*pools*).
3. The trust securitizes the pools and issues MBS against them.

Both RMBS and CMBS have interest rate risk, prepayment risk, and default risk. All fixed-income securities have interest rate risk. A fixed coupon bond loses value in a rising interest rate environment. Prepayment risk come from the fact that many residential mortgages can be prepaid and refinanced for lower interest rates. As interest rates fall, mortgage rates fall, and homeowners prepay their old loans for newer ones with lower interest rates. Fixed-income instruments generally benefit from a falling interest rate environment, but MBS might not because the lower interest rates might precipitate refinancing. For instance, an investor may hold an MBS with a high coupon. As interest rates fall, the MBS gets fully prepaid and the investor receives his principal back long before the legal maturity of the bond. Now he must reinvest in a lower interest rate environment, thereby earning a lower coupon than he previously had. A regular fixed-income security does not have this risk. Because of this prepayment risk, MBS prices may level off or fall when rates decrease below a certain level in contrast to regular fixed income instruments.

This is referred to as "negative convexity" as it goes against the usual inverse relationship of prices and yields common in bonds (see [Tuckman, 2012]). Default risk arises when borrowers fail to pay scheduled interest and principal payments, which adversely affects the cash-flow characteristics of the MBS with which they are associated.

The "American dream" is often made up of purchasing a house, purchasing a car, purchasing consumer goods, and sending children to college (purchasing an education). These components are all realized through loans. Homes are purchased through mortgages. Cars are purchased through auto loans from dealerships. Goods and services are purchased through credit cards. Education is purchased through student loans. This has led to a massive issuance of financial instruments generically called *asset-backed securities* (ABS). Bonds "backed" by mortgages are called MBS. Bonds backed by auto loan payments are called auto loan ABS. The other big ABS types are credit cards, student loans, home equity loans (put the equity of your home up for yet another loan), manufactured housing, and so on. Any and every type of loan can be securitized. One of the main purposes of securitization is to provide *liquidity* for these loans. No investor wishes to buy a single $20,000 car loan or a $100,000 home loan. They are willing to buy an asset comprised of a diversified pool of a thousand such loans. This in turn allows banks to offer more such loans and then sell them off as ABS. By selling off the loan, the bank does not need the capital to actually fund the loan thereby transferring all the risk to the end investor of such ABS instruments.

To encourage mortgage securitization (thereby enabling the American dream), the US government created three major federally chartered mortgage corporations (securitization trusts): Ginnie Mae, Fannie Mae, and Freddie Mac. The Government National Mortgage Association (GNMA, hence "Ginnie Mae") is a wholly owned government corporation within the Department of Housing and Urban Development (HUD). It issues mortgage bonds backed by the full faith and credit of the US government. Ginnie Mae guarantees the timely payment of principal and interest on MBS backed by loans insured by the government agencies such as Federal Housing Administration and the Department of Veterans Affairs. This guarantee removes the default risk of these bonds, thereby providing lower mortgage rates for homeowners because investors in these bonds do not require a credit risk premium to purchase the bonds. The US government is taking the credit risk of residential home buyers so that investors will be willing to give home loans through MBS. This only happens in the United States and not in Canada, Great Britain, Europe, and other comparable countries.

US government *agency bonds* are debt obligations issued by *government-sponsored enterprises* (GSEs). GSEs are independent organizations sponsored by the federal government and established with a public purpose. GSEs include the Federal Home Loan Banks (FHLB) and the Federal Farm Credit Banks (FFCB), which are systems comprising regional banks. The Federal National Mortgage Association (FNMA or "Fannie Mae") and the Federal Home Loan Mortgage Corporation (FHLMC/GOLD or "Freddie Mac") are privately owned corporations created by the federal government to provide liquidity and increase available credit in the mortgage markets. Before the 2008 financial crisis, the main difference between GSE bonds and Ginnie Mae bonds was that GSE debt was solely the obligation of the issuer and carried greater credit risk than US-backed agency bonds (Ginnie Mae bonds are often considered agency bonds). During the 2008 crisis, the US government bailed out both Fannie Mae and Freddie Mac, indicating their equal importance with respect to Ginnie Mae.

Bloomberg Price Quotes: 30Y MBS

For "vanilla" or "generic" 30-year pools (GNMA/GOLD/FNMA) with coupons of 3.0%–3.5%, the prices posted on the BTMM screen by the primary dealers are called *To-Be-Announced* (TBA) bonds (see Figure 1-38). This is due to the fact that the actual pools of mortgage loans are not yet known. These are forward prices for the next three delivery months because the underlying pools haven't been created yet. Only the issuing agency, coupon, maturity, par dollar amount, and settlement dates have been agreed upon. The TBA trading convention enables a heterogeneous market consisting of thousands of different MBS pools backed by millions of individual mortgages to be reduced to only a few liquid contracts. The Bloomberg quotes list the agency, coupon, bid price, offer price, and change from the previous close. Similar to Treasury futures, TBAs trade on a "cheapest to deliver" basis. On settlement date, the seller will select which MBS in their inventory they will deliver to the buyer. The seller has a clear incentive to deliver the lowest-valued securities that satisfy the terms of the trade.

Figure 1-38. *Agency MBS Quotes. Used with permission of Bloomberg L.P. Copyright© 2014. All rights reserved.*

Appendix: Daycount Conventions

Daycount fractions are needed for all interest rate calculations where an interest rate is quoted as an annualized number (which is almost always the case). Interest rate payments are almost always paid over time periods of less than a year. The actual interest rate amount paid will be $r \cdot \Delta t$. How does one calculate Δt? It is generically seen as

$$\Delta t = \frac{\text{time within the payment period}}{\text{time within a year}} \qquad (1.56)$$

Both the numerator and denominator have different conventions ("basis") based on the calculation methodology that grew from specific asset classes. Unfortunately, the financial world has not been able to agree on one convention for all such calculations. For instance, corporate bonds tend to use a 30/360 basis, which assumes all whole months have 30 days and a year has 360 days. This convention is easy to calculate by hand and predates the use of computers and calculators. Here, a three month period has a daycount fraction given by

$$\Delta t = \frac{3 \cdot 30}{360} = \frac{90}{360} = \frac{1}{4} \qquad (1.57)$$

CHAPTER 1 — FINANCIAL INSTRUMENTS

Other methods will calculate the numerator or denominator using the actual (*act*) number of days between payment periods, such as the exact number of days between March 13 and June 13 (a quarterly payment). The number of days in this case is 92. If the basis convention is act/360, the 3-month period daycount fraction is given by

$$\Delta t = \frac{act}{360} = \frac{92}{360} \qquad (1.58)$$

More complications arise from weekends and special holidays. Wall Street systems have databases of future holidays for several countries around the world. One can never make an interest rate payment on a holiday. The most common types of daycount basis are

- $\frac{30}{360}$
- $\frac{act}{360}$
- $\frac{act}{365}$
- $\frac{act}{364}$
- $\frac{act}{act}$

LIBOR is calculated on an act/360 basis. Treasury bills also use act/360. Treasury bonds and notes use act/365. It should be noted that having a daycount *off* by one day can cause large errors as Wall Street deals in billions of dollars of notional risk.

Problems

1.1: Create an implied volatility calculator using Black's formula

- A simplified discount factor may be used that is comprised of only one interest rate r—namely, $df(0,T) = \frac{1}{1+r \cdot T}$ —where T is the maturity of the option.
- If using Excel, $N(d)$ is the function NORM**S**DIST().
- The forward rate for stocks can be approximated by

$$F_T = S_0[1 + r \cdot T]\exp[-d \cdot T]$$
$$S_0 = \text{spot stock value} \qquad (1.59)$$
$$d = \text{continously compounded dividends}$$

- Remember to have two models: one with σ as an input, and one with the option market price as an input.

CHAPTER 1 ■ FINANCIAL INSTRUMENTS

- For the Black formula calculator, use the following data:

$$\text{Put Option Price} = ?$$
$$\text{Spot Price S\&P 500} = 1314.49$$
$$K = \text{ATM("at the money")} \tag{1.60}$$
$$T = 180 \text{ days} \quad \sigma = 20.252\%$$
$$r = 0.78525\% \quad d = 2.211\%$$

- For the implied volatility calculator, use the following data:

$$\text{Call Option Price} = 23.47$$
$$\text{Spot Price S\&P 500} = 1314.25$$
$$K = \text{ATM("at the money")} \tag{1.61}$$
$$T = 30 \text{ days} \quad \sigma_{imp} = ?$$
$$r = 0.261\% \quad d = 2.886\%$$

- It is important to differentiate the various components of your model as outlined in Figure 1-39. Inputs and outputs will change depending on whether one is calculating a price or a volatility.

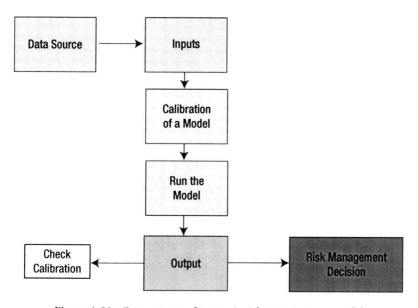

Figure 1-39. Components of a generic risk management model

51

Further Reading

Bouchaud, J.-P., and M. Potters. *Theory of Financial Risk and Derivative Pricing.* 2nd ed. Cambridge: Cambridge University Press, 2003.

Hull, J. C. *Risk Management and Financial Institutions.* 3rd ed. Hoboken, NJ: John Wiley & Sons, 2012.

Tuckman, B., and A. Serrat. *Fixed Income Securities.* 3rd ed. Hoboken, NJ: John Wiley & Sons, 2012.

CHAPTER 2

Building a Yield Curve

Financial institutions use *yield curves* (also called *discount curves*) to calculate the present value of all future cash flows (positive or negative) coming from the financial instruments held on the firm's balance sheet. The purpose of discounting future cash flows comes from the concept of the *time value of money*. Cash is not a static investment. It grows by earning interest or loses value by being charged interest as borrowed money. The process of discounting includes this nonstatic behavior. Yield curves are needed for multiple currencies because interest rates vary from country to country. One can also have more than one yield curve for a specific currency such as a US Treasury curve, a US LIBOR curve, and an OIS fed funds curve.

The three main uses of a yield curve are to:

- Calculate discount factors
- Calculate implied interest rates
- Be used in stochastic interest rate models (Chapter 4)

The three main constraints on a yield curve are that it:

- Must exactly reprice its input market instruments (calibration points)
- Must give reasonable values for market instruments not used for calibration
- Preferably have two relatively continuous first and second derivatives (needed for stochastic short-rate models)

The standard LIBOR yield curve used by all US banks or brokerage firms is created using the following market instruments as *calibration points*:

1. LIBOR cash rates [O/N (overnight), 1W, 1M, 2M, 3M]
2. 90D eurodollar futures (going out to five years)
3. Swap rates (starting from 5Y swaps)

The choice of calibration instruments is largely driven by liquidity considerations. LIBOR rates with tenors exceeding 6M exist, but they are generally not used. Eurodollar futures can go out past 5Y and one can also find short-dated swaps under 5Y, but these are less liquid and not generally used in the construction of yield curves.

Even though pure LIBOR-based discounting has long been used on Wall Street, the financial crisis of 2008 led to technical nuances such that one needs to take into account the counterparty and collateralization of swaps that materially affect the discounting methodology of swaps and other financial instruments. These issues are explored in the "OIS Discounting" section of Chapter 7.

Overview of Yield Curve Construction

Recall that if one invests $1 for three months earning 3M LIBOR, the final value of the investment at the end of three months will be

$$\text{Final Value} = \$1 \cdot (1 + \delta L)$$

$$\text{where } \delta = \frac{\text{actual days in three month period}}{360} \quad (2.1)$$

$$L = \text{3M LIBOR} \, .$$

If one had been given the final value and needed to calculate the present value, the correct discount factor would clearly be

$$df(0, 3M) = \frac{1}{1 + \delta L} \, . \quad (2.2)$$

Furthermore, to receive exactly $1 in three months, one would invest $[1/(1 + \delta L)]$ today. Therefore, a discount factor can be defined as the price today ($t = 0$, where t denotes time) of a *zero coupon* bond that pays $1 at maturity, $t = T$. This discount factor will be denoted as $df(0, T)$. For example, if $T = 3M$, a LIBOR-based discount factor is given by (2.2). Other tenors need a combination of LIBOR rates. This is the so-called *bootstrapping method* of building up discount curves tenor by tenor starting from the shortest time horizon. Nonetheless, to calculate the present value of a cash flow at some future time T, one multiplies it by the discount factor $df(0, T)$. Discount factors need not start at time $t = 0$. Forward-starting discount factors are given by ($0 < t < T$)

$$df(t, T) = \frac{df(0, T)}{df(0, t)} \, . \quad (2.3)$$

Clearly, $df(t, t) = 1$, $\forall t$.

The bootstrapping method for calculating discount factors is as follows:

1. Calculate discount factors $df(0, t_i)$, $t_i \leq 3M$, from cash LIBOR rates (O/N, 1W, 1M, 2M, 3M).

2. Calculate discount factors $df(0, t_i)$, $3M < t_i < 5Y$, from 3M eurodollar futures going out to five years using previously calculated discount factors.

3. Use swap rates to calculate discount factors $df(0, t_i)$, $t_i > 5Y$, on swap cash flow dates (semiannual), while interpolating swap rates on cash flow dates not covered by another quoted market swap rate (one will need all semiannual discount factors).

4. Interpolate the above calculated discrete discount factors $\{df(0, t_i), \forall t_i\}$ to generate $df(0, t)$'s for all daily points in the future.

CHAPTER 2 ■ BUILDING A YIELD CURVE

> **Note** The interpolation methods for swap rates and discount factors can be different—for example, one can be linear and the other cubic.

Yield curves are often graphically shown as a curve of interest rates versus time. Even though this is visually correct, a yield curve is a set of discount factors, and most financial analytic libraries store the daily discount factors and not the rates used to calibrate the curve, because the curve is mostly used for finding the present value of cash flows. When a yield curve is shown as a curve of interest rates versus time, it is often a continuously compounded interest rate that is shown, such that

$$df(0, t_i) = \exp(-r_i \cdot t_i) \quad . \tag{2.4}$$

Another method of looking at interest rates is to calculate the continuously compounded forward rate

$$df(t_i, t_{i+1}) = \exp\{-f(t_i, t_{i+1})[t_{i+1} - t_i]\} \tag{2.5}$$

or, if one assumes a instantaneous continuously compounded forward rate function,

$$df(t, T) = \exp\left\{-\int_t^T f(t, \tau) d\tau\right\} \quad . \tag{2.6}$$

Cash LIBOR Rates

The front end of the curve is constructed using simply compounded term LIBOR rates where one can use a simple cash rate formula

$$df(0, t_i) = \frac{1}{1 + \delta_i L_i}$$

L_i = O/N, 1W, 1M, 2M, 3M Spot Libor   (2.7)

δ_i = Act/360 daycount factor from 0 to t_i .

Figure 2-1 indicates the nature of these discount factors with the x-axis showing the term LIBOR rates going out further and further in time and the y-axis showing the discount factors distance from 1 (the no-discounting level). As time increases, this distance grows even for flat interest rates: this is the fundamental decreasing nature of discount factors.

CHAPTER 2 ■ BUILDING A YIELD CURVE

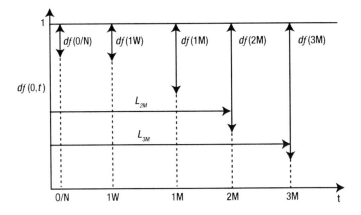

Figure 2-1. Term LIBOR rate discount factors

For instance,

$$df(0, 6M) = \frac{1}{1+\delta_{6M}L_{6M}} < df(0, 3M) = \frac{1}{1+\delta_{3M}L_{3M}} \quad . \tag{2.8}$$

One can get implied LIBOR rates from discount factors as follows:

$$L_j = \left[\frac{1}{df(0, t_j)} - 1\right]\frac{1}{\delta_j}$$

L_j = Spot LIBOR set at $t = 0$

δ_j = act/360 daycount fraction from $t = 0$ to t_j .

(2.9)

If one has constructed the yield curve correctly, the input calibration points should be recovered exactly using (2.9).

90D Eurodollar Futures

Recall from Chapter 1 that a 90D eurodollar futures contract is a futures on a forward-starting 3M LIBOR rate. This forward can produce a forward-starting discount factor. One needs to bootstrap this forward-starting discount factor into a term discount factor.

Before this method is shown, a comment about the difference between futures and *forward rate agreements* (FRAs), or simply *forwards*, is in order. As discussed in Chapter 1, futures are traded on exchanges, marked to market daily, and margined daily, leading to higher P&L fluctuations. Forwards are OTC-traded and entail both market and credit risk. They are not margined, and marked-to-market (MTM) gains and losses are not transferred between the respective counterparties. Even though forwards are less liquid than futures, the increased P&L volatility and daily margining requirements of futures contracts make them more expensive than forwards in the sense that the futures tend to have a slightly higher implied LIBOR rate than do forwards. Furthermore, the gains from future contracts are realized in cash immediately (via MTM at the exchange) and can be reinvested at prevailing interest rates, making the actual P&L dependent on ever-changing interest rates. There are no intermediate cash flows in a forward contract. This difference between futures and FRAs can be calculated using the volatility of interest rates (the *convexity adjustment*), but it is beyond the scope of this chapter and is model-dependent. Here, it will be assumed that the 90D eurodollar futures can be approximated as FRAs. For more information, see (Tuckman, 2012).

Assuming the 90D eurodollar futures exactly overlap (such that the maturity on one futures contract coincides exactly with the start of the next futures contract), the first forward-starting discount factor to be calculated is

$$df(3M, 6M) = \frac{df(0, 6M)}{df(0, 3M)} \quad . \tag{2.10}$$

This equation must be inverted because one needs $df(0, 6M)$. Suppose the first futures has a market price of $F(3M - 6M) = 99.25$. Assume the actual number of days is 90 between the 3M and 6M points. The required discount factor bootstrapped using the previously calculated discount factor $df(0, 3M)$ is

$$df(0, 6M) = \frac{df(0, 3M)}{1 + \delta_{3M\text{-}6M} L_{3M\text{-}6M}} \tag{2.11}$$

where

$$df(0, 3M) \rightarrow \text{known from Cash LIBOR Rates}$$
$$\delta_{3M\text{-}6M} = 90/360 \tag{2.12}$$
$$L_{3M\text{-}6M} = 0.75\% \quad .$$

The next discount factor $df(0, 9M)$ uses the value calculated in (2.11) and the next futures contract. This process is repeated until the 5Y swap calibration point begins.

Again, assuming the 90D eurodollar futures exactly overlap, the generic equation to use is

$$df(0, t_j) = \frac{df(0, t_{j-1})}{1 + \delta_j L_j}$$
F_{j-1} = Futures with settlement at t_{j-1} (2.13)
$$L_j = \frac{100 - F_{j-1}}{100} = \text{3M foward LIBOR at } t_{j-1}$$
δ_j = act/360 daycount fraction from t_{j-1} to t_j .

The forward-starting nature of this method in respect of both the rates and the discount factors is indicated in Figure 2-2.

CHAPTER 2 ■ BUILDING A YIELD CURVE

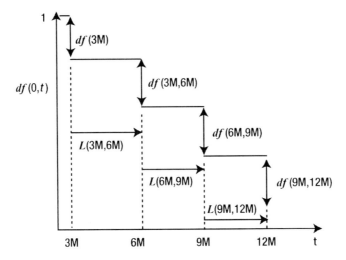

Figure 2-2. *Forward 3M LIBOR rate discount factors*

The maturity dates and starting dates of futures do not necessarily overlap precisely. There are simple interpolation methods to fill in the gaps, but they are not very instructive and are not presented here.

Finally, the implied forward 3M LIBOR rates are

$$L_j = \left[\frac{df(0, t_{j-1})}{df(0, t_j)} - 1\right]\frac{1}{\delta_j} \tag{2.14}$$

L_j = 3M foward LIBOR set at t_{j-1}^{flt}

δ_j = Act/360 daycount fraction from t_{j-1}^{flt} to t_j^{flt} .

Once again, calibrated points must be exactly reproduced by this equation.

Swaps

Swaps are more complicated than either cash or futures, inasmuch as they involve multiple cash flows instead of just one. Market swap rates are for par swaps, so that the floating leg simplifies and is not a problem except for the discount factor at maturity as shown in Chapter 1, (Equation 1.26). The fixed leg has to be analyzed more carefully because it has semiannual swap payments, and therefore semiannual discount factors. Begin with the first swap: the 5Y swap. If one assumes that the last futures ended at the (4Y + 9M) point, then one already has every semiannual discount factor needed for the swap except the one at the 5Y maturity point. Recall the swap formula from Chapter 1:

$$S \cdot DV01 = 1 - df(0, T)$$

$$DV01 = \sum_{i=1}^{n} \Delta_i \, df(0, t_i) \qquad (2.15)$$

$\Delta_i = 30/360$ daycount fraction.

For the 5Y swap, one has $t_n = T = 5Y$. Since that the cash flows here are semiannual, one has $n=10, \Delta_i = 1/2$. Because every semiannual discount factor except the one at maturity has already been constructed from cash rates and futures, one must separate the maturity discount factor out from the expression,

$$\sum_{i=1}^{n-1} S_{5Y} \Delta_i \, df(0, t_i) + S_{5Y} \Delta_n \, df(0, t_n) = 1 - df(0, t_n) \qquad (2.16)$$

Solving for $df(0, t_n)$ gives

$$df(0, t_n) = \frac{1 - \sum_{i=1}^{n-1} S_{5Y} \Delta_i \, df(0, t_i)}{1 + S_{5Y} \Delta_n} \qquad (2.17)$$

Note that this formula is valid for any swap tenor, not just a 5Y swap. (For a 7Y swap, for example, $S_{7Y}, n = 14$). Say one has the 5Y swap rate, $S_{5Y} = 0.75\%$.

$$df(0, t_{10} = 5Y) = \frac{1 - \sum_{i=1}^{n-1} S_{5Y} \Delta_i \, df(0, t_i)}{1 + S_{5Y} \Delta_n} \qquad (2.18)$$

As the cash flows are semiannual, this swap has 10 discount factors,

$$n = 10$$
$$\Delta_i = \frac{1}{2}, \quad \Delta_n = \frac{1}{2}$$
$$df(0, t_1) = df(0, 6M)$$
$$df(0, t_2) = df(0, 12M)$$
$$df(0, t_3) = df(0, 18M)$$
$$df(0, t_4) = df(0, 24M) \qquad (2.19)$$
$$df(0, t_5) = df(0, 30M)$$
$$df(0, t_6) = df(0, 36M)$$
$$df(0, t_7) = df(0, 42M)$$
$$df(0, t_8) = df(0, 48M)$$
$$df(0, t_9) = df(0, 54M)$$
$$df(0, t_{10}) = df(0, 60M)$$

The first nine discount factors are already known at this stage via the bootstrapping of discount factors from cash rates and futures.

The first swap is the easiest to handle. The next most liquid swap is 7Y. Unfortunately, one needs the 5.5Y, 6Y, and 6.5Y discount factors before one can calibrate the 7Y swap rate. How does one get these intermediate discount factors? What is often done is to interpolate between the available swap rates at the necessary semiannual cashflow points 5.5Y, 6Y, and 6.5Y and calibrate these interpolated swaps to get the needed discount factors. Then one can calibrate the market input 7Y swap. This interpolation process has to continue. Even if the next market quote is an 8Y rate, one must interpolate to get the 7.5Y discount factor. The two most common interpolation methods are linear and cubic. Linear interpolation is done as follows. Given a set of swap rates at specific times $S(t_k)$, the swap rate between times t_k and t_{k+1} using linear interpolation is given by

$$S(t) = AS(t_k) + BS(t_{k+1})$$
$$A = \frac{t_{k+1} - t}{t_{k+1} - t_k}, \quad B = 1 - A \quad (2.20)$$
$$t_k \leq t \leq t_{k+1}$$

If needed, the last available swap rate (usually 30Y) can be extrapolated out farther—say, to 40Y—although financial instruments usually do not go out that far into the future.

Generic Discount Factors

Once a set of discount factors has been calibrated to all market calibration inputs, a methodology to get a discount factor for any time in the future is needed. This is the case as cash flows from the vast array of financial instruments on the balance sheet of a bank occur on almost every day in the future (going out to at least thirty years). The typical way to calculate these noncalibrated discount factors is to use linear interpolation on the natural logarithm of the calibrated discount factors, $\ln[df(t_i)]$. For instance, from bootstrapping, one should already have the 2.5Y and 2.75Y discount factors from calibrating the respective eurodollar futures contracts. What is the 2.7Y discount factor? The linear interpolation method is

$$t_i = 2.5, \quad t = 2.7, \quad t_{i+1} = 2.75$$
$$\ln[df(t)] = A\ln[df(t_i)] + B\ln[df(t_{i+1})]$$
$$A = \frac{t_{i+1} - t}{t_{i+1} - t_i}, \quad B = 1 - A \quad (2.21)$$
$$df(t) = \exp(\ln[df(t)])$$

CHAPTER 2 ■ BUILDING A YIELD CURVE

This methodology effectively leads to piecewise constant continuously compounded forward rates. One can see this by first writing the discount factors in terms of continuously compounded spot interest rates:

$$df(t) = \exp(-r_t \cdot t)$$
$$\ln[df(t)] = A\ln[df(t_i)] + B\ln[df(t_{i+1})]$$
$$r_t \cdot t = Ar_i \cdot t_i + Br_{i+1} \cdot t_{i+1} \quad (2.22)$$
$$r_t \cdot t = \left[\frac{t_{i+1} - t}{t_{i+1} - t_i}\right] r_i \cdot t_i + \left[\frac{t - t_i}{t_{i+1} - t_i}\right] r_{i+1} \cdot t_{i+1} \quad .$$

Now write an expression for a forward-starting discount factor $df(t, t_{i+1})$, $t > 0$ using a continuously compounded forward rate:

$$df(t, t_{i+1}) = \frac{df(0, t_{i+1})}{df(0, t)} = \exp\{-f(t, t_{i+1})[t_{i+1} - t]\} = \exp(-r_{i+1} \cdot t_{i+1}) \exp(r_t \cdot t) \quad . \quad (2.23)$$

Matching the exponents of this expression and using the linear interpolation result from (2.22) produce the desired result:

$$-f(t, t_{i+1})[t_{i+1} - t] = -r_{i+1} \cdot t_{i+1} + r_t \cdot t$$
$$-f(t, t_{i+1})[t_{i+1} - t] = -r_{i+1} \cdot t_{i+1} + \left[\frac{t_{i+1} - t}{t_{i+1} - t_i}\right] r_i \cdot t_i + \left[\frac{t - t_i}{t_{i+1} - t_i}\right] r_{i+1} \cdot t_{i+1}$$
$$-f(t, t_{i+1})[t_{i+1} - t] = -\left[\frac{t_{i+1} - t_i}{t_{i+1} - t_i}\right] r_{i+1} \cdot t_{i+1} + \left[\frac{t_{i+1} - t}{t_{i+1} - t_i}\right] r_i \cdot t_i + \left[\frac{t - t_i}{t_{i+1} - t_i}\right] r_{i+1} \cdot t_{i+1} \quad (2.24)$$
$$-f(t, t_{i+1})[t_{i+1} - t] = -\left[\frac{t_{i+1} - t}{t_{i+1} - t_i}\right] r_{i+1} \cdot t_{i+1} + \left[\frac{t_{i+1} - t}{t_{i+1} - t_i}\right] r_i \cdot t_i$$
$$f(t, t_{i+1}) = \left[\frac{t_{i+1}}{t_{i+1} - t_i}\right] r_{i+1} + \left[\frac{t_i}{t_{i+1} - t_i}\right] r_i \quad .$$

Because $f(t, t_{i+1})$ is independent of t, linear interpolation of the logarithm of discount factors leads to piecewise constant continuously compounded forward rates.

Problems
Problem 2.1: Build a Simple Yield Curve
Calibrate a yield curve using the market inputs given in Figure 2-3.

CHAPTER 2 ■ BUILDING A YIELD CURVE

TO	JAN 1 2012	%
CASH	1W	0.206200
	1M	0.296300
	2M	0.428200
	3M	0.580500
FUTURES	MAR(3M-6M)	99.440000
	JUN(6M-9M)	99.400000
	SEPT(9M-12M)	99.370000
	DEC(12M-15M)	99.345000
	MAR(15M-18M)	99.350000
	JUN(18M-21M)	99.330000
SWAPS	2 yr	0.649000
	3 yr	0.755000
	4 yr	0.956000
	5 yr	1.196000

Figure 2-3. Yield curve calibration inputs

1. Bootstrap the discount factors for all the calibration points in Figure 2-3.
2. Produce discount factors at the following noncalibration times given in Figure 2-4.

T
1.8
2.3
2.7
3.1
3.3
4.2
4.7

Figure 2-4. Noncalibration times (in years)

3. Reproduce the 3Y swap rate calibration point using your discount factors.
4. Produce a continuously compounded yield curve using (2.4)—i.e., a graph of r_i versus t_i.

Make the following assumptions:

- Dates overlap perfectly—i.e., the 3M cash rate ends just when the first futures begins.
- The daycount basis for all rates is 30/360—i.e., 3M = 0.25 Years.
- All times are relative—i.e., the actual dates such as "Jan 1, 2012" don't matter and may be ignored. This relaxed assumption is true only for this exercise. In practice, actual dates, holiday calendars, etc. need to be taken into account.

Note The quotes are in the same format as the Bloomberg quotes in Chapter 1, such that all rates convert to percentages (e.g., 0.20620 → 0.20620% = 0.0020620). All times should be converted to units of years (e.g., 18M = 1.5Y).

Further Reading

Bouchaud, J.-P., and M. Potters. *Theory of Financial Risk and Derivative Pricing*, 2nd ed. Cambridge: Cambridge University Press, 2003.

Tuckman, B., and A. Serrat. *Fixed Income Securities*, 3rd ed. Hoboken, NJ: John Wiley & Sons, 2012.

CHAPTER 3

Statistical Analysis of Financial Data

Chapters 1 and 2 presented various financial instruments in the form of market data familiar to Wall Street traders—namely, Bloomberg screens. Chapter 3 lays the mathematical foundation for the valuation of financial instruments, which depends in the first place on an analysis of the likelihood of future events using the tools of statistics and probability. This chapter shows you how to perform a statistical analysis of a given financial instrument by first identifying a suitable probability distribution and then calibrating it appropriately. Finally, this chapter discusses Risk measures such as *value at risk, conditional value at risk,* the *term structure of statistics, temporal autocorrelations,* and *volatility convexity.*

Tools in Probability Theory

Probability theory deals with mathematical models of processes whose outcomes are uncertain (random). One must define what these outcomes are and assign appropriate probabilities to every outcome. Certain formal mathematical definitions using set-theoretic notation follow, which equip the reader to study the extensive literature on probability theory.[1] Figure 3-1 tabulates the translation between set theory and probability theory.

---

[1] See, for example, Patrick Billingsley, *Probability and Measure,* Anniversary Ed., John Wiley and Sons, 2012; S. R. S. Varadhan, *Probability Theory,* American Mathematical Society, 2001.

Notation	Set Theory	Probability Concept
Ω	Collection of elements	Sample Space of all possible outcomes
ω	$\omega \in \Omega$	Elementary outcome or event
A	$A \subset \Omega$	Event that the outcomes in the set A occurs
A^c	Complement of A	Event that *no* outcome in the set A occurs
$A \cup B$	Union of A and B	Events in either A or B occur
$A \cap B$	Intersection of A and B	Events in both A and B occur
$\emptyset$	Empty set	Impossible Event

Figure 3-1. *Set-theoretic notation and probability*

- *Sample space* Ω: The set of all possible outcomes or elementary events w of some process is called the *sample space*. This sample space forms a mathematical *set*. For example,

  - The process of coin tossing has a sample space: $\Omega = \{H,T\}$.
  - The process of dice throwing has a sample space: $\Omega = \{1,2,3,4,5,6\}$.

- *Events* $A \subset \Omega$: Not every interesting observable of a random process is an elementary outcome. One may be interested in a combination of outcomes. Therefore, one defines an event A as a subset of the sample space. When throwing dice, possible events could be

  - an even number $A = \{2,4,6\}$
  - not an even number $A = \{2,4,6\}^c$
  - an even number less than 4, $A = \{2,4,6\} \cap \{1,2,3\}$

  Obviously, the basic sample elements of the sample space can be events, such that $A = \omega = \{2\}$.

- *σ-Algebra*: Simply choosing an interesting set of events is not sufficient for defining probabilities. The set of events needs to form a closed system under the set-theoretic operations of union and intersection. A *σ-algebra* is the set of all possible *countable* unions and intersections of a chosen set of events. This collection of events $\Im$ satisfies the following four conditions:

  a. $\Omega \in \Im$
  b. If $A_1, A_2, A_3, \ldots \in \Im$ then $\bigcup_{i=1}^{A_i} \in \Im$

CHAPTER 3 ■ STATISTICAL ANALYSIS OF FINANCIAL DATA

  c. If $A_1, A_2, A_3, \ldots \in \Im$ then $\bigcap_{i=1}^{A_i} \in \Im$

  d. If $A \in \Im$ then $A^c \in \Im$

■ **Note** Condition (c) can be derived from (d) and (b).[2]

For example, if A is any subset of Ω, then $\Im = \{\varnothing, A, A^c, \Omega\}$ is a σ-algebra.

- *Probability Measure*: Now that a mathematically consistent set of events has been given (the σ-algebra $\Im$), one can assign probabilities to these events. There are a few basic restrictions on probabilities that are intuitively obvious but must be stated precisely in a mathematical way. First, probabilities must lie between 0 and 1. There are no negative probabilities, and there is no such thing as being more than 100% certain of some event. Also, the impossible event $\varnothing$ has a probability of 0. The probability of any event happening (that is, Ω) is clearly 100%. Finally, the probability of two *disjoint* or mutually exclusive events occurring must equal the sum of the probabilities of the individual events. A probability measure P on $(\Omega, \Im)$ is a function $P: \Im \to [0,1]$ such that

  a. $P(\varnothing) = 0, P(\Omega) = 1$

  b. If $A_1, A_2, A_3, \ldots \in \Im$ and $A_i \cap A_j = \varnothing$, then

$$P\left(\bigcup_i A_i\right) = \sum_i P(A_i) \quad . \qquad (3.1)$$

The triplet $(\Omega, \Im, P)$ is called a *probability space*.

Assigning probabilities to the σ-algebra $\Im$ is often straightforward. For example, for coin tossing one has $\Omega = \{H, T\}$, $\Im = \{\varnothing, H, T, \Omega\}$ and

$$P(\varnothing) = 0, P(H) = p, P(T) = 1 - p, P(\Omega) = 1 \quad . \qquad (3.2)$$

If the coin is unbiased, $p = 0.5$.

- *Random Variables*: To create a mathematical model of probability, one must deal with numerical constructs and not symbols such as H and T. A *random variable* is a variable whose possible values are *numerical* outcomes of a random phenomenon (such as tossing a coin).

---

[2] For discussion of countability conditions, see, for example, Patrick Billingsley, *Probability and Measure*, Anniversary Ed. John Wiley and Sons, 2012.

A random variable is a function $X: \Omega \to \Re$ with the property that

$$\{\omega \in \Omega : X(\omega) \leq x\} \in \mathfrak{I}, \forall x \in \Re \quad . \tag{3.3}$$

Basically, a random variable assigns a real valued number to an event from the sample space Ω.
Example: Coin tossing

$$\Omega = \{H, T\} \quad X(\omega) = \begin{cases} 1 & \omega = H \\ 0 & \omega = T \end{cases} . \tag{3.4}$$

Example: Marks on an exam

$$\Omega = \{A, B, C, F\} \quad X(\omega) = \begin{cases} 1 & \omega = A \\ 2 & \omega = B \\ 3 & \omega = C \\ 4 & \omega = F \end{cases} . \tag{3.5}$$

- *Distribution Function:* Now that a random variable has been defined, it is clear that it is more likely to be found in certain subsets of $\Re$ depending on the probability space $(\Omega, \mathfrak{I}, P)$ and the mapping X. What one really wants is the distribution $F(x)$ of the likelihood of X taking on certain values. One could define $F(x)$ as being the probability that the random number X equals a particular number x. This does not work in general, and therefore the more appropriate definition is

$$F_X(x) = \text{probability that } X \text{ does not exceed } x \quad . \tag{3.6}$$

Therefore, the distribution function of a random variable X is the function $F: \Re \to [0,1]$ given by

$$F_X(x) = P(X \leq x) \quad . \tag{3.7}$$

such that

i. $P(X > x) = 1 - F(x)$
ii. $P(x < X \leq y) = F(y) - F(x)$
iii. If $x < y$ then $F(x) \leq F(y)$
iv. $\lim_{x \to -\infty} F(x) \to 0$, $\lim_{x \to \infty} F(x) \to 1$.

Two types of random variables will be discussed in the remainder of this chapter: *discrete* and *continuous*.

- *Discrete Random Variable*: A random variable X is called discrete if it takes values in some countable subset $\{x_1, x_2, ..., x_n\}$ of $\Re$. It has a *density function* $f: \Re \to [0,1]$ given by $f(x) = P(X = x)$. The distribution function for a discrete variable is

$$F(x) = \sum_{x_i \leq x} f(x_i) \quad . \tag{3.8}$$

with the *normalization* condition (the probability of all discrete events)

$$\sum_{\forall i} f(x_i) = 1 \quad . \tag{3.9}$$

- *Continuous Random Variable*: A random X is called continuous if its distribution function can be expressed as

$$F(x) = \int_{-\infty}^{x} f(u) du \quad x \in \Re \quad , \tag{3.10}$$

with a density function $f: \Re \to [0, \infty)$ with the properties

  i. $\int_{-\infty}^{\infty} f(x) dx = 1$ normalization

  ii. $P(X = x) = 0, \ \forall x \in \Re$ (probability of getting precisely a specific real number is zero)

  iii. $P(a \leq X \leq b) = \int_a^b f(x) dx$

One can think of $f(x)dx$ as a differential element of probability, such that

$$P(x < X < x + dx) = F(x + dx) - F(x) \cong f(x) dx \tag{3.11}$$

Several popular discrete and continuous distribution functions are described as follows:

- *Binomial Distribution*: Let a random variable X take values 1 and 0 with probabilities p and $1-p$ (known as a Bernoulli trial). The discrete density function is $f(0) = 1-p, f(1) = p$. Perform n independent trials $\{X_1 ... X_n\}$ and count the total numbers of 1's, such that $Y = X_1 + X_2 + ... X_n$. The density function of Y is

$$f(k) = P(Y = k) = \binom{n}{k} p^k (1-p)^{n-k}, \quad k = 0, 1, ..., n \tag{3.12}$$

with the binomial coefficient

CHAPTER 3 ■ STATISTICAL ANALYSIS OF FINANCIAL DATA

$$\binom{n}{k} = \frac{n!}{k!(n-k)!} \quad . \tag{3.13}$$

One can check that this probability mass function has the proper normalization

$$\sum_{k=0}^{n} f(k) = \sum_{k=0}^{n} \binom{n}{k} p^k (1-p)^{n-k} = \sum_{k=0}^{n} \binom{n}{k} (1-p)^n \left(\frac{p}{1-p}\right)^k \quad . \tag{3.14}$$

Using the identity

$$\sum_{k=0}^{n} \binom{n}{k} x^k = (1+x)^n \quad , \tag{3.15}$$

the desired result is obtained

$$(1-p)^n \sum_{k=0}^{n} \binom{n}{k} \left(\frac{p}{1-p}\right)^k = (1-p)^n \left[1 + \frac{p}{1-p}\right]^n = (1-p)^n \left[\frac{1}{1-p}\right]^n = 1 \quad . \tag{3.16}$$

In finance, the binomial distribution is used in the *binomial tree model* (Chapter 4).

- *Poisson Distribution*: This is another counting-type discrete probability distribution that considers the random count of a given number of *independent* events occurring in a fixed interval (space or time) with a known average occurrence rate. Poisson distributions are found in financial processes with sudden large moves in price (*jumps*) or in credit default situations (Chapter 6). A discrete random variable Y with a Poisson distribution with parameter λ has a probability mass function given by

$$f(k) = P(Y = k) = \frac{\lambda^k}{k!} e^{-\lambda}, \quad k = 0, 1, \ldots, n, \quad \lambda > 0 \quad . \tag{3.17}$$

- *Normal (Gaussian) Distribution*: As the ubiquitous distribution of probability theory, the normal distribution has been overused on account of its simplicity. Its use in finance is also fraught with peril. A large portion of this chapter is dedicated to describing why *not* to use the following distribution and to providing alternative distributions with better properties for describing financial data:

$$f(x)dx = \frac{1}{\sqrt{2\pi\sigma^2}} \exp\left(-\frac{(x-\mu)^2}{2\sigma^2}\right) dx, \quad x \in \Re, \sigma > 0 \quad . \tag{3.18}$$

This distribution is often denoted as $N(\mu, \sigma^2)$. Note that by substituting $y = \dfrac{x-\mu}{\sigma}$, $dy = \dfrac{dx}{\sigma}$, the foregoing reduces to $N(0,1)$ for the variable y (because $-\infty<x<\infty$). Therefore, if one has an $N(0,1)$ variable y, one can create an $N(\mu, \sigma^2)$ variable by the transformation $x = \mu + \sigma y$.

- *Log-normal Distribution*: This is another popular but overused distribution seen in finance, suffering from many of the same problems as the normal distribution.

$$f(x)dx = \frac{1}{\sqrt{2\pi\sigma^2}} \exp\left(-\frac{[\ln(x)-\mu]^2}{2\sigma^2}\right)\frac{dx}{x}, \quad x \in \Re, x>0 \quad . \tag{3.19}$$

The reason this is called the *log-normal distribution* is that the natural logarithm of the variable x is normally distributed. This is easy to see by substituting $y = \ln(x)$, $dy = \dfrac{dx}{x}$ into (3.19).

- *Gamma Distribution*: This has become a popular distribution in finance in conjunction with the *variance-gamma* model [Glasserman, 2003]. It is a two-parameter continuous distribution given by

$$f(x) = \frac{\lambda}{\Gamma(\alpha)}(\lambda x)^{\alpha-1}e^{-\lambda x}, \quad x \in \Re, x>0 \;\; \lambda>0, \;\; \alpha>0 \quad , \tag{3.20}$$

where the gamma function is

$$\Gamma(p) = \int_0^\infty t^{p-1}e^{-t}\,dt \quad . \tag{3.21}$$

- *Beta Distribution*: This continuous distribution differs from the ones above in that the range of the underlying random variable is between zero and one. A financial variable with this property is the recovery rates of defaulted bonds (0% to 100%). This will be explained later in this chapter. The density function has two parameters and is given by

$$f(x) = \frac{\Gamma(p+q)}{\Gamma(p)\Gamma(q)}x^{p-1}(1-x)^{q-1}, \quad 0<x<1, \;\; p,q>0 \quad , \tag{3.22}$$

or, when written in terms of the beta function,

$$f(x) = \frac{1}{B(p,q)}x^{p-1}(1-x)^{q-1}, \quad 0<x<1, \;\; p,q>0 \quad . \tag{3.23}$$

where the beta function is

$$B(p,q) = \int_0^1 t^{p-1}(1-t)^{q-1}\, dt \quad . \tag{3.24}$$

One can check the normalization condition as follows:

$$\int_0^1 f(x)\, dx = \frac{1}{B(p,q)} \int_0^1 x^{p-1}(1-x)^{q-1}\, dx = \frac{B(p,q)}{B(p,q)} = 1 \quad . \tag{3.25}$$

- *Generalized Student's-t Distribution*: This is a three-parameter (μ, ν, λ) continuous distribution that will be used later in this chapter. Historically, the random variable is denoted as t rather than the more traditional x. The probability density function is

$$f(t) = \frac{\Gamma\left(\dfrac{\nu+1}{2}\right)}{\Gamma\left(\dfrac{\nu}{2}\right)} \sqrt{\dfrac{\lambda}{\nu\pi}} \left(1 + \dfrac{\lambda(t-\mu)^2}{\nu}\right)^{-\frac{\nu+1}{2}} \quad . \tag{3.26}$$

where the parameter ν is often referred to as the *degrees of freedom*. (Note that this is still a one-dimensional probability distribution.)

Moments of a Distribution

What does one want to measure in a probabilistic system? One can either measure a specific value of a random variable (for example, the number of heads that come up with multiple coin tosses), or one can construct some sort of average of the random variable itself. If X_n is the value of a random variable from the n_{th} trial of that variable, the (obvious) average of this variable after N trials is

$$\bar{X}_N = \frac{1}{N} \sum_{n=1}^{N} X_n \tag{3.27}$$

In the limit of a very large number of trials, by the law of large numbers $\bar{X}_N$ approaches the *mean* or *expected value* $E[X]$ of the random variable X,

$$\lim_{N \to \infty} \bar{X}_N = \lim_{N \to \infty} \frac{1}{N} \sum_{n=1}^{N} X_n = E[X] \quad . \tag{3.28}$$

The mean or expected value of a discrete random variable X is given by

CHAPTER 3 ■ STATISTICAL ANALYSIS OF FINANCIAL DATA

$$E[X] = \sum_x x f(x) \quad . \tag{3.29}$$

For continuous random variables, one has

$$E[X] = \int_{x \in \Re} x f(x) dx \quad . \tag{3.30}$$

The *expectation operator* has the following *linearity property*. If X and Y are random variables and a, b and c are constants, then

$$E[aX + bY + c] = a E[X] + b E[Y] + c \quad . \tag{3.31}$$

The expectation is often called the *first moment* of a distribution. If n is a positive integer, the nth moment m_n of a random variable X is

$$m_n = E[X^n] \quad . \tag{3.32}$$

Moments can describe the *shape* of a density function. Consider the symmetric Gaussian density function. The first moment $\mu = E[X]$ of this density function is where the shape of the density function is centered. The second moment $\sigma^2 = E[(X - \mu)^2]$ is a measure of the *width* of the density function, describing the probability of how far the random numbers can deviate from the mean μ. For $n > 2$, it is common to calculate the *normalized central moments*

$$\frac{E[(X - \mu)^n]}{\sigma^n} \quad . \tag{3.33}$$

where $\mu = E[X]$ and $\sigma^2 = E[(X-\mu)^2]$.

σ^2 is called the *variance*, and σ is the *standard deviation*. These moments are dimensionless quantities and are invariant to any linear change of scale of the random variable X. The next two moments are the most critical to risk management: the third moment, *skewness*, and the fourth moment, *kurtosis*. Skewness describes the asymmetry of the shape of the density function; kurtosis describes the "thickness" or "fatness" of the tails of the density function. Financial return data are often described by their empirical moments. The standard deviation of financial return data is called the *volatility* of returns. Moments are the primary method for determining the suitability of using a distribution to represent empirical facts. Matching the moments of empirical data to the moments of a theoretical distribution is one of the key calibration methods discussed below.

What are the moments of the commonly used Gaussian distribution

$$f(x) = \frac{1}{\sqrt{2\pi\sigma^2}} \exp\left(-\frac{x^2}{2\sigma^2}\right) \sim N(0, \sigma^2) \quad ? \tag{3.34}$$

To calculate the moments, the following integral relation proves useful

CHAPTER 3 ■ STATISTICAL ANALYSIS OF FINANCIAL DATA

$$\int_{-\infty}^{\infty} \exp(-ax^2)\,dx = \sqrt{\frac{\pi}{a}} \quad . \tag{3.35}$$

Its proof is as follows. First, take a square of the left-hand side and make a transformation to polar coordinates:

$$I = \int_{-\infty}^{\infty} \exp(-ax^2)\,dx = \sqrt{\frac{\pi}{a}}$$

$$I^2 = \int_{-\infty}^{\infty} \exp(-ax^2)\,dx \int_{-\infty}^{\infty} \exp(-ay^2)\,dy = \int_{-\infty}^{\infty}\int_{-\infty}^{\infty} \exp\left[-a(x^2+y^2)\right]dx\,dy \tag{3.36}$$

$$x = r\cos(\theta)$$
$$y = r\sin(\theta)$$

Recall that making a transformation requires calculating the Jacobian of the transformation:

$$dx\,dy = \begin{vmatrix} \dfrac{\partial x}{\partial r} & \dfrac{\partial y}{\partial r} \\ \dfrac{\partial x}{\partial \theta} & \dfrac{\partial y}{\partial \theta} \end{vmatrix} dr\,d\theta$$

$$\begin{vmatrix} \dfrac{\partial x}{\partial r} & \dfrac{\partial y}{\partial r} \\ \dfrac{\partial x}{\partial \theta} & \dfrac{\partial y}{\partial \theta} \end{vmatrix} = \begin{vmatrix} \cos(\theta) & \sin(\theta) \\ -r\sin(\theta) & r\cos(\theta) \end{vmatrix} = r\cos^2(\theta) + r\sin^2(\theta) = r \tag{3.37}$$

Calculating the integral in polar coordinates is straightforward:

$$\int_{-\infty}^{\infty}\int_{-\infty}^{\infty} \exp\left[-a(x^2+y^2)\right]dx\,dy = \int_{0}^{2\pi}\int_{0}^{\infty} \exp\left[-ar^2\right] r\,dr\,d\theta$$

$$I^2 = \int_{0}^{2\pi}\int_{0}^{\infty} \exp\left[-ar^2\right] r\,dr\,d\theta = -\frac{1}{2a} 2\pi \exp\left[-ar^2\right]\Big|_0^{\infty} = \frac{\pi}{a} \tag{3.38}$$

$$I = \int_{-\infty}^{\infty} \exp(-ax^2)\,dx = \sqrt{\frac{\pi}{a}}$$

From this relation, one has, using $a = 1/(2\sigma^2)$, the normalization constraint of the density function

$$\int_{-\infty}^{\infty} f(x)\,dx = \int_{-\infty}^{\infty} \frac{1}{\sqrt{2\pi\sigma^2}} \exp\left(-\frac{x^2}{2\sigma^2}\right)dx = \frac{\sqrt{2\pi\sigma^2}}{\sqrt{2\pi\sigma^2}} = 1 \quad . \tag{3.39}$$

How can one use the integral relation to calculate moments as powers of x are needed in the integrand? One can use the following trick to calculate all the moments.

CHAPTER 3 ■ STATISTICAL ANALYSIS OF FINANCIAL DATA

Take a derivative of the integral relation (both left- and right-hand sides) with respect to a (not x)

$$\int_{-\infty}^{\infty} x^2 \exp(-ax^2)\,dx = \frac{1}{2}\sqrt{\frac{\pi}{a^3}} \; . \tag{3.40}$$

A power of x^2 has been obtained. This relation will be useful when calculating the second moment. One can repeat this process on the above result to get all the even powers of X

$$\int_{-\infty}^{\infty} x^4 \exp(-ax^2)\,dx = \frac{3\sqrt{\pi}}{4} a^{-\frac{5}{2}} \; . \tag{3.41}$$

Odd powers of the integral are zero because the integrand is an even function and the range of the integration is from $-\infty$ to ∞. The positive and negative parts of the integral cancel each other out.

The variance of the Gaussian distribution using (3.37) is

$$E[X^2] = \int_{-\infty}^{\infty} \frac{x^2}{\sqrt{2\pi\sigma^2}} \exp\left(-\frac{x^2}{2\sigma^2}\right) dx = \frac{1}{\sqrt{2\pi\sigma^2}} \frac{1}{2}\sqrt{\pi(2\sigma^2)^3} = \sigma^2 \; . \tag{3.42}$$

The third moment, *skewness*, of the Gaussian distribution is zero because all odd powers of the required integral are zero.

The fourth moment, kurtosis, of the Gaussian distribution is

$$\frac{E[(X-\mu)^4]}{\{E[(X-\mu)^2]\}^2} = \frac{E[X^4]}{\sigma^4} = \frac{1}{\sigma^4}\frac{1}{\sqrt{2\pi\sigma^2}}\frac{3\sqrt{\pi}}{4}(2\sigma^2)^{\frac{5}{2}} \to \frac{E[X^4]}{\sigma^4} = 3 \; . \tag{3.43}$$

■ **Note** All normal distributions have a kurtosis of 3.

Kurtosis is a measure of how peaked a distribution is and how heavy (*fat*) its tails are. A high kurtosis distribution has a sharper peak and longer, fatter tails, whereas a low kurtosis distribution has a more rounded peak and shorter, thinner tails (Figure 3-2). A higher kurtosis distribution means more of the variance is the result of rare extreme deviations as opposed to frequent modestly sized deviations. Kurtosis risk is commonly referred to as *fat-tail risk*.

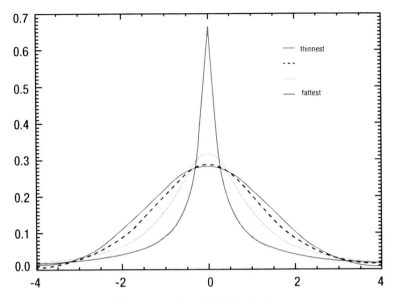

Figure 3-2. Fat-tailed distributions

▪ **Caution**   Not recognizing the importance of kurtosis risk has precipitated crises at many Wall Street firms, such as Long-Term Capital Management, Lehman Brothers, Bear Stearns, and Merrill Lynch.

How peaked a distribution and how fat the tails of a distribution are with respect to a normal distribution, which has a kurtosis of 3, is measured by the *excess kurtosis*

$$\frac{E[(X-\mu)^4]}{\{E[(X-\mu)^2]\}^2} - 3 \quad . \tag{3.44}$$

(In many statistical systems, such as the one in Microsoft Excel, the kurtosis calculation is in fact the excess kurtosis.)

The normal distribution has serious shortcomings as a model for changes in market prices of an asset. In virtually all markets, the distribution of observed market price changes displays far higher peaks and heavier tails than can be captured with a normal distribution. Nassim Taleb, a former Wall Street derivatives trader, developed the *black swan theory of rare events* to explain the disproportionate role of high-impact, hard-to-predict, and rare events that are beyond the realm of normal expectations in history, science, finance, and technology—such as the rise of the personal computer, the Internet, World War I, and the

September 11 attacks. Taleb summarizes his criteria for identifying a black swan event as follows:[3]

> What we call here a Black Swan is an event with the following three attributes. First, it is an outlier, as it lies outside the realm of regular expectations, because nothing in the past can convincingly point to its possibility. Second, it carries an extreme impact. Third, in spite of its outlier status, human nature makes us concoct explanations for its occurrence after the fact, making it explainable and predictable.

Taleb contends that banks and trading firms are very vulnerable to hazardous black swan events and are exposed to losses beyond those predicted by their defective models (often based on normal and log-normal distributions). In connection with the third attribute of black swans, note that Taleb advanced his theory *before* the mortgage crisis of 2008.

Creating Random Variables and Distributions

Before dealing with real financial data, it is useful first to generate random variables on a computer and create distributions from these generated numbers. The generated random variables can be seen as *synthetic data* and the methods of creating distributions from them will lead naturally to the moment-matching calibration methods of the following section. Because real data is rarely clean and precise, some practice with idealized data is helpful in learning the concepts. The generation of *pseudo* and *quasi* random numbers and their use in *Monte Carlo* simulations is of fundamental importance in financial engineering (Chapter 4). This section will describe a very straightforward method for generating random numbers using Microsoft Excel.[4]

The Inverse Transform Method

The *inverse transform method* is a basic method for sampling random numbers from a specific distribution given an *invertible* expression for the distribution and a method for generating continuous uniform random numbers between 0 and 1. The idea is to sample a uniform number U between 0 and 1, interpret it as a probability, and assign a random number x from a pre-specified distribution by choosing the smallest number x such that $P(X \leq x) \geq U$. As probabilities lie between 0 and 1, U needs to lie between 0 and 1.

---

[3]Nassim Taleb, *The Black Swan: The Impact of the Highly Improbable*. Random House, 2007.
[4]For other methods of generating random numbers, see Paul Glasserman, *Monte Carlo Methods in Financial Engineering*. Springer, 2003.

Suppose one wants to sample random numbers from a cumulative distribution function $F_X(x) = P(X \leq x)$. Because $F_X(x)$ is a non-decreasing function, the inverse function, if it exists, may be defined for any value U between 0 and 1 as $F_X^{-1}(U) = \inf\{x : F_X(x) \geq U, 0 < U < 1\}$.

Note that $P(F_X^{-1}(U) \leq x) = P(U \leq F_X(x))$ by the fact that $F_X(x)$ is monotonic. Finally, $P(U \leq F_X(x)) = F_X(x)$ as U is assumed to be uniformly distributed, indicating that $F_X^{-1}(U)$ follows the desired distribution.

One can generate a uniform random number between 0 and 1 and interpret it as a probability. This probability can then be seen as the result of a specific random number that can be found by using the *inverse* distribution on the generated probability. The inverse transform sampling method has the following steps:

1. Generate a probability from a standard uniform distribution

$$\rightarrow U \sim \text{Unif}\,[0,1] \quad (3.45)$$

2. Associate a random number with this probability using the inverse transformation

$$\rightarrow x = F_X^{-1}(U)$$

This can be done for any random variable where the inverse transformation is known and can be calculated explicitly. For Gaussian variables $N(\mu, \sigma^2)$, the distribution function

$$F_X(x) = \int_{-\infty}^{x} f(s)\,ds = \frac{1}{\sqrt{2\pi\sigma^2}} \int_{-\infty}^{x} \exp\left(-\frac{(s-\mu)^2}{2\sigma^2}\right) ds \quad (3.46)$$

does not have an explicit expression for the inverse distribution. Yet approximate formulas exist for the Gaussian distribution inverse function for any desired accuracy. Microsoft Excel has the following two functions, indicated by the arrow, that allow one to create $N(\mu, \sigma^2)$ random variables in a spreadsheet

$$U \sim \text{Unif}\,[0,1] \rightarrow \text{RAND}()$$
$$x = F^{-1}(U) \rightarrow \text{NORMINV}(U, \mu, \sigma) \quad (3.47)$$

These Excel functions RAND() and NORMINV() are good for demonstration and testing purposes but are not accurate enough for real-world use. Figure 3-3 shows an example of the spreadsheet use of these functions (see Problem 3-1). The empirical moments of the random numbers generated must be compared to the theoretical moments. It is critical that one checks the moments of the random variables produced versus the theoretical ones given by the inputs μ and σ. Remember that the purpose here is to produce random numbers that have the characteristics of the Gaussian distribution. This convergence will depend upon how many random numbers are produced and how accurate the random number generator is. The random number generator in Excel, RAND(), is poor and is not recommended for genuine use. The number of random observations one needs to generate is dependent on the distribution in question, but in general for fat-tailed distributions more random numbers are needed to fully "experience" the distribution. An order-of-magnitude estimate is that one needs to produce at least one million numbers for true convergence (which is not possible in Excel).

CHAPTER 3 ■ STATISTICAL ANALYSIS OF FINANCIAL DATA

	INPUTS	
	Mean	0.05
	Sigma	0.25

Excel Function	OUTPUTS		Excel Function
average()	Mean	0.050195	
stdev()	Stdev	0.24993	
kurt()	Ex-Kurt	-0.00087	
	Uniform	Normal	
RAND()	0.101931	-0.26766	NORMINV(U, Mean, Sigma)
RAND()	0.6825198	0.168689	NORMINV(U, Mean, Sigma)
RAND()	0.5792655	0.100004	NORMINV(U, Mean, Sigma)
RAND()	0.7289174	0.202386	NORMINV(U, Mean, Sigma)
RAND()	0.4770257	0.035595	NORMINV(U, Mean, Sigma)
RAND()	0.2032693	-0.1575	NORMINV(U, Mean, Sigma)
RAND()	0.4303552	0.006133	NORMINV(U, Mean, Sigma)
RAND()	0.4106028	-0.0065	NORMINV(U, Mean, Sigma)
RAND()	0.7526418	0.220707	NORMINV(U, Mean, Sigma)
RAND()	0.8049862	0.264892	NORMINV(U, Mean, Sigma)
RAND()	0.0697711	-0.31937	NORMINV(U, Mean, Sigma)
RAND()	0.7581072	0.225057	NORMINV(U, Mean, Sigma)
RAND()	0.6383251	0.138496	NORMINV(U, Mean, Sigma)
RAND()	0.0770063	-0.30638	NORMINV(U, Mean, Sigma)
RAND()	0.7943755	0.255424	NORMINV(U, Mean, Sigma)

Figure 3-3. Excel functions for the inverse transform method for normal variables

■ **Note** RAND() will produce a new uniformly [0,1] distributed random number every time the Excel spreadsheet is recalculated.

Creating a Density Function: Histograms and Frequencies

Theoretical density functions are mimicked by histograms when dealing with finite amounts of empirical data. A *histogram* is a graphical representation of an approximate density function for an underlying random variable. The histogram groups nearby data into discrete buckets and counts the number of data points, called *frequencies*, in a predetermined bucket. Graphically, a histogram is a set of these frequencies pictured as adjacent rectangles over discrete intervals called *bins*, as shown in Figure 3-4. Each rectangle has a height equal to the frequency over that interval and a width equal to the bin size. The appropriate bin size and number of bins depend on the empirical data at hand. If the bin size is too gross, the histogram will not represent some of the subtle points of the true density function because too many data points will put into the same bin. If the bin size is too fine, one will not get a histogram because the frequencies in each bucket will be too small. Unfortunately, there is no systematically best method to choose the number of bins and bin size. It depends on the number of empirical points as well as how spread out these points are in the sample space. You could use the empirical standard deviation to estimate this spread of data, but you would miss the fat tail characteristics of the data unless you calculate the empirical kurtosis and any skew properties. You need to experiment with different ranges of bins and bin sizes and choose a histogram that best communicates the shape of the empirical distribution.

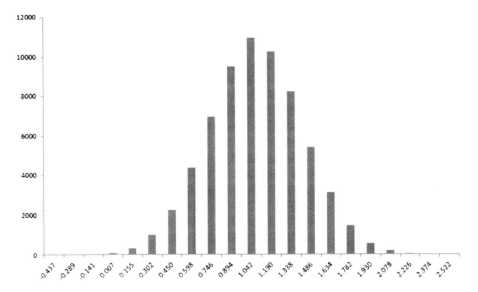

Figure 3-4. Raw histogram

Some rules of thumb are good to start with when creating a histogram. If $x_1, x_2, \ldots, x_n$ are the set of n data points, the basic relationship between bins and bin width is

$$\text{bin width} = \frac{\max(x) - \min(x)}{\text{number of bins}} \qquad (3.48)$$

where one can start with the estimate

$$\text{number of bins} = \sqrt{n} \text{ or } n^{1/3} \qquad (3.49)$$

(See Problem 3-1.)
There are two methods in Excel for creating a histogram, depending on the nature of the data—whether *static* or *dynamic*.

Excel Histogram-Creating Method: Static Data

For static data, one can use the Histogram tool in the Excel Data Analysis toolkit (Figure 3-5). The inputs are the predetermined bin range that has the number of bins with their specific attachment and detachment points and the empirical data that will be counted against these bins (Figure 3-6). Figure 3-7 shows the output bin range with the respective frequency count. These frequencies need to be *normalized*, as discussed in the section after next.

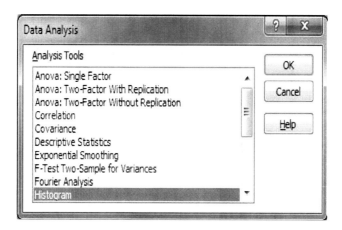

Figure 3-5. Excel Histogram tool in Data Analysis

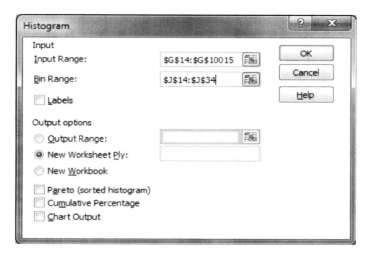

Figure 3-6. Excel Histogram tool inputs

CHAPTER 3 ■ STATISTICAL ANALYSIS OF FINANCIAL DATA

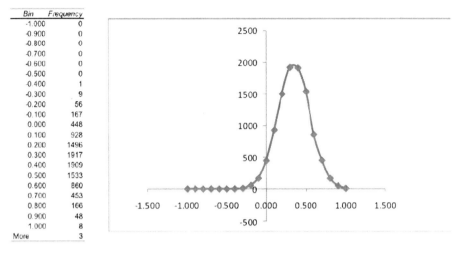

Figure 3-7. *Excel Histogram tool output*

Excel Histogram-Creating Method: Dynamic Data

If one's empirical data are continually changing, the static histogram method described above can become tiresome. The Excel array function *FREQUENCY(data array, bin array)* can be used and is readily able to recalculate when the inputs change, making it a dynamic function. For array functions, one must use CTRL-SHIFT-ENTER over the array space in Excel (usually beside the bin array). This method is ideal for creating a density function from randomly generated normal variables, such as the ones illustrated in Figure 3-3, as the function RAND() produces new numbers on every update of the spreadsheet.

Normalization of a Histogram

Raw frequencies do not equal a density function. A density function must have the property $\int_{-\tau_c}^{\tau_c} f(x)dx = 1$. Therefore, one must convert raw frequencies into normalized frequencies. Because one is dealing with discrete data, all integrals are turned into summations whereby

$$\int_{-\tau_c}^{\tau_c} \to \sum \quad . \tag{3.50}$$

such that

$$dx \to \Delta x \to (Bin\ Size) \tag{3.51}$$

CHAPTER 3 ■ STATISTICAL ANALYSIS OF FINANCIAL DATA

The first step is to find the total area under the raw histogram. One can then normalize the raw frequencies to get normalized frequencies such that the resulting area under the normalized empirical density curve is one (Figure 3-8). The steps are as follow.

Bin Size 0.144777723		Area under Curve	Normalized
Bins	Excel Frequency Function	9409.03	1.0000
-1.048	1	0.14	0.00
-0.903	5	0.72	0.00
-0.758	25	3.62	0.00
-0.613	109	15.78	0.01
-0.469	303	43.87	0.03
-0.324	856	123.93	0.09
-0.179	1885	272.91	0.20
-0.034	3750	542.92	0.40
0.110	6323	915.43	0.67
0.255	8717	1262.03	0.93
0.400	10417	1508.15	1.11
0.545	10457	1513.94	1.11
0.690	8961	1297.35	0.95
0.834	6246	904.28	0.66
0.979	3796	549.58	0.40
1.124	1912	276.82	0.20
1.269	809	117.13	0.09
1.413	287	41.55	0.03
1.558	107	15.49	0.01
1.703	20	2.90	0.00
1.848	5	0.50	0.00

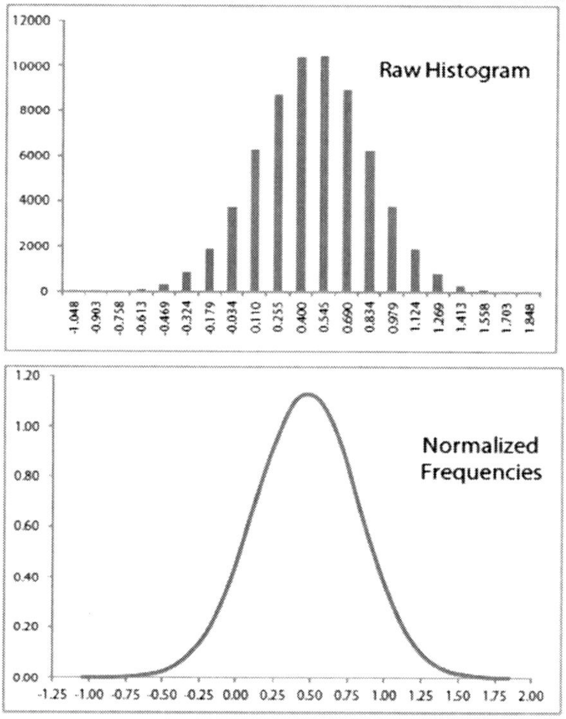

Figure 3-8. Example of bins, frequencies, and normalization of empirical densities

CHAPTER 3 ■ STATISTICAL ANALYSIS OF FINANCIAL DATA

1) Area under the normalized empirical density curve:

$$\text{Area} = \sum (Frequency) \cdot (Bin\ Size)$$
$$\text{Area} = \int_{-\infty}^{\infty} f(x)dx \rightarrow \sum f(x)\Delta x \quad (3.52)$$
$$= \sum (Frequency) \cdot (Bin\ Size)$$

2) Normalize frequencies by the area:

$$Frequency \rightarrow \frac{Frequency}{Area} \quad (3.53)$$
$$= Normalized\ Frequency$$

3) Perform a check of the area of the final distribution:

$$\text{Area} = \sum (Normalized\ Frequency) \cdot (Bin\ Size) = 1$$
$$\rightarrow \int_{-\infty}^{\infty} f(x)dx = 1 \quad (3.54)$$

With these normalized frequencies, one can calculate empirical moments—the mean, variance, and kurtosis—as follows, using the ordered bins of the discretized x-space (Figure 3-8) and assuming the random variable x is either in the middle or at one endpoint of the appropriate bin.

1. $\text{Mean} = E[x] = \int_{-\infty}^{\infty} x f(x) dx \rightarrow \sum x(Normalized\ Frequency)(Bin\ Size)$

2. $\text{Var} = E(x - \mu)^2 = E[x^2]$
$$= \int_{-\infty}^{\infty} x^2 f(x) dx \rightarrow \sum x^2 (Normalized\ Frequency)(Bin\ Size),$$
$$\sigma = \sqrt{Var}$$

3. $\text{Kurt} = \dfrac{E[x^4]}{\sigma^4} = \dfrac{\int_{-\infty}^{\infty} x^4 f(x) dx}{\sigma^4} \rightarrow \dfrac{\sum x^4 (Normalized\ Frequency)(Bin\ Size)}{\sigma^4}$

Mixture of Gaussians: Creating a Distribution with High Kurtosis

Modeling heavy tails is a critical skill in risk management. High peaks and heavy tails are a characteristic of many financial markets with small to medium price changes during most times, interrupted by occasional large price moves. Even though the Gaussian distribution does not capture these features, a simple extension of the Gaussian distribution exhibiting a higher kurtosis than three is a mixture of two or more normal density functions. Consider the following dual mixture,

$$qN(0,\sigma_1^2)+(1-q)N(0,\sigma_2^2), \quad q \in (0,1) \tag{3.55}$$

$$f(x) \rightarrow \frac{q}{\sqrt{2\pi\sigma_1^2}}\exp\left(-\frac{x^2}{2\sigma_1^2}\right)+\frac{1-q}{\sqrt{2\pi\sigma_2^2}}\exp\left(-\frac{x^2}{2\sigma_2^2}\right). \tag{3.56}$$

This is *not* simply adding two random variates. What this produces is a distribution of a random variable drawn from $N(0, \sigma_1^2)$ with probability q and drawn from $N(0, \sigma_2^2)$ with probability $1-q$. A mixed Gaussian distribution is the weighted sum of Gaussian *densities*. It is a three-parameter (q, σ_1, σ_2) distribution. The moments can be calculated using the moments for simple normal distributions. First, check the normalization,

$$\int_{-\infty}^{\infty} f(x)\,dx = \int_{-\infty}^{\infty}\left[\frac{q}{\sqrt{2\pi\sigma_1^2}}\exp\left(-\frac{x^2}{2\sigma_1^2}\right)+\frac{1-q}{\sqrt{2\pi\sigma_2^2}}\exp\left(-\frac{x^2}{2\sigma_2^2}\right)\right]dx = q+(1-q)=1 \tag{3.57}$$

Next, calculate the mean

$$E[x] = \int_{-\infty}^{\infty} x\,f(x) = \int_{-\infty}^{\infty}\left[\frac{q}{\sqrt{2\pi\sigma_1^2}}\exp\left(-\frac{x^2}{2\sigma_1^2}\right)+\frac{1-q}{\sqrt{2\pi\sigma_2^2}}\exp\left(-\frac{x^2}{2\sigma_2^2}\right)\right]x\,dx = 0 \tag{3.58}$$

This result is not surprising because the individual means of the two densities are zero. Next comes the variance,

$$E[x^2] = \int_{-\infty}^{\infty} x^2\,f(x) = \int_{-\infty}^{\infty}\left[\frac{q}{\sqrt{2\pi\sigma_1^2}}\exp\left(-\frac{x^2}{2\sigma_1^2}\right)+\frac{1-q}{\sqrt{2\pi\sigma_2^2}}\exp\left(-\frac{x^2}{2\sigma_2^2}\right)\right]x^2\,dx$$
$$= q\sigma_1^2 + (1-q)\sigma_2^2 = \sigma^2 \tag{3.59}$$

Like the mean, the skew is zero because the individual densities have zero skew. Finally, the kurtosis, using the above result is

$$\text{kurt} = \frac{E[x^4]}{\sigma^4} = \frac{\int_{-\infty}^{\infty} x^4 f(x)}{\sigma^4} = \frac{3(q\sigma_1^4 + (1-q)\sigma_2^4)}{[q\sigma_1^2 + (1-q)\sigma_2^2]^2}. \tag{3.60}$$

Therefore, the variance and kurtosis of the three-parameter mixed Gaussian distribution are, respectively,

$$\sigma^2 = q\sigma_1^2 + (1-q)\sigma_2^2 \tag{3.61}$$

and

$$\text{kurt} = \frac{3(q\sigma_1^4 + (1-q)\sigma_2^4)}{\sigma^4} \quad . \tag{3.62}$$

Figures 3-9 and 3-10 compare a mixed Gaussian density function with that of $N(0,1)$.

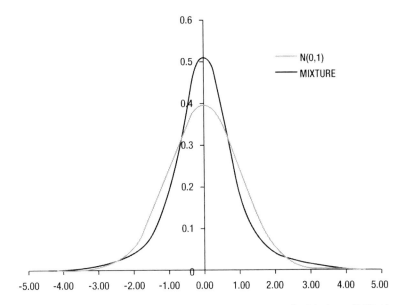

Figure 3-9. Mixed Gaussian density function compared with that of $N(0,1)$

CHAPTER 3 ■ STATISTICAL ANALYSIS OF FINANCIAL DATA

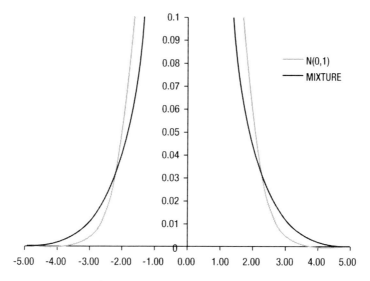

Figure 3-10. *Detail of mixed Gaussian density function compared with that of N(0,1)*

The next two sections describe two methods for creating a mixed Gaussian distribution function in Excel: a *random variable approach* using the inverse transform method and a *density approach* (see Problem 3-2).

Random Variable Approach

One can use the inverse transform method to create two series of normal variables with standard deviations of σ_1 and σ_2, each involving a series of calls to RAND(). Then one can use a third series of calls to RAND() to determine which of the two normal variables just created make up the mixture, such that

$$\text{if } (RAND() < q) \text{ choose } N(0, \sigma_1^2), \text{ else choose } N(0, \sigma_2^2) \quad . \tag{3.63}$$

Figure 3-11 shows a sample spreadsheet with this structure, in which the final column displays the outcome of the (3.63) relation. Here again, it is critical that you check the moments of the random variables produced versus the theoretical ones given by expressions (3.58), (3.59), and (3.60) based on the three inputs q, σ_1, and σ_2. Remember that the purpose here is to produce random numbers that have the characteristics of the mixed Gaussian distribution. The distribution is described by its moments (3.58), (3.59), and (3.60) (the mean and skew are zero), and the accuracy of this method is determined by the proximity of the moments resulting from the random numbers to the theoretical density function. The same strictures in respect of the inadequacy of RAND() and the deficiency in the number of random variables generated in Excel apply here as are noted in the section "The Inverse Transform Method."

87

CHAPTER 3 ■ STATISTICAL ANALYSIS OF FINANCIAL DATA

								q	30.0%
								sigma	16.4%
	sigma1	30.0%			sigma2	10.0%		EX KURT	3.488
	Mean	0.00			Mean	0.00		Mean	0.00
	Stdev	30.0%			Stdev	10.0%		Stdev	18.5%
	Ex Kurt	0.02			Ex Kurt	0.03		Ex Kurt	3.35
RAND()	0.763206	0.214996	NORMINV()	RAND()	0.438846	-0.01539	NORMINV()	RAND()	0.832596	-0.01539
RAND()	0.896701	0.378892	NORMINV()	RAND()	0.492447	-0.00198	NORMINV()	RAND()	0.231416	0.378892
RAND()	0.588111	0.065807	NORMINV()	RAND()	0.010766	-0.22985	NORMINV()	RAND()	0.464458	-0.22985
RAND()	0.872683	0.34175	NORMINV()	RAND()	0.661572	0.041676	NORMINV()	RAND()	0.07792	0.34175
RAND()	0.192086	-0.261071	NORMINV()	RAND()	0.202936	-0.08312	NORMINV()	RAND()	0.089089	-0.26107
RAND()	0.877642	0.348983	NORMINV()	RAND()	0.666807	0.043111	NORMINV()	RAND()	0.506796	0.043111
RAND()	0.581804	0.061953	NORMINV()	RAND()	0.856947	0.10667	NORMINV()	RAND()	0.741928	0.10667
RAND()	0.371439	-0.098413	NORMINV()	RAND()	0.962552	0.17811	NORMINV()	RAND()	0.478481	0.17811
RAND()	0.28791	-0.16785	NORMINV()	RAND()	0.470122	-0.0075	NORMINV()	RAND()	0.971649	-0.0075
RAND()	0.942911	0.473907	NORMINV()	RAND()	0.860661	0.108329	NORMINV()	RAND()	0.102874	0.473907
RAND()	0.667973	0.130296	NORMINV()	RAND()	0.644384	0.03702	NORMINV()	RAND()	0.453096	0.03702
RAND()	0.752297	0.20452	NORMINV()	RAND()	0.589336	0.022584	NORMINV()	RAND()	0.155939	0.20452
RAND()	0.155501	-0.303937	NORMINV()	RAND()	0.623826	0.031555	NORMINV()	RAND()	0.473341	0.031555

Figure 3-11. *Random variable approach in Excel to generate mixed normal variables*

Density Approach

The density approach directly models the density function rather than the random numbers themselves. For a density function $f(x)$, one begins with discretizing the x-space. This will depend on the level and range of the moments of the density function in question. For a Gaussian density function, the range of x is theoretically $-\infty$ to ∞. Yet for most empirical values of the first two moments μ and σ, the realistic range will be substantially smaller because the tails of the density function exponentially decay. For example, for a normal distribution with a $\mu=0$ and $\sigma=100\%$, the discretized x-space will be from about -4.0 to 4.0. Density values outside this range will be essentially zero. Therefore, one must be careful when discretizing the x-space. Once the x-values are known, it is a simple matter to calculate the density directly using the expression for $f(x)$. Afterwards, one should check that the theoretical moments have actually been produced by the discrete mixed density function using the formulas (3.64)–(3.66) (also in Figure 3-12), analogous to those adduced in the "Normalization of a Histogram" section.

CHAPTER 3 STATISTICAL ANALYSIS OF FINANCIAL DATA

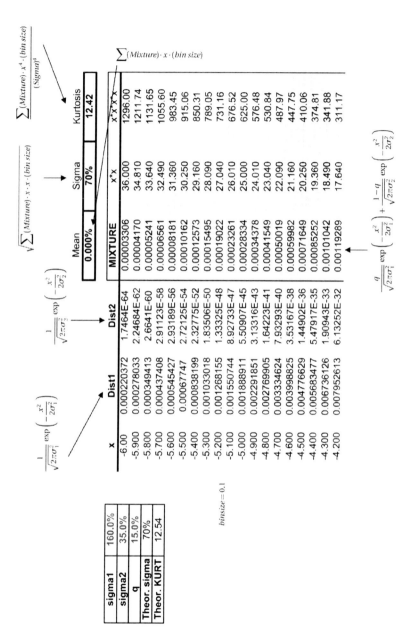

Figure 3-12. Mixed Gaussian density approach in Excel

89

$$\text{Mean} = E[x] = \int_{-\infty}^{\infty} x f_{mixture}(x)\, dx \to \sum x (Mixture)(Bin\ Size) \qquad (3.64)$$

$$\text{Var} = E[(x-\mu)^2] = E[x^2] = \int_{-\infty}^{\infty} x^2 f_{mixture}(x)\, dx \to \sum x^2 (Mixture)(Bin\ Size), \qquad (3.65)$$

$$\sigma = \sqrt{\text{Var}}$$

$$\text{Kurt} = \frac{E[x^4]}{\sigma^4} = \frac{\int_{-\infty}^{\infty} x^4 f_{mixture}(x)\, dx}{\sigma^4} \to \frac{\sum x^4 (Mixture)(Bin\ Size)}{\sigma^4} \qquad (3.66)$$

Skew Normal Distribution: Creating a Distribution with Skewness

Recall the definition of *skewness*,

$$\frac{E[(X-\mu)^3]}{\left(\sqrt{E[(X-\mu)^2]}\right)^3}. \qquad (3.67)$$

Skewness is another very important moment that is often ignored on Wall Street at great risk. Commonly used distributions and their third moments follow:

> *Gaussian distribution skew = 0*
>
> *Mixed Gaussian distribution skew = 0*
>
> *Student's-t distribution skew = 0*

Figure 3-13 shows several density functions with positive and negative skew. The centered symmetric one (dashed line) has no skew. The two distributions to the left of center have negative skew even though they are leaning to the right. The negative skew here is manifested by the longer tail to the left. The reverse is true for the density functions with positive skew.

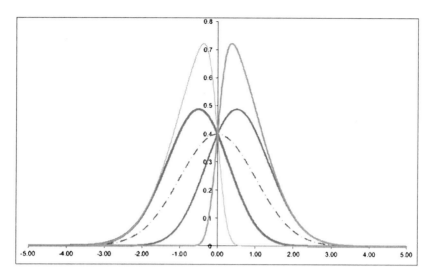

Figure 3-13. Density functions with skew

A skewed normal distribution is created by taking a $N(0,1)$ density function and changing the shape of it with a skewing function. A simple skewing function is given by

$$\Phi_{\text{skew}}(\alpha x) = \frac{1}{2}\left[1+\text{erf}\left(\frac{\alpha x}{\sqrt{2}}\right)\right] = \frac{1}{\sqrt{2\pi}} \int_{-\infty}^{\alpha x} \exp\left(-\frac{s^2}{2}\right) ds \quad . \tag{3.68}$$

where erf is the error function. This is easily recognizable as the distribution function of a Gaussian variable. Multiply this skewing function with that of a $N(0,1)$ density function

$$N(0,1) \rightarrow \phi(x) = \frac{1}{\sqrt{2\pi}} \exp\left(-\frac{x^2}{2}\right) \quad ,$$

$$f(x) = 2\phi(x)\Phi_{\text{skew}}(\alpha x) = \frac{1}{\pi} \exp\left(-\frac{x^2}{2}\right) \int_{-\infty}^{\alpha x} \exp\left(-\frac{s^2}{2}\right) ds \quad . \tag{3.69}$$

This is a one-parameter (α) skewed density function. It is illustrated in Figure 3-13 for several values of α. Positive values of α provide positive skew, and negative values of α provide negative skew. The moments of this distribution can be written in terms of its one parameter as follows:

$$\text{Define } \delta = \frac{\alpha}{\sqrt{1+\alpha^2}} \sqrt{\frac{2}{\pi}}$$

$$E[X] = \delta$$

$$Var[X] = \left(1 - \delta^2\right)$$

$$Skew[X] = \frac{4-\pi}{2} \frac{\delta^3}{\left(1-\delta^2\right)^{3/2}}$$

$$Kurt[X] = 2(\pi-3) \frac{\delta^4}{\left(1-\delta^2\right)^2} + 3$$

(3.70)

Calibrating Distributions through Moment Matching

Finding an appropriate probability distribution that can describe the future events of a certain type of financial instrument comes down to properly characterizing the statistical properties of some aspect of that financial instrument—for instance, the return characteristics of a stock. The historical financial time-series data of stock returns are best described by their empirical moments such as mean, variance, skew, kurtosis as well as empirical temporal moments such as the autocorrelation of returns, squared returns, and so forth (discussed in the "Autocorrelation" section). Any distribution that purports to describe data with a certain set of empirical moments must possess similar theoretical moments to characterize the data properly. If any key moments are missing from the distribution, any analysis based on the distribution must be faulty. The key objection of the black swan critique to the commonly used distributions is that their poor representation of the fat tails of financial data resulted in a colossal risk management failure at many Wall Street firms. To calibrate a distribution properly to represent empirical data, one must match the crucial empirical moments to the theoretical moments of the distribution. If the theoretical moments are lacking, the resulting statistical analysis of these data using the theoretical distribution may be faulty.

Calibrating a Mixed Gaussian Distribution to Equity Returns

A key aspect in analyzing financial data is to fit the distribution of returns for some asset to a known fat-tailed distribution such as the mixed Gaussian distribution. Here we use the density approach. The mixed Gaussian has three parameters, σ_1, σ_2, and q. One can use these to match the second and fourth moments of the empirical distribution (variance and

CHAPTER 3 ■ STATISTICAL ANALYSIS OF FINANCIAL DATA

kurtosis). The empirical distribution can be scaled to have zero mean as the moments are all mean adjusted.

Step 1: Create an Empirical Distribution

i. Obtain the financial time-series data of the stock in question. The amount of data will depend on the nature of the analysis. Generally, if you want to represent all historical features of the data, using as much data as possible is suggested.

ii. If P_t is the asset price at time t, create either a natural-log return time series $r_t = \ln\left(\dfrac{P_t}{P_{t-1}}\right)$ or simple return time series $r_t = \left(\dfrac{P_t}{P_{t-1}} - 1\right)$. For small stock moves, these returns will be almost similar.

iii. Estimate the mean of these returns $\bar{r} = E[r_t]$.

iv. Calculate mean adjusted returns $\tilde{r}_t = r_t - \bar{r}$. These zero-mean returns will be fit to a mixed normal distribution.

v. Estimate the empirical standard deviation $\sigma_{empirical}$ and $\text{kurt}_{empirical}$ of $\tilde{r}_t$. Note that other empirical moments (such as skew) exist but cannot be fit to the mixed Gaussian distribution.

vi. To get some "visuals" on the data, create an appropriately normalized density function of the mean adjusted returns (as described previously). Calculate the variance and kurtosis from the empirical density function to make sure that it matches the variance and kurtosis of the empirical data. The accuracy will depend on the number of data points, number of bins, and so on. (The purpose of this substep is really for visual inspection of the data versus the theoretical distribution. It is not a requirement for moment matching.)

$$\sigma^2_{emp\,den} = \sum x^2 (Empirical\ Density)(Bin\ Size)$$
$$\text{Kurt}_{emp\,den} = \dfrac{\sum x^4 (Empirical\ Density)(Bin\ Size)}{\sigma^4_{emp\,den}} \qquad (3.71)$$

Step 2: Match the Theoretical Moments to the Empirical Moments

Because there are two moments to match with three parameters for the Gaussian mixture, you must fix one of the parameters and solve for the other two. Solving for all three will give a family of solutions, some of which may not be the fit you are looking for (check

93

this by inspecting the graph of the fit, such as Figure 3-14). Assuming that σ_2 is fixed, one must solve for q and σ_1 such that

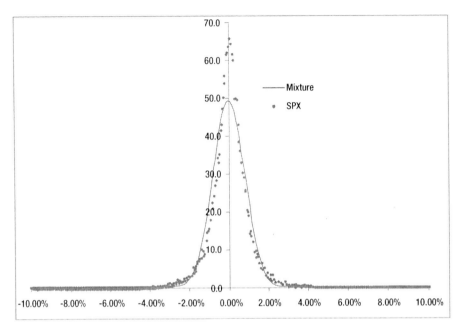

Figure 3-14. S&P 500 discrete empirical density function versus mixed Gaussian

$$\sigma_{theoretical}(q,\sigma_1) = \sqrt{q\sigma_1^2 + (1-q)\sigma_2^2} = \sigma_{empirical} \qquad (3.72)$$

$$\text{kurt}_{theoretical}(q,\sigma_1) = \frac{3(q\sigma_1^4 + (1-q)\sigma_2^4)}{[q\sigma_1^2 + (1-q)\sigma_2^2]^2} = \text{kurt}_{empirical} \qquad (3.73)$$

Unfortunately, these equations cannot be inverted explicitly to solve for q and σ_1 and must be solved by alternate means, such as those described in the next two sections.

Fitting by Hand

i. Create a graph of both the empirical density function and the theoretical mixed normal density function, as illustrated in Figure 3-14. (See Problem 3-3.)

ii. Adjust σ_1 and q to best-fit the standard deviation and kurtosis of the empirical data. Do this by adjusting (by hand) these parameters until the theoretical moments match the empirical ones. A visual inspection of the graph will help. This fit will not be perfect.

CHAPTER 3 ■ STATISTICAL ANALYSIS OF FINANCIAL DATA

Chi-Squared Fitting

Use the Solver function in Excel to calibrate σ_1, σ_2, and q to the moments. Create the following weighted *chi-squared* function

$$\chi^2(q,\sigma_1) = w_1 \cdot [\text{kurt}_{theoretical}(q,\sigma_1) - \text{kurt}_{empirical}]^2 + w_2 \cdot [\sigma_{theoretical}(q,\sigma_1) - \sigma_{empirical}]^2 \quad , \quad (3.74)$$

which needs to be made as small as possible to have a good match of moments. This method is called *chi-squared minimization*, (3.75). The weights w_i are chosen to scale the levels properly, such that each term in the chi-squared function is on equal footing (see Problem 3-3). Use the Solver function in Excel to solve for σ_1 and q, as shown in Figure 3-15.

$$\underset{\text{By changing } q \& \sigma_1}{\text{Minimize}} \chi^2(q,\sigma_1) \quad (3.75)$$

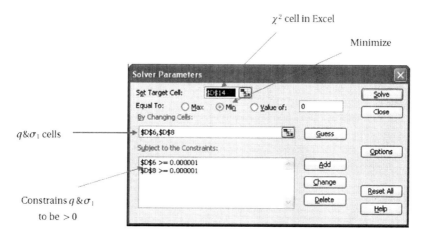

Figure 3-15. *The Solver function in Excel*

Calibrating a Generalized Student's-*t* Distribution to Equity Returns

The basic Student's-*t* density function is given by one parameter v,

$$f(t) = \frac{\Gamma\left(\frac{v+1}{2}\right)}{\sqrt{v\pi}\,\Gamma\left(\frac{v}{2}\right)} \left(1 + \frac{t^2}{v}\right)^{-\frac{v+1}{2}} \quad . \quad (3.76)$$

95

The generalized version is given by three parameters μ, ν, and λ. The mean is captured by μ, whereas λ provides a length scale,

$$f(t) = \frac{\Gamma\left(\frac{\nu+1}{2}\right)}{\Gamma\left(\frac{\nu}{2}\right)}\sqrt{\frac{\lambda}{\nu\pi}}\left(1 + \frac{\lambda(t-\mu)^2}{\nu}\right)^{-\frac{\nu+1}{2}} . \quad (3.77)[5]$$

Note that t is the random variable keeping with tradition and should not be confused with time. The mean, variance, and kurtosis of this distribution are given by

$$E[t] = \mu, \quad \text{Var}[t] = \frac{1}{\lambda}\frac{\nu}{\nu-2}, \quad \text{kurt}[t] = \frac{6}{\nu-4} + 3 . \quad (3.78)$$
$$\nu > 4$$

This distribution has no skew. Note that the variance only exists for $\nu > 2$, whereas the kurtosis exists for $\nu > 4$. Unlike the mixed Gaussian distribution, the moment-matching equations

$$\text{Var}[t] = \frac{1}{\lambda}\frac{\nu}{\nu-2} = \sigma^2_{empirical} \quad (3.79)$$

$$\text{kurt}[t] = \frac{6}{\nu-4} + 3 = \text{kurt}_{empirical} \quad (3.80)$$

can be inverted explicitly to give the following moment-matching formulas:

$$\nu = \frac{6}{\text{kurt}_{empirical} - 3} + 4$$
$$\lambda = \frac{1}{\sigma^2_{empirical}}\left[\frac{\nu}{\nu-2}\right] \quad (3.81)$$

Figures 3-16 and 3-17 illustrate a method of moments calibration of the Euro Stoxx 50 index known as SX5E (see Problem 3-4). Figure 3-17 is a log graph (base 10) of Figure 3-16 (y-axis) to visually bring out the fit of the tails of the distribution. The method to create a log scale in Excel is shown in Figure 3-18.

---

[5] Repeats (3.26).

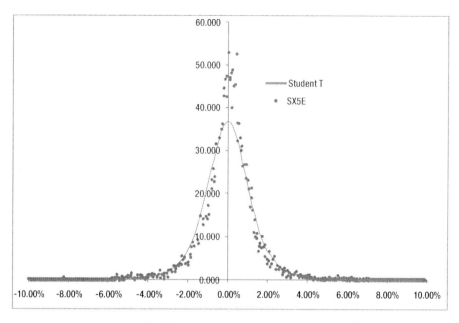

Figure 3-16. *Method of moments fit for the SX5E Index (Euro Stoxx 50) to a Student's-t distribution*

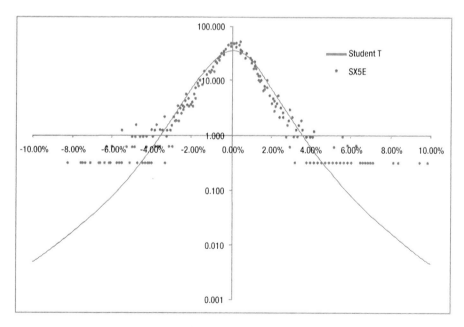

Figure 3-17. *Log graph of a method of moments fit for the SX5E Index to a Student's-t distribution*

CHAPTER 3 ■ STATISTICAL ANALYSIS OF FINANCIAL DATA

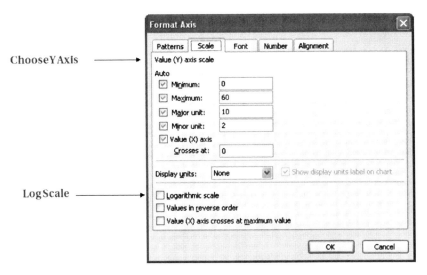

Figure 3-18. Creating a log scale in Excel

Calibrating a Beta Distribution to Recovery Rates of Defaulted Bonds

Probability distributions are used for all sorts of financial analysis, not just modeling financial returns. When corporate or government bonds default, they stop paying their coupon payments (see Chapter 6 for further discussion). The value of the defaulted bond does not necessarily become zero but has a value known as a *recovery rate*. This recovery rate is based on many factors, including the possibility of recovering some amount of cash from the issuer in bankruptcy court. These recovery rates range from 0% to 100% and are random variables because they are unknown until a default event happens. Therefore, modeling recovery rates is important when dealing with defaultable bonds, and one needs a distribution where the variables go from 0 to 1. An example of such a distribution is the two-parameter beta distribution introduced in (3.22),

$$f(x) = \frac{x^{p-1}(1-x)^{q-1}}{B(p,q)} \quad x \in [0,1]$$

$$\text{Beta Function} = B(p,q) = \int_0^1 t^{p-1}(1-t)^{q-1}\, dt = \frac{\Gamma(p)\Gamma(q)}{\Gamma(p+q)} \quad (3.82)$$

$$\Gamma(p) = \int_0^\infty t^{p-1} e^{-t}\, dt, \quad \Gamma(p+1) = p\Gamma(p), \quad \Gamma(p) = (p-1)\Gamma(p-1)$$

Its moments are given by

$$E[X^k] = \int_0^1 x^k f(x)dx = \int_0^1 \frac{x^{(p+k)-1}(1-x)^{q-1}}{B(p,q)} dx = \frac{B(p+k,q)}{B(p,q)}$$

$$E[X] = \frac{B(p+1,q)}{B(p,q)} = \frac{\frac{\Gamma(p+1)\Gamma(q)}{\Gamma(p+q+1)}}{\frac{\Gamma(p)\Gamma(q)}{\Gamma(p+q)}} = \frac{p\Gamma(p)\Gamma(p+q)}{(p+q)\Gamma(p+q)\Gamma(p)}$$

(3.83)

$$E[X] = \frac{p}{p+q}$$

$$Var(X) = \frac{pq}{(p+q+1)(p+q)^2}$$

$$Skew(X) = \frac{2(q-p)\sqrt{p+q+1}}{(p+q+2)\sqrt{pq}}$$

$$Kurt(X) = \frac{6[(p-q)^2(p+q+1) - pq(p+q+2)]}{pq(p+q+2)(p+q+3)} + 3$$

(3.84)

Assuming one has an historical recovery rate data R_i per bond type (see Table 3-1), one can calculate the empirical moments,

$$\bar{R} = \frac{1}{N}\sum_{i=1}^{N} R_i, \quad \sigma^2 = \frac{1}{N}\sum_{i=1}^{N}(R_i - \bar{R})^2 \quad . \quad (3.85)$$

Using the moment-matching method to calibrate the beta distribution,

$$\frac{p}{p+q} = \bar{R}, \quad \frac{pq}{(p+q+1)(p+q)^2} = \sigma^2 \quad . \quad (3.86)$$

one can solve for the parameters p and q explicitly,

$$p = \bar{R}\left(\frac{\bar{R}(1-\bar{R})}{\sigma^2} - 1\right) \quad (3.87)$$

$$q = (1-\bar{R})\left(\frac{\bar{R}(1-\bar{R})}{\sigma^2} - 1\right) \quad . \quad (3.88)$$

Table 3-1 presents the results of this calibration.

CHAPTER 3 ■ STATISTICAL ANALYSIS OF FINANCIAL DATA

Table 3-1. *Statistics for Recovery Rates (%) Upon Default (1970-2000)*

	Mean	SD	p	q
Bank Loans				
Senior Secured	64.0	24.4	1.84	1.03
Senior Unsecured	49.0	28.4	1.03	1.07
Bonds				
Senior Secured	52.6	24.6	1.64	1.48
Senior Unsecured	46.9	28.0	1.02	1.16
Senior Subordinate	34.7	24.6	0.95	1.79
Subordinate	31.6	21.2	1.20	2.61
Junior Subordinate	22.5	18.7	0.90	3.09
Preferred Stock	18.1	17.2	0.73	3.28

Source: A. M. Berd and V. Kapoor, "Digital Premium," *Journal of Derivatives*, 10 (2003), 66-76.

Figures 3-19 and 3-20 illustrate two calibrated density functions of recovery rates.

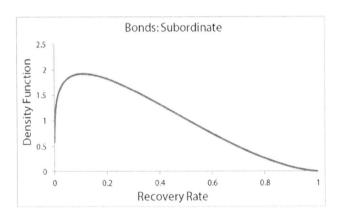

Figure 3-19. *Beta distribution for recovery rates from defaulted subordinate bonds*

CHAPTER 3 ■ STATISTICAL ANALYSIS OF FINANCIAL DATA

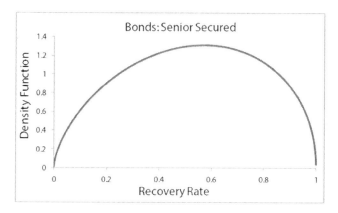

Figure 3-20. *Beta distribution for recovery rates from defaulted senior secured bonds*

Basic Risk Measures

Measuring and controlling risk is a major concern for all financial institutions. With better measurement, an institution can chart and take a more prudent path to risk management. Financial risk is typically associated with the statistical uncertainty of the final outcome of the valuation of financial positions. An objective measure of this risk is needed to handle the "rare events" in which the true financial risk resides. No single risk measurement can give the complete picture of potential losses in the future. There are generically three large types of financial risk: *market risk*, *credit risk*, and *operational risk*. Furthermore, many subdivisions of these risk types exist. Market risk encompasses all the well-known risks that attend the trading of financial securities, such as the price risk of stocks, the volatility risk of options (Chapter 5), the interest risk of fixed income instruments, the foreign exchange risk of currency transactions, and the prepayment risk of mortgages. Credit risk deals with losses arising from defaults and bankruptcy. Operational risk deals with losses arising from business operations failures such as in the informational technology (IT) area or the legal department. Credit and operational risk will be further explored in Chapters 6 and 7.

The *probability of extreme losses* is of great concern. A typically used but poor risk measurement of extreme losses used on Wall Street and prescribed by many regulators around the globe is the *value at risk* (VaR). Suppose one has a distribution of daily returns of some asset (say the S&P 500). One can ask, "What is the probability of a daily return being less than 7%?" Statistically, this means

$$F(-0.07) = P(r \leq -0.07) = \int_{-\infty}^{-0.07} f(r)dr \quad . \tag{3.89}$$

■ **Caution** This value is highly dependent on the tail of the distribution $F(x) = P(X \leq x)$ that is being used to model the returns (such as Gaussian, mixed Gaussian, or Student's-t).

CHAPTER 3 ▪ STATISTICAL ANALYSIS OF FINANCIAL DATA

The more typical question is, "What is the loss amount (negative return) at the 95% confidence interval?" This is referred to as a *95% VaR number*. It means "What is the return level r_{95} where 95% of the returns are greater than this level?" Mathematically, this is

$$1 - 0.95 = 0.05 = P(r \leq r_{95}) = \int_{-\infty}^{r_{95}} f(r)\,dr \quad . \tag{3.90}$$

or equivalently

$$0.95 = P(r > r_{95}) = \int_{-r_{95}}^{\infty} f(r)\,dr \quad . \tag{3.91}$$

VaR is the level of loss (e.g., r_{95}) corresponding to a certain probability of loss (e.g., 5%). VaR is usually calculated at the 95%, 99%, and 99.9% levels. These levels are highly dependent on the tail of the distribution. Figure 3-21 shows a distribution function of returns with the VaR(95) point indicated.

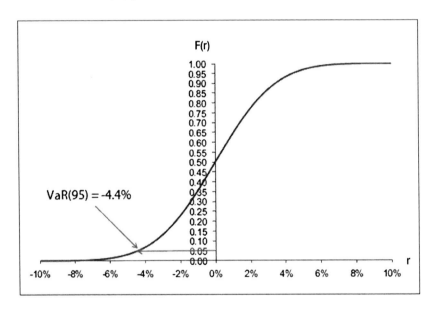

Figure 3-21. *A cumulative distribution function of returns with VaR(95) indicated*

Generally speaking, given a distribution of returns $F(r)$ and a confidence level (percentile) α, VaR (α) is the smallest number r_α such that the probability of the return r is less than r_α is at most $1-\alpha$,

$$\text{VaR}_\alpha = \sup\{r_\alpha \in \Re : P(r \leq r_\alpha) \leq 1-\alpha\} = \sup\{r_\alpha \in \Re : F(r_\alpha) \leq 1-\alpha\} \quad . \tag{3.92}$$

■ **Caution** Much of the literature and nomenclature on Wall Street deals with "loss" distributions in which the loss is mathematically a positive number, such as "a loss of 100K." The foregoing definition for VaR must be changed appropriately.[6]

One of the main problems with VaR is that it cannot answer the following question: "If the VaR(80) return is (negatively) exceeded (a 20% chance), what is the realized loss?" This VaR tells one the cut-off at which 80% of the returns are higher than the cut-off. The real question is, what are the negative returns in the remaining 20% of the distribution? This number will depend on the thickness of that tail of the distribution. Figure 3-22 shows two distributions having the same VaR(80) point but clearly different loss levels once this common point is reached. The fat-tailed distribution has a thicker tail and is more risky than the normal distribution even though they both have the same VaR(80).

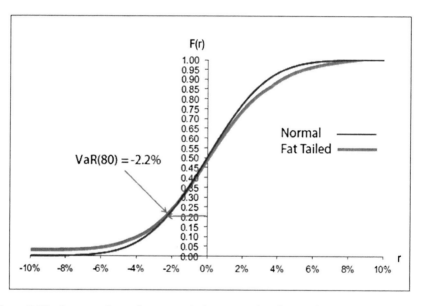

Figure 3-22. A comparison of two cumulative return distribution functions with identical VaR(80) points indicated

---

[6]See A. J. McNeil, R. Frey, and P. Embrechts, *Quantitative Risk Management.* Princeton University Press, 2005.

103

CHAPTER 3 ■ STATISTICAL ANALYSIS OF FINANCIAL DATA

The most straightforward way to get a better risk measure is to calculate the area under the tail to the left of the VaR$_a$ point. That is, "What is the average of the losses *if* the VaR$_a$ point is exceeded?" This is called *conditional VaR* (CVaR) *or expected shortfall*,

$$\text{CVaR}(\alpha) = \frac{\int_{-\infty}^{r_a} r \cdot f(r)\,dr}{\int_{-\infty}^{r_a} f(r)\,dr} \quad . \tag{3.93}$$

Note that this formula is similar to taking the expectation value of r in the region $-\infty$ to r_a except the density function is *not* normalized in this region. Therefore, one must divide by the area of this region, which is the denominator in (3.93). For instance, CVaR(95) equals

$$\text{CVaR}(95) = \frac{\int_{-\infty}^{r_{95}} r \cdot f(r)\,dr}{\int_{-\infty}^{r_{95}} f(r)\,dr} = \frac{\int_{-\infty}^{r_{95}} r \cdot f(r)\,dr}{0.05} \quad . \tag{3.94}$$

Calculating VaR and CVaR from Financial Return Data

Estimating VaR and CVaR from return data, whether historic or simulated, is a straightforward process. This section describes how to calculate VaR and CVaR from historical data as an educational exercise. In reality, all risk is in the future and therefore VaR and CVaR are calculated using simulations of events in the future, which are described in Chapter 4.

Note that the time scale of the returns dictates the time scale of the risk measure. Daily returns provide daily VaR and CVaR numbers. Weekly returns provide weekly VaR and CVaR numbers. Here are the following steps for historical VaR and CVaR:

1. Get the set of return data (historic or simulated).

2. Sort the returns from lowest to highest and number them as in Figure 3-23. The sorted data are called the "order statistics" of the set of return data, where 1 = L(1) = the smallest value among the returns, 2 = L(2) = the next larger value, ...

1	-22.928%
2	-9.498%
3	-9.382%
4	-9.229%
5	-8.670%
6	-7.951%
7	-7.141%
8	-7.072%
9	-7.037%
10	-6.977%

Figure 3-23. Sorted and numbered returns (a count of 15,432)

3. Get the total number of returns (15,432 in the example in Figures 3-23 to 3-25).

CHAPTER 3 ■ STATISTICAL ANALYSIS OF FINANCIAL DATA

4a. Approximate the VaR(99) as → $L(\lfloor (1-99\%)*(Total\ Count) \rfloor) = L(\lfloor .01*15432 \rfloor) = L(154) = 2.638\%$. It is an approximation because the data are discrete and finite.

4b. Approximate the VaR(99.9) as → $L(\lfloor (1-0.999)*Total\ Count \rfloor) = L(\lfloor .001*15432 \rfloor) = L(15) = -6.324\%$

151	-2.647%	12	-6.876%
152	-2.645%	13	-6.341%
153	-2.643%	14	-6.339%
154	-2.638%	15	-6.324%
155	-2.634%	16	-6.033%
156	-2.633%	17	-5.939%
157	-2.625%	18	-5.560%

Figure 3-24. *VaR(99) and VaR(99.9) sorted returns*

5a. CVaR(99)

$$CVaR(99) = \frac{\int_{-\infty}^{r_{99}} r \cdot f(r)\,dr}{0.01} \approx \left(\frac{1}{154}\right) \sum_{i=1}^{154} return \quad . \quad (3.95)$$

5b. CVaR(99.9)

$$CVaR(99.9) = \frac{\int_{-\infty}^{r_{99.9}} r \cdot f(r)\,dr}{0.001} \approx \left(\frac{1}{15}\right) \sum_{i=1}^{15} return \quad (3.96)$$

$$Sum = -128.70\%$$

$$CVaR(99.9) \approx \left(\frac{1}{15}\right) Sum = -8.580\% \quad (3.97)$$

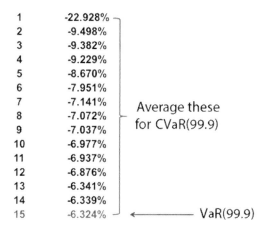

Figure 3-25. *Calculating VaR(99.9) and CVaR(99.9) from sorted returns*

The purpose of this section has been to give you a sense of the basic risk measures used on Wall Street. VaR is a large subject, and many complications arise for calculating such numbers for portfolios of correlated assets.[7]

The Term Structure of Statistics

The moment calculations described so far have not made any mention of the type of financial return one was analyzing other than assuming equity-style daily returns. The question of the temporal aspect of the returns is important. The standard deviation of daily S&P 500 returns is very different from that of weekly or monthly returns. Hedge funds, for example, do not generally have daily returns, as they only report the *net asset value* (NAV) of their funds on a monthly basis. Whatever happened in the fund during the month is unknown, and calculating moments using monthly returns will provide monthly statistics that do not capture the intra-month activity. On the other hand, an investor who wishes to hold a hedge fund for several years may not care about intra-month statistics. The temporal nature of the return must fit the temporal nature of the investors' *holding horizon*. High-frequency traders who use automated platforms to trade many times a day do not care for daily returns and daily statistics. The statistical nature of intra-day returns, daily returns, monthly returns, and so on are all very different.

A term structure of log returns is given by the following expression with two time components, t and T,

$$r_T(t) = \ln\left(\frac{P(t+T)}{P(t)}\right), \quad T = 1, 2, 3, \ldots \quad (3.98)$$

The small t labels the return within the time series as before. The larger T indicates the term structure and stays constant for a specific calculation. For example, if you had a time series of daily prices $P(t)$, you could create a time series of three-day returns $r_3(t)$ by setting $T = 3$ in (3.98). $r_3(0)$ would be the first return in the three-day time series being the return from time $t = 0$ to time $t = 3$. The next element in the time series would be $r_3(1)$, which is the three-day return between time $t = 1$ and time $t = 4$.

The Term Structure of the Mean

Each return series $\{r_1(t)\}$, $\{r_2(t)\}$, $\{r_3(t)\}$, ... has its own set of moments. The term structure of the first moment is given by

$$\mu(T) = E[r_T(t)] \quad . \quad (3.99)$$

Therefore, each return series $\{r_1(t)\}$, $\{r_2(t)\}$, $\{r_3(t)\}$, ... has means given by $\mu(1)$, $\mu(2)$, $\mu(3)$, and so on.

---

[7] See A. J. McNeil, R. Frey, and P. Embrechts, *Quantitative Risk Management*. Princeton University Press, 2005.

The Term Structure of Skew

The *term structure of skew* is an important temporal moment to calculate for many types of investments. It is given by

$$skew(T) = E\left[\left\{\frac{r_T(t) - \mu(T)}{\sigma(T)}\right\}^3\right] \quad . \tag{3.100}$$

Note that this involves calculating the term structure of means and volatility (see (3.102) below). Figure 3-26 shows the term structure of skew for the S&P 500 starting from daily returns ($T = 1$) all the way to yearly returns ($T = 252$).

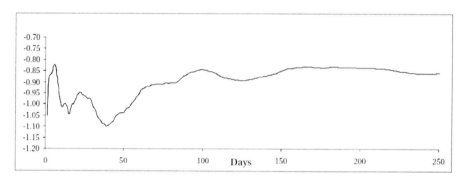

Figure 3-26. *Term structure of skew for the S&P 500 Index, 1961–2011*

Figure 3-26 indicates that one is more susceptible to greater negative skew, on average, when holding the S&P 500 for fewer than 100 days. Now consider Figure 3-27a. This is the NAV graph of a *multi-asset proprietary* ("prop") *index* based upon the *dynamic portfolio allocation* (DPA) method described in the next section. Figure 3-27b illustrates the term structure of skew of returns for the multi-asset DPA prop index. Note that, compared to the S&P 500, the skew is not as negative but, more importantly, the skew becomes positive after around 175 days. This change is clearly due to the nature of the trading strategy used by this prop index. For an investor, therefore, a longer holding horizon is advisable to get the full benefit of this prop index.

CHAPTER 3 ■ STATISTICAL ANALYSIS OF FINANCIAL DATA

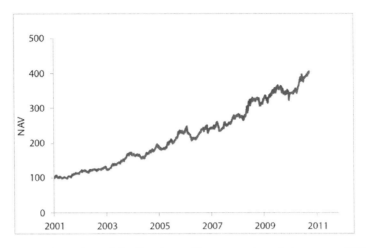

Figure 3-27a. *Dynamic portfolio allocation multi-asset proprietary index strategy, 2001–2011*

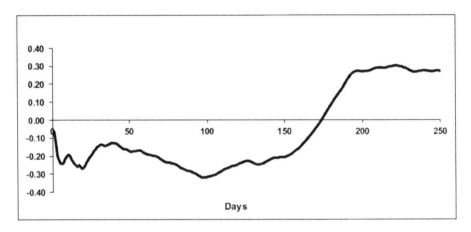

Figure 3-27b. *Term structure of skew of returns for the dynamic portfolio allocation multi-asset proprietary index strategy, 2001–2011*

The Term Structure of Kurtosis

The *term structure of kurtosis* is an important temporal moment to calculate for many types of investment. It is given by the natural generalization of the skew expression,

$$kurt(T) = E\left[\left\{\frac{r_T(t) - \mu(T)}{\sigma(T)}\right\}^4\right] \quad . \tag{3.101}$$

The term structure of kurtosis for the S&P 500 index is depicted in Figure 3-28.

CHAPTER 3 ▪ STATISTICAL ANALYSIS OF FINANCIAL DATA

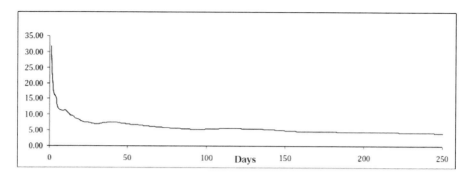

Figure 3-28. Term structure of kurtosis for the S&P 500 index, 1961–2011

Note that the kurtosis of the S&P 500 starts at a number very close to 30 but decays to about 6 for longer holding periods. For short-dated trading, one is clearly exposed to large moves. This graph indicates that daily hedging of S&P 500 option positions would require a model that captured the fat-tailed risk illustrated here. Even holding the index for longer periods of time does not bring the kurtosis down to the ubiquitous 3 of a normal distribution. On the other hand, the term structure of kurtosis for the DPA prop strategy *starts* at 6 and disappears to 3 quickly as shown in Figure 3-29.

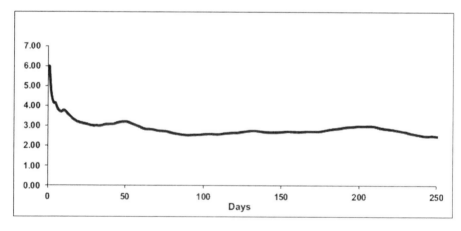

Figure 3-29. Term structure of kurtosis for the dynamic portfolio allocation multi-asset proprietary index strategy, 2001–2011

The prop index has a trading strategy that drastically reduces the kurtosis of asset returns while providing a positive skew for longer holding periods.

The Term Structure of Volatility

The term structure of volatility also has a natural expression given by,

$$\sigma_r^2(T) = E\left[\left\{r_T(t) - \mu(T)\right\}^2\right] \quad . \tag{3.102}$$

The difference with volatility is that it tends to scale with time T. Therefore, a comparison of the value of $\sigma_r^2(T)$ for several values of T is not entirely appropriate. One can multiply this expression by $\sqrt{(T)}$ or find a suitable method to make the expression scaleless. Volatility by itself is symmetric to positive and negative changes. In reality, an investor is interested in the volatility of positive moves versus the volatility of negative moves. Positive and negative changes are seen with respect to the expected change $\mu(T)$ and not with respect to zero. Therefore, one may define something called an "up" volatility as the square root of the variance of those changes greater than $\mu(T)$,

The Term Structure of "Up" Volatility

$$\sigma_r^{2+}(T) = E\left[\left\{r_T(t) - \mu(T)\right\}^2 | r_T(t) > \mu(T)\right] \tag{3.103}$$

"Down" volatility has a similar expression.

The Term Structure of "Down" Volatility

$$\sigma_r^{2-}(T) = E\left[\left\{r_T(t) - \mu(T)\right\}^2 | r_T(t) < \mu(T)\right] \tag{3.104}$$

The purpose now is to see the term structure of "up" and "down" volatility *scaled* by the regular symmetric volatility,

$$\frac{\sigma_r^+(T)}{\sigma_r(T)} \tag{3.105}$$

and

$$\frac{\sigma_r^-(T)}{\sigma_r(T)} \quad . \tag{3.106}$$

Figure 3-30 illustrates these two Risk measures for the S&P 500 Index. The scaled down volatility does not improve with the holding horizon. In fact, it becomes a larger fraction of the regular volatility as time goes by.

CHAPTER 3 ■ STATISTICAL ANALYSIS OF FINANCIAL DATA

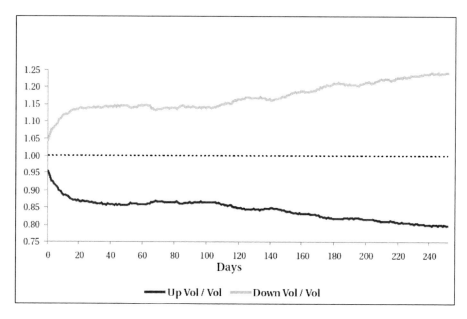

Figure 3-30. *Term structure of "up" and "down" volatility for the S&P 500 index, 1961–2011*

A more desirable effect happens for the DPA prop strategy, as shown in Figure 3-31, where the "down" and "up" volatilities cross after a certain point, where the up volatility makes up a bigger fraction than the down volatility. This indicates that, on average, moves that are bigger than the mean change are biased upward rather than downward.

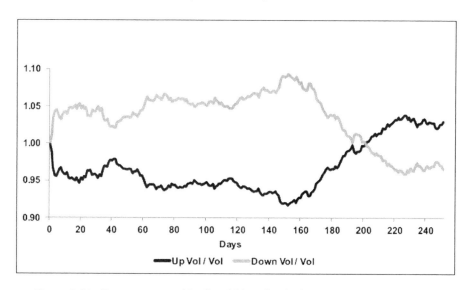

Figure 3-31. *Term structure of "up" and "down" volatility for the dynamic portfolio allocation multi-asset proprietary index strategy, 2001–2011*

111

CHAPTER 3 ▪ STATISTICAL ANALYSIS OF FINANCIAL DATA

The term structure of statistics are very important to calculate when analyzing a cash-like investment. Even the P&L (profit and loss) of a trading book or trading strategy based on derivatives can be effectively analyzed by calculating the term structure of statistics. Such moments are also used for investments such as hedge funds and fund-of-funds, where only monthly NAVs are given.

Autocorrelation

Autocorrelation is the correlation of a signal with itself as a function of the time separation between observations. In finance, autocorrelations are used to analyze memory in the return time series of an asset. For many assets classes, pure returns have little autocorrelation, but squared returns show distinct properties that come from *volatility clustering*. This refers to the phenomenon of certain financial assets having periods of high volatility, medium volatility, and low volatility while mean-reverting to some long-term mean. For these assets, large price changes tend to be followed by further large price changes, whereas periods of calm have some temporal stability.

Autocorrelations are very similar to the concept of a *covariance* (cov) and *correlation* (ρ) between two random variables X and Y and are given by the following expressions:

$$\text{cov}(X,Y) = E[(X - E(X))(Y - E(Y))] = E[XY] - E[X]E[Y]$$

$$\rho(X,Y) = \frac{\text{cov}(X,Y)}{\sigma(X)\sigma(Y)} \qquad (3.107)$$

Both these concepts require the *theory of joint distributions*, which is outlined in this chapter's appendix. For the purposes here, a definition of autocorrelation and its empirical estimation will suffice. For serious readers, an understanding of the material in the appendix is very important for financial engineering applications. The correlation between a return time series and the returns time series itself lagged by a pre-specified time lag τ is given by

$$\rho(r(t), r(t+\tau)) = \frac{E[\{r(t) - \mu(r(t))\}\{r(t+\tau) - \mu(r(t+\tau))\}]}{\sigma[r(t)]\sigma[r(t+\tau)]} \qquad (3.108)$$

$$\tau = time\ lag$$

For a discrete set of data $r(1), r(2),..., r(n)$, an estimate of the autocorrelation of lagged returns may be obtained as follows:

$$\rho(r(t), r(t+\tau)) = \frac{1}{(n-\tau)} \frac{\sum_{t=1}^{n-\tau} [r(t) - \mu(r(t))][r(t+\tau) - \mu(r(t+\tau))]}{\sigma[r(t)]\sigma[r(t+\tau)]} \qquad (3.109)$$

CHAPTER 3 ▪ STATISTICAL ANALYSIS OF FINANCIAL DATA

The autocorrelation of financial returns often does not reveal much structure. The autocorrelation of squared returns may however provide evidence of memory in the squared return time series,

$$\rho(r^2(t), r^2(t+\tau)) = \frac{E[\{r^2(t) - \mu(r^2(t))\}\{r^2(t+\tau) - \mu(r^2(t+\tau))\}]}{\sigma[r^2(t)]\sigma[r^2(t+\tau)]} \quad . \quad (3.110)$$

The empirical estimation is similar to the previous expression,

$$\rho(r^2(t), r^2(t+\tau)) = \frac{1}{(n-\tau)} \frac{\sum_{t=1}^{n-\tau}[r^2(t) - \mu(r^2(t))][r^2(t+\tau) - \mu(r^2(t+\tau))]}{\sigma[r^2(t)]\sigma[r^2(t+\tau)]} \quad . \quad (3.111)$$

Figure 3-32 illustrates how one would calculate autocorrelations in Excel using the function Correl().

Date	SX5E	Daily Return r	Daily Return Squared r*r
10/21/2011	2337.51	2.8938%	0.0837%
10/20/2011	2271.77	-2.5025%	0.0626%
10/19/2011	2330.08	1.0088%	0.0102%
10/18/2011	2306.81	-0.3921%	0.0015%
10/17/2011	2315.89	-1.6808%	0.0282%
10/14/2011	2355.48	0.9843%	0.0097%
10/13/2011	2332.52	-1.6706%	0.0279%
10/12/2011	2372.15	2.4258%	0.0588%
10/11/2011	2315.97	-0.2081%	0.0004%
10/10/2011	2320.8	2.2744%	0.0517%
10/7/2011	2269.19	0.9076%	0.0082%
10/6/2011	2248.78	3.1825%	0.1013%
10/5/2011	2179.42	4.2241%	0.1784%
10/4/2011	2091.09	-2.2051%	0.0486%
10/3/2011	2138.24	-1.9003%	0.0361%
9/30/2011	2179.66	-1.4816%	0.0220%
9/29/2011	2212.44	1.6447%	0.0271%
9/28/2011	2176.64	-0.7926%	0.0063%
9/27/2011	2194.03	5.3126%	0.2822%
9/26/2011	2083.35	2.8292%	0.0800%
9/23/2011	2026.03	1.5172%	0.0230%
9/22/2011	1995.75	-4.8959%	0.2397%
9/21/2011	2098.49	-1.9585%	0.0384%
9/20/2011	2140.41	2.1139%	0.0447%
9/19/2011	2096.1	-2.9260%	0.0856%
9/16/2011	2159.28	0.1698%	0.0003%
9/15/2011	2155.62	3.4674%	0.1202%
9/14/2011	2083.38	2.2950%	0.0527%
9/13/2011	2036.64	2.0867%	0.0435%
9/12/2011	1995.01	-3.7933%	0.1439%
9/9/2011	2073.67	-4.1476%	0.1720%

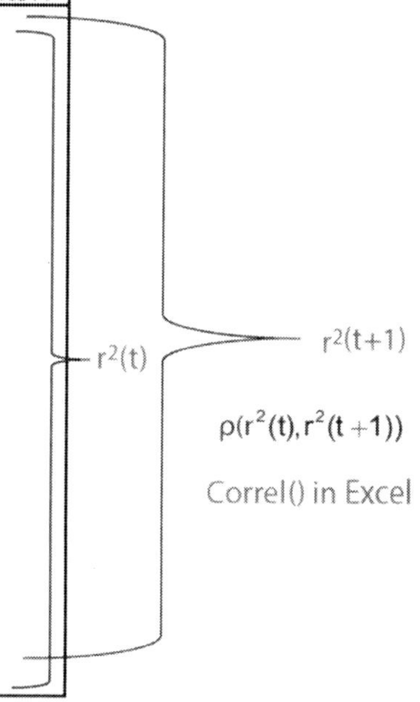

$r^2(t)$ $r^2(t+1)$

$\rho(r^2(t), r^2(t+1))$

Correl() in Excel

Figure 3-32. *How to calculate autocorrelation in Excel*

Figure 3-33 illustrates the autocorrelation of returns and squared returns of the S&P 500 index (SPX). Note the pronounced structure and slow decay of the autocorrelation of squared returns. Because squared returns are used in the calculation volatility, this empirical feature is directly related the phenomenon of *volatility clustering*, a required feature for successful volatility traders. Stochastic processes that capture this feature are presented in Chapter 4.

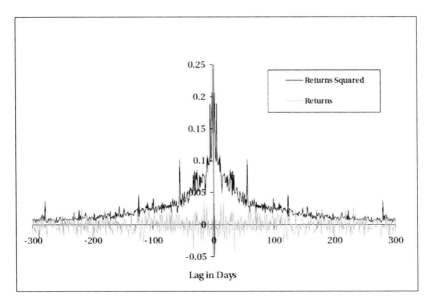

Figure 3-33. The autocorrelation of returns and squared returns of the S&P 500 index, 1/1950–4/2011

Dynamic Portfolio Allocation

The preceding section introduced many temporal statistics that could be used to analyze index returns such as those from the S&P 500 and a DPA proprietary index. In general, the statistical properties of the DPA prop index were far more favorable for an investor than those of the S&P 500. The question now is how does one incorporate these statistics effectively into creating a trading strategy index such as the DPA prop index? This section outlines in broad strokes how this should be done. As with most investment advice, there are no guarantees. Rather, the term structure of statistics can be used as a relative value risk measure to compare strategies against each other and incorporate them into already existing strategies to greatly improve their performance. This section briefly describes the well-known but relatively poorly performing *modern portfolio theory* of Markowitz and how the term structure of statistics can be used to improve its performance.

Modern Portfolio Theory

There is nothing "modern" about modern portfolio theory. In its original form, it is an outdated and poorly performing static method for portfolio allocation.[8] This theory of portfolio selection attempts to maximize portfolio expected returns for a given amount of portfolio risk, or minimize risk for a predetermined level of expected return, by prescribing a methodology for allocating various assets to a portfolio. If one treats single-period returns for various securities

---

[8]H. Markowitz, *Portfolio Selection: Efficient Diversification of Investments* (Cowles Foundation Monograph No. 16), Yale University Press, 1968.

as random variables (usually Gaussian in this methodology), one can assign them expected returns, standard deviations (volatilities), and correlations. Based on these, one can calculate the expected return and volatility of any portfolio constructed from these securities. This method treats expected return and volatility as the basic building blocks for risk and reward. Out of the universe of possible portfolios, certain ones will optimally balance risk and reward (the Markowitz "efficient frontier"). An investor should select a portfolio that lies on this efficient frontier. This efficient frontier is the "border" of highest expected returns for a given level of volatility (see Figure 3-34). There exist many portfolios on the inside of this frontier line that produce the same volatility with a lower expected return.

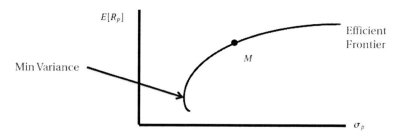

Figure 3-34. *Markowitz efficient frontier of portfolio volatility σ_p versus portfolio expected return, $E[R_p]$*

Consider a portfolio P of n assets with relative weights w_i and stochastic returns R_i. Its mean return is given by

$$\mu_P = E[R_P] = \sum_{i=1}^{n} w_i E[R_i] = \sum_{i=1}^{n} w_i \mu_i \quad . \qquad (3.112)$$

The portfolio variance is given by (using the definition of covariance (3.141))

$$\begin{aligned}
\sigma_p^2 &= E[(R_P - \mu_P)^2] = E\left[\left\{\sum_{i=1}^{n} w_i (R_i - \mu_i)\right\}^2\right] \\
&= E\left[\sum_{i=1}^{n} w_i (R_i - \mu_i) \sum_{j=1}^{n} w_j (R_j - \mu_j)\right] \\
&= E\left[\sum_{i=1}^{n}\sum_{j=1}^{n} w_i w_j (R_i - \mu_i)(R_j - \mu_j)\right] \qquad (3.113) \\
&= \sum_{i=1}^{n}\sum_{j=1}^{n} w_i w_j E\left[(R_i - \mu_i)(R_j - \mu_j)\right] \\
&= \sum_{i=1}^{n}\sum_{j=1}^{n} w_i w_j \operatorname{cov}(R_i, R_j) \\
&= \sum_{i=1}^{n}\sum_{j=1}^{n} w_i w_j \rho_{ij} \sigma_i \sigma_j
\end{aligned}$$

For two assets, this reduces to

$$\sigma_p^2 = E[(R_p - \mu_p)^2] = E\left[\left\{\sum_{i=1}^{2} w_i(R_i - \mu_i)\right\}^2\right] \qquad (3.114)$$
$$= w_1^2 \operatorname{var}(R_1^2) + w_2^2 \operatorname{var}(R_2^2) + 2w_1 w_2 \operatorname{cov}(R_i, R_j)$$
$$= w_1^2 \sigma_1^2 + w_2^2 \sigma_2^2 + 2w_1 w_2 \sigma_1 \sigma_2 \rho$$

The two-asset portfolio variance, with the constraint that $w_1 + w_2 = 1$ (no leverage, but short selling allowed), can be used to solve for the minimum variance weight as indicated by the arrow in Figure 3-34:

$$\sigma_p^2 = w_1^2 \sigma_1^2 + w_2^2 \sigma_2^2 + 2w_1 w_2 \sigma_1 \sigma_2 \rho$$
$$w_2 = 1 - w_1 \qquad (3.115)$$

The minimum portfolio variance weights are found by taking a derivative of the above function with respect to the unknown weight w_1 and finding the solution to the minimization equation,

$$\frac{d}{dw_1}[\sigma_p^2] = \frac{d}{dw_1}\left[w_1^2 \sigma_1^2 + (1-w_1)^2 \sigma_2^2 + 2w_1(1-w_1)\sigma_1 \sigma_2 \rho\right] = 0 \qquad (3.116)$$

$$\frac{d}{dw_1}[\sigma_p^2] = \left[2w_1 \sigma_1^2 - 2(1-w_1)\sigma_2^2 + 2(1-w_1)\sigma_1 \sigma_2 \rho - 2w_1 \sigma_1 \sigma_2 \rho\right] = 0$$

$$w_1\left[2\sigma_1^2 + 2\sigma_2^2 - 2\sigma_1 \sigma_2 \rho - 2\sigma_1 \sigma_2 \rho\right] - 2\sigma_2^2 + 2\sigma_1 \sigma_2 \rho = 0$$

$$w_1^{\text{Minimum}} = \frac{\sigma_2^2 - \sigma_1 \sigma_2 \rho}{\left[\sigma_1^2 + \sigma_2^2 - 2\sigma_1 \sigma_2 \rho\right]} \qquad (3.117)$$

$$w_2^{\text{Minimum}} = 1 - w_1^{\text{Minimum}} = \frac{\sigma_1^2 - \sigma_1 \sigma_2 \rho}{\left[\sigma_1^2 + \sigma_2^2 - 2\sigma_1 \sigma_2 \rho\right]}$$

The weights w_1^{Minimum} and w_2^{Minimum} are the solutions to the minimum variance point indicated in Figure 3-34.

Modern portfolio theory has also been used to argue for the benefits of diversification. The basic (traditional) diversification argument comes in two standard cases:

1. Assume zero correlation between assets and an equally weighted portfolio,

$$w_i = \frac{1}{n}, \ \operatorname{cov}(R_i, R_j) = 0 \qquad . \qquad (3.118)$$

CHAPTER 3 ■ STATISTICAL ANALYSIS OF FINANCIAL DATA

Substituting these simplifications into (3.113) gives

$$\sigma_p^2 = \sum_{i=1}^{n} \frac{1}{n^2} \sigma_i^2 = \frac{1}{n} \sum_{i=1}^{n} \frac{\sigma_i^2}{n} \quad . \tag{3.119}$$

Define

$$<\sigma_i^2>_{\text{average}} = \sum_{i=1}^{n} \frac{\sigma_i^2}{n} \quad . \tag{3.120}$$

Then the portfolio variance becomes

$$\sigma_p^2 = \frac{1}{n} <\sigma_i^2>_{\text{average}} \quad . \tag{3.121}$$

The traditional diversification indicates one should add as many assets to one's portfolio as possible. Mathematically, this becomes the limit as the number of assets grows infinitely large,

$$\lim_{n \to \infty} \sigma_p^2 = \lim_{n \to \infty} \frac{1}{n} <\sigma_i^2>_{\text{average}} = 0 \quad . \tag{3.122}$$

In modern portfolio theory, variance is the only measure of risk. Therefore, the above argument leads to a diversification argument. Unfortunately, in reality, variance is *not* the only measure of risk.

2. *An equally weighted portfolio.*

This time, the correlation comes in to play:

$$\sigma_p^2 = \sum_{i=1}^{n} \sum_{j=1}^{n} \frac{1}{n^2} \text{cov}(R_i, R_j)$$

$$= \frac{1}{n} \sum_{i=1}^{n} \frac{\sigma_i^2}{n} + \frac{1}{n} \sum_{i=1}^{n} \sum_{j \ne i}^{n} \frac{\text{cov}(R_i, R_j)}{n}$$

$$= \frac{1}{n} <\sigma_i^2>_{\text{average}} + \frac{n-1}{n} <\text{cov}(R_i, R_j)>_{\text{average}} \tag{3.123}$$

where $<\text{cov}(R_i, R_j)>_{\text{average}} = 2 \sum_{i}^{n} \sum_{j: i<j}^{n} \frac{\text{cov}(R_i, R_j)}{n(n-1)}$

117

CHAPTER 3 ■ STATISTICAL ANALYSIS OF FINANCIAL DATA

Once again, the traditional diversification argument leads to the limit as the number of assets grows infinitely large,

$$\lim_{n\to\infty}\left\{\frac{1}{n}<\sigma_i^2>_{average}+\frac{n-1}{n}<\text{cov}(R_i,R_j)>_{average}\right\}=<\text{cov}(R_i,R_j)>_{average} \quad . \quad (3.124)$$

Therefore, the correlation between assets has placed a limit on the traditional diversification argument, as one would intuitively expect.

Key Problems with Modern Portfolio Theory

The following is a short list of weaknesses that arise in the original version of modern portfolio theory. Some of these are addressed in the DPA method.

I. It does not use the term structure of statistics.
 - There is no mention of holding horizons for assets.

II. Assets returns are usually assumed to be Gaussian.
 - It is missing both skewness and kurtosis (that is, it is missing fat tails).

III. The correlations between assets are fixed and constant forever.
 - This is clearly false, especially when the market is crashing.

IV. The risk is represented by volatility only.
 - It assumes that high volatility usually leads to higher risk. This is not necessarily true because many short traders prefer high-volatility regimes.
 - There is no mention of credit risk. Therefore, emerging market assets would be indistinguishable from other assets.

The DPA method seeks to improve on the obvious weaknesses of the modern portfolio theory. It also requires portfolio rules that are systematic in nature. *Systematic trading strategies* have become very popular because they are rule-based and often can be executed electronically directly through an exchange. For any strategy, a set of systematic trading rules eliminates any need for idiosyncratic trading "skill" of any one individual or individuals. These rules can also be explained generically to a client purchasing such a strategy. The number of investors who are willing to buy "black-box" strategies with almost no information about the strategy except an NAV graph has decreased substantially since the 2008 crisis. DPA attempts to optimize a function I of several weighted variables, not just the return of the portfolio. This is schematically given by (see Figure 3-35)

$$I = \omega_1 E[R_p] + \omega_2 \text{Skew}[R_p] + \omega_3 \text{Kurt}[R_p] + \cdots \quad . \quad (3.125)$$

CHAPTER 3 ■ STATISTICAL ANALYSIS OF FINANCIAL DATA

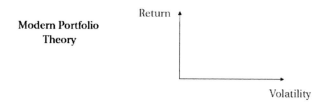

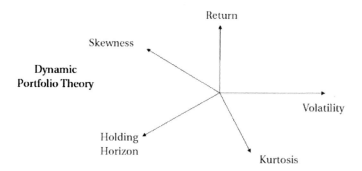

Figure 3-35. Modern portfolio theory versus dynamic portfolio allocation

Following is an outline of systematic trading rules followed by a DPA-type strategy.

Generic Rules to Dynamic Portfolio Allocation with Volatility Targets

I. The strategy should have separate volatility targets for long-only portfolios versus long-short portfolios.

II. One must choose assets consistent with the volatility target. If one has a 5% volatility target, one cannot expect to use the S&P 500 index in the portfolio. Minimum volatility levels are needed to trade stocks or emerging market assets.

III. The strategy will periodically reallocate the portfolio to the one with the highest returns within a volatility target. The exact nature of this periodicity (the trading horizon) is determined by the term structure of statistics.

- A pre-specified trailing window of historical returns may be used to perform this periodic optimization.

IV. One may have a long-only preference first, thereafter moving to a long-short portfolio.

- One may first look for long-only portfolios that give a minimum target return and, failing this, move onto a long-short portfolio.

119

CHAPTER 3 ■ STATISTICAL ANALYSIS OF FINANCIAL DATA

V. One clearly needs a higher volatility (vol) target for short portfolios.

- The empirical *leverage effect* shows that negative returns (when short selling is profitable) lead to higher volatilities, thereby requiring a higher vol target. Large positive returns may also lead to an increase in market volatility but not as much as negative returns and therefore, the leverage effect is a description of market asymmetry

VI. One should move to cash if no suitable portfolio can be found.

- In a directionless market that has nothing to offer, don't take risk unnecessarily.

Consider a two-asset portfolio consisting of the S&P 500 and a cash account earning the federal funds rate. Rebalance this portfolio according to the DPA rules just described (creating long and short portfolios of the S&P 500 using two target volatilities, etc.). Figure 3-36 shows this portfolio, called the S&P 500 DPA index, versus the S&P 500 index. While leading to a somewhat more moderate return, the S&P 500 DPA index shows far less swings that the S&P 500.

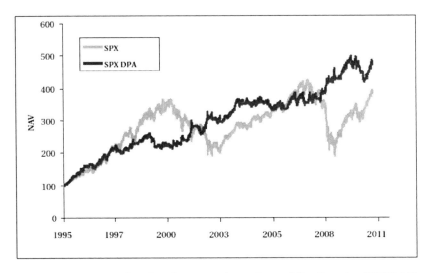

Figure 3-36. *S&P 500 (SPX) and S&P 500 dynamic portfolio allocation (SPX DPA), 1995–2011. Scaled to 100 on 1/1/1995*

What effect does the DPA method have on the volatility of the S&P 500? Figure 3-37 is a scatter plot of all the 42-day period returns versus the annualized volatility within that 42-day period. The S&P 500 has periods of very high vol (> 70%), and these high-vol periods almost always lead to negative returns, as can be seen by the dark trend line sloping downward. The S&P 500 DPA index has 42-day volatilities all less than 24%. Furthermore, periods of high vol may lead to positive returns as indicated by the upward-sloping dark trend line. The S&P 500 has *negative volatility convexity* whereas the S&P 500 DPA strategy has *positive volatility convexity*. That is, on average, high vol regimes tend to be skewed to positive returns. Volatility convexity can be a very powerful Risk measure.

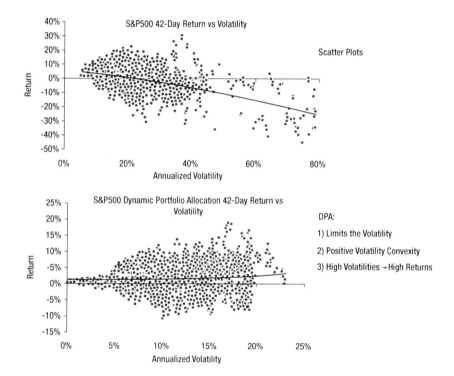

Figure 3-37. *Scatter plots of 42-day returns of S&P 500 and S&P 500 DPA versus their respective 42-day annualized volatilities*

Furthermore, one should compare the term structure of statistics between these two indices. Figure 3-38 illustrates the superior term structure of skew and kurtosis of the S&P 500 DPA index leading to better risk characteristics than the S&P 500. The term structure of statistics is an important tool in the risk management of trading strategies.

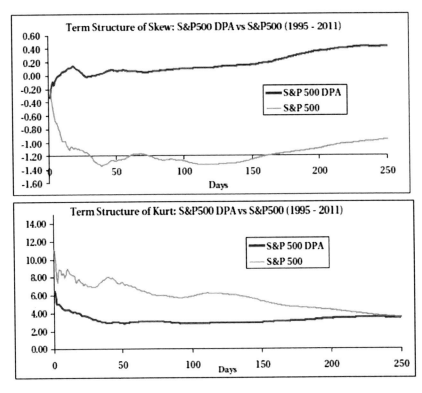

Figure 3-38. *The term structure of skewness and kurtosis of S&P 500 versus S&P 500 DPA, 1995-2011*

Figure 3-39 compares the autocorrelation of squared returns of these two indices. The rapid disappearance of the autocorrelation of squared returns of the S&P 500 DPA index indicates that dynamic rebalancing has limited the volatility of volatility. Furthermore, by limiting the temporal memory of the volatility of volatility, potential fat-tailed returns have been reduced with longer holding horizons.

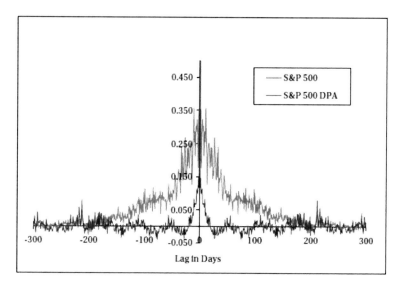

Figure 3-39. *The autocorrelation of squared returns of S&P 500 versus S&P 500 DPA, 1995-2011*

A similar exercise is performed on the MSCI Emerging Markets Index iShares (EEM). Figures 3-40 to 3-43 show the resulting NAV graphs and term structure of statistics.

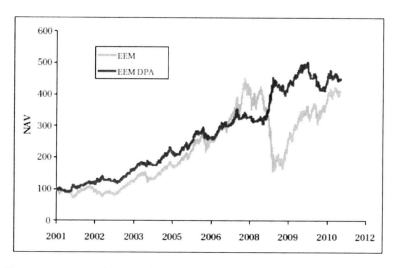

Figure 3-40. *NAV of EEM and EEM DPA , 2001-2012. Scaled to 100 on 1/1/2001*

CHAPTER 3 ■ STATISTICAL ANALYSIS OF FINANCIAL DATA

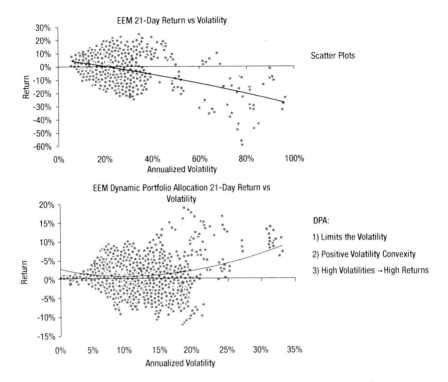

Figure 3-41. *Scatter plots of 42-day returns of EEM and EEM DPA versus their respective 42-day annualized volatilities*

CHAPTER 3 ■ STATISTICAL ANALYSIS OF FINANCIAL DATA

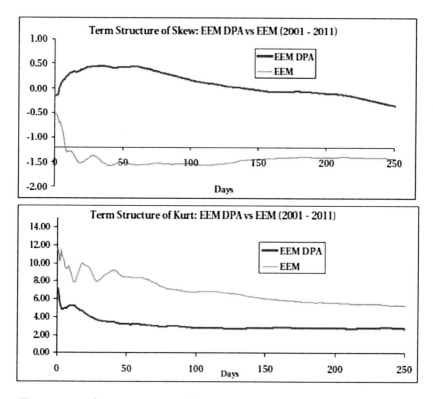

Figure 3-42. *The term structure of skewness and kurtosis of EEM versus EEM DPA*

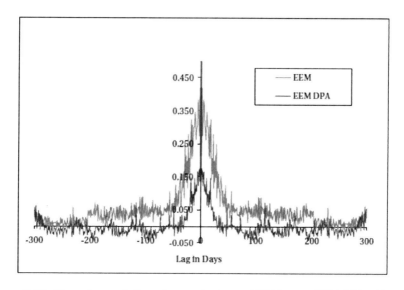

Figure 3-43. *The autocorrelation of squared returns of EEM versus EEM DPA, 1995-2011*

Appendix. Joint Distributions and Correlation

This appendix is a brief introduction to several probability concepts that are needed when dealing with two (or more) random variables. The key concepts touched on in this chapter and discussed here are those of covariances and correlations.[9]

Joint Distribution Function

For any two random variables X and Y, the joint distribution function is given by $F: \Re \times \Re \to [0,1]$ where

$$F(x,y) = P\{X \leq x, Y \leq y\} \quad . \qquad (3.126)$$

Here the brackets $\{X \leq x, Y \leq y\}$ are used to denote the intersection $(X \leq x) \cap (Y \leq y)$ of events.

Joint Density Function

Two random variables X and Y are jointly continuous if there exists a function $f(x,y): \Re \times \Re$ such that

$$F(x,y) = \int_{-\infty}^{y} \int_{-\infty}^{x} f(s,t)\, ds\, dt \quad . \qquad (3.127)$$

The function $f(x,y)$ is called the joint probability density function of X and Y having the following properties:

a. $f(x,y) \geq 0, \quad \forall (x,y) \in \Re \times \Re$

b. $\int_{-\infty}^{\infty} \int_{-\infty}^{\infty} f(x,y)\, dx\, dy = 1$

Example: Is the following a joint density function,

$$f(x,y) = \begin{cases} x+y, & \forall (x,y) \in [0,1] \\ 0 & \text{otherwise} \end{cases} ? \qquad (3.128)$$

---

[9] For mathematically rigorous definitions using σ-algebras and concepts of measurability, see P. Billingsley, *Probability and Measure*, Anniversary Ed., John Wiley and Sons, 2012.

Property (a) is clearly satisfied. What about property (b)?

$$\int_{-\infty}^{\infty}\int_{-\infty}^{\infty} f(x,y)\,dx\,dy = \int_0^1\int_0^1 (x+y)\,dx\,dy = \int_0^1 \left[0.5x^2 + xy\right]_0^1 dy$$
$$= \int_0^1 (0.5+y)\,dy = 0.5y + 0.5y^2 \big|_0^1 = 0.5 + 0.5 = 1 \qquad (3.129)$$

Example: Is the following a joint density function,

$$f(x,y) = x^a y^{1-a}, \quad \forall (x,y) \in [0,1], \ a \in (0,1) \quad ? \qquad (3.130)$$

Property (a) is satisfied. What about property (b)?

$$\int_0^1 \int_0^1 x^a y^{1-a}\,dx\,dy = \int_0^1 \left[\frac{x^{a+1}}{a+1} y^{1-a}\right]_0^1 dy$$
$$= \int_0^1 \left[\frac{1}{a+1} y^{1-a}\right] dy = \frac{1}{(a+1)(2-a)} \qquad (3.131)$$

Therefore, one should redefine $f(x,y)$ to make it a density function as

$$f(x,y) = (2 + a - a^2) x^a y^{1-a} \ . \qquad (3.132)$$

Marginal Distribution Function

Given a joint distribution $f(x,y)$, the marginal distribution functions of X and Y are

$$F_X(x) = P(X \le x) = \lim_{y \to \infty} F(x,y) = F(x,\infty)$$
$$F_Y(y) = P(Y \le y) = \lim_{x \to \infty} F(x,y) = F(\infty, y) \qquad (3.133)$$
$$F_X(x) = P(X \le x) = \int_{-\infty}^{x} \left(\int_{-\infty}^{\infty} f(u,y)\,dy\right) du$$

The corresponding marginal density functions are

$$f_X(x) = \int_{-\infty}^{\infty} f(x,y)\,dy \quad f_Y(y) = \int_{-\infty}^{\infty} f(x,y)\,dx \ . \qquad (3.134)$$

(3.134) basically says that one should be left with the probability density function of one variable, say x, if one integrates out all the probabilities of the other variable. Completely removing the randomness of one variable should leave the other variable intact.

CHAPTER 3 ■ STATISTICAL ANALYSIS OF FINANCIAL DATA

Example: Consider a circle of radius R centered at (0,0). A point is randomly selected from within this circle such that all regions in the circle of equal area are equally likely to contain the point. Let (X, Y) denote the coordinates of the chosen point. The joint density function of X and Y is given by

$$f(x,y) = \begin{cases} c & \text{if } x^2 + y^2 \leq R^2 \\ 0 & \text{otherwise} \end{cases} \quad (3.135)$$

1. Find c

$$\iint_{x^2+y^2 \leq R^2} f(x,y)\,dx\,dy = 1 = \int_0^{2\pi}\int_0^R f(r,\theta)r\,dr\,d\theta = c\int_0^{2\pi}\int_0^R r\,dr\,d\theta = c\pi R^2 \quad (3.136)$$

$$c = \frac{1}{\pi R^2}$$

2. Find the marginal density of X

$$f_X(x) = \int_{-\sqrt{(R^2-x^2)}}^{\sqrt{(R^2-x^2)}} f(x,y)\,dy = c2\sqrt{(R^2-x^2)} = \frac{2\sqrt{(R^2-x^2)}}{\pi R^2}, \quad x^2 \leq R^2 \quad (3.137)$$

3. Let D be the distance from the origin to the point (X, Y), such that $D = \sqrt{X^2 + Y^2}$. Find $P\{D \leq a\}, a \in \Re$

$$F((x,y) \in D) = \int_0^{2\pi}\int_0^a f(r,\theta)r\,dr\,d\theta = c2\pi\frac{a^2}{2} = \frac{a^2}{R^2} \quad (3.138)$$

4. Find $E[D]$

$$\int_0^{2\pi}\int_0^R r\,f(r,\theta)r\,dr\,d\theta = 2\pi c\frac{R^3}{3} = \frac{2}{3}R \quad (3.139)$$

Independence

The introduction of joint probabilities has assumed that the randomness of the variables X and Y are connected to each other. In general, the occurrence of some value of X will affect that value of Y. In certain cases, these variables may be independent. The mathematical definition of independence is as follows.

Given a joint distribution $F(x,y)$, X and Y are independent if and only if

$$F(x,y) = F_X(x)F_Y(y), \quad \forall (x,y) \in \Re \times \Re$$
or (3.140)
$$f(x,y) = f_X(x)f_Y(y)$$

Covariance and Correlation

A concept closely related to independence is correlation. The autocorrelation of squared returns was used in this chapter to describe volatility clustering. Given a joint density function, the correlation of two variables is defined as the scaled covariance of these two variables.

$$\text{cov}(X,Y) = E[(X - E(X))(Y - E(Y))] = E[XY] - E[X]E[Y]$$
$$\rho(X,Y) = \frac{\text{cov}(X,Y)}{\sqrt{\text{var}(X)\text{var}(Y)}} \quad (3.141)$$

Note that if $X = Y$, the covariance reduces to the familiar variance formula and the correlation goes to one. More importantly, *independent variables are uncorrelated but uncorrelated variables are not necessarily independent.*

Cauchy-Schwarz Inequality

$$|E[XY]|^2 \le E[X^2]E[Y^2] \rightarrow |\text{cov}(X,Y)|^2 \le \text{var}(X)\text{var}(Y) \quad (3.142)$$

This inequality restricts the correlation between two variables to be between 1 and −1.
Example: Consider the following joint *Density function*:

$$f(x,y) = \begin{cases} \dfrac{2e^{-2x}}{x} & 0 \le x < \infty, \ 0 \le y < x \\ 0 & \text{otherwise} \end{cases} \quad (3.143)$$

The task is to find cov (X, Y). Because cov $(X,Y) = E[XY] - E[X]E[Y]$, one first needs to calculate the marginal densities:

$$f_X(x) = \int_0^x \frac{2e^{-2x}}{x} dy = \frac{2e^{-2x}}{x} y \Big|_0^x = 2e^{-2x}$$

$$E[X] = \int_0^\infty 2xe^{-2x} dx = -xe^{-2x}\Big|_0^\infty + \int_0^\infty e^{-2x} dx = -\frac{e^{-2x}}{2}\Big|_0^\infty = \frac{1}{2}$$
(3.144)

$$E[Y] = \int_0^x f_Y(y)\, y\, dy = \int_0^x \int_0^x \frac{2e^{-2x}}{x}\, y\, dx\, dy = \int_0^x \frac{2e^{-2x}}{x} \frac{x^2}{2}\, dx$$

$$E[Y] = \int_0^x x e^{-2x}\, dx = \frac{1}{4} \qquad (3.145)$$

$$E[XY] = \int_0^x \int_0^x \frac{2e^{-2x}}{x}\, xy\, dy\, dx = \int_0^x e^{-2x} x^2 = \left. \frac{-e^{-2x}}{2} x^2 \right|_0^x + \int_0^x e^{-2x} x\, dx = \frac{1}{4}$$

$$\operatorname{cov}(X,Y) = E[XY] - E[X]E[Y] = \frac{1}{4} - \frac{1}{2} \cdot \frac{1}{4} = \frac{1}{8}$$

Example: Consider the bivariate Gaussian distribution

$$f(x,y) = \frac{1}{2\pi\sqrt{1-\rho^2}} \exp\left(-\frac{1}{2(1-\rho^2)}(x^2 - 2\rho xy + y^2)\right) . \qquad (3.146)$$

What is the marginal distribution of Y? One must integrate out the x variable,

$$f_Y(y) = \frac{1}{2\pi\sqrt{1-\rho^2}} \int_{-\infty}^{\infty} \exp\left(-\frac{1}{2(1-\rho^2)}(x^2 - 2\rho xy + y^2)\right) dx . \qquad (3.147)$$

First, complete the squares of the exponent:

$$-\frac{1}{2(1-\rho^2)}(x^2 - 2\rho xy + y^2) = -\frac{1}{2(1-\rho^2)}\left[(x-\rho y)^2 - \rho^2 y^2 + y^2\right]$$

$$= -\frac{1}{2(1-\rho^2)}(x-\rho y)^2 - \frac{1}{2} y^2 \qquad (3.148)$$

Let $z = x - \rho y$, $dz = dx$.

$$f_Y(y) = \frac{1}{2\pi\sqrt{1-\rho^2}} \int_{-\infty}^{\infty} \exp\left(-\frac{z^2}{2(1-\rho^2)} - \frac{y^2}{2}\right) dz$$

$$= \frac{1}{\sqrt{2\pi}} \exp\left(\frac{-y^2}{2}\right) \frac{1}{2\pi\sqrt{1-\rho^2}} \int_{-\infty}^{\infty} \exp\left(-\frac{z^2}{2(1-\rho^2)}\right) dz \qquad (3.149)$$

$$= \frac{1}{\sqrt{2\pi}} \exp\left(\frac{-y^2}{2}\right)$$

where the relation $\int_{-\infty}^{\infty} \exp(-ax^2)\, dx = \sqrt{\frac{\pi}{a}}$ has been used. The marginal distribution is as expected where $y \sim N(0,1)$. What is the covariance between X and Y?

$$\text{cov}(X,Y) = \frac{1}{2\pi\sqrt{1-\rho^2}} \int_{-\infty}^{\infty}\int_{-\infty}^{\infty} xy \exp\left(-\frac{1}{2(1-\rho^2)}(x^2 - 2\rho xy + y^2)\right) dx\, dy \qquad (3.150)$$

$$= \frac{1}{2\pi\sqrt{1-\rho^2}} \int_{-\infty}^{\infty}\int_{-\infty}^{\infty} xy \exp\left(-\frac{1}{2(1-\rho^2)}(x-\rho y)^2 - \frac{1}{2}y^2\right) dx\, dy$$

Make the following change of variables:

$$z = x - \rho y, \quad w = y$$

$$dx\, dy = \begin{vmatrix} \frac{\partial x}{\partial z} & \frac{\partial y}{\partial z} \\ \frac{\partial x}{\partial w} & \frac{\partial y}{\partial w} \end{vmatrix} dz\, dw = \begin{vmatrix} 1 & 0 \\ \rho & 1 \end{vmatrix} dz\, dw = dz\, dw \qquad (3.151)$$

Using the fact that all odd powers of Gaussian integrals are zero, one is left with

$$= \frac{1}{2\pi\sqrt{1-\rho^2}} \int_{-\infty}^{\infty}\int_{-\infty}^{\infty} \rho w^2 \exp\left(-\frac{z^2}{2(1-\rho^2)} - \frac{1}{2}w^2\right) dz\, dw$$

$$= \frac{1}{\sqrt{2\pi}} \int_{-\infty}^{\infty} \rho w^2 \exp\left(-\frac{1}{2}w^2\right) dw \qquad (3.152)$$

$$\text{cov}(X,Y) = \frac{\rho}{\sqrt{2\pi}} \cdot \frac{1}{2}\sqrt{2^3\pi} = \rho$$

where the relation $\int_{-\infty}^{\infty} x^2 \exp(-ax^2) dx = \frac{1}{2}\sqrt{\frac{\pi}{a^3}}$ has been used. This shows that the use of the symbol ρ as the correlation in the bivariate density function was appropriate.

Conditional Distribution and Density Functions

The conditional distribution function of Y given $X = x$, denoted as $F_{Y|X}(y|x)$ or $P(Y \leq y | X = x)$, is

$$F_{Y|X}(y|x) = \int_{s=-\infty}^{y} \frac{f(x,s)}{f_X(x)} ds, \quad f_{Y|X}(y|x) = \frac{f(x,y)}{f_X(x)} \qquad (3.153)$$

CHAPTER 3 ■ STATISTICAL ANALYSIS OF FINANCIAL DATA

Conditional Expectation

Let $\phi(x) = E[Y \mid X = x]$. Then $\phi(x)$ is the conditional expectation of Y given X.

In basic probability theory, the conditional expectation is calculated as

$$E[Y \mid X = x] = \int_{-\infty}^{\infty} y f_{Y\mid X}(y \mid x) dy$$

Example: Calculate the conditional density function and conditional expectation of the variable Y for the bivariate normal distribution:

$$f(x,y) = \frac{1}{2\pi\sqrt{1-\rho^2}} \exp\left(-\frac{1}{2(1-\rho^2)}(x^2 - 2\rho xy + y^2)\right)$$

$$f_X(x) = \frac{1}{\sqrt{2\pi}} \exp\left(\frac{-x^2}{2}\right) \tag{3.154}$$

$$f_{Y\mid X}(y \mid x) = \frac{f(x,y)}{f_X(x)}$$

Once again, complete the squares of the resulting exponent,

$$-\frac{1}{2(1-\rho^2)}(x^2 - 2\rho xy + y^2) + \frac{x^2(1-\rho^2)}{2(1-\rho^2)} = -\frac{(y^2 - 2\rho xy + \rho^2 x)}{2(1-\rho^2)} = -\frac{(y-\rho x)^2}{2(1-\rho^2)}$$
$$f_{Y\mid X}(y \mid x) = \frac{1}{\sqrt{2\pi(1-\rho^2)}} \exp\left[-\frac{(y-\rho x)^2}{2(1-\rho^2)}\right] \tag{3.155}$$

$$E[Y \mid X = x] = \int_{-\infty}^{\infty} y f_{Y\mid X}(y \mid x) dy = \int_{-\infty}^{\infty} \frac{y}{\sqrt{2\pi(1-\rho^2)}} \exp\left[-\frac{(y-\rho x)^2}{2(1-\rho^2)}\right] dy$$
$$= \int_{-\infty}^{\infty} \frac{z + \rho x}{\sqrt{2\pi(1-\rho^2)}} \exp\left[-\frac{z^2}{2(1-\rho^2)}\right] dz = \rho x \int_{-\infty}^{\infty} \frac{1}{\sqrt{2\pi(1-\rho^2)}} \exp\left[-\frac{z^2}{2(1-\rho^2)}\right] dz = \rho x \tag{3.156}$$

Again, recall that the expectation of odd powers of Gaussian variables is zero.

In more general measure theoretic approaches, the conditional expectation $E\{X\mid Y\}$ is written without the dummy variable x and is a random variable itself. (See Billingsley, 2012.) $E[Y \mid X=x] = \rho x$, is intuitively correct as ρ is the correlation between X and Y.

CHAPTER 3 ■ STATISTICAL ANALYSIS OF FINANCIAL DATA

Convolution

One often hears the statement that the sum of Gaussian variables is again Gaussian. If X and Y have a joint distribution function $f(x, y)$, then $Z = X + Y$ has a density function given by

$$f_Z(z) = \int_{-\infty}^{\infty} f(x, z-x)dx \quad . \tag{3.157}$$

If X and Y are independent,

$$f_Z(z) = \int_{-\infty}^{\infty} f_X(x) f_Y(z-x)dx = \int_{-\infty}^{\infty} f_X(z-y) f_Y(y)dy \quad . \tag{3.158}$$

Note that convolution is often written as

$$f_Z = f_X * f_Y \quad . \tag{3.159}$$

Example: One can use the convolution property of joint density functions to prove the statement that the sum of Gaussian variables is Gaussian.

Let X and Y be independent $N(0,1)$ variables. What is the density function of $Z = X + Y$?

$$f_Z(z) = \frac{1}{2\pi} \int_{-\infty}^{\infty} \exp\left[-\frac{x^2}{2} - \frac{(z-x)^2}{2}\right] dx \tag{3.160}$$

Complete the squares:

$$x^2 + (z-x)^2 = 2x^2 + z^2 - 2zx = \left(\sqrt{2}x - \frac{z}{\sqrt{2}}\right)^2 + \frac{z^2}{2} \quad . \tag{3.161}$$

Make the following change of variables,

$$v = \sqrt{2}x - \frac{z}{\sqrt{2}}, dx = \frac{dv}{\sqrt{2}} \tag{3.162}$$

Finally,

$$f_Z(z) = \frac{1}{2\sqrt{\pi}} \exp\left(-\frac{z^2}{4}\right) \int_{-\infty}^{\infty} \frac{1}{2\sqrt{\pi}} \exp\left[-\frac{v^2}{2}\right] dv = \frac{1}{2\sqrt{\pi}} \exp\left(-\frac{z^2}{4}\right) \quad . \tag{3.163}$$

Therefore, as expected, the resultant variance is the sum of individual variances, i.e., $Z \sim N(0,2)$. The sum of Gaussian variables is again a Gaussian variable.

> **Caution** Do not confuse the sum of Gaussian variables with the mixed Gaussian distribution, which is the weighted sum of Gaussian *densities*.

Problems

Problem 3-1. Create a Gaussian Random Number Generator in Excel

This model will have two inputs: σ and μ. Use the inverse transform method to create a series of normal variables with a mean of μ and standard deviation of σ. Use the Histogram tool in the Data Analysis toolbox of Excel to create a density function for one static example *or* use the Excel array function "**FREQUENCY**(data array, bin array)" and **CTRL-SHIFT-ENTER** to create a density function for dynamic data. See Figures 3-5 to 3-8.

- Make sure to normalize the histogram-generated density function.
- Choose the bins and bin sizes carefully (try different ranges). They will depend on the mean and σ. Start by getting the MIN and MAX points of the generated random numbers and then divide the space in between them into a certain number of bins (say, 40). See equations (3.48) and (3.49).
- Generate at least 65,000 random numbers.
- Calculate the mean, standard deviation, and kurtosis of the generated random numbers. Compare them to the inputs. Did the process converge?

Problem 3-2. Create a Mixture of Gaussians in Excel
Method One: Random Variable Approach

The model will have three inputs σ_1, σ_2, and q (assume means of zero): Use the inverse transform method to create two series of normal variables with standard deviations of σ_1 and σ_2, each involving a series of calls to RAND(). Then, use a third series of calls to RAND() to determine which of the two normal variables just created make up the mixture,

$$\text{if } (RAND() < q) \text{ choose } N(0, \sigma_1^2), \text{ else choose } N(0, \sigma_2^2) \qquad (3.164)$$

- Generate at least 65,000 numbers.
- Calculate the mean, standard deviation, and excess kurtosis for all three distributions.

- Check the resultant mixture versus the theoretical formulas for convergence.

$$\sigma^2 = q\sigma_1^2 + (1-q)\sigma_2^2 \quad \text{kurt} = \frac{3(q\sigma_1^4 + (1-q)\sigma_2^4)}{\sigma^4} \qquad (3.165)$$

Method Two: Density Approach

This approach directly models the mixed Gaussian density function rather than the random numbers themselves.

$$f(x) \to \frac{q}{\sqrt{2\pi\sigma_1^2}} \exp\left(-\frac{x^2}{2\sigma_1^2}\right) + \frac{1-q}{\sqrt{2\pi\sigma_2^2}} \exp\left(-\frac{x^2}{2\sigma_2^2}\right) \qquad (3.166)$$

- The model will have three inputs (assume means of zero): σ_1, σ_2, and q.
- Choose the discretized x-space carefully.
- Graph all three distributions.
- Use the density approach formulas for the moments (3.64)-(3.66) and check them against the theoretical values. If the match is poor, it could be due to a poor choice of the discretized x-space.

Problem 3-3. Calibrate S&P 500 Returns to a Mixed Normal in Excel

Use both the random variable approach and the density method. For the random variable approach, also create a theoretical histogram.

- Download S&P 500 historical prices from 1950 to the present (using Bloomberg or Thomson Reuters if possible).
- Calibrate the two parameters σ_1 and q via the method of moments.
- As an initial guess, let $\sigma_2 = 0.8\%$. The range of the other two variables will be $\sigma_1 \in [1\%, 10\%]$, $q \in [1\%, 10\%]$. Using another choice of σ_2 can change these ranges. Experiment with different values.
- Let $\sigma_2 = 0.8\%$, $w_1 = 1$, $w_2 = 10000$, if using the Excel Solver.
- Choose the discretized x-space carefully (start with -25% to 25% in increments of 0.05%).
- Graph both empirical and theoretical distributions as in Figure 3-44. Also, graph a log version of this graph to see how well the distribution fits the tail data.

CHAPTER 3 ■ STATISTICAL ANALYSIS OF FINANCIAL DATA

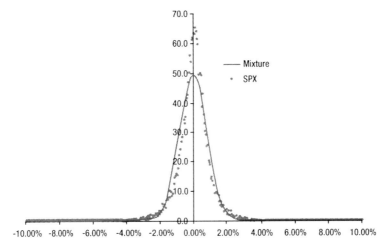

Figure 3-44. *Empirical data versus a theoretical fit of a mixed Gaussian density function*

Problem 3-4. Calibrate SX5E Returns to a Student's-t distribution in Excel

- Download SX5E historical prices from 1987 to the present (using Bloomberg or Thomson Reuters if possible).
- Calibrate the two parameters υ and λ via the explicit moment-matching formulas.
- Choose $\mu = 0$ (the returns should have been mean adjusted at this stage).
- Choose the discretized x-space carefully.
- Graph both empirical and theoretical distributions using a log graph.
- Use the Excel function GAMMALN(), which is the natural log of $\Gamma(p)$

$$\Gamma(p) = \exp(\text{GAMMALN}(p))$$

$$f(x) = \frac{\Gamma\left(\frac{\upsilon+1}{2}\right)}{\Gamma\left(\frac{\upsilon}{2}\right)} \sqrt{\frac{\lambda}{\upsilon\pi}} \left(1 + \frac{\lambda(x-\mu)^2}{\upsilon}\right)^{-\frac{\upsilon+1}{2}} \qquad (3.167)$$

Problem 3-5. Create a Skew Normal Distribution in Excel

Use the density method approach to create a skew normal distribution in Excel.

- Your model will have one input parameter a

$$f_{skew\,normal}(x) = 2\phi(x)\Phi(\alpha x) = \frac{1}{\pi}\exp\left(-\frac{x^2}{2}\right)\int_{-\infty}^{\alpha x} \exp\left(-\frac{s^2}{2}\right) ds \quad . \tag{3.168}$$

Excel Function NORMSDIST()

- Choose your discretized x-space carefully (start with -15 to 15 in increments of 0.10, as in Figure 3-45).

				Mean	Var	Skew	Kurtosis
				-0.7741	40.1%	-0.784	0.633
PI	3.141593						
alpha	-4.0	x	N(0,1)	Skew Normal	(x-mu)*(x-mu)	(x-mu)^3	(x-mu)^4
delta	-0.7741	-15.00	5.531E-50	1.10614E-49	202.377	-2879.007	40956.58
Th Mean	-0.7741	-14.900	2.466E-49	4.93266E-49	199.542	-2818.720	39817.06
Theor.Var	40.1%	-14.800	1.089E-48	2.17775E-48	196.727	-2759.280	38701.49
Theor. Skew	-0.784	-14.700	4.76E-48	9.51903E-48	193.932	-2700.682	37609.53
Theor. Ex KURT	0.633	-14.600	2.06E-47	4.1194E-47	191.157	-2642.919	36540.83
		-14.500	8.825E-47	1.76495E-46	188.401	-2585.986	35495.08
		-14.400	3.743E-46	7.48666E-46	185.666	-2529.876	34471.94
		-14.300	1.572E-45	3.14413E-45	182.951	-2474.584	33471.07
		-14.200	6.536E-45	1.30729E-44	180.256	-2420.103	32492.16
		-14.100	2.691E-44	5.38142E-44	177.581	-2366.429	31534.88
		-14.000	1.097E-43	2.19321E-43	174.925	-2313.553	30598.91
		-13.900	4.425E-43	8.84956E-43	172.290	-2261.471	29683.93
		-13.800	1.768E-42	3.53524E-42	169.675	-2210.177	28789.63

Figure 3-45. *Skew normal discrete density approach in Excel*

- Compare the theoretical mean, variance, skew, and kurtosis given in (3.70) to the empirical ones using the density approach formulas analogous to (3.64)-(3.66). For instance,

$$Var = E[(x-\mu)^2] = E[x^2] = \int_{-\infty}^{\infty} x^2 f_{skew\,normal}(x)dx$$
$$\rightarrow \sum x^2 (Skew\ Normal)(Bin\ Size) \tag{3.169}$$

(If the match is poor, it could be due to a poor choice of the discretized x-space.)

- Graph the result, as in Figure 3-46.

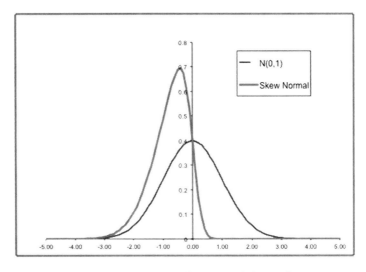

Figure 3-46. *Normal versus skew normal density functions*

Problem 3-6. VaR and CVaR

Calculate VaR and CVaR for daily returns for

    i.   S&P 500 (from 1950)

    ii.   SX5E (from 1987)

Fill in the following table for both S&P 500 and SX5E:

VaR Point	VaR Result	CVaR Result
95.00%		
99.00%		
99.90%		

Problem 3-7. Term Structure of Statistics

1. Calculate the following term structures statistics (Days 1 to 252) for the SX5E index. Provide graphs similar to the ones in this chapter.

$$skew(T) = E\left[\left\{\frac{r_T(t) - \mu(T)}{\sigma(T)}\right\}^3\right] \quad kurt(T) = E\left[\left\{\frac{r_T(t) - \mu(T)}{\sigma(T)}\right\}^4\right] \quad (3.170)$$

$$\left[\frac{\sigma_r^+(T)}{\sigma_r(T)}\right] \quad \left[\frac{\sigma_r^-(T)}{\sigma_r(T)}\right]$$

■ **Hint** To make life easier, use the OFFSET function in Excel, illustrated in Figure 3-47. (This function returns an array, *not* a number in a single cell.)

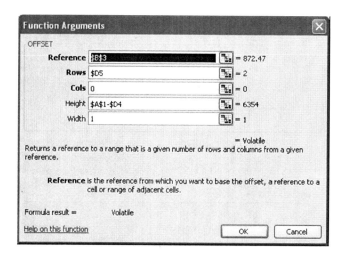

Figure 3-47. The OFFSET function in Excel

2. Create a scatter plot of rolling 21-day returns versus (annualized) 21-day volatilities (see formulas that follow). That is, one compares a specific 21-day return to the volatility of that same 21-day period in question. Provide graphs similar to the ones in this chapter.

$$r_{21}(t) = \ln\left(\frac{P(t+21)}{P(t)}\right), \quad t = 0, 1, \ldots, n \quad (3.171)$$

CHAPTER 3 ■ STATISTICAL ANALYSIS OF FINANCIAL DATA

$$\text{Let } r(t) = \ln\left(\frac{P(t+1)}{P(t)}\right), \quad Vol_{21}^{Annualized} = \left(\sqrt{\frac{\sum_{t=1}^{21}(r(t)-E[r(t)])^2}{20}}\right)\sqrt{252}$$

3. Calculate the autocorrelation of squared returns up to 300 lag days. Provide graphs similar to the ones in this chapter.

$$\rho(r^2(t), r^2(t+\tau)) = \frac{E[\{r^2(t)-E(r^2(t))\}\{r^2(t+\tau)-E(r^2(t+\tau))\}]}{\sqrt{\text{var}[r^2(t)]\text{var}[r^2(t+\tau)]}} \qquad (3.172)$$

$$\tau = \text{time lag}$$

Use the CORREL() function in Excel along with the OFFSET() function.

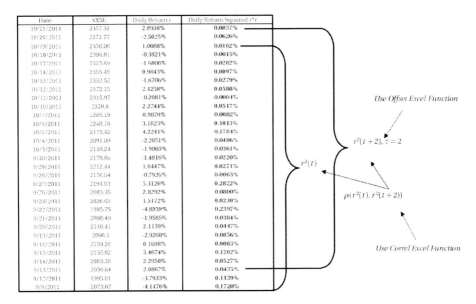

Figure 3-48. *Example of two-day lag calculation of autocorrelation in Excel*

140

References

Berd, A. M. and V. Kapoor. "Digital Premium." *Journal of Derivatives* 10, no. 3 (2003): 66–76.
Billingsley, P. *Probability and Measure*, Anniversary ed. New York: John Wiley and Sons, 2012.
Gardiner, C. W. *Handbook of Stochastic Methods*, 2nd ed. New York: Springer-Verlag, 1997.
Glasserman, Paul. *Monte Carlo Methods in Financial Engineering*. New York: Springer, 2003.
Grimmett, G. R. and D. R. Strizaker. *Probability and Random Processes*, 3rd ed. New York: Oxford University Press, 2001.
Markowitz, H. *Portfolio Selection: Efficient Diversification of Investments* (Cowles Foundation Monograph No. 16). New Haven, CT: Yale University Press, 1968.
McNeil, A. J., R. Frey, and P. Embrechts. *Quantitative Risk Management*. Princeton, NJ: Princeton University Press, 2005.

CHAPTER 4

Stochastic Processes

In the previous chapter, distributions were calibrated to historical data, and risk measures such as VaR and CVaR were calculated. Yet the valuation of financial products and the associated risk measures all deal with events in the *future*. Bonds, stocks, options, and so forth all have potential cash flows in the future, and therefore one needs a method to generate distributions at arbitrary times in the future, as indicated in Figure 4-1. This is the purpose of a *stochastic* (or *random*) *process*, which represents the evolution of a random variable in time.

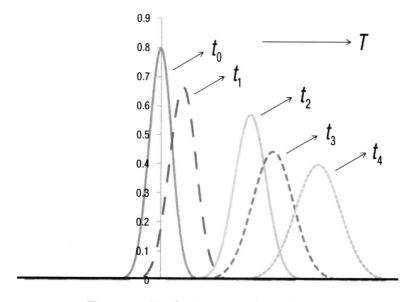

Figure 4-1. Distributions moving forward in time

Stochastic Calculus

This section gives a brief introduction to a very large field in probability theory: *stochastic calculus*. Further explanations may be found in this chapter's appendices and references.

CHAPTER 4 ■ STOCHASTIC PROCESSES

A *stochastic process* with state space S is a collection of S-valued random variables $\{X_t : t \in T\}$ defined on the same probability space $(\Omega, \Im, P)$. The set T is called its *parameter set*. If $T = N = \{0, 1, 2, \ldots\}$, the process is called *discrete*. If T is not countable, the process is called *continuous*. The index t often represents time, and then one thinks of X_t as the state of the process at time t. The state space is usually $\Re$ and then the process is real-valued. A *stochastic process* is fully statistically determined by its nth -order *joint distribution function*

$$P(X_{t_1} \leq x_{t_1}; X_{t_2} \leq x_{t_2}; X_{t_3} \leq x_{t_3}; \ldots; X_{t_n} \leq x_{t_n}) \quad . \tag{4.1}$$

This is a very general joint distribution function for every random variable in the future. It obeys the standard rules of conditional distributions

$$\begin{aligned} & P(X_{t_n} \leq x_{t_n} \mid X_{t_{n-1}} \leq x_{t_{n-1}}; X_{t_{n-2}} \leq x_{t_{n-2}}; \ldots; X_{t_1} \leq x_{t_1}) \\ & = \frac{P(X_{t_1} \leq x_{t_1}; X_{t_2} \leq x_{t_2}; X_{t_3} \leq x_{t_3}; \ldots; X_{t_n} \leq x_{t_n})}{P(X_{t_1} \leq x_{t_1}; X_{t_2} \leq x_{t_2}; X_{t_3} \leq x_{t_3}; \ldots; X_{t_{n-1}} \leq x_{t_{n-1}})} \quad . \end{aligned} \tag{4.2}$$

One can make a few simplifying assumptions about this joint distribution function. The most common one is as follows.

A *Markov process* is a stochastic process $\{X_t : t \in T\}$ that is fully characterized by a conditional probability and a one-point probability function,

$$\begin{aligned} & P(X_{t_n} \leq x_{t_n} \mid X_{t_{n-1}} \leq x_{t_{n-1}}; X_{t_{n-2}} \leq x_{t_{n-2}}; \ldots; X_{t_1} \leq x_{t_1}) \\ & = P(X_{t_n} \leq x_{t_n} \mid X_{t_{n-1}} \leq x_{t_{n-1}}) \quad . \end{aligned} \tag{4.3}$$

This type of process has no "memory" of the past. The future process X_{t_n} at t_n depends only upon the current $X_{t_{n-1}}$ position. The Markov process does not care how it got to the current position at time t_{n-1}. It should be noted that this is not always a desirable feature when one uses stochastic processes to represent real financial processes, as discussed in subsequent sections of this chapter. What other restrictions can one make on the joint distribution function (4.1)? It is often useful to have a process where the nature of the distribution does not change as time evolves—that is, the amount of randomness the process experiences over a certain fixed period of time, say Δt, does not change over time. This requirement can be made mathematically strict with the following restriction.

A stochastic process $\{X_t : t \in T\}$ is called a *stationary stochastic process* if for $\forall \tau$

$$\begin{aligned} & P(X_{t_1+\tau} \leq x_{t_1+\tau}; X_{t_2+\tau} \leq x_{t_2+\tau}; X_{t_3+\tau} \leq x_{t_3+\tau}; \ldots; X_{t_n+\tau} \leq x_{t_n+\tau}) = \\ & P(X_{t_1} \leq x_{t_1}; X_{t_2} \leq x_{t_2}; X_{t_3} \leq x_{t_3}; \ldots; X_{t_n} \leq x_{t_n}) \quad . \end{aligned} \tag{4.4}$$

A stationary stochastic process is statistically invariant under time translations (τ in equation (4.4)). Strict stationarity is seldom observed in practice. Rather, a stochastic process is *weakly stationary* if its first two moments (mean and variance) are finite and independent of t and the covariance function (autocorrelation function) $\text{cov}(X_t, X_{t+s})$ is a function of s for all t. Such a process is also called a *second-order stationary stochastic process* (up to the second order, moments do not change with time).

One of the first such stochastic processes was discovered by Robert Brown in 1827. He noticed that tiny pollen particles suspended in water exhibit a continuous but very jittery and irregular motion. Hence came the name *Brownian motion*. The first quantitative descriptions of Brownian motion were given by Louis Bachelier in 1900 and by Albert Einstein in 1905 and put on firm mathematical ground by Norbert Wiener in 1923. Brownian motion, also called a *Wiener process*, is the canonical example of a stochastic process.

Wiener Stochastic Process

A *Wiener stochastic process* W_t (standard Brownian motion) has the following properties:

i. $W_0 = 0$ (with probability 1)

ii. The increments $W_{t_i} - W_{t_{i-1}}$, $\forall i$ are independent random variables

iii. The increments are normally distributed with mean zero and variance $t-s$, $W_t - W_s \sim N(0, t-s)$

iv. With probability one, $t \mapsto W_t$ is continuous on $[0, \infty)$

Property (i) basically says that there is no process (randomness) at time $t=0$; one must have $t>0$ for a random process to take effect. Property (ii) leads to the Markov property. Property (iii) gives the distribution of increments (Gaussian) and says that the variance is proportional to time. This physically makes sense, for it is intuitively clear that the random nature of the process should increase as one evolves further in time, thereby creating a larger variance when measured from the initial time point. Property (iii) also implies that the increments are stationary: that is, the distribution of $W_t - W_s$ is the same as the distribution of W_{t-s}. Every increment $W_t - W_s$ separated by the same amount of time $\Delta t = t - s$ has the same variance given by $t-s$. For example, all daily increments in the future have the same variance. Property (iii) is the key condition as it states that the distribution of Brownian motion is Gaussian. If one doesn't state an explicit distribution but rather requires stationarity, such that Properties (i), (ii), and (iv) are as above but Property (iii) is instead

iii. The increments $W_{t_i} - W_{t_{i-1}}$, $\forall i$ are stationary random variables,

one is left with the more general *Lévy process*. Property (iv) of a Wiener process states that paths are continuous with respect to the time index, but it should be pointed out that this process is nowhere differentiable in the traditional calculus sense. Therefore, an alternative *stochastic calculus* must be introduced. This non-differentiability comes from the fact that Brownian motion is *self-similar*—that is, it looks the same at every length scale and cannot be reduced to straight lines at infinitesimal scales (Figure 4-2).

CHAPTER 4 ■ STOCHASTIC PROCESSES

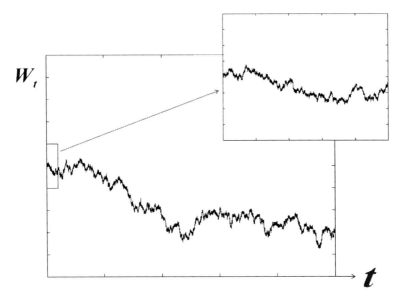

Figure 4-2. *Self-similarity of Brownian motion at all scales*

How does the autocorrelation function for Brownian motion look? Let $s < t$

$$\text{cov}(W_s, W_t) = E[W_s W_t] = E[W_s \{(W_t - W_s) + W_s^2\}] \\ = E[W_s(W_t - W_s)] + E[W_s^2] \qquad (4.5)$$

Using the above properties, one has

$$\text{cov}(W_s, W_t) = E[W_s^2] = s \qquad (4.6)$$

Therefore, a pure Wiener process has a trivial autocorrelation function, which is sometimes referred to as *white noise*.

Since the Wiener process W_t is self-similar at every length scale and cannot be reduced to straight lines at infinitesimal scales, functions of W_t inherit this same property. Heuristically, standard calculus on functions of regular variables works because one can construct tangent lines at points of the function and calculate a slope at that tangent point. At infinitesimal distances, this slope turns into the derivative at that point. As evident in Figure 4-2, the tangent concept will not work for functions of W_t. Thus the field of stochastic calculus was born. Stochastic calculus is a very large and difficult area of mathematics with an extensive literature (see this chapter's references for some excellent examples). In fact, there seems to be a plethora of mathematical finance books that consist of 90% math and 10% finance. Because the purpose here is to concentrate on financial concepts, only a very brief sketch of stochastic calculus is given (without proofs).

To create some intuition, consider the following relation,

$$W_t \to \sqrt{t}\, \varepsilon_t, \quad \varepsilon_t \sim N(0,1) \quad . \tag{4.7}$$

Note that for all t, ε_t are identical and *independent* Gaussian variables with mean zero and variance one. It is straight forward to verify that this substitution satisfies the properties of a Wiener variable,

$$E[W_t] = E[\sqrt{t}\,\varepsilon_t] = \sqrt{t}\, E[\varepsilon_t] = 0 \tag{4.8}$$

and

$$\mathrm{Var}[W_t] = E[(W_t - E[W_t])^2] = E[W_t^2] = t\, E[(\varepsilon_t)^2] = t \quad . \tag{4.9}$$

Using the fact that $W_0 = 0 \cdot \varepsilon_0 = 0$, and the independence of ε_t, the relation given in (4.7) satisfies all the properties of a Wiener process. Therefore, this process somehow acts as a $N(0,1)$ independent random number times a scaling factor of $\sqrt{t}$.

Quadratic Variation

Consider an even partition of the time interval $[0, T]$,

$$0 = t_0 < t_1 < t_2 < \cdots < t_n = T, \Delta t = t_i - t_{i-1} \quad . \tag{4.10}$$

Let W_t be Brownian motion and consider the sum of squared changes,

$$Q_n(T) = \sum_{i=1}^{n} [\Delta W_{t_i}]^2, \quad \Delta W_{t_i} = W_{t_i} - W_{t_{i-1}} \quad . \tag{4.11}$$

The *quadratic variation* of the stochastic process W_t is defined as the limit as the time interval Δt goes to zero while the number of partitions n goes to infinity

$$\langle W, W \rangle_T \equiv \lim_{\substack{\Delta t \to 0 \\ n \to \infty}} Q_n(T) \quad . \tag{4.12}$$

Theorem: The quadratic variation of a Wiener process is given by

$$\langle W, W \rangle_T \equiv \lim_{\substack{\Delta t \to 0 \\ n \to \infty}} Q_n(T) = \lim_{\substack{\Delta t \to 0 \\ n \to \infty}} \sum_{i=1}^{n} [W_{t_i} - W_{t_{i-1}}]^2 = T \tag{4.13}$$

with probability one. Given (4.7), this should not be surprising.

Stochastic Integrals

Rather than starting with stochastic differentiation, the quadratic variation theorem in the preceding section can assist in defining stochastic integrals. Recall from regular calculus that integrals are really infinite sums (the Riemann integral). Consider the following basic integral and its limit as a sum,

$$\int_0^T W_t \, dW_t \to \lim_{\substack{\Delta t \to 0 \\ n \to \infty}} \sum_{i=0}^{n-1} W_{t_i}(W_{t_{i+1}} - W_{t_i}) \quad . \tag{4.14}$$

The sum can be rewritten as follows,

$$\sum_{i=0}^{n-1} W_{t_i}(W_{t_{i+1}} - W_{t_i}) = \frac{1}{2} \sum_{i=0}^{n-1} \left[W_{t_{i+1}}^2 - W_{t_i}^2 - (W_{t_{i+1}} - W_{t_i})^2 \right]$$

$$= \frac{1}{2} W_T^2 - \frac{1}{2} W_0^2 - \frac{1}{2} \sum_{i=0}^{n-1} (W_{t_{i+1}} - W_{t_i})^2 \quad . \tag{4.15}$$

Using the properties of a Wiener process and the theorem on quadratic variation, one has (in the quadratic variation limit)

$$\int_0^T W_t \, dW_t = \frac{1}{2} W_T^2 - \frac{1}{2} T \quad . \tag{4.16}$$

Notice the extra term $-T/2$ when compared with the regular calculus result. One should be aware that these integrals are stochastic as W_t is a random process. Just as in regular calculus, one would like rules to make integration easier than taking explicit sums all the time. The following results (stated without proof) are of great assistance in doing stochastic integrals.

First Moment (Mean)

Consider a function of a Wiener process $f(t, W_t)$. The *first moment of the integral* of this function with respect to a Wiener process is given by

$$E\left[\int_0^T f(t, W_t) \, dW_t \right] = 0 \quad . \tag{4.17}$$

Second Moment (Variance)

Consider a function of a Wiener process $f(t, W_t)$. The *second moment of the integral* (aka *Ito's isometry*) of this function with respect to a Wiener process is given by

$$E\left[\left(\int_0^T f(t, W_t) \, dW_t \right)^2 \right] = E\left[\int_0^T f(t, W_t)^2 \, dt \right] \quad . \tag{4.18}$$

Second Moment (Covariance)

Consider two functions of a Wiener process $f(t, W_t)$ and $g(t, W_t)$. The *covariance* (aka *Ito's isometry*) of the integrals of these random functions with respect to a Wiener process satisfies for $s < t$,

$$E\left[\int_0^s f(u, W_u) dW_u \int_0^t g(v, W_v) dW_v\right] = E\left[\int_0^s f(t, W_t) g(t, W_t) dt\right] \quad . \tag{4.19}$$

Ito's Lemma

Consider a function of a Wiener process $f(t, W_t)$. Ito's lemma states that

$$f(t, W_t) = f(0, W_0) + \int_0^t \frac{\partial f}{\partial s}(s, W_s) ds + \int_0^t \frac{\partial f}{\partial w}(s, W_s) dW_s + \frac{1}{2}\int_0^t \frac{\partial^2 f}{\partial w^2}(s, W_s) d\langle W_s, W_s \rangle \quad . \tag{4.20}$$

The derivative of the quadratic variation of the final term reduces to $d\langle W_s, W_s \rangle \to ds$ using the theorem of quadratic variations of a Wiener process. Although this integral equation may appear odd, the derivative version of Ito's lemma will seem more natural. First, two examples of this integral version are given.

1. $$f(W_t) = W_t^2$$

    $$f(t, W_t) = \int_0^t \frac{\partial f}{\partial w}(W_s) dW_s + \frac{1}{2}\int_0^t \frac{\partial^2 f}{\partial w^2}(W_s) d\langle W_s, W_s \rangle \tag{4.21}$$

    $$W_t^2 = 2\int_0^t W_s dW_s + \int_0^t ds$$

    Bringing the stochastic integral to the left-hand side gives the familiar result from our explicit sum above,

    $$\int_0^t W_s dW_s = \frac{1}{2}W_t^2 - \frac{t}{2} \quad . \tag{4.22}$$

2. $$f(t, W_t) = f_0 \exp\left[\left(\mu - \frac{\sigma^2}{2}\right)t + \sigma W(t)\right]$$

    $$f(t, W_t) = f_0 + \int_0^t f(s, W_s)\left(\mu - \frac{1}{2}\sigma^2\right)ds + \int_0^t f(s, W_s)\sigma\, dW_s + \frac{1}{2}\int_0^t f(s, W_s)\sigma^2 ds \quad . \tag{4.23}$$

    This reduces to

    $$f(t, W_t) = f_0 + \int_0^t f(s, W_s)\mu\, ds + \int_0^t f(s, W_s)\sigma\, dW_s \quad . \tag{4.24}$$

CHAPTER 4 ■ STOCHASTIC PROCESSES

Now take a "derivative" of the above expression. Symbolically, one is left with

$$df(t,W_t) = \mu f(t,W_t)dt + \sigma f(t,W_t)dW_t \quad , \qquad (4.25)$$

where

$$f(t,W_t) = f_0 \exp\left[\left(\mu - \frac{\sigma^2}{2}\right)t + \sigma W(t)\right] \quad . \qquad (4.26)$$

Equation (4.25) may be seen as the derivative of the Wiener function (4.24). In the same way, Ito's lemma may be written in a differential form, as shown in the next section.

Ito's Lemma (Differential Form)

Consider a function of a Wiener process $f(t,W_t)$. The following relationship holds.

$$df(t,W_t) = \frac{\partial f(t,W_t)}{\partial t}dt + \frac{\partial f(t,W_t)}{\partial W_t}dW_t + \frac{1}{2}\frac{\partial^2 f(t,W_t)}{\partial W_t^2}dt \quad . \qquad (4.27)$$

(Extra Ito Term points to the third term.)

Note that the first two terms in the preceding expression are from regular calculus, whereby the total derivative of a regular function $f(t,x)$ is given by

$$df(t,x) = \frac{\partial f(t,x)}{\partial t}dt + \frac{\partial f(t,x)}{\partial x}dx \quad . \qquad (4.28)$$

The fact that W_t is a Wiener process creates the third term in Ito's lemma. The following three examples make this clear.

1. $f(W_t) = W_t^2$

$$\begin{aligned}\frac{\partial f(W_t)}{\partial t} &= 0 \\ \frac{\partial f(W_t)}{\partial W_t} &= 2W_t \\ \frac{\partial^2 f(W_t)}{\partial W_t^2} &= 2 \\ df(W_t) &= 2W_t\, dW_t + dt\end{aligned} \qquad (4.29)$$

2. $f(W_t) = exp[W_t]$

$$\frac{\partial f(W_t)}{\partial t} = 0$$

$$\frac{\partial f(W_t)}{\partial W_t} = exp[W_t]$$

$$\frac{\partial^2 f(W_t)}{\partial W_t^2} = exp[W_t] \qquad (4.30)$$

$$df(W_t) = f(W_t)dW_t + \frac{f(W_t)}{2}dt$$

3. $f(t, W_t) \equiv S_t = S_0 \exp\left[\left(\mu - \frac{\sigma^2}{2}\right)t + \sigma W_t\right]$

$$\frac{\partial f(t, W_t)}{\partial t} = \left(\mu - \frac{\sigma^2}{2}\right) S_t$$

$$\frac{\partial f(t, W_t)}{\partial W_t} = \sigma S_t$$

$$\frac{\partial^2 f(t, W_t)}{\partial W_t^2} = \sigma^2 S_t \qquad (4.31)$$

$$dS_t = \left(\mu - \frac{\sigma^2}{2}\right) S_t \, dt + \sigma S_t \, dW_t + \frac{1}{2}\sigma^2 S_t \, dt$$

$$dS_t = \mu S_t \, dt + \sigma S_t \, dW_t$$

This is often taken as a (rather poor) stochastic model for stock returns (as discussed in the second half of this chapter)—hence the use of the **S** letter.

Often the above machinery is shown for a more general stochastic process than that of a pure Wiener process. Such a process is called an *Ito process*, given by

$$X(t) = X(0) + \int_0^t \alpha(s, X_s) ds + \int_0^t \beta(s, X_s) dW(s) \quad . \qquad (4.32)$$

This most general form of an Ito process, with coefficients that depend upon the stochastic process X_t, is beyond the scope of this book, but a simplified version is given below to help the reader with some of the more mathematical finance literature.

Generalized Wiener Process

$$X(t) = X(0) + \int_0^t \alpha(s)\,ds + \int_0^t \beta(s)\,dW(s) \quad . \tag{4.33}$$

The above simplified version of an Ito process assumes that $\alpha(s)$ and $\beta(s)$ are functions of time, whereas the general version relaxes this constraint as in (4.32) [Shreve 2004B]. Once again, the quadratic variation plays a key role in the stochastic calculus of these processes.

The quadratic variation of a generalized Wiener process is given by

$$\langle X_t, X_t \rangle = \int_0^t \beta_s^2 \, ds \quad . \tag{4.34}$$

Consider a function of the generalized Wiener process $f(t, X_t)$. Ito's lemma states that

$$\begin{aligned}f(t,X_t) &= f(0,X_0) + \int_0^t \frac{\partial f}{\partial t}(s,X_s)\,ds + \int_0^t \frac{\partial f}{\partial x}(s,X_s)\alpha(s)\,ds \\&+ \int_0^t \frac{\partial f}{\partial x}(s,X_s)\beta(s)\,dW_s + \frac{1}{2}\int_0^t \frac{\partial^2 f}{\partial x^2}(s,X_s)\,d\langle X_s, X_s\rangle \quad .\end{aligned} \tag{4.35}$$

This relationship also holds when $\alpha(s)$ and $\beta(s)$ are adapted stochastic processes that depend on X_t, such as the Ito process of (4.32). The exact definitions are beyond the scope of this book [Shreve 2004B].

The following are two sections present very important examples of Ito's lemma that will be used in the remainder of this chapter.

Log Normal Process

Consider the following Ito process

$$S_t = S_0 + \int_0^t \mu S_s \, ds + \int_0^t \sigma S_s \, dW_s \tag{4.36}$$

and the natural logarithm of this process $f(t, S_t) = \ln[S_t]$. Applying Ito's lemma gives

$$\begin{aligned}f(t,S_t) &= f(0,X_0) + \int_0^t \frac{\partial f}{\partial x}(s,X_s)\mu S_s\,ds \\&+ \int_0^t \frac{\partial f}{\partial x}(s,X_s)\sigma S_s\,dW_s + \frac{1}{2}\int_0^t \frac{\partial^2 f}{\partial x^2}(s,X_s)\sigma^2 S_s^2\,ds\end{aligned} \tag{4.37}$$

$$f(t, S_t) = \ln[S_0] + \int_0^t \frac{1}{S_s} \mu S_s \, ds$$
$$+ \int_0^t \frac{1}{S_s} \sigma S_s \, dW_s + \frac{1}{2} \int_0^t \frac{-1}{S_s^2} \sigma^2 S_s^2 \, ds$$
$$\ln[S_t] = \ln[S_0] + \int_0^t \mu \, ds + \int_0^t \sigma \, dW_s - \frac{1}{2} \int_0^t \sigma^2 \, ds \qquad (4.38)$$
$$\ln\left[\frac{S_t}{S_0}\right] = \left(\mu - \frac{\sigma^2}{2}\right) t + \sigma W_t$$

Therefore, the exact explicit solution of our Ito process is

$$S_t = S_0 \exp\left[\left(\mu - \frac{\sigma^2}{2}\right) t + \sigma W_t\right] \quad . \qquad (4.39)$$

Ornstein-Uhlenbeck Process: White Noise versus Colored Noise

As shown in the "Wiener Stochastic Process" section, a pure Wiener process has a trivial autocorrelation function (white noise). The *Ornstein-Uhlenbeck* (OU) process is somewhat more interesting in its autocorrelation features. It can be integrated exactly. The process is given by

$$dX_t = \theta(\mu - X_t) dt + \sigma \, dW_t \quad . \qquad (4.40)$$

Let $f(t, X_t) = X_t \exp(\theta t)$ and apply Ito's lemma. First, get the correct α and β for Ito's integral relation (these can be read off the specific Ito process).

$$X_t = X_0 + \int_0^t \theta(\mu - X_s) ds + \int_0^t \sigma \, dW_s \quad ,$$
$$f(t, X_t) = f(0, X_0) + \int_0^t \frac{\partial f}{\partial t}(s, X_s) ds + \int_0^t \frac{\partial f}{\partial x}(s, X_s) \theta(\mu - X_s) ds \qquad (4.41)$$
$$+ \int_0^t \frac{\partial f}{\partial x}(s, X_s) \sigma \, dW_s$$

Calculate the explicit derivatives,

$$X_t \exp(\theta t) = X_0 + \int_0^t \theta X_s \exp(\theta s) ds + \int_0^t \exp(\theta s) \theta(\mu - X_s) ds + \int_0^t \exp(\theta s) \sigma \, dW_s \quad . \quad (4.42)$$

CHAPTER 4 ■ STOCHASTIC PROCESSES

Two terms cancel in the above expression, leaving

$$X_t \exp(\theta t) = X_0 + \int_0^t \exp(\theta s)\theta\, \mu\, ds + \int_0^t \exp(\theta s)\sigma\, dW_s$$

$$X_t e^{\theta t} = X_0 + \mu(e^{\theta t} - 1) + \int_0^t e^{\theta s}\sigma\, dW_s \qquad (4.43)$$

Multiplying through by $e^{-\theta t}$ gives

$$X_t = X_0 e^{-\theta t} + \mu(1 - e^{-\theta t}) + \int_0^t e^{\theta(s-t)}\sigma\, dW_s \qquad (4.44)$$

With this expression, one may calculate some moments of the OU process. Recalling the first moment relation for functions of Wiener processes,

$$E\left[\int_0^T f(t, W_t)\, dW_t\right] = 0 \qquad (4.45)$$

one obtains the mean of a OU process

$$E[X_t] = X_0 e^{-\theta t} + \mu(1 - e^{-\theta t}) \qquad (4.46)$$

Using Ito's isometry,

$$E\left[\left(\int_0^T f(t, W_t)\, dW_t\right)^2\right] = E\left[\int_0^T f(t, W_t)^2\, dt\right] \qquad (4.47)$$

one may calculate the variance of an OU process,

$$\text{Var}[X_t] = E[(X_t - E[(X_t)])^2]$$

$$\text{Var}[X_t] = E\left[\left(\int_0^t e^{\theta(s-t)}\sigma\, dW_s\right)^2\right]$$

$$\text{Var}[X_t] = E\left[\left(\int_0^t e^{2\theta(s-t)}\sigma^2\, ds\right)\right] \qquad (4.48)$$

$$= \left.\frac{\sigma^2}{2\theta} e^{2\theta(s-t)}\right|_0^t$$

$$= \frac{\sigma^2}{2\theta}\left[1 - e^{-2\theta t}\right]$$

154

Finally, one may calculate the covariance (autocorrelation function) as follows:

$$\text{cov}(X_s, X_t) = E[(X_s - E[X_s])(X_t - E[X_t])]$$

$$\text{cov}(X_s, X_t) = E\left[\int_0^s e^{\theta(u-s)} \sigma dW_u \int_0^t e^{\theta(v-t)} \sigma dW_v\right] \quad (4.49)$$

$$\text{cov}(X_s, X_t) = \sigma^2 e^{-\theta(s+t)} E\left[\int_0^s e^{\theta u} dW_u \int_0^t e^{\theta v} dW_v\right]$$

Using Ito's isometry (covariance version) $(s < t)$,

$$E\left[\int_0^s f(u, W_u) dW_u \int_0^t g(v, W_v) dW_v\right] = E\left[\int_0^s f(t, W_t) g(t, W_t) dt\right] \quad , \quad (4.50)$$

one obtains the desired expression,

$$\text{cov}(X_s, X_t) = \sigma^2 e^{-\theta(s+t)} E\left[\int_0^s e^{2\theta u} du\right] = \sigma^2 e^{-\theta(s+t)} \int_0^s e^{2\theta u} du$$

$$\text{cov}(X_s, X_t) = \frac{\sigma^2}{2\theta} e^{-\theta(s+t)} \left[e^{2\theta s} - 1\right] \quad . \quad (4.51)$$

The dependence on the latter time t indicates true autocorrelation. A process having a nontrivial autocorrelation function is often called a *colored noise* process. This process is used in the discussion of statistical arbitrage in the "Statistical Modeling of Trading Strategies" section.

Geometric Brownian Motion and Monte Carlo Simulations

This section discusses a very common model for stock returns: *geometric Brownian motion*. It is being presented mainly for pedagogical reasons, as it has many weaknesses addressed in the following section on GARCH models. Geometric Brownian motion has a differential form given by

$$dS_t = \mu S_t \, dt + \sigma S_t \, dW_t \quad (4.52)$$

and an explicit solution derived in the previous section using Ito's lemma,

$$S_t = S_0 \exp\left[\left(\mu - \frac{\sigma^2}{2}\right)t + \sigma W_t\right] \quad (4.53)$$

Stock Price at time = t

Drift Term – Annualized mean rate of return

Annualized Volatility

Wiener Process

CHAPTER 4 ▪ STOCHASTIC PROCESSES

This is often called a *log-normal process* because the log returns of S_t are normally distributed, as can be seen by taking the log of the above solution,

$$\ln\left[\frac{S_t}{S_0}\right] = \left(\mu - \frac{\sigma^2}{2}\right)t + \sigma W_t \qquad (4.54)$$

As pointed out earlier, since $W_t \sim N(0, t)$ and therefore $E[W_t] = 0$, $\text{Var}(W_t) = t$, one can always make the following substitution $W_t \to \sqrt{t}\varepsilon, \varepsilon \sim N(0,1)$. For example,

$$\text{Var}[W_t] = E[W_t^2] = \int_{-\infty}^{\infty} t\varepsilon^2 \frac{1}{\sqrt{2\pi}} \exp\left[-\frac{\varepsilon^2}{2}\right] d\varepsilon = \frac{t}{\sqrt{2\pi}} \frac{\sqrt{\pi}}{2} 2^{3/2} = t \qquad (4.55)$$

One can use a similar technique to calculate the *moments of geometric Brownian motion*. Start with the first moment,

$$E[S_t] = S_0 \exp\left[\left(\mu - \frac{\sigma^2}{2}\right)t\right] E\left[\exp(\sigma W_t)\right] \qquad (4.56)$$

$$\exp[\sigma W_t] \to \exp\left[\sigma\sqrt{t}\,\varepsilon\right] \qquad (4.57)$$

$$E[S_t] = S_0 \exp\left[\left(\mu - \frac{\sigma^2}{2}\right)t\right] \int_{-\infty}^{\infty} \exp\left[\sigma\sqrt{t}\,\varepsilon\right] \frac{1}{\sqrt{2\pi}} \exp\left[-\frac{\varepsilon^2}{2}\right] d\varepsilon$$

Completing the squares of the exponential term reduces this to a familiar integral,

$$E[S_t] = S_0 \exp\left[\left(\mu - \frac{\sigma^2}{2}\right)t\right] \int_{-\infty}^{\infty} \frac{1}{\sqrt{2\pi}} \exp\left[-\frac{(\varepsilon - \sigma\sqrt{t})^2}{2}\right] \exp\left[\frac{\sigma^2 t}{2}\right] d\varepsilon$$

$$E[S_t] = S_0 \exp(\mu t) \int_{-\infty}^{\infty} \frac{1}{\sqrt{2\pi}} \exp\left[-\frac{(\varepsilon - \sigma\sqrt{t})^2}{2}\right] d\varepsilon \qquad (4.58)$$

$$E[S_t] = S_0 \exp(\mu t)$$

The following very useful integral relation for exponentiated Gaussian variables comes in handy for all moments of the log-normal stock process. Let z denote a standard $N(0, 1)$ Gaussian variable and λ a constant. Then,

$$E[\exp(\lambda Z)] = \frac{1}{\sqrt{2\pi}} \int_{-\infty}^{\infty} \exp[\lambda \varepsilon] \exp\left[-\frac{\varepsilon^2}{2}\right] d\varepsilon \qquad (4.59)$$

Once again, complete the squares of the exponential term,

$$E[\exp(\lambda Z)] = \frac{1}{\sqrt{2\pi}} \int_{-\infty}^{\infty} \exp\left[\frac{\lambda^2}{2}\right] \exp\left[-\frac{(\varepsilon-\lambda)^2}{2}\right] d\varepsilon = \exp\left[\frac{\lambda^2}{2}\right] \quad . \quad (4.60)$$

Therefore, for any integer n,

$$E[S_t^n] = S_0^n \exp\left[n\left(\mu - \frac{\sigma^2}{2}\right)t\right] E\left[\exp(n\sigma\sqrt{t}\varepsilon)\right]$$

$$E[S_t^n] = S_0^n \exp\left[n\left(\mu - \frac{\sigma^2}{2}\right)t\right] \exp\left(n^2\sigma^2 \frac{t}{2}\right) \quad . \quad (4.61)$$

For $n=1$,

$$E[S_t] = S_0 \exp\left[\left(\mu - \frac{\sigma^2}{2}\right)t\right] \exp\left(\sigma^2 \frac{t}{2}\right) = S_0 \exp(\mu t) \quad , \quad (4.62)$$

as in (4.57). Next is the variance,

$$\text{Var}[S_t] = E[S_t^2] - E[S_t]E[S_t] = S_0^2 \exp(2\mu t)[\exp(\sigma^2 t) - 1] \quad . \quad (4.63)$$

Since the expressions for higher moments begin to look complicated, let $S_0 = 1$ and $\mu = 0$. These simplifications lead to

$$S_t = \exp\left[\sigma W_t - \frac{\sigma^2}{2}t\right]$$

$$E[S_t^n] = \exp\left[\frac{n(n-1)\sigma^2 t}{2}\right] \quad . \quad (4.64)$$

It immediately follows that

$$E[S_t] = 1$$
$$E[S_t^2] = e^{\sigma^2 t}$$
$$\text{Var}[S_t] = e^{\sigma^2 t} - 1 \quad (4.65)$$
$$\sigma[S_t] \equiv \sigma_t = \sqrt{e^{\sigma^2 t} - 1} \quad .$$

These moments are what one would expect. But what about the skewness of geometric Brownian motion?

$$E[S_t^3] = e^{3\sigma^2 t}$$
$$\text{Skew}[S_t] = \frac{1}{\sigma_t^3}\left[e^{3\sigma^2 t} - 3e^{\sigma^2 t} + 2\right] \quad . \quad (4.66)$$

While the skewness is not zero, it cannot be calibrated because it is completely determined by the variance σ. It is somewhat an artifact of structure of the exact solution. Remember that the log-normal returns are Gaussian variables without skew and excess kurtosis. Also, for most reasonable values of σ, $\sigma^2 t$ is relatively small, so that one can take a first-order expansion of the exponentials in the numerator as follows (the denominator stays finite):

$$\text{Skew}[S_t] = \frac{1}{\sigma_t^3}\left[1 + 3\sigma^2 t - 3 - 3\sigma^2 t + 2\right] \to 0 \quad . \tag{4.67}$$

Therefore, the skew is practically negligible. The kurtosis can be derived in a similar fashion:

$$E[S_t^4] = e^{6\sigma^2 t}$$
$$\text{Kurt}[S_t] = \frac{1}{\sigma_t^4}\left[e^{6\sigma^2 t} - 4e^{3\sigma^2 t} + 6e^{\sigma^2 t} - 3\right] \tag{4.68}$$

The kurtosis also cannot be calibrated because it is completely determined by the variance σ. A first-order expansion shows that it too is negligible,

$$\text{Kurt}[S_t] = \frac{1}{\sigma_t^4}\left[1 + 6\sigma^2 t - 4 - 12\sigma^2 t + 6 + 6\sigma^2 t - 3\right] \to 0 \quad . \tag{4.69}$$

The autocorrelation function is the final moment that needs to be calculated. Start with the covariance of two stock prices on the *same process*, one at time t and one at time $t + \tau$,

$$S_t = \exp\left[\sigma W_t - \frac{\sigma^2}{2}t\right]$$
$$S_{t+\tau} = S_t \exp\left[\sigma(W_{t+\tau} - W_t) - \frac{\sigma^2}{2}\tau\right] \quad . \tag{4.70}$$

The stationarity condition of a Wiener process means $W_{t+\tau} - W_t = W_\tau = \sqrt{\tau}Z$. Therefore, the covariance of these two stock prices at two different temporal points is

$$E[S_t S_{t+\tau}] = E[S_t^2 e^{\sigma\sqrt{\tau}Z - \sigma^2/2\tau}]$$
$$= E[S_t^2]E[e^{\sigma\sqrt{\tau}Z - \sigma^2/2\tau}] \tag{4.71}$$
$$= e^{\sigma^2 t}e^{-\sigma^2/2\tau}e^{\sigma^2/2\tau} = e^{\sigma^2 t} \quad .$$

As this depends only on the earlier time t, one concludes that geometric Brownian motion has a trivial autocorrelation function (white noise). Therefore, the main features of stock returns that include fat tails and autocorrelation of squared returns (volatility clustering) are not found in geometric Brownian motion.

Creating Random Stock Paths in Excel

The purpose of a stochastic process is to generate distributions in the future (Figure 4-1). The stochastic calculus framework above gives a firm mathematical basis to do this, but unfortunately most stochastic processes cannot be integrated exactly in terms of expected values, unlike most of the examples provided so far. How does one approximate a stochastic process when exact integration is not possible? The solution was given by physicists working on the Manhattan Project at the Los Alamos National Laboratory in the 1940s. Their solution was to generate random samples from a specific probability distribution using a computer (which was very primitive at the time). These samples, called *simulations*, could be seen as synthetic experiments of phenomena that followed this probability distribution (they were looking at neutron diffusion). The statistics of these simulations could be interpreted as features of the real phenomena if the calibration of the distribution closely matched that of the phenomena in question. These synthetic simulations were called *Monte Carlo* (MC) simulations. MC methods now have wide use in simulations, optimization, numerical integration, and the fields of computational physics, chemistry, biology, and finance. A brief introduction to this method using Excel is given in this section.

Once again, the prescription $W_t \to \sqrt{t}\,\varepsilon_t, \varepsilon_t \sim N(0,1)$ is used. The inverse transform method described in Chapter 3 is used to generate identically distributed and independent $\varepsilon_t's$ via the Excel functions RAND() and NORMSINV(). As with most things calculated on a computer, one must go to a discrete time setting, such as the following discrete version of geometric Brownian motion,

$$dW_t \to \Delta W_t = \sqrt{\Delta t}\,\varepsilon_t, \quad \varepsilon_t \sim N(0,1)$$
$$\Delta S_t = S_t(\mu \Delta t + \sigma \sqrt{\Delta t}\,\varepsilon_t) \qquad (4.72)$$

Here the Δ refers to a finite change in the variable within the discrete *time step* Δt. Δt could be in days, weeks, months, years, and so forth. For daily simulation, $\Delta t = 1/252$ as there are roughly 252 trading days in a year. For monthly simulation, $\Delta t = 1/12$. If the two input parameters μ and σ are annualized, as they often are, Δt must also be annualized. The formula above for ΔS_t provides the methodology for going from one time step to the next for one specific simulation through time called a *path*. One MC path through time in Excel is schematically given by

$$t = 0 \quad S_0$$
$$t = 1 \quad S_1 = S_0 + S_0(\mu \Delta t + \sigma\sqrt{\Delta t}\,\varepsilon_0) \quad \varepsilon_0 \to \text{NORMSINV(RAND())}$$
$$t = 2 \quad S_2 = S_1 + S_1(\mu \Delta t + \sigma\sqrt{\Delta t}\,\varepsilon_1) \quad \varepsilon_1 \to \text{NORMSINV(RAND())} \qquad (4.73)$$
$$t = 3 \quad S_3 = S_2 + S_2(\mu \Delta t + \sigma\sqrt{\Delta t}\,\varepsilon_2) \quad \varepsilon_2 \to \text{NORMSINV(RAND())}$$
$$\ldots$$

Figure 4-3 shows several MC paths in time with superscripts identifying the particular stock path. For clarity, the paths shown in Figure 4-2 do not cross, but in real simulations they may cross multiple times. Each time slice in Figure 4-2 is a distribution of stock prices, and therefore Figure 4-3 is the realization of Figure 4-1.

CHAPTER 4 ■ STOCHASTIC PROCESSES

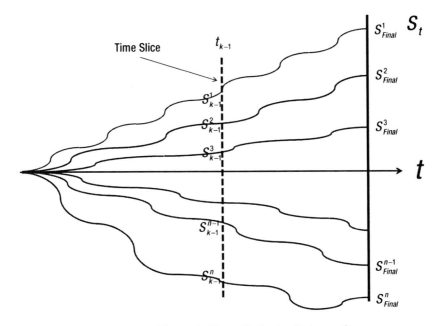

Figure 4-3. Schematic Monte Carlo simulation paths

Figure 4-4 illustrates how an Excel spreadsheet would look with time going across horizontally and different paths going down vertically. It is crucial to keep the order of the paths because the step-by-step discrete stochastic process is path-dependent.

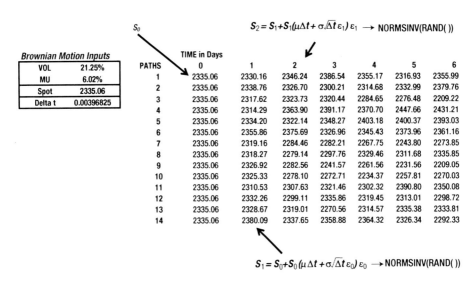

Figure 4-4. Brownian motion Monte Carlo simulation of SX5E in Excel

CHAPTER 4 ■ STOCHASTIC PROCESSES

The actual paths generated by Excel are shown in Figure 4-5.

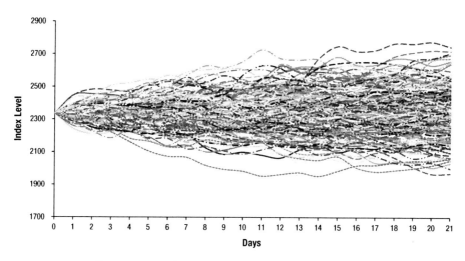

Figure 4-5. 21-day MC simulation paths of SX5E in Excel

The following is an example of a calibration and generation procedure for MC paths, along with a risk calculation using VaR and CVaR.

1. The inputs of annualized μ, σ, and S_0 may be calibrated to a stock or an index (say, SX5E). Because of the choice of discretization in (4.72), one should use simple historical returns (as opposed to log), such that

$$r_{t+1} = \frac{\Delta S_t}{S_t} = \frac{S_{t+1} - S_t}{S_t} = \mu \Delta t + \sigma \sqrt{\Delta t} \varepsilon_t \quad . \tag{4.74}$$

Because $E[r_t] = \mu \Delta t$ and $\Delta t = \dfrac{1}{252}$, μ is calibrated as

$$\rightarrow \mu = \text{Average(daily simple returns)} \bullet 252 \quad . \tag{4.75}$$

Also, because $E[(r_t - \bar{r})^2] = \sigma^2 \Delta t$, the volatility is calibrated as

$$\rightarrow \sigma = \text{STDEV(daily simple returns)} \bullet \sqrt{252} \quad . \tag{4.76}$$

S_0 is the last available price for the index in question.

161

2. Use the prescription in (4.73) to generate 65,000 paths for 21 time steps.

3. *Calibration and Generation Check.* For the 21st day return, the Mean, Stdev, and Kurt should be close to the inputs, with Kurt = 3 for Brownian Motion. The 21st day return will be

$$r_{21} = \frac{S_{21}^{MC} - S_0}{S_0} \quad . \tag{4.77}$$

Here $\Delta t = \frac{21}{252}$. Therefore,

$$\rightarrow \mu^{MC} = \text{Average}(21 \text{ day simple MC returns}) \cdot \frac{252}{21} \approx \mu \tag{4.78}$$

$$\rightarrow \sigma^{MC} = \text{STDEV}(21 \text{ day simple MC returns}) \cdot \sqrt{\frac{252}{21}} \approx \sigma \tag{4.79}$$

The level of convergence between the simulated μ^{MC} and σ^{MC} and the input ones is determined by the quality of the random numbers and the number of paths generated. A detailed discussion on MC simulations and convergence may be found in Glasserman [2003].

4. For the 21st MC return, one can calculate the 99% and 99.9% *VaR* and *CVaR* (Chapter 3).

■ **Note** This is a simplified version of the main methodology of the VaR and CVaR risk management tools used throughout Wall Street. Massive correlated Monte Carlo simulations of more complicated stochastic processes are used for all asset classes throughout the bank to assess the VaR and CVaR risk numbers of these assets classes.

The discretization method of (4.72) is the simplest approximation one can make for geometric Brownian motion (4.52). Yet the exact solution (4.53) can lead to a better discretization method, given by

$$dW_t \rightarrow \Delta W_t = \sqrt{\Delta t}\, \varepsilon_t, \quad \varepsilon_t \sim N(0,1)$$

$$S_t + \Delta S_t = S_t \exp\left[\left(\mu - \frac{\sigma^2}{2}\right)\Delta t + \sigma\sqrt{\Delta t}\, \varepsilon_t\right] \quad . \tag{4.80}$$

Note that because of the nature of the exact solution (4.53) and the condition of stationarity, one need not go through a series of time steps if one is looking for a distribution at only one time in the future. For instance, in Step 4 above, where VaR and CVaR are calculated for the 21st Monte Carlo return, one may generate only one distribution at the 21st point by using $\Delta t = 21/252$ in the above equation, such that

$$S_{21} = S_0 \exp\left[\left(\mu - \frac{\sigma^2}{2}\right)\left(\frac{21}{252}\right) + \sigma\sqrt{\frac{21}{252}}\,\varepsilon_t\right] \quad . \quad (4.81)$$

The discretization method used in (4.72) is called the *Euler-Maruyama method*. For a general Ito process,

$$dX_t = \alpha(t, X_t)dt + \beta(t, X_t)dW_t \quad , \quad (4.82)$$

it is given by

$$X_{t+1} = X_t + \alpha(t, X_t)\Delta t + \beta(t, X_t)\Delta W_t \quad . \quad (4.83)$$

For a geometric Brownian motion stock process, $X_t = S_t$, $\alpha(t, X_t) = \mu S_t$, and $\beta(t, X_t) = \sigma S_t$. An improved discretization method over (4.83) is the following *Milstein method*:

$$X_{t+1} = X_t + \alpha(t, X_t)\Delta t + \beta(t, X_t)\Delta W_t + \frac{1}{2}\beta(t, X_t)\frac{\partial}{\partial X_t}\beta(t, X_t)[(\Delta W_t)^2 - \Delta t] \quad , \quad (4.84)$$

which for the stock process becomes

$$S_{t+1} = S_t + \mu S_t \Delta t + \sigma S_t \Delta W_t + \frac{1}{2}\sigma^2 S_t[(\Delta W_t)^2 - \Delta t] \quad . \quad (4.85)$$

The foregoing can also be derived from a first-order expansion in Δt of the exact solution (4.80). For most Ito processes, the exact solution does not exist, so discretization methods such as these are important (see Kloeden and Platen [1999] for higher-order expansions).

GARCH Process for Stock Returns

GARCH is the acronym for a *generalized autoregressive conditional heteroskedasticity* model appropriate if an autoregressive moving average model is assumed for conditional variances.

GARCH(1,1)

In the lognormal process for stock returns considered in the preceding section, the volatility of the process σ was considered a constant. In reality, this is very far from the truth. Volatility is constantly changing. A Wall Street derivative trader is constantly trading "vol". This expression is used for those who make profits from buying and selling options with a view on the *implied volatilities* of these options. Others trade implied volatility versus realized volatility through variance swaps, which are swaps that essentially swap a preset fixed volatility (implied) versus a floating volatility (realized). These traders are rarely taking a view on whether an option will expire in the money or not. They buy 3-6 month options and hold them only for several days or weeks. A simple trade is to be long vol by buying options (calls and/or puts) while delta-hedging. The hope is that the implied volatility will increase, such that the positions can be sold for a higher price at a not-so-later date (so as not to lose on the time value of the option). Going short vol is selling options when one believes that the implied volatility is high and will decrease in the near future when these options will be bought back to close the short positions.

Clearly, a better model than geometric Brownian motion is needed to address the empirical facts of changing volatility. Volatility, unlike stock prices, does not continually go up or down. Rather, volatility is like an interest rate that fluctuates within a band. There are periods of low volatility, medium volatility, and high volatility. For a specific stock or index, these regions are somewhat centered around a long-term volatility that is the characteristic volatility of that specific stock or index. For instance, the characteristic volatility of the S&P 500 is around 12%, whereas the NASDAQ has a higher vol of around 15%. Furthermore, volatility tends to cluster into regions of high, medium, and low volatility. That is, the volatility tomorrow has some correlation to the volatility today. Volatility is of course a measurement of the price movement of a stock or index. It is an empirical fact that large downward price moves tend to lead to regions of higher volatilities, called the *leverage effect*, rather than large upward moves. How can one capture all these facets in one model? The most straightforward way is to simply let today's *variance* σ_t^2 have a weighting to yesterday's variance σ_{t-1}^2, yesterday's price move ε_{t-1}, and the characteristic long-term variance σ^2 as follows:

$$\sigma_t^2 = W_1 \sigma^2 + W_2 \sigma_{t-1}^2 + W_3 \varepsilon_{t-1}^2 \quad . \tag{4.86}$$

Because $\varepsilon_t \sim N(0,1)$, one needs to scale it by the standard deviation of the process. Therefore, one should really write

$$\sigma_t^2 = W_1 \sigma^2 + W_2 \sigma_{t-1}^2 + W_3 \sigma_{t-1}^2 \varepsilon_{t-1}^2 \tag{4.87}$$

with weights, such that

$$W_1 + W_2 + W_3 = 1, \rightarrow W_1 = 1 - W_2 - W_3 \quad . \tag{4.88}$$

The traditional notation for GARCH(1,1) uses $\beta = W_2$ and $\alpha = W_3$, and therefore $W_1 = 1 - \alpha - \beta$. "(1,1)" stands for a dependence on the previous day's vol and price move. If one took into account the two previous days' vol and price move, one would have GARCH(2,2).

- The *GARCH(1,1)* model: The asset and its volatility evolve as follows:

$$\Delta S_t = S_t(\mu \Delta t + \sigma_t \sqrt{\Delta t}\, \varepsilon_t)$$
$$\sigma_t^2 = (1 - \alpha - \beta)\sigma^2 + \sigma_{t-1}^2(\beta + \alpha \varepsilon_{t-1}^2) \tag{4.89}$$
$$\varepsilon_t \sim N(0,1)$$

CHAPTER 4 ■ STOCHASTIC PROCESSES

It is important to note that the ε_{t-1} is not a new random variable for σ_t but the exact random variable used for ΔS_{t-1}.

- The *Autoregressive Term*: $\alpha \sigma_{t-1}^2 \varepsilon_{t-1}^2$. This term makes the conditional variance at time t a function of the actual innovation (change) of the previous time period $t-1$. This produces the effect that periods of big moves or small moves are clustered together (volatility clustering). This also leads to a high kurtosis or fat-tailed distribution.

- The *Generalized Term*: $\beta \sigma_{t-1}^2$. This term produces a richer autocorrelation term structure of squared returns, as shown below.

- This is one of the simplest examples of a *stochastic volatility model*.

- *Parameter Restrictions*: The parameters α and β have the following restrictions (which are clear if one considers them as weights):

$$(\alpha + \beta) < 1$$
$$0 < \alpha < 1 \quad (4.90)$$
$$0 < \beta < 1 \quad .$$

One can calculate the long-term unconditional variance using two different methods. In the first method, one starts with the variance of a return at time t,

$$r_t = \frac{\Delta S_t}{S_t} = (\mu \Delta t + \sigma_t \sqrt{\Delta t}\, \varepsilon_t)$$
$$\overline{r} = E[r_t] = \mu \Delta t \quad (4.91)$$

Consider the variance of the mean adjusted return,

$$\hat{r}_t = r_t - \overline{r}$$
$$\mathrm{Var}(\hat{r}_t) = E[\hat{r}_t^2] - E[\hat{r}_t]^2 = E[\hat{r}_t^2]$$
$$\hat{r}_t^2 = \sigma_t^2 \Delta t\, \varepsilon_t^2 \quad (4.92)$$
$$\mathrm{Var}(\hat{r}_t) = E[\sigma_t^2 \Delta t\, \varepsilon_t^2] = E[\sigma_t^2 \Delta t] E[\varepsilon_t^2] = E[\sigma_t^2 \Delta t] \quad .$$

Using the GARCH variance, $\sigma_t^2 = (1 - \alpha - \beta)\sigma^2 + \sigma_{t-1}^2(\beta + \alpha \varepsilon_{t-1}^2)$, one finds

$$\mathrm{Var}(\hat{r}_t) = E[\sigma_t^2 \Delta t] = (1-\alpha-\beta)\sigma^2 \Delta t + \beta E[\sigma_{t-1}^2 \Delta t] + \alpha E[\sigma_{t-1}^2 \varepsilon_{t-1}^2 \Delta t]$$
$$\mathrm{Var}(\hat{r}_t) = (1-\alpha-\beta)\sigma^2 \Delta t + \beta E[\hat{r}_{t-1}^2] + \alpha E[\hat{r}_{t-1}^2] \quad . \quad (4.93)$$

Therefore, one has a recursive relationship for $\mathrm{Var}(\hat{r}_t)$,

$$\mathrm{Var}(\hat{r}_t) = (1-\alpha-\beta)\sigma^2 \Delta t + (\alpha + \beta)\mathrm{Var}(\hat{r}_{t-1}) \quad (4.94)$$

For the unconditional variance of a weakly stationary stochastic process, the long-term unconditional variance should have the property that

$$\lim_{t\to\infty}\text{Var}(\hat{r}_t) = \text{Var}(\hat{r}_{t-1})$$
$$\lim_{t\to\infty}\text{Var}(\hat{r}_t) = (1-\alpha-\beta)\sigma^2\Delta t + (\alpha+\beta)\text{Var}(\hat{r}_t)$$
$$\lim_{t\to\infty}\text{Var}(\hat{r}_t)[1-(\alpha+\beta)] = (1-\alpha-\beta)\sigma^2\Delta t \quad (4.95)$$
$$\lim_{t\to\infty}\text{Var}(\hat{r}_t) \to \sigma^2$$

Therefore, σ is the long-term volatility of the GARCH(1,1) process.

Another way to see this is as follows. Rewrite the GARCH(1,1) variance equation for time $t+n$ as

$$\sigma_{t+n}^2 - \sigma^2 = \alpha\left(\sigma_{t+n-1}^2\varepsilon_{t+n-1}^2 - \sigma^2\right) + \beta(\sigma_{t+n-1}^2 - \sigma^2) \quad (4.96)$$

Taking an expected value on both sides gives

$$E\left[\sigma_{t+n}^2 - \sigma^2\right] = (\alpha+\beta)E\left[\sigma_{t+n-1}^2 - \sigma^2\right] \quad (4.97)$$

Using this repeatedly backwards in time until time t results in

$$E\left[\sigma_{t+n}^2\right] = \sigma^2 + (\alpha+\beta)^n E\left[\sigma_t^2 - \sigma^2\right] \quad (4.98)$$

Therefore, in the long-term limit

$$\lim_{n\to\infty} E\left[\sigma_{t+n}^2\right] = \sigma^2, \quad (4.99)$$

using the fact that $(\alpha+\beta) < 1$.

Calibration

The GARCH(1,1) model can be calibrated by a *method of moments fit to empirical returns*. The model has six parameters to calibrate:

$$\begin{aligned}
S_0 &= \text{initial stock price} \\
\mu &= \text{mean stock return} \\
\sigma_0 &= \text{initial stock volatility} \\
\sigma &= \text{long term stock volatility} \\
\alpha &= \text{Autoregressive coefficient} \\
\beta &= \text{Generalized coefficient}
\end{aligned} \quad (4.100)$$

Step 1: The mean return, initial volatility, and long-term volatility are matched to the empirical mean and the short- and long-term standard deviations of the historical stock returns,

$$r_t = \frac{\Delta S_t}{S_t} \rightarrow \text{historical returns} \quad (4.101)$$

$$\bar{r} = E[r_t] = \mu \Delta t \quad (4.102)$$

$$\sigma_r^2 = E[(r_t - \bar{r})^2 \mid \text{Use All the Data}] = \sigma^2 \Delta t \quad (4.103)$$

$$E[(r_t - \bar{r})^2 \mid \text{Use Only Recent Returns}] = \sigma_0^2 \Delta t \quad (4.104)$$

The long-term variance is calculated using all possible data to capture the long-term trend of the underlying asset. The initial volatility calculation is more dependent on the actual asset or risk measure one is investigating with this model. For instance, if one is pricing one-month options using daily data, one may choose to use the last 21 days of data to calculate the initial volatility. For 10-day CVaR calculations, one may choose to use the last 10 days of data. Note that these equations are valid for other types of temporal data, such as weekly or monthly.

Step 2: Fit the *kurtosis* of returns and the *autocorrelation of squared returns* to get α and β.

GARCH(1,1) has an exact expression for the kurtosis of returns. By matching this expression to the empirical kurtosis, one has a much better representation of the fat tails of the distribution of returns than that of geometric Brownian motion. The theoretical formula for the kurtosis is

$$\kappa(\alpha, \beta) = \frac{E[\hat{r}^4]}{\sigma_r^4} = \frac{3}{\left[1 - \frac{2\alpha^2}{1-(\alpha+\beta)^2}\right]} \quad . \quad (4.105)$$

One should appreciate the fact that such a simple expression exists making moment matching possible. For the vast majority of stochastic processes, such formulas do not exist, and one is left to calibrate with less precise ways, such as the maximum-likelihood method (see Chapter 8).

The other empirical fact that is missing in geometric Brownian motion is the autocorrelation of squared returns. Once again, GARCH(1,1) has an exact expression for this second-order moment. Let Δt be the time step between data points (daily, monthly, and so on). The autocorrelation of squared returns for a certain number of time steps h (or lags) is given by

$$\rho_{\hat{r}^2}(h) = \frac{E\left[\left(\hat{r}^2(t+h\Delta t) - \sigma_r^2\right)\left(\hat{r}^2(t) - \sigma_r^2\right)\right]}{E\left[\left(\hat{r}^2(t) - \sigma_r^2\right)^2\right]} = \begin{cases} \dfrac{\alpha\left[1-(\alpha+\beta)^2 + \alpha(\alpha+\beta)\right]}{1-(\alpha+\beta)^2 + \alpha^2}, & h=1 \\ (\alpha+\beta)\rho_{\hat{r}^2}(h-1), & h>1 \end{cases} \quad (4.106)$$

It is clear that with only two parameters, one cannot match point by point every autocorrelation, $\rho_{\hat{r}^2}, \forall h$. Instead, one matches a sum of autocorrelations,

$$\Gamma(n, \alpha, \beta) = \sum_{h=1}^{n} \rho_{\hat{r}^2}(h) \quad . \quad (4.107)$$

CHAPTER 4 ■ STOCHASTIC PROCESSES

This is called the *volatility clustering time*. It is the area under the curve of the empirical autocorrelation function (see Figure 4-6). It is also an *average* time measure of when the autocorrelation of squared returns begins to disappears and therefore gives an indication of the time over which the volatility of the underlying tends to *cluster*. The choice of the number of autocorrelations summed is dependent on the empirical autocorrelation function. For instance, in Figure 4-6, the empirical autocorrelation disappears around 120 days, and therefore one would set $n = 120$.

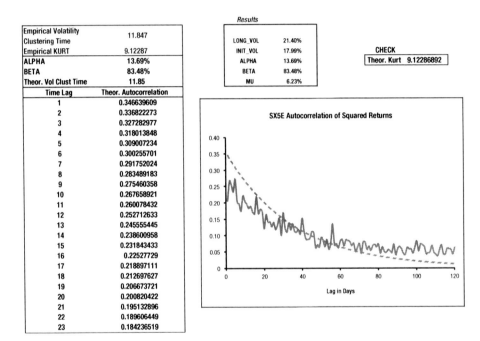

Figure 4-6. Calibration of GARCH(1,1) to the SX5E Index in Excel. The dashed line is the autocorrelation function produced by a calibrated GARCH(1,1) model whereas the solid line is the empirical autocorrelation

One is left with matching the empirical kurtosis κ_{emp} and the empirical volatility clustering time $\Gamma(n)_{emp}$ a judicious choice of α and β. In order to fit the kurtosis exactly $\kappa(\alpha, \beta) = \kappa_{emp}$, solve for α in equation (4.105) in terms of β and κ_{emp}

$$\alpha = \frac{\sqrt{(\kappa_{emp} - 3)[\kappa_{emp}(3 - 2\beta^2) - 3]} - \beta(\kappa_{emp} - 3)}{3(\kappa_{emp} - 1)} \quad (4.108)$$

Now, solve for β such that

$$\Gamma(n, \alpha, \beta) = \Gamma(n)_{emp} \quad , \quad (4.109)$$

and use this β in equation (4.108) to obtain α.

The GARCH(1,1) model can be calibrated to all types of temporal data. Figure 4-7 shows the empirical versus the calibrated GARCH(1,1) autocorrelation function (ACF) of squared returns for a *monthly hedge fund index* comprised of many individual hedge funds. The empirical returns are monthly NAVs, and therefore the lag times are in steps of months. The fit here is clearly better than that of SX5E in Figure 4-6. The smoothness of the fit and high autocorrelation indicate the well-known fact that hedge funds tend to smooth their P&L over time to give the impression of consistent monthly returns. (Some hedge funds may actually achieve this, but it is rare.)

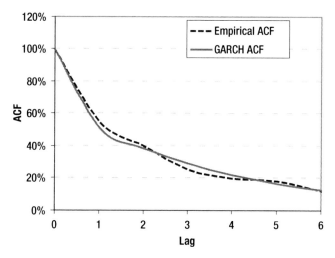

Figure 4-7. Empirical versus theoretical GARCH(1,1) autocorrelation of squared returns for a monthly hedge fund index

The GARCH(1,1) Model for the "Traditional" Term Structure of Volatility

In this section, a formula is derived for the traditional term structure of volatility that comes from the market where different implied volatilities are used for option prices with different maturities but with the same underlying asset and strike. This is an artifact of the inferior Black-Scholes model (Appendix A of this chapter). This is not the same as the term structure of statistics discussed in Chapter 3, where moments were calculated on different *lagged returns*, such as one-day, two-day, or three-day returns. These types of returns are very important and were used to calibrate the autocorrelation of the GARCH(1,1) model. The GARCH(1,1) model can also provide a more traditional view of the temporal progression of annualized daily volatilities (if one calibrated monthly data, these volatilities would be monthly). This is the case because the volatility in this model is stochastic and changes as time goes by. The short-term volatility is given by the short-term vol input $\sigma(0)$.

The long-term volatility is given by the long vol input σ. The stochastic volatility is anchored between these two points. It can certainly be greater or less than these two on a path-by-path basis, but on average it is between these two points, as the following will show.

Start with $t=0$ (today) in equation (4.98). Also, let

$$\gamma = \ln\frac{1}{\alpha+\beta} \quad . \tag{4.110}$$

An estimate of the instantaneous variance in n days from now is given by

$$E[\sigma_n^2] = V(n) = \sigma^2 + e^{-\gamma n}[V(0)-\sigma^2] \quad . \tag{4.111}$$

The average variance between today $t=0$ and time T is the time average integral of this expression,

$$\frac{1}{T}\int_0^T V(n)\,dn = \sigma^2 + \frac{1-e^{-\gamma T}}{\gamma T}[V(0)-\sigma^2] \quad . \tag{4.112}$$

Therefore, the average term structure of annualized volatility is

$$\hat{\sigma}(T) = \left[\sigma^2 + \frac{1-e^{-\gamma T}}{\gamma T}\left(\sigma(0)^2 - \sigma^2\right)\right]^{\frac{1}{2}}, \tag{4.113}$$

with the expected long-term limit

$$\lim_{T\to\infty}\hat{\sigma}(T) = \sigma \quad . \tag{4.114}$$

Note the interplay between the long vol and short vol. The second term in equation (4.113) is simply a time-weighted difference between the long-term and short-term variance.

Statistical Modeling of Trading Strategies

Stochastic processes are not used just to model asset returns for calculating risk (VaR, CVaR) or pricing derivatives (Chapter 5). They are also used in the modeling of systematic trading strategies. Systematic trading strategies are rules-based trading strategies that execute trades based on some algorithm (often mathematical) that provides dynamic buy and sell signals. It is called *systematic* because it relies on the algorithmic signals rather than the financial manager's trading ability. Trades are systematically executed according to the algorithmic signal without manager intervention. Systematic trading strategies often come down to the following broad features:

Methodology or Algorithm: This is basically the algorithm that is used to generate trading signals and forms the backbone of the strategy—whether statistical arbitrage, volatility arbitrage, momentum-driven long-short strategies, or machine learning. Regardless of the mathematical sophistication of the strategy, the key to getting investors for the strategy lies here. One has to convince them, in general (without showing them a backtest), that the methodology makes financial sense. Is the methodology applicable to the asset classes that are being considered? Can one realistically execute the methodology in the market? One can't, for example, achieve high-frequency trading on a hedge fund. Why is the chosen algorithm better than other ones for the asset classes that are being considered? All these issues must be addressed for a successful trading strategy.

Data Sets: Financial data are needed for both the backtest and live signal generation. Cleaning raw data is always necessary. Are the cleaning methodologies (such as volume adjustments or outlier adjustments) consistent with the trading algorithm? Is any useful information being lost? Are the data being distorted to make the trading algorithm work better? Data must be obtained from reliable sources such as Bloomberg and Thomson Reuters and easily accessible though APIs that are usually connected to the algorithmic signal generation system.

Backtesting and Risk Assessment: This is always the most nebulous part of a systematic trading strategy. One always needs a realistic backtest that includes transactions and hedge slippage costs, but very few investors are going to trust it. Investors are often sold on the methodology rather than a spectacular backtest. A few years of real live performance is the true seller of strategies. Nonetheless, a backtest is necessary and it has to be relatively stable. The proof of stability comes from running the algorithm through crisis periods such as the 1998 Russian crisis, 9/11, the dot-com bust, and the sub-prime crisis of 2008. The term structure of statistics (Chapter 3) plays a large role in the risk assessment. What are the term structures of mean, volatility, skew, and kurtosis of the backtest? What are the drawdown characteristics (largest drop over any time period)? How does the "up" volatility compare with the "down" volatility? What are the historic VaR and CVaR over various time periods? Once live, the trading strategy must continue to calculate these risk numbers and potentially simulate future results with realistic stochastic processes such as GARCH(1,1) in order to assess future tail risk.

An Automated Execution System: A majority of systematic trading strategies have automated trade execution systems. Buy and sell signals are generated by the algorithm, and these are sent to an execution system that feeds directly to multiple exchanges and executes trade orders electronically without human intervention. Such an approach is critical for risk management because of the precise nature of executing trades at specific price levels and trade size and rapid stop-loss and system shutdown abilities.

One very popular systematic trading strategy is called *statistical arbitrage*. The following sections present a simplified version of a statistical arbitrage strategy described in a paper by Avellaneda and Lee (2010). The main concepts are pairs trading and mean reversion.

Pairs Trading

Pairs trading is a generic methodology of going long one asset and going short another asset (a *long-short pair*). When dealing with stocks, these tend to have either similar characteristics or come from the same industry. The main assumption here is that one is expecting the returns of these two stocks to track each other to a certain extent. The simplest mathematical relation to investigate is the linear regression equation between the returns of the two stocks in a long-short pair. Recall that the linear regression formula for a time series r_t^P versus r_t^Q is given by

$$r_t^P = \beta_0 + \beta r_t^Q + \varepsilon_t \quad . \tag{4.115}$$

The linear regression algorithm tries to find the coefficients β_0 and β such that the sum of squared residuals ε_t is minimized,

$$\text{Minimize} \sum_{t=1}^{n} \varepsilon_t^2 = \sum_{t=1}^{n} (r_t^P - \beta_0 - \beta r_t^Q)^2 \quad . \tag{4.116}$$

Basically, one is fitting the best-fit line through a set of points as illustrated in Figure 4-8.

CHAPTER 4 ■ STOCHASTIC PROCESSES

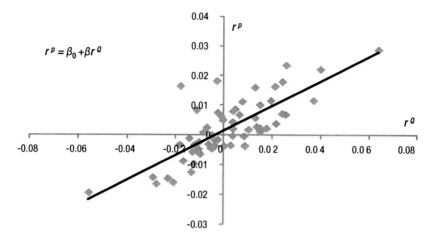

Figure 4-8. *Linear regression*

Let P_t and Q_t denote the corresponding price time series for the pair of stocks. The linear regression equation on returns is given by

$$\ln\left(\frac{P_t}{P_0}\right) = \alpha t + \beta \ln\left(\frac{Q_t}{Q_0}\right) + X_t \quad . \tag{4.117}$$

This is a very common equation and is known as *beta-adjusting* one stock with another. The key to this equation is the *residual* term X_t. Pairs trading comes down to investigating the behavior of the residual term as time evolves. The differential form of this equation is

$$\frac{dP_t}{P_t} = \alpha \, dt + \beta \frac{dQ_t}{Q_t} + dX_t \quad . \tag{4.118}$$

Consider the following scenario. Suppose that, after beta-adjusting stock P with Q over a certain period of time, the residual term X_t is fairly positive. This means that P has overperformed its cousin Q. In the *mean reverting* paradigm, this overperformance cannot last because these stocks are similar in nature and their market valuations must converge. Therefore, it is a good time to go short P (it is overvalued) and go long Q (which is undervalued relative to P). Conversely, if the residual term X_t is fairly negative, this means that P has underperformed its relative pair Q, and one should go long P and short Q. The mean reverting concept is associated with market overreaction: assets are temporarily over- or undervalued with respect to their peers. In this method, one has statistically measured a time series of spreads between two correlated assets and invested in overbought or undersold spreads.

CHAPTER 4 ■ STOCHASTIC PROCESSES

A straightforward generalization of the concept of pairs trading described above is to adapt the method to indices and ETFs made up of groups of similar stocks:

$$\ln\left(\frac{S_t}{S_0}\right) = \alpha t + \beta \ln\left(\frac{I_t}{I_0}\right) + X_t, \quad (4.119)$$

$$S_t = \text{stock}, \quad I_t = \text{ETF Index}$$

These stocks are in a certain industry sector—such as financials, biotechnology, or health care—and are expected to provide similar returns over a certain period of time. When certain stocks perform differently from the sector returns, the mean reverting paradigm can be invoked. For instance, relative value sector ETF pairs trading involves beta-adjusting every stock within an ETF to that ETF and identifying undervalued or overbought stocks with respect to that sector. One goes long one unit of an undervalued stock and goes short β units of the ETF. If the mean reverting assumption holds, the undervalued stock will start to perform similarly to its sector returns (the ETF), and one will make money on this long–short pair. By always beta-adjusting the position, one is creating a market sector of factor-neutral trading strategy. This is an important fact to remember. This is a relative value trade, where one is taking a view not on the outright performance of a sector but on the relative performance of a stock within the sector with respect to the sector as a whole. Several stocks maybe held long or short relative to the ETF. Often, these beta-adjusted ETF positions almost net themselves out and the trading book looks like a portfolio of long and short stocks. Not every stock within an ETF will be used. For instance, one usually restricts trading to stocks with a market capitalization of at least US$1 billion. Also, minimum weight thresholds of the stock within an ETF are sometimes required. A stock that makes up less than 2% of an ETF may be ignored.

Models for Residuals: Mean Reverting Ornstein-Uhlenbeck Process

In the mean reverting paradigm described in the preceding section, one looks at the residual of the beta-adjusted process to determine whether to go long or short:

$$\ln\left(\frac{S_t}{S_0}\right) = \alpha t + \beta \ln\left(\frac{I_t}{I_0}\right) + X_t,$$

$$\frac{dS_t}{S_t} = \alpha\, dt + \beta \frac{dI_t}{I_t} + dX_t \quad (4.120)$$

$$S_t = \text{stock}, \quad I_t = \text{ETF Index}$$

If the residual X_t is relatively positive (relative to some mean), one goes short the stock S and long the index because one believes X_t will revert back to its mean level. If the residual X_t is relatively negative, one goes long the stock S and short the index. To quantify what one means by "relatively positive," "relatively negative," and the "mean of the residual," one needs to calibrate a stationary stochastic process to the residuals and create a trading strategy based on this process. The process that is used for modeling the residual is a mean reverting OU process,

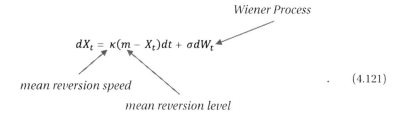

(4.121)

The second term of this equation should be familiar from geometric Brownian motion. The first term is the drift term. If X_t is less than its *mean reversion level m*, the drift term becomes positive, thereby pushing the next step closer to m on average (the next step is still random because of the second term). If X_t is greater than its *mean level m*, the drift term becomes negative pushing the next step on average downwards to m. As κ multiplies the distant between X_t and m, a large κ creates a large drift term, thereby making X_t approach m faster. Therefore, κ is called the *mean reversion speed*. The OU process has a simple solution and can be calibrated by linear regression. The solution, as derived in the "Ornstein-Uhlenbeck Process" section above (Equation 4.44), is

$$X_{t+\Delta t} = e^{-\kappa \Delta t} X_t + m(1-e^{-\kappa \Delta t}) + \sigma \int_t^{t+\Delta t} e^{-\kappa(t+\Delta t-s)} dW_s \quad . \tag{4.122}$$

It possesses the following moments (which are used for moment matching calibration):

$$E[X_t] = X_0 e^{-\kappa t} + m(1-e^{-\kappa t}) \qquad \mathrm{Var}[X_t] = \frac{\sigma^2}{2\kappa}[1-e^{-2\kappa t}] \quad , \tag{4.123}$$

with a covariance function for **s < t** given by

$$\mathrm{cov}(X_s, X_t) = E[X_s X_t] - E[X_s]E[X_t]$$
$$\mathrm{cov}(X_s, X_t) = \frac{\sigma^2}{2\kappa} e^{-\kappa(s+t)} \left[e^{2\kappa s} - 1 \right] \quad . \tag{4.124}$$

Equilibrium Statistics

In the limit of t going to ∞, one finds that the *equilibrium* probability distribution for the OU process is Gaussian with

$$E[X_t]_{eq} = m \qquad \sigma_{eq}^2 = \mathrm{Var}[X_t]_{eq} = \frac{\sigma^2}{2\kappa} \quad . \tag{4.125}$$

ETF Factor-Neutral Calibration and Trading Strategy

The steps to implement a *factor-neutral ETF statistical arbitrage strategy* between a sector ETF (say, XLK-Technology Sector ETF) and a stock (say, Sun Microsystems) are as follow.

CHAPTER 4 ▪ STOCHASTIC PROCESSES

Step 1: Create return time series for XLK and SUN,

$$r_t^{SUN} = \ln\left(\frac{S_t^{SUN}}{S_{t-1}^{SUN}}\right), \quad r_t^{XLK} = \ln\left(\frac{I_t^{XLK}}{I_{t-1}^{XLK}}\right) . \qquad (4.126)$$

Step 2: Perform linear regression for times $t = 1, 2, ..., 60$. The number of time steps used is an input and must be chosen carefully depending upon the temporal characteristics of the pair and the overall trading strategy. The number 60 is used for illustrative purposes:

$$r_t^{SUN} = \beta_0 + \beta r_t^{XLK} + \varepsilon_t, \quad t = 1, 2, ..., 60 . \qquad (4.127)$$

Step 3: Define the *residual process* as

$$X_t = \sum_{k=1}^{t} \varepsilon_k, \quad t = 1, 2, ..., 60 . \qquad (4.128)$$

The residual process is a running sum of the residuals at each of the 60 time steps. The last one is zero,

$$X_{60} = \sum_{k=1}^{60} \varepsilon_k = 0 , \qquad (4.129)$$

as a result of the regression in Step 2. One could have easily defined the residual process as a sum of less than 60 time step residuals.

Step 4: Perform linear regression on a *1-day-lagged residual process* for times $t = 1, 2, ..., 60$

$$X_{t+1} = a + b X_t + \zeta_{t+1}, \quad t = 1, 2, ..., 59 . \qquad (4.130)$$

By comparing this step to the OU process solution,

$$X_{t+\Delta t} = e^{-\kappa \Delta t} X_t + m(1 - e^{-\kappa \Delta t}) + \sigma \int_t^{t+\Delta t} e^{-\kappa(t+\Delta t - s)} dW_s , \qquad (4.131)$$

a calibration has been performed where OU parameters $\kappa, m,$ and σ are given related to empirical parameters $a, b,$ and $\text{var}(\zeta)$ by the following relations:

$$\begin{array}{ll} a = m(1 - e^{-\kappa \Delta t}) & \kappa = -\ln(b) \times 252 \\ b = e^{-\kappa \Delta t} & m = \dfrac{a}{1-b} \\ \text{var}(\zeta) = \sigma^2 \dfrac{1 - e^{-2\kappa \Delta t}}{2\kappa} & \sigma = \sqrt{\dfrac{\text{var}(\zeta) \times 2\kappa}{1 - b^2}} \end{array} \qquad (4.132)$$

Step 5: Determine the *s-score*. This is the key step where one defines the *trading signal* of the algorithm.

Using the equilibrium variance,

$$\sigma_{eq}^2 = \text{Var}[X_t]_{eq} = \frac{\sigma^2}{2\kappa} , \qquad (4.133)$$

it follows that

$$\sigma_{eq} = \sqrt{\frac{\text{var}(\zeta)}{1-b^2}} \quad . \quad (4.134)$$

The following s-score is the statistical measure that indicates how far the residual has moved from its mean. Its level determines whether one goes long or short a stock. The s-score is theoretically defined as

$$s = \frac{X(t)-m}{\sigma_{eq}} \quad . \quad (4.135)$$

The s-score measures the distance from the mean reversion level m of the co-integrated residual $X(t)$ as illustrated in Figure 4-9. It measures how far a stock has moved from its equilibrium level with respect to its ETF pair. It has been scaled by the long-term standard deviation σ_{eq} of the residual process similar to that of the traditional Sharpe ratio of investment returns.

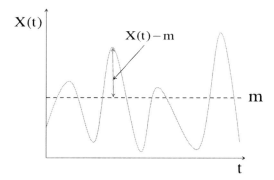

Figure 4-9. *A distance measure for going long or short in the OU framework*

Finally, the trading signal strategy is given by a set of trading rules relative to the s-score trading signal. The whole strategy comes down to these rules (the numbers are just sample levels and are proprietary for any real strategy):

$$\begin{array}{lll} \text{buy to open if} & s < \bar{s}_{bo} & \bar{s}_{bo} = -1.75 \\ \text{sell to close if} & s > \bar{s}_{sc} & \bar{s}_{sc} = -0.25 \\ \text{sell to open if} & s > \bar{s}_{so} & \bar{s}_{so} = 2.00 \\ \text{buy to close if} & s < \bar{s}_{bc} & \bar{s}_{bc} = 1.25 \end{array} \quad (4.136)$$

"Buy to open" means going long one unit of stock (SUN) and going short β units of the ETF XLK to open a trade.

"Sell to close" means going reverse the "buy to open" trade (closing this trade).

"Sell to open" means going short one unit of stock (SUN) and going long β units of the ETF XLK to open a trade.

"Buy to close" means going reverse the "sell to open" trade (closing this trade).

These rules, graphically depicted in Figure 4-10, must be backtested rigorously. Note that the levels where one closes trades are not zero, as one might naively expect. One cannot wait for the residual to back exactly to the mean; instead, it affords some cushioning when getting out of a trade, in case the market moves too quickly.

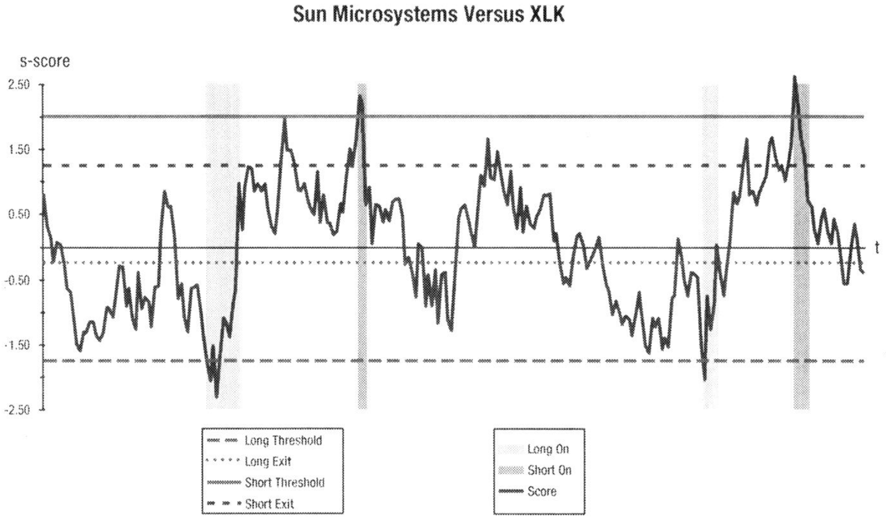

Figure 4-10. *Evolution of an s-score in 2002 and the corresponding long short trades*

Including the Drift Term

In the calibration in the preceding section, the drift term αdt from equation (4.120) was not included. This is often the case because it is small compared to the residual term dX. Occasionally, however, a stock may have an expected excess return above the market (for instance, a star stock such as Apple). In such a case, one can capture this drift in the s-score as follows. By combining (4.120) with the OU process (4.121), the full residual drift of the beta-adjusted process is

$$\alpha dt + \kappa(m - X_t)dt \quad . \tag{4.137}$$

This can be rewritten as

$$\kappa\left(\frac{\alpha}{\kappa} + m - X_t\right)dt = \kappa\left(\frac{\alpha}{\kappa} - \sigma_{eq}s\right)dt \quad . \tag{4.138}$$

Thus, the *drift-adjusted modified s-score* is given by

$$S_{mod} = s - \frac{\alpha}{\kappa\sigma_{eq}} . \quad (4.139)$$

Another way to see this is to write

$$\frac{dS_t}{S_t} = \beta \frac{dI_t}{I_t} + d\varepsilon_t , \quad (4.140)$$

where

$$d\varepsilon_t = \alpha dt + dX_t . \quad (4.141)$$

What is the conditional expectation of this residual term?

$$E[d\varepsilon_t | X_t] = \alpha dt + \kappa(m - X_t)dt$$
$$= \alpha dt - \kappa\sigma_{eq} s dt \quad (4.142)$$
$$= -\kappa\sigma_{eq}\left(s - \frac{\alpha}{\kappa\sigma_{eq}}\right)dt = -\kappa\sigma_{eq} S_{mod} dt .$$

Clearly, the s-score gets reduced by the residual drift. For instance, a relatively positive s-score may indicate a shorting of the stock. Yet if this stock has a significant positive drift with respect to the index, the s-score should be reduced by this drift, which is what the modified s-score accomplishes.

Hints for Constructing Market-Neutral Portfolios

A statistical arbitrage strategy trades not just one specific long-short pair but many such pairs. Figure 4-10 indicates that the specific trade of SUN versus XLK is off most of the time. Therefore, one needs many such pairs in order to create a successful strategy. The statistical nature of this strategy comes both from using a statistical model and from trading many pairs such that, on average statistically, the strategy makes money. When creating a portfolio of pair trades, the following should be kept in mind:

- Use a large diversified universe of traded securities (for example, use as many non-overlapping sector ETFs as can be found).
- Calculate s-scores for all pairs and trade only those with the best signals.
- Monitor the closing of trades carefully via the s-scores. (Getting out of trades at the right time is often the real secret of making money.)
- Maintain sector neutrality. (Don't ignore the betas to the ETFs.)
- Use only modest risk capital leverage—say, 2 (such that for $1 dollar of risk capital, one can go long $2 and short $2).
- Monitor the volatility of the net trading strategy. Many clients need a trading strategy with an annualized volatility of 10–15%.

The Rolling NAV Equation

To provide a backtest of a trading strategy, one needs to perform a time-evolution of the P&L of the net trading strategy. One simplified method for doing this is to use the following equation:

$$E_{n+1} = E_n + rE_n \Delta t + \sum_{i=1}^{N} Q_{i,n} R_{i,n} - \left(\sum_{i=1}^{N} Q_{i,n} \right) r\Delta t - \sum_{i=1}^{N} |Q_{i,n+1} - Q_{i,n}| \chi \quad , \tag{4.143}$$

$$Q_{i,n} \propto \Lambda E_n \xi_{i,n} \quad , \tag{4.144}$$

where

> E_n : Equity at the beginning of period n
> r : Fed Funds or Libor
> Δt : the time (in years) within a period
> $Q_{i,n}$: dollars invested in the i-th stock / index at the beginning of period n (4.145)
> $R_{i,n}$: total return of i-th stock / index over the period n
> χ : bid – offer spread and transaction cost
> Λ : Leverage Coefficient = 2 * max fraction of equity in any one position
> $\xi_{i,n}$: 0, +1, −1, depending upon position (none, long, short)

This is a very "risk capital"-type formula. It tries to calculate the return on equity (cash or cash-like instruments which constitute the initial risk capital E_0) that the strategy earns over time. It is fully return-based. By using the *total return* of a stock or index, it is including dividends that are earned when going long (or paid when going short). In this equation, Λ includes a leverage of 2 and a diversification component that limits the amount of risk capital that can be allocated to any one position. It is just an approximation inasmuch as the leverage can change depending on the position and ongoing margin calls. Furthermore, risk capital is not necessarily equally distributed among all positions. Also, the fourth term assumes that one gets the same interest rate from proceeds from a short sale as the interest rate one pays to borrow money. This is never true and depends upon the margining agreements set up for the strategy (such as the prime brokerage used). Nonetheless, this equation has minimally all the necessary terms to calculate the P&L of the strategy.

An Example of a Statistical Arbitrage Trading Strategy Pitch

An example follows of a statistical arbitrage trading strategy pitch, called *[Stat Arb]*, that describes the features of the strategy in a manner than may be suitable for investors.

[Stat Arb] aims to capture the mean reversion of large-cap US equities across all market regimes while maintaining sector neutrality.

- [Stat Arb] is a medium-frequency long/short systematic trading strategy that monetizes the mean reversion of S&P 500 stocks to sector ETF spreads.
- Liquidity
  - [Stat Arb] trades only S&P 500 constituents and Sector SPDR ETFs, which are widely viewed to be liquid.
  - Throughout the hypothetical backtesting period from 2000 to 2010, [Stat Arb] maintained an average money market balance of 93% of equity.
- Transparency
  - [Stat Arb] employs a simple and transparent factor model developed by Avellaneda and Lee (2010).
  - Pricing of the trading universe is transparent.
  - Daily NAVs are available.
- Risk Control
  - Daily hedging ensures sector neutrality with respect to nine sectors.
  - Leverage is modest (maximum: 1.50×).
  - Drawdown, skewness, and kurtosis characteristics are excellent.
  - [Stat Arb] has low correlation to the S&P 500.

[Stat Arb] has a significantly improved risk/return profile on a hypothetical historical basis, as indicated in Figure 4-11.

CHAPTER 4 ■ STOCHASTIC PROCESSES

Annualized Monthly Return Statistics (01/2000 to 12/2009)	[Stat Arb]	S&P 500 Total Return	HFRI	HFRI Market Neutral
Mean	13.5%	0.4%	6.5%	4.2%
Volatility	5.7%	16.1%	6.9%	3.1%
Sharpe Ratio[1]	1.8	-0.2	0.5	0.3
Correlation to S&P 500	8.4%	100.0%	73.9%	5.5%
Max Drawdown	2.9%	50.9%	21.4%	9.2%
Up Months (out of 120)	99	70	81	86
Skewness	1.1	-0.6	-0.6	-0.3
Up Kurtosis	8.7	3.3	5.7	5.9
Down Kurtosis	3.6	4.9	7.9	6.3

Source: Bloomberg, Hedge Fund Research (HFRI and HFRI Market Neutral)

(1) Sharpe Ratios are calculated using 3-month US Treasury yields as the risk-free benchmark
(2) All figures calculated using end-of-month data

Figure 4-11. *[Stat Arb] return statistics and comparable markets indices*

[Stat Arb] exhibits a superior risk-return return profile on a hypothetical historical basis as indicated in Figure 4-12.

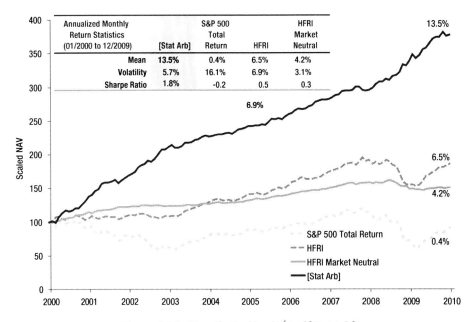

Figure 4-12. *Hypothetical backtest of [Stat Arb]*

The trading universe is widely viewed to be liquid and represents a diverse range of market sectors and geographic exposures.

[Stat Arb] trades the constituents of the S&P 500, which are generally well capitalized and highly liquid.

[Stat Arb] hedges sector risk daily by allocating to the nine Sector SPDR ETFs in Figure 4-13. These are well-known benchmarks that provide both transparency and adequate liquidity.

Sector	ETF	Number of Constituents	Indicative ETF Spread
Consumer Discretionary	XLY	81	3 bps
Consumer Staples	XLP	41	4 bps
Energy	XLE	38	2 bps
Financial	XLF	79	7 bps
Healthcare	XLV	52	3 bps
Industrial	XLI	56	3 bps
Materials	XLB	32	3 bps
Technology	XLK	85	5 bps
Utilities	XLU	36	3 bps

Figure 4-13. The universe of traded assets of [Stat Arb] and bid-offer spreads

Excess cash is allocated to a money market component.

- The money market component accrues at the Fed Funds rate on an Actual/360 day count convention.

- A fixed 0.95% adjustment factor, notional transaction costs, and leverage costs are all deducted from the money market component.

Filters

[Stat Arb] employs several filters and modifications to augment signals and control risk.

- κ is the speed of mean reversion, and τ is the characteristic time scale for mean reversion of the process. [Stat Arb] enter trades only when the expected mean-reversion time scale is low and exits trades if κ falls past a critical threshold,

$$\tau = \frac{1}{\kappa}$$
$$\tau < \tau_{max}$$
(4.146)

- For instance, the estimation window for calibration is 60 days. Therefore, one chooses a mean reversion time of less than half of this time, such that

$$\tau_{max} = \frac{30}{252}$$
$$\kappa > \frac{252}{30} \quad . \quad (4.147)$$

- [Stat Arb] incorporates *volume information* by looking at the daily trading volume and comparing it to the 10-day rolling average. This amplifies the s-score on low-volume days and reduces the s-score on high-volume days. This prevents the model from detecting high-volume true news events (such as M&A announcements) as anomalous excursions and trading against them:

10 Day Moving Average $\rightarrow$
$$\langle V \rangle_t^{avg} = \frac{1}{10} \sum_{i=t-10}^{t-1} V_i$$
$$\hat{r}_t = r_t \left[\frac{\langle V \rangle_t^{avg}}{V_t} \right] \quad . \quad (4.148)$$

- Finally, [Stat Arb] uses realized correlation as a proxy for systematic risk. When systematic factors explain a large portion of returns, [Stat Arb] has little predictive power and does not trade the risky name.

Figure 4-14 illustrates the effects of these filters on the hypothetical backtest of [Stat Arb].

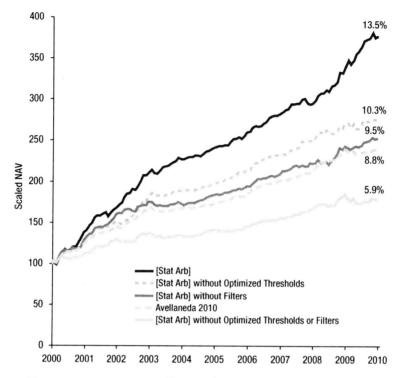

Figure 4-14. *Comparison of [Stat Arb] with and without certain filters*

i. [Stat Arb] employs several filters and an asymmetric entry-exit rule.
ii. [Stat Arb without optimized thresholds] uses simple symmetric entry-exit rules.
   - Enter trades when the co-integrated spread is more than 1.5 standard deviations from its theoretical mean.
   - Exit trades when the spread converges to within 0.5 standard deviations.
iii. [Stat Arb without filters] takes on riskier trades.
   - It does not normalize scores to reduce model bias.
   - It does not require fast mean reversion.
   - It does not consider volume data.
   - It does not avoid systemically risky stocks.

Appendix A. Black-Scholes with Holes

This appendix gives a brief derivation of the standard Black-Scholes European option formula. Note that the whole derivation is based on several assumptions that are often not true—that is, *holes*. These holes include the following:

1. Perfect delta hedging with no hedge slippage. This means that a delta-hedged portfolio Π is riskless and therefore earns a risk-free rate r over a short period of time (clearly not true when one has high skew or kurtosis),

$$\Pi = C - \Delta S \tag{4.149}$$

$$\Delta \Pi = r \Pi \Delta t \quad . \tag{4.150}$$

2. No transaction costs or bid-offer spread (obviously not true)
3. Instantaneous hedging (often not true)
4. Infinite liquidity (obviously not true)

These false assumptions lead to the so-called *risk-neutral* paradigm, wherein effectively the asset-specific mean return μ for the geometric Brownian motion process is replaced by a continuously compounded risk-free rate r (see Glasserman [2003] and Shreve [2008B] for deeper mathematical arguments for this replacement):

$$S_T = S \exp\left[\left(r - \frac{\sigma^2}{2}\right)T + \sigma W_T\right] \quad . \tag{4.151}$$

Here one can make the usual replacement $W_T \to \sqrt{T}\epsilon$. The corresponding log returns of the underlying asset are normally distributed as follows,

$$\ln \frac{S_T}{S} \sim N[\left(r - \frac{\sigma^2}{2}\right)T, \sigma^2 T] \quad . \tag{4.152}$$

Recall that a normal variable can always be created from a $N(0,1)$ variable ϵ. Therefore,

$$z = \ln \frac{S_T}{S} = \left(r - \frac{\sigma^2}{2}\right)T + \sigma\sqrt{T}\epsilon \tag{4.153}$$

and

$$S_T = S \exp(z) = S \exp\left[\left(r - \frac{\sigma^2}{2}\right)T + \sigma\sqrt{T}\epsilon\right] \quad . \tag{4.154}$$

One can also show that this theory reduces everything down to one discounted expected value of an option payoff (Glasserman [2003], Shreve [2004B]). For European call options, one has (using a discount factor of the form $\exp(-rT)$)

$$C(S,K,T) = e^{-rT} E[\text{Max}(S_T - K, 0)] = e^{-rT} \int_{-\infty}^{\infty} \text{Max}(S_T - K, 0) f(S_T) dS_T \tag{4.155}$$

and using (4.154),

$$C(S,K,T) = e^{-rT} \int_{-\infty}^{\infty} \text{Max}\left(S\exp\left[\left(r-\frac{\sigma^2}{2}\right)T + \sigma\sqrt{T}\epsilon\right] - K, 0 \right) \frac{e^{-\epsilon^2/2}}{\sqrt{2\pi}} d\epsilon \quad . \tag{4.156}$$

At this stage, the constraint on ϵ that satisfies the Max condition is needed,

$$S\exp\left[\left(r-\frac{\sigma^2}{2}\right)T + \sigma\sqrt{T}\epsilon\right] > K \tag{4.157}$$

$$\exp\left[\left(r-\frac{\sigma^2}{2}\right)T + \sigma\sqrt{T}\epsilon\right] > \frac{K}{S} \tag{4.158}$$

$$\left[\left(r-\frac{\sigma^2}{2}\right)T + \sigma\sqrt{T}\epsilon\right] > \ln\frac{K}{S} \tag{4.159}$$

$$\sigma\sqrt{T}\epsilon > \ln\frac{K}{S} - \left(r-\frac{\sigma^2}{2}\right)T \tag{4.160}$$

$$\epsilon > \frac{\ln\frac{K}{S} - \left(r-\frac{\sigma^2}{2}\right)T}{\sigma\sqrt{T}} \tag{4.161}$$

$$\epsilon > -\left[\frac{-\ln\frac{K}{S} + \left(r-\frac{\sigma^2}{2}\right)T}{\sigma\sqrt{T}}\right] \tag{4.162}$$

$$\epsilon > -\left[\frac{\ln\frac{S}{K} + \left(r-\frac{\sigma^2}{2}\right)T}{\sigma\sqrt{T}}\right] = -d_2 \quad . \tag{4.163}$$

Now, one can eliminate the Max from the integral using the above condition,

$$C(S,K,T) = e^{-rT} \int_{-d_2}^{\infty} \left(S\exp\left[\left(r-\frac{\sigma^2}{2}\right)T + \sigma\sqrt{T}\epsilon\right] - K \right) \frac{e^{-\epsilon^2/2}}{\sqrt{2\pi}} d\epsilon \quad . \tag{4.164}$$

Using the fact that the Gaussian distribution is symmetric, one can flip the limits of the integrand, keeping in mind that the sign in front of the ϵ will change because it is an odd function.

CHAPTER 4 ■ STOCHASTIC PROCESSES

$$C(S,K,T) = e^{-rT} \int_{-\infty}^{d_2} \left(S\exp\left[\left(r - \frac{\sigma^2}{2}\right)T - \sigma\sqrt{T}\epsilon\right] - K \right) \frac{e^{-\epsilon^2/2}}{\sqrt{2\pi}} d\epsilon \qquad (4.165)$$

$$C(S,K,T) = e^{-rT} \int_{-\infty}^{d_2} S\exp\left[\left(r - \frac{\sigma^2}{2}\right)T - \sigma\sqrt{T}\epsilon\right] \frac{e^{-\epsilon^2/2}}{\sqrt{2\pi}} d\epsilon - e^{-rT}KN(d_2) \qquad (4.166)$$

$$C(S,K,T) = S \int_{-\infty}^{d_2} \exp\left[-\frac{(\epsilon + \sigma\sqrt{T})^2}{2}\right] \frac{1}{\sqrt{2\pi}} d\epsilon - e^{-rT}KN(d_2) \quad . \qquad (4.167)$$

Making the following substitution

$$\tilde{\epsilon} = \epsilon + \sigma\sqrt{T}$$
$$d\tilde{\epsilon} = d\epsilon \qquad (4.168)$$
$$d_1 = d_2 + \sigma\sqrt{T} \quad ,$$

one is left with

$$C(S,K,T) = SN(d_1) - e^{-rT}KN(d_2) \quad . \qquad (4.169)$$

Appendix B. Moment Matching and Binomial Trees

A *binomial tree* is a discrete approximation to a stochastic process. Much like MC simulation, the tree represents possible asset prices in the future. It is much simpler than MC simulation, but such tree approximations do not exist for a general Ito process and are sometimes too simple for risk management purposes. For a detailed discussion, see Shreve [2004A]. Figure 4-15 shows the first step of a binomial tree where the stock price can either go up to a level Su with probability p, or down to a level Sd with probability $1 - p$.

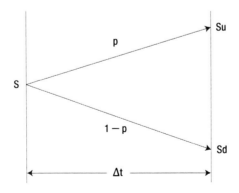

Figure 4-15. *One step of a binomial tree*

One has three unknown parameters to calibrate, p, u, and d. The standard risk-neutral binomial tree is calibrated by moment matching the mean and variance of a risk-neutral lognormal process (the other moments, such as skew or kurtosis, are negligible as shown in (4.67) and (4.69)). The moment matching derivation is given below. It should be pointed out that the exact formulas produced here are rarely seen in the finance literature (only approximate formulas are given). Recall that the exact solution of a lognormal stock process is given by

$$S_T = S\exp\left[\left(r - \frac{\sigma^2}{2}\right)T + \sigma W_T\right] \quad , \tag{4.170}$$

with moments

$$E[S_T] = S\exp(rT) \quad . \tag{4.171}$$

and

$$\text{Var}[S_T] = S^2 \exp(2rT)[\exp(\sigma^2 T) - 1] \quad . \tag{4.172}$$

Unfortunately, with three unknown parameters to calibrate, one can only set two moment matching conditions—one for the mean and one for the variance:

$$S\exp(r\Delta t) = p(Su) + (1-p)(Sd) \quad , \tag{4.173}$$

$$\begin{aligned} S^2 \exp(2r\Delta t)[\exp(\sigma^2 \Delta t) - 1] &= \text{Var}[S_{\Delta t}] \\ &= E[S_{\Delta t}^2] - (E[S_{\Delta t}])^2 \\ &= p(Su)^2 + (1-p)(Sd)^2 - (S\exp(r\Delta t))^2 \end{aligned} \quad . \tag{4.174}$$

These moment matching conditions become two equations with three unknowns:

$$\begin{aligned} \exp(r\Delta t) &= pu + (1-p)d \\ \exp[(2r+\sigma^2)\Delta t] &= p(u)^2 + (1-p)(d)^2 \end{aligned} \quad . \tag{4.175}$$

From these, one gets two equations for the up probability p,

$$\begin{aligned} p &= \frac{\exp(r\Delta t) - d}{u - d} \\ p &= \frac{\exp[(2r+\sigma^2)\Delta t]) - d^2}{u^2 - d^2} \\ &= \frac{\exp[(2r+\sigma^2)\Delta t]) - d^2}{(u+d)(u-d)} \end{aligned} \quad . \tag{4.176}$$

To solve these, one usually adds an *ad hoc* constraint. A common one is

$$u = \frac{1}{d} \quad . \tag{4.177}$$

Equating the above equations for p gives

$$\frac{\exp[(2r+\sigma^2)\Delta t])-d^2}{(u+d)} = \exp(r\Delta t)-d \quad . \tag{4.178}$$

Using the extra *ad hoc* constraint provides a quadratic equation for d,

$$\exp[(2r+\sigma^2)\Delta t])-d^2 = (\exp(r\Delta t)-d)\left(\frac{1}{d}-d\right)$$

$$= \frac{\exp(r\Delta t)}{d} + d\exp(r\Delta t) - 1 - d^2 \tag{4.179}$$

$$d\exp[(2r+\sigma^2)\Delta t]) = \exp(r\Delta t) + d^2\exp(r\Delta t) - d \tag{4.180}$$

$$d^2 - \{\exp[(r+\sigma^2)\Delta t] + \exp[-r\Delta t]\}d + 1 = 0 \quad . \tag{4.181}$$

One can solve this exactly using the standard quadratic formula,

$$ax^2 + bx + c = 0$$

$$x = \frac{-b \pm \sqrt{b^2 - 4ac}}{2a} \quad . \tag{4.182}$$

The explicit solution is

$$d = \frac{\{\exp[(r+\sigma^2)\Delta t] + \exp[-r\Delta t]\} - \sqrt{\{\exp[(r+\sigma^2)\Delta t] + \exp[-r\Delta t]\}^2 - 4}}{2} \quad . \tag{4.183}$$

p and u then follow from (4.176) and (4.177). It is easy to show that u also satisfies the same quadratic equation with the *plus sign* solution. The well-known *approximate* solution can be derived from the above exact solution. Expand the b term above to the first power of Δt,

$$b \approx -[1 + r\Delta t + \sigma^2 \Delta t + 1 - r\Delta t] = -[2 + \sigma^2 \Delta t] \tag{4.184}$$

$$d = \frac{-b - \sqrt{b^2 - 4}}{2} \approx \frac{[2+\sigma^2\Delta t] - \sqrt{4 + 4\sigma^2\Delta t - 4}}{2} \tag{4.185}$$

$$d \approx \frac{[2+\sigma^2\Delta t] - 2\sigma\sqrt{\Delta t}}{2} = 1 - \sigma\sqrt{\Delta t} + \frac{1}{2}\sigma^2\Delta t \quad . \tag{4.186}$$

This expression appears to have the first three terms of a exponential series, and one can set

$$d \approx \exp[-\sigma\sqrt{\Delta t}] \quad . \tag{4.187}$$

CHAPTER 4 ■ STOCHASTIC PROCESSES

Therefore, a binomial tree can be approximately moment-matched to a lognormal process using the expressions,

$$d = e^{-\sigma\sqrt{\Delta t}}, u = e^{\sigma\sqrt{\Delta t}}, p = \frac{e^{r\Delta t} - d}{u - d} \quad . \tag{4.188}$$

Using this tree, one can price options in a risk-neutral framework. Consider a two-step tree for a call option struck at K as shown in Figure 4-16. In the risk-neutral paradigm where delta hedging is miraculously perfect, the call prices at each time node are calculated working one's way backwards in time as follows. At maturity time T, the call price at each node is given by

$$C(T) = MAX[S_T - K, 0] \quad . \tag{4.189}$$

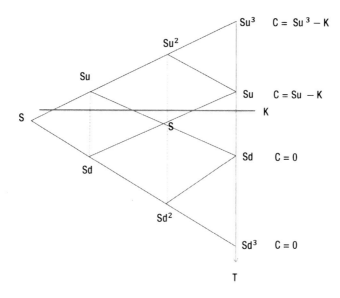

Figure 4-16. *Two-step binomial tree for a call option*

At $T-1$, the call price at each node is given by

$$C(T-1) = e^{-r\Delta t}[pC_T^u + (1-p)C_T^d] \quad . \tag{4.190}$$

For the three nodes at time $T-1$, one has

$$\begin{aligned} C(T-1) &= e^{-r\Delta t}[p(Su^3 - K) + (1-p)(Su - K)] \\ C(T-1) &= e^{-r\Delta t}[p(Su - K) + (1-p)(0)] = e^{-r\Delta t}[p(Su - K)] \\ C(T-1) &= 0 \end{aligned} \tag{4.191}$$

CHAPTER 4 ■ STOCHASTIC PROCESSES

For the two nodes at time $T-2$, one has

$$C(T-2) = e^{-2r\Delta t}\left(p[p(Su^3-K)+(1-p)(Su-K)]+(1-p)[p(Su-K)]\right) \quad (4.192)$$
$$C(T-2) = e^{-2r\Delta t}[p^2(Su-K)]$$

Finally, the call price at inception is

$$C(0) = e^{-3r\Delta t}p\left(p[p(Su^3-K)+(1-p)(Su-K)]+(1-p)[p(Su-K)]\right) + e^{-3r\Delta t}(1-p)[p^2(Su-K)] \quad (4.193)$$

Problems

Problem 4-1. Create a Brownian Motion Process for Stock Returns Using Monte Carlo Simulations in Excel

1. The inputs are the annualized μ, σ, and S_0 that must be calibrated to an index (say, SX5E). Because of the choice of discretization in (4.71), one should use simple historical returns (as opposed to log),

$$r_{t+1} = \frac{\Delta S_t}{S_t} = \frac{S_{t+1}-S_t}{S_t} \quad (4.194)$$

Since $E[r_t] = \mu \Delta t$ and $\Delta t = \frac{1}{252}$, μ is calibrated as

$$\rightarrow \mu = \text{Average(daily simple returns)} \bullet 252 \quad (4.195)$$

Also as $E[(r_t - \bar{r})^2] = \sigma^2 \Delta t$, the volatility is calibrated as

$$\rightarrow \sigma = \text{STDEV(daily simple returns)} \bullet \sqrt{252} \quad (4.196)$$

S_0 will be the last available price for the index in question.

2. Use the prescription in (4.72) to generate 65,000 paths for 21 time steps.

3. *Calibration and Generation Check.* For the 21st day return, the Mean, Stdev, and Kurt should be close to the inputs, with Kurt = 3 for Brownian Motion. The 21st day return will be

$$r_{21} = \frac{S_{21}^{MC} - S_0}{S_0} \quad (4.197)$$

Here $\Delta t = \frac{21}{252}$. Therefore,

$$\rightarrow \mu^{MC} = \text{Average(21 day simple MC returns)} \bullet \frac{252}{21} \approx \mu \quad (4.198)$$

$$\to \sigma^{MC} = \text{STDEV}(21\text{ day simple MC returns}) \cdot \sqrt{\frac{252}{21}} \approx \sigma \quad . \quad (4.199)$$

The level of convergence between the simulated μ^{MC} and σ^{MC} and the input ones is determined by the quality of the random numbers and the number of paths generated. A detailed discussion on MC simulations and convergence can be found in Glasserman [2003].

4. For the 21st MC return, one can calculate the 99% and 99.9% VaR and CVaR as described in Chapter 3.

Problem 4-2. Ito's Lemma

Assume that W_t is Brownian Motion. Use Ito's Lemma to find $df(t, W_t)$.

1. $f(t, W_t) = e^{\frac{t}{2}} \cos(W_t)$
2. $f(t, W_t) = [W_t + t] e^{-W_t - \frac{t}{2}}$

Problem 4-3. Calibrate a GARCH(1,1) Process for SX5E

1. Find μ from $\bar{r} = \mu \Delta t$ where $\Delta t = \dfrac{1}{252}$.
2. Find σ from $E[(r_t - \bar{r})^2] = \sigma^2 \Delta t$.
3. Find the recent 21-day annualized volatility: $E[(r_t - \bar{r})^2 \,|\, \text{Last 21 Days}] = \sigma_0^2 \Delta t$.
4. Use the methodology described in this chapter to calibrate α and β.
5. Provide a graph of the theoretical versus empirical autocorrelation fit as in Figure 4-7.
6. Provide a graph of the term structure of volatility using (4.113).

Problem 4-4. Create a GARCH(1,1) Simulator in Excel

- Use the calibrated parameters of Problem 4-3.
- Generate 65,000 paths for 100 days.
- One must prove that the resulting model creates MC paths with a kurtosis of the 100th-day MC return that approximately matches the inputs based on the calibrated parameters α and β. The match depends upon the convergence of the MC simulation. The more paths one has, the better the convergence.

Problem 4-5. Volume Adjustment for Pairs Trading for MCD versus XLY

Perform a rolling 60-day linear regression of volume adjusted returns of MCD versus XLY (MCD: McDonald's, XLY: Consumer Discretionary Sector SPDR ETF),

$$\hat{r}_t^{MCD} = \beta_0 + \beta \hat{r}_t^{XLY} + \varepsilon_t, \quad t = 1, 2, \ldots, 60, \quad (4.200)$$

where

$$\hat{r}_t^{MCD} = \ln\left(\frac{S_t^{MCD}}{S_{t-1}^{MCD}}\right)\left[\frac{\langle V^S \rangle_t^{avg}}{V_t^S}\right], \quad \hat{r}_t^{XLY} = \ln\left(\frac{I_t^{XLY}}{I_{t-1}^{XLY}}\right)\left[\frac{\langle V^I \rangle_t^{avg}}{V_t^I}\right] \quad (4.201)$$

$$10 \text{ Day Moving Average} \rightarrow \langle V \rangle_t^{avg} = \frac{1}{10}\sum_{i=t-10}^{t-1} V_i \quad .$$

References

Avellaneda, Marco, and Lee, Jeong-Hyun. 2010. "Statistical Arbitrage in the US Equities Market." *Quantitative Finance*, 10, 1–22.

Glasserman, Paul. 2003. *Monte Carlo Methods in Financial Engineering*. New York: Springer.

Kloeden, Peter E., and Platen, Eckhard. 1999. *Numerical Solution of Stochastic Differential Equations*. Berlin: Springer.

Shreve, Steven. 2004A. *Stochastic Calculus for Finance I*. New York: Springer.

Shreve, Steven. 2004B. *Stochastic Calculus for Finance II*. New York: Springer.

CHAPTER 5

Optimal Hedging Monte Carlo Methods

Leverage in the financial markets is one of the oldest techniques to increase one's gains in an investment. It has also has lead to colossal losses and defaults. Leverage within an investment exists when an investor is exposed to a higher capital base than his or her original capital inlay. The margin mechanism of buying futures, as explained in Chapter 1, is a typical example of leverage. One posts margin of 5%–15% of the futures contract value but is exposed to 100% of the gains or losses of the notional amount of the futures contract. Exchanges will reduce the risk of this leverage in futures contracts by remargining daily using margin calls. Derivatives securities are another way to increase leverage. The call and put options described in Chapter 1 are standard ways to go long or short an underlying asset using leverage. A call option costing $5 and expiring $10 in the money creates a 200% return on investment. If this call expires out of the money, the loss is 100%.

The stylized empirical facts of *fat tails, term structure of moments, autocorrelation of squared returns, volatility clustering*, and the *leverage effect* (not to be confused with the more generic leverage being discussed here) are brought to the forefront when dealing with leveraged financial products. For instance, say an investor has bought an unlevered stock position worth $100. If this stock drops by 20% in one day (a fat-tailed event), the investor has lost 20% of their investment, which is a substantial but not huge loss. If on the other hand, the investor had spent $100 on at-the-money call options, the stock drop would have had a much larger effect on the marked-to-market value of these levered products (the exact loss depending on time to expiration, volatility, etc.). If these options were close to expiry, the loss could have approached 100%. Yet in the Black-Scholes world alluded to in Chapter 4, none of these stylized facts were taken into account when pricing options. The *optimal hedging Monte Carlo* (OHMC) methodology presented here is a framework to allow for realistic option pricing without the largely inaccurate assumptions needed in the standard *risk-neutral pricing* framework.

Philosophically, the OHMC method has the following scenario in mind when pricing a derivative security. Suppose someone undertakes to trade derivatives on his own.

- What's the first thing this trader will need? *Risk capital.*
- Who will be the investor (the provider of risk capital)?
- What will be the required return on this risk capital?

One of the main goals of the OHMC method is to quantify the question of risk capital using a fully simulated P&L distribution of a hedging strategy for a derivative security. This chapter deals with the question of what exactly is a hedging strategy.

Dynamic Hedging and Replication

Dynamic hedging is the periodic hedging of a nonlinear financial instrument (i.e., an option) with linear instruments like spot instruments and futures or with other nonlinear instruments. The amount of the linear hedge is generically called the *delta*. The deltas of the nonlinear position are calculated and executed using either linear or other nonlinear instruments. The original nonlinear position along with its delta hedge yields an instantaneous zero delta risk position. For instance, a short call option is delta hedged with a long position in the underlying asset. A short put option is delta hedged with a short position in the underlying. The direction of these hedges can be assessed by the direction of the payoff the hedger is trying to simulate or replicate with the chosen linear hedge. A sold call position is a levered long position in the underlying for the holder and therefore the seller must also go long in order to replicate its payoff. A sold put position exposes the seller to a levered short position in the underlying and therefore, he must also go short in order to replicate the investment he has sold. However, as the underlying asset value changes, the delta of the nonlinear position changes, indicating its implied leverage, while that of a linear hedge stays the same. Therefore, the deltas no longer offset, and the linear hedge has to be adjusted (increased or decreased) to restore the offsetting delta hedge. This process of continually adjusting a linear position to maintain a delta hedge is one aspect of dynamic hedging. Dynamic hedging also refers to the hedging of the changing volatility exposure of an option (called vega hedging) or the changing of the delta position itself (gamma hedging). These types of hedges may involve other derivatives (see [Bouchaud, 2003]). Figure 5-1 indicates that geometrically, dynamic replication is attempting to replicate the curved option value with tangent lines that represent the deltas.

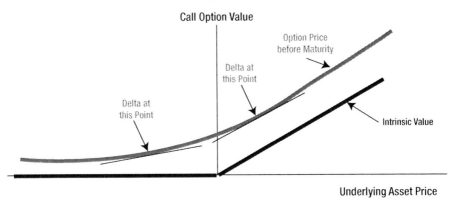

Figure 5-1. The changing delta of a call option

Standard option pricing methodologies, such as risk-neutral pricing and Black-Scholes formulas, assume that dynamic hedging works perfectly and therefore the hedger has effectively replicated the option payoff with linear instruments. They make assumptions,

CHAPTER 5 ■ OPTIMAL HEDGING MONTE CARLO METHODS

which are largely inaccurate, of instantaneous perfect delta-hedging with no friction costs: no bid-offer spread, no transaction cost, no liquidity premium, no hedge slippage. Hedge slippage is one of the biggest risks when trading options. In real-life delta hedging, the hedge is rarely perfect and cannot be changed continuously. Therefore, losses may occur between discrete delta hedging points. This can clearly be seen in Figure 5-1 where a large move in the underlying can change the slope of a tangent line substantially. This hedge slippage needs to be quantified, and this is exactly what the OHMC method provides. For those who believe that continuous-slippage free delta hedging is a reasonable approximation, a five-day minute-by-minute tick graph of the S&P 500 in August 2011 (shown in Figure 5-2) should convince them otherwise.

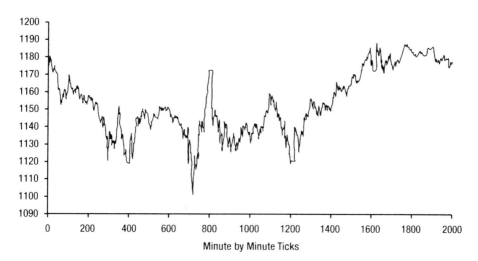

Figure 5-2. *A five-day minute-by-minute tick graph of the S&P 500. The return kurtosis is 13.06*

Therefore, the main points to consider are as follows:

- Perfect replication is not possible.
  - Excess kurtosis (jumpiness) in asset returns is the rule rather than the exception (see Figure 5-2).
  - Liquidity is not a panacea.
    - Even if one could hedge every tick, the kurtosis of asset returns can be high (i.e., 13.06 in Figure 5-3).
    - The underlying asset can be illiquid: hedging intervals can be on the order of hours, days, or months (hedge funds).
  - Significant residual risks in terms of hedge slippage exist.
- One needs to address hedging directly and evaluate the attempted cost of replication and compensation for irreducible risks.

197

- Derivative prices are viewed as a synthesis of average hedging costs plus a risk premium for unhedgable risks associated with illiquidity and high return kurtosis.

- The OHMC method focuses on the cost of derivatives replication by explicitly analyzing the mechanics of dynamic hedging.

- The OHMC method estimates
  - The average hedging cost
  - The hedge slippage distribution
  - A P&L volatility minimizing hedge ratio

- The role of asset kurtosis and volatility clustering of asset returns may be assessed by various models, such as
  - GARCH(1,1)
  - EGARCH, APARCH, etc.

- To assess the risk capital associated with a derivatives trade, a specific solvency target using the P&L distribution (tail losses) will be defined.

The key differences between the standard risk-neutral approach and the OHMC approach are summarized in Table 5-1.

Table 5-1. Differences in approach

Characteristics	Risk-Neutral Approach	OHMC
Hedging and replication	Assumes perfect replication. There is no mention of residual risks such as hedge slippage. Assumes continuous friction-less hedging.	Seeks to minimize hedging error and assess residual risks. Addresses hedging frequency and transaction costs.
Stochastic process	Requires a risk free (detrended) martingale process.	Places no restrictions on the process (could be non-Markovian, fat-tailed, etc.)
Risk management	Sensitivity based (delta, gamma, vega, dv01).	A full P&L back-testing is performed with the residual risk distribution being produced.

Source: Petrelli et al. (2008)

The standard risk-neutral quantitative analyst ("quant") makes sure his option model is calibrated "to the market." This is often done through the implied Black-Scholes volatility surface as described for caps and swaptions in Chapter 1. The risk-neutral methodology does not attempt to quantify replication errors but rather hides all real-world features and risks into one magic implied volatility. Furthermore, these implied volatilities are calibrated from vanilla options and then blithely used to price and risk-manage exotic derivatives. This simply hides the residual risks coming from hedge slippage, resulting in a remarkably

CHAPTER 5 ■ OPTIMAL HEDGING MONTE CARLO METHODS

poor risk-management practice associated with risk-neutral-based derivatives modeling and trading. The OHMC method allows a quantification of risks associated with trading and hedging options and therefore provides an analytic tool to determine which options in the market are "cheap" and which ones are "expensive." This is the heart of true options and volatility trading. Simply making one's model fit the market may be necessary for mark-to-market purposes, but it provides little in terms of real risk management and risk capital analysis (Petrelli et al. 2010).

Wealth Change Equations: Spot, Forwards, and Options

The basic mechanism of the OHMC method deals with the wealth change equation of a self-financing portfolio. A *self-financing portfolio* is one in which there is no exogenous infusion or withdrawal of cash. Any new asset purchases must be financed by the available assets in the portfolio—that is, they must be self-financed. It is instructive to derive the wealth change equation for spot and forward instruments before moving onto derivatives. Start with a simple portfolio consisting of a risky asset s_n and a risk-less bank balance b_n which earns a continuously compounded interest rate of r. Let the time parameter be sliced up into equal intervals of $t_n = n\Delta t$. The wealth equation at time t_n is given by

$$W_n = \Phi_n s_n + b_n , \qquad (5.1)$$

where Φ_n is the amount of risky asset s_n held at time t_n. The change in wealth between time t_n and time t_{n+1} is

$$W_{n+1} - W_n = \Phi_n [s_{n+1} - s_n] + b_n [e^{r\Delta t} - 1] . \qquad (5.2)$$

Note that the hedge amount is kept at Φ_n when comparing to W_{n+1} in order to evaluate the effect of the hedge from time t_n to t_{n+1}. Using (5.1) to eliminate b_n gives

$$W_{n+1} - W_n = \Phi_n [s_{n+1} - s_n] + (W_n - \Phi_n s_n)[e^{r\Delta t} - 1] . \qquad (5.3)$$

$$W_{n+1} - W_n = \Phi_n s_{n+1} - \Phi_n s_n e^{r\Delta t} + W_n [e^{r\Delta t} - 1] . \qquad (5.4)$$

Rearranging terms gives

$$W_{n+1} - W_n e^{r\Delta t} = \Phi_n s_{n+1} - \Phi_n s_n e^{r\Delta t} . \qquad (5.5)$$

Now define a time t_n *wealth change equation* as follows

$$\Delta W(n, n+1) = W_{n+1} e^{-r\Delta t} - W_n . \qquad (5.6)$$

This is a fundamental equation that compares the discounted value of the portfolio at time t_{n+1} with the portfolio value at time t_n. For the spot portfolio, one has

$$\Delta W(n, n+1) = \Phi_n [s_{n+1} - s_n e^{r\Delta t}] e^{-r\Delta t} . \qquad (5.7)$$

199

This is the fundamental wealth change equation for a spot position present-valued to time t_n. It is clearly the basic P&L equation for a spot position of an amount of Φ_n of the risky asset s_n. Note that Φ_n can be a negative amount, indicating a short position. A similar equation will appear in the OHMC formulation for the delta hedging of an option position. Note that if one discounts the wealth changes appropriately, there is no need for the bank balance term.

Now that the one-time-step wealth change formula has been derived, can one find an expression for the wealth change over all time steps? Much like the binomial tree model described in Chapter 4, all such calculations in the OHMC framework will start at maturity and work their way backward in time. At maturity $t_N = N\Delta t$, (5.5) reads as follows:

$$W_N = W_{N-1} e^{r\Delta t} + \Phi_{N-1}[s_N - s_{N-1} e^{r\Delta t}] \quad . \tag{5.8}$$

At $t_{N-1} = (N-1)\Delta t$ one has

$$W_{N-1} = W_{N-2} e^{r\Delta t} + \Phi_{N-2}[s_{N-1} - s_{N-2} e^{r\Delta t}] \quad . \tag{5.9}$$

Substituting this into (5.8) gives

$$W_N = W_{N-2} e^{2r\Delta t} + \Phi_{N-1}[s_N - s_{N-1} e^{r\Delta t}] + \Phi_{N-2} e^{r\Delta t}[s_{N-1} - s_{N-2} e^{r\Delta t}] \quad . \tag{5.10}$$

Continuing in this manner until $t = 0$ produces the following:

$$W_N = W_0 e^{Nr\Delta t} + \sum_{n=0}^{N-1} \Phi_n e^{r[N-n-1]\Delta t}[s_{n+1} - s_n e^{r\Delta t}] \quad . \tag{5.11}$$

This makes perfect financial sense. The wealth change of a stock position is the initial cash amount accrued up to maturity plus the sum of changes in the stock position and stock price appropriately discounted. A similar formula linking the initial wealth amount to the final wealth amount will be derived for forwards and options (which will form the basis of the OHMC methodology). Note that no assumptions have been made on the stock position and the hedge and that both s_n and Φ_n follow *stochastic processes*.

Forward Contracts

Consider the portfolio of a seller of a forward contract f_n

$$W_n = \Phi_n s_n + f_n \quad . \tag{5.12}$$

The forward contract has a payoff at maturity $t_N = N\Delta t$ of

$$f_N = F - s_N \quad . \tag{5.13}$$

CHAPTER 5 ■ OPTIMAL HEDGING MONTE CARLO METHODS

where F is the forward price (which turns into a strike price when dealing with options). The wealth balance equation at maturity is (there is no new hedge position Φ_N at maturity as the contract has expired)

$$W_N = \Phi_{N-1} s_N + F - s_N \quad . \tag{5.14}$$

The previous time-step wealth equation is given by

$$W_{N-1} = \Phi_{N-1} s_{N-1} + f_{N-1} \quad . \tag{5.15}$$

Therefore, *starting backwards from maturity*, one can calculate the wealth change equation for each time step starting with

$$\begin{aligned}\Delta W(N-1,N) &= W_N e^{-r\Delta t} - W_{N-1} \\ &= [\Phi_{N-1} s_N + f_N] e^{-r\Delta t} - [\Phi_{N-1} s_{N-1} + f_{N-1}] \quad .\end{aligned} \tag{5.16}$$

Note that the hedge position is kept at Φ_{N-1} when comparing to W_N in order to evaluate the effect of the hedge from time $N-1$ to N. Substituting for f_n with the payoff at maturity (5.13) produces

$$\begin{aligned}\Delta W(N-1,N) &= [\Phi_{N-1} s_N + F - s_N] e^{-r\Delta t} - [\Phi_{N-1} s_{N-1} + f_{N-1}] \\ &= \Phi_{N-1}[s_N e^{-r\Delta t} - s_{N-1}] + [F - s_N] e^{-r\Delta t} - f_{N-1} \quad .\end{aligned} \tag{5.17}$$

The reason for starting at maturity and working backwards in time should be clear: one knows the payoff structure at maturity. Whether it is a spot position, a forward position, or a European option payoff, the maturity wealth change equation is relatively easy to write down.

The key idea here is to *solve for both Φ_n and f_n at each time step*. Risk managers would like to know the value of the financial contract and the hedge amount at each time step. The time zero contract value will be the contract price at initiation. Note that risk-neutral methods tend to give only the contract value f_0 without explicitly looking at the hedge Φ_n because they live in the perfect hedging world of the risk-neutral measure. The time zero hedge will be the amount a trader must execute to hedge the initial trade. To solve for these two functions, one needs two conditions or constraints. Suppose one of the conditions is

$$E[\Delta W(n, n+1)] = 0 \quad . \tag{5.18}$$

This constraint makes financial sense, because it basically says that at each time step the expected wealth change is zero. That is, the forward is being priced "fairly" between the buyer and the seller of the forward contract. The use of expectations is due to the fact that both s_n and Φ_n are stochastic processes. Ideally, one would need another constraint to solve for two functions (i.e., two unknowns need two equations). For futures one can guess a possible solution to (5.18) applied (5.17) by setting $\Phi_{N-1} = 1$. Using this ansatz, one is left with the simplified equation

$$E[\Delta W(N-1,N)] = E[-s_{N-1} + Fe^{-r\Delta t} - f_{N-1}] = 0 \quad . \tag{5.19}$$

CHAPTER 5 ■ OPTIMAL HEDGING MONTE CARLO METHODS

which has a generic solution of

$$f_{N-1} = Fe^{-r\Delta t} - s_{N-1} \quad . \tag{5.20}$$

This is true for any stochastic path taken by s_{N-1}. Continuing backward in time with the next wealth change equation gives

$$\Delta W(N-2, N-1) = W_{N-1}e^{-r\Delta t} - W_{N-2} = [\Phi_{N-2}s_{N-1} + f_{N-1}]e^{-r\Delta t} - [\Phi_{N-2}s_{N-2} + f_{N-2}] \quad . \tag{5.21}$$

Using the solution to f_{N-1} leaves one with

$$\Delta W(N-2, N-1) = \Phi_{N-2}[s_{N-1}e^{-r\Delta t} - s_{N-2}] + [Fe^{-r\Delta t} - s_{N-1}]e^{-r\Delta t} - f_{N-2} \quad . \tag{5.22}$$

Setting $\Phi_{N-2} = 1$, the constraint (5.18) requires that

$$E[\Delta W(N-2, N-1)] = E[-s_{N-2} + Fe^{-2r\Delta t} - f_{N-2}] = 0 \quad , \tag{5.23}$$

with the solution of

$$f_{N-2} = Fe^{-2r\Delta t} - s_{N-2} \quad . \tag{5.24}$$

Continuing in this manner until today $t = 0$ produces the solution ($\Phi_n = 1$)

$$f_0 = Fe^{-rN\Delta t} - s_0 = Fe^{-rt_N} - s_0 \quad . \tag{5.25}$$

Since the fair value of this forward contract must be zero today, the forward price is given by

$$F = s_0 e^{rt_N} \quad . \tag{5.26}$$

This is the well known no-arbitrage fair value strike price for a forward contract. Here, it has been derived in a systematic manner consistent with every time step. Its illustrative purpose is to smooth the way to a derivation for contracts with option-like payoffs.

Similar to the spot position derivation, an expression for the wealth change over all time steps can be found. Starting backwards from maturity, (5.16) can be rewritten as

$$W_N = W_{N-1}e^{r\Delta t} + f_N - f_{N-1}e^{r\Delta t} + \Phi_{N-1}[s_N - s_{N-1}e^{r\Delta t}] \quad . \tag{5.27}$$

Similarly, the next time step follows,

$$W_{N-1} = W_{N-2}e^{r\Delta t} + f_{N-1} - f_{N-2}e^{r\Delta t} + \Phi_{N-2}[s_{N-1} - s_{N-2}e^{r\Delta t}] \quad . \tag{5.28}$$

Substituting this into the previous equation results in

$$W_N = W_{N-2}e^{2r\Delta t} + f_N - f_{N-1}e^{r\Delta t} + f_{N-1}e^{r\Delta t} - f_{N-2}e^{2r\Delta t}$$
$$+ \Phi_{N-1}[s_N - s_{N-1}e^{r\Delta t}] + \Phi_{N-2}e^{r\Delta t}[s_{N-1} - s_{N-2}e^{r\Delta t}]$$
$$= W_{N-2}e^{2r\Delta t} + f_N - f_{N-2}e^{2r\Delta t} + \Phi_{N-1}[s_N - s_{N-1}e^{r\Delta t}] + \Phi_{N-2}e^{r\Delta t}[s_{N-1} - s_{N-2}e^{r\Delta t}] \quad . \quad (5.29)$$

Continuing this process until $t = 0$ produces the desired expression (with $f_N = F - s_N$)

$$W_N = W_0 e^{Nr\Delta t} + [F - s_N] - f_0 e^{Nr\Delta t} + \sum_{n=0}^{N-1} \Phi_n e^{r[N-n-1]\Delta t}[s_{n+1} - s_n e^{r\Delta t}] \quad . \quad (5.30)$$

Once again, if the constraint for the wealth change from the beginning $t = 0$ to the end $t = t_N$ is

$$E[\Delta W(0, N)] = 0 \quad . \quad (5.31)$$

then

$$f_0 = e^{-Nr\Delta t} E\left\{[F - s_N] + \sum_{n=0}^{N-1} \Phi_n e^{r[N-n-1]\Delta t}[s_{n+1} - s_n e^{r\Delta t}]\right\} \quad . \quad (5.32)$$

Can one solve the above for both F and Φ_n for general stochastic processes s_n and Φ_n? For forward contracts, one can, using the previous discovered solution of $\Phi_n = 1$. It will be shown that for options, the solution is not so trivial, which leads to the OHMC methodology. With $\Phi_n = 1$, each of the terms in the sum of (5.32) cancel except for the first and last,

$$f_0 = e^{-Nr\Delta t} E\{[F - s_N] + [s_N - s_0 e^{Nr\Delta t}]\} \quad . \quad (5.33)$$

All stochastic terms cancel, leaving

$$f_0 = e^{-Nr\Delta t}[F - s_0 e^{Nr\Delta t}] \quad . \quad (5.34)$$

As before, the fair value at the initiation of a forward contract is $f_0 = 0$ and therefore

$$F = s_0 e^{Nr\Delta t} \quad . \quad (5.35)$$

European Options

The wealth change equations of the previous section have a natural analogue for options. The pattern is as follows:

$$\text{Cash} \to f_N = b_N$$
$$\text{Forward} \to f_N = F - s_N$$
$$\text{Call Option} \to f_N = C_N = \text{Max}[s_N - K, 0]$$
$$\text{Put Option} \to f_N = P_N = \text{Max}[K - s_N, 0] \quad . \quad (5.36)$$

It is straightforward to show that (5.30) has an analogous counterpart for a short call option given by

$$W_N = W_0 e^{Nr\Delta t} - \text{Max}[s_N - K, 0] + C_0 e^{Nr\Delta t} + \sum_{n=0}^{N-1} \Phi_n e^{r[N-n-1]\Delta t}[s_{n+1} - s_n e^{r\Delta t}] \quad . \quad (5.37)$$

Once again, if the constraint for the wealth change is the familiar fair value condition $E[\Delta W(0, N)]$, then one is left with

$$C_0 = e^{-Nr\Delta t} E\left\{ \text{Max}[s_N - K, 0] - \sum_{n=0}^{N-1} \Phi_n e^{r[N-n-1]\Delta t}[s_{n+1} - s_n e^{r\Delta t}] \right\} \quad . \quad (5.38)$$

analogous to (5.32) for forward contracts.

Because of the Max condition, the stochastic parts of this expression cannot be eliminated with a specific choice of Φ_n as was the case for forward contracts. This Max term is the standard one you see in books on risk-neutral pricing. The second and far more important term is the sum of delta hedges. This second term is *not* assumed to be zero in the OHMC methodology as opposed to the risk-neutral method of perfect replication where this second term magically disappears. Here, the option price is dependent on a particular hedging strategy and therefore carries residual risk because no general hedging strategy can be perfect. One can come up with an optimal hedging strategy that can attempt to minimize the risk but not fully eliminate it. Therefore, contrary to the risk-neutral methodology, there is no unique option price. An option price is dependent on a trader's hedging strategy and his view of the asset's future volatility, which is implicit in the type of stochastic process chosen and calibrated for the underlying asset s_n. The OHMC method can estimate the residual risk coming from any hedging strategy and use the risk distribution for pricing and risk capital purposes. The next section studies a particular choice of an optimized hedging strategy in detail.

The OHMC Optimization Problem and Solution Methodology

This section presents a specific optimal hedging strategy along with a Monte Carlo solution methodology. Some of the simplifications used above—such as continuously compounded interest rates, simple payoffs, and zero dividends—are addressed here. Consider the one-time-step wealth change equation of an option seller who will hedge his position. The option is European-style but may have other intermediate cash payments. The underlying is assumed to pay discrete dividends. Two different yield curves will be used. *df* will denote discount factors coming from the standard discounting yield curve (LIBOR or Fed funds), whereas *Df* will denote discount factors coming from the repo curve or borrowing cost curve of the underlying asset (see Chapter 1 for repo definitions). Finally, the change in wealth will be written in a way suitable for the optimization methodology. The change in wealth of the option seller position comes from two sources, the option part and the hedge.

$$\Delta W(t_k, t_{k+1}) = \Delta W^{option}(t_k, t_{k+1}) + \Delta W^{hedge}(t_k, t_{k+1}) \quad . \quad (5.39)$$

CHAPTER 5 ■ OPTIMAL HEDGING MONTE CARLO METHODS

The option part will be written as

$$\Delta W^{option}(t_k, t_{k+1}) = \underbrace{C(s_k, t_k)}_{\text{option mark at } t_k} - G(t_k) \tag{5.40}$$

$$G(t_k) = \underbrace{C(s_{k+1}, t_{k+1})}_{\text{option mark at } t_{k+1}} \underbrace{df(t_k, t_{k+1})}_{\substack{\text{risk-free} \\ \text{discount} \\ \text{factor}}} + \underbrace{P(t_{k+1})}_{\substack{\text{intermediate} \\ \text{payout at } P(t_{k+1})}} df(t_k, t_{k+1}) \tag{5.41}$$

The term $P(t_{k+1})$ is included in (5.41) for any intermediate payouts or cash flows, so that the OHMC framework could be applied to a wide range of situations. For vanilla options, this term is zero and for a European call option, $C(s_{maturity}, t_{maturity}) = \text{Max}[s_{maturity} - K, 0]$, as in (5.36).

The wealth change of the hedge position is given as

$$\Delta W^{hedge}(t_k, t_{k+1}) = \Phi(s_k, t_k) \underbrace{H(t_k)}_{\text{hedge amount at } t_k} \tag{5.42}$$

$$H(t_k) = \left(\underbrace{s_{k+1}}_{\text{asset value at } t_{k+1}} - \frac{\overbrace{s_k}^{\text{asset value at } t_k}}{Df(t_k, t_{k+1})} \right) df(t_k, t_{k+1}) + \underbrace{\pi(t_{k+1})}_{\text{dividends at } t_{k+1}} df(t_k, t_{k+1}) \tag{5.43}$$

$$\text{borrow-cost discount factor}$$

The OHMC Optimization Problem

The goal here is to find $C(s_k, t_k)$ and $\Phi(s_k, t_k)$ for every time step, just as it was the case for forward contracts. For forwards, the constraint (5.18) was sufficient to solve the problem. For options however, the stochastic terms cannot easily be canceled by a judicious choice of $\Phi(s_k, t_k)$, and therefore another condition will be needed to fully specify the optimization problem. This second condition is what characterizes the nature of the optimal hedge. A well-known condition is one that *minimizes the variance* of the wealth change at every time step. Another potential condition is one that constrains the wealth change to be no worse than a predefined number called the expected shortfall minimization condition

[Petrelli et al., 2006]. This type of constraint requires a maximum allowed CVaR on the wealth change at each time step. There have also been attempts at using global constraints. Here, the following *constrained optimization* problem will be investigated.

Find:

$$C(s_k, t_k) \text{ and } \Phi(s_k, t_k) \tag{5.44}$$

such that the wealth change variance is minimized along with satisfying the fair value constraint,

$$\begin{aligned}\textbf{minimize:} \quad & E[\{\Delta W(t_k,t_{k+1}) - E[\Delta W(t_k,t_{k+1})]\}^2] \\ \textbf{constraint:} \quad & E[\Delta W(t_k,t_{k+1})] = 0\end{aligned} \tag{5.45}$$

Clearly, one needs two conditions to solve for the two unknown functions. Because one is trying to find two functions with respect to a minimization condition, functional derivatives used in the *calculus of variations* will take the place of ordinary derivatives. First, a suitable Monte Carlo framework for evaluating the stochastic processes underlying the wealth change equation will be discussed. The methodology used is very similar in spirit of the binomial tree model of Chapter 4. The generic steps are as follows.

The OHMC Technique

1. Simulate all Monte Carlo paths for all time steps for the specific stochastic process chosen for the underlying asset, such as GARCH(1,1). This is similar to creating the full binomial tree first before starting the option pricing.

2. Starting from the option maturity, work backwards in time solving for the option value $C(s_k, t_k)$ and the optimal hedge $\Phi(s_k, t_k)$ at each time step. Much like the binomial tree, the European option value at maturity will be the European payoff for the specific MC path. The method to solve for $C(s_k, t_k)$ and $\Phi(s_k, t_k)$ at other time steps is the Lagrange multiplier technique described below.

3. Calculate the total wealth change distribution by keeping track of the total wealth change path by path,

$$\Delta W_0(0,T) = \sum_{k=0}^{N-1} \Delta W_{t_k}(t_k, t_{k+1}) df(0, t_k) \tag{5.46}$$

This is illustrated in Figure 5-3, where the superscripts of the asset price denote a particular MC path.

CHAPTER 5 ■ OPTIMAL HEDGING MONTE CARLO METHODS

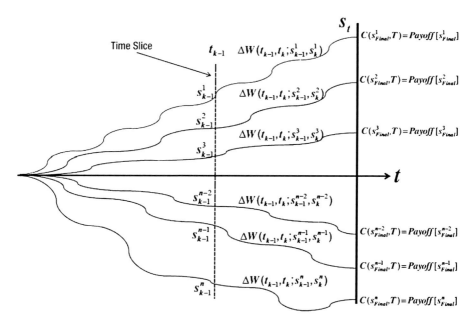

Figure 5-3. *The OHMC simulation approach*

Basis Function Expansions and the Lagrange Multiplier Technique

The OHMC optimization problem is theoretically infinite-dimensional as both the option value and hedge amount depend on the continuous underlying spot value. Even in the Monte Carlo approach, solving for the option value $C(s_k, t_k)$ and the optimal hedge amount $\Phi(s_k, t_k)$ that satisfy (5.45) would be very difficult because one is usually dealing with a minimum of 1,000,000 MC paths. The number of paths needed is driven not just by the desired accuracy of the OHMC method but also by the underlying fat-tailed MC process. To completely capture rare events with the underlying stochastic process, one needs many MC paths. A finite-dimensional reduction of the state space is necessary to make the problem tractable. That is, rather than dealing with 1,000,000 equity prices at any one time, these equity prices can be represented by a finite set of functions that span the equity state space. Start by dividing up the state space into numerically ordered non-overlapping elements that are identified by their endpoints, called *nodes*. The number of these ordered nodal locations $s_k(j)$ will be far fewer than the number of MC paths. *Basis functions* can now be defined at these nodal locations. The range of nodal values for which a basis function has a

CHAPTER 5 ■ OPTIMAL HEDGING MONTE CARLO METHODS

nonzero value defines the *support* of the function. First consider the following *linear basis functions* defined at M nodal locations $s_k(j)$ ordered from the lowest to the highest equity values,

$$\Omega_j(s_k) = \begin{cases} \dfrac{s_k - s_k(j-1)}{s_k(j) - s_k(j-1)}, & s_k(j-1) \leq s_k \leq s_k(j) \\ \dfrac{s_k(j+1) - s_k}{s_k(j+1) - s_k(j)}, & s_k(j) \leq s_k \leq s_k(j+1) \\ 0, & \text{otherwise} \end{cases} \quad (5.47)$$

These basis functions have support only at the *nearest neighbor* nodal points that are bounding the specific stock value s_k. Note that in an MC simulation with several time steps, each time step will have its own set of basis functions. At a specific time step t_k, a function of s_k can be represented as an expansion over the above M basis functions as follows:

$$f(s_k) = \sum_{j=0}^{M-1} a_j \Omega_j(s_k) \quad (5.48)$$

Due to the nearest neighbor support of the linear basis functions above, this expansion reduces to using two basis functions identified by the adjacent nodal locations to s_k, $s_k(j^*) \leq s_k \leq s_k(j^*+1)$,

$$f(s_k) = a_{j^*} \Omega_{j^*}(s_k) + a_{j^*+1} \Omega_{j^*+1}(s_k) \quad (5.49)$$

The unknown coefficients are the values of the function $f(s_k)$ at the particular nodal locations $s_k(j^*)$,

$$a_{j^*} = f(s_k(j^*)) \quad (5.50)$$

Figures 5-4 and 5-5 illustrate the use of linear basis functions to approximate the function $s^2 \exp[s^{-2}]$.

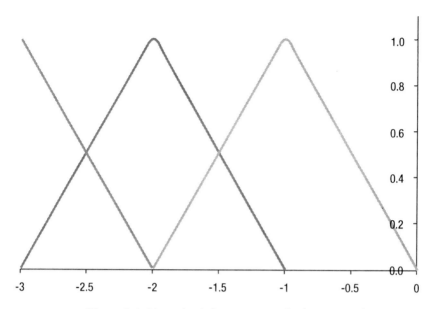

Figure 5-4. *Linear basis functions at nodes (−3, −2, −1, 0)*

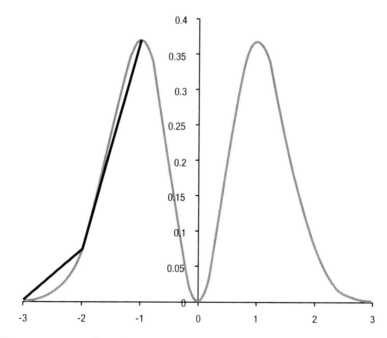

Figure 5-5. *Linear basis function expansion of $s^2 \exp[s^{-2}]$. The straight lines are the approximation to the curve*

CHAPTER 5 ■ OPTIMAL HEDGING MONTE CARLO METHODS

From Figure 5-5, it is clear that the approximation of the function in question will depend on the type of basis functions used and the number of nodes chosen. For linear basis functions, the approximation improves as more nodes are used. Using too many nodes (relatively speaking) defeats the purpose of the approximation as one is trying to reduce the dimensionality of the problem in question. Therefore, one can alternately choose more complex basis function to improve the fit while keeping the dimensionality low. One such type of basis function is the *Hermite cubic polynomial*. This representation offers *two functions per node* as follows:

$$\omega_j(s_k) = \begin{cases} \frac{[s_k - s_k(j-1)]^2}{[s_k(j) - s_k(j-1)]^3} \{2[s_k(j) - s_k] + [s_k(j) - s_k(j-1)]\}, & s_k(j-1) \leq s_k \leq s_k(j) \\ \frac{[s_k(j+1) - s_k]^2}{[s_k(j+1) - s_k(j)]^3} \{2[s_k - s_k(j)] + [s_k(j+1) - s_k(j)]\}, & s_k(j) \leq s_k \leq s_k(j+1) \\ 0, \text{ otherwise} \end{cases}$$

(5.51)

$$\tilde{\omega}_j(s_k) = \begin{cases} \frac{[s_k - s_k(j-1)]^2}{[s_k(j) - s_k(j-1)]^2} [s_k - s_k(j)], & s_k(j-1) \leq s_k \leq s_k(j) \\ \frac{[s_k(j+1) - s_k]^2}{[s_k(j+1) - s_k(j)]^2} [s_k - s_k(j)], & s_k(j) \leq s_k \leq s_k(j+1) \\ 0, \text{ otherwise} \end{cases}$$

(5.52)

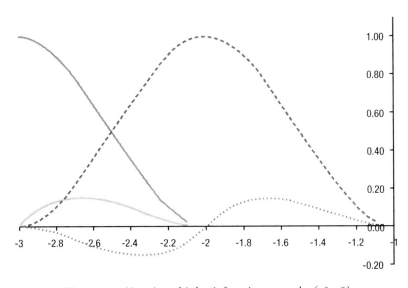

Figure 5-6. *Hermite cubic basis functions at nodes (-3, -2)*

At a specific time step t_k, a function of s_k can be represented as an expansion over the above M Hermite cubic basis functions as follows

$$f(s_k) = \sum_{j=0}^{M-1} \left(a_j \omega_j(s_k) + b_j \tilde{\omega}_j(s_k) \right) \quad . \tag{5.53}$$

Due to the nearest neighbor support of the linear basis functions, this expansion reduces to using four basis functions identified by the adjacent nodal locations to s_k, $s_k(j^*) \leq s_k \leq s_k(j^* + 1)$,

$$f(s_k) = a_{j^*} \omega_{j^*}(s_k) + b_{j^*} \tilde{\omega}_{j^*}(s_k) + a_{j^*+1} \omega_{j^*+1}(s_k) + b_{j^*+1} \tilde{\omega}_{j^*+1}(s_k) \quad . \tag{5.54}$$

The unknown coefficients are the value of the function $f(s_k)$ and its derivative at the particular nodal location $s_k(j^*)$,

$$a_{j^*} = f(s_k(j^*)), \quad b_{j^*} = \frac{df(s_k(j^*))}{ds_k} \quad . \tag{5.55}$$

Figures 5-6 and 5-7 illustrate the use of Hermite cubic basis functions to approximate the function $s^2 \exp[s^{-2}]$.

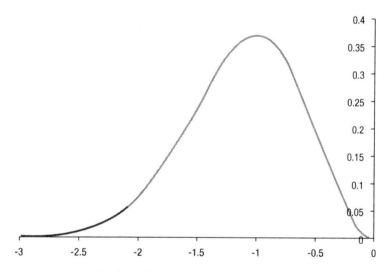

Figure 5-7. *Hermite cubic basis function expansion of $s^2 \exp[s^{-2}]$. The fit is at the far left side of the graph (the darker curve)*

Now a finite dimensional representation of the option value and hedge functions can be found using an expansion of either linear or cubic basis functions (where the superscripts on the expansion coefficients now carry explicitly the time index),

$$C(s_k, t_k) = \sum_{j=0}^{M_C - 1} a_j^k A_j(s_k) \quad \Phi(s_k, t_k) = \sum_{j=0}^{M_\Phi - 1} b_j^k B_j(s_k) \quad . \tag{5.56}$$

211

The basis functions A_j for the option and those of the hedge B_j need not be the same. The numbers of basis functions used for the option and the hedge, M_C and M_Φ, need not be the same either.

Recall that the wealth change equation is given by:

$$\Delta W(t_k, t_{k+1}) = C(s_k, t_k) - G(t_k) + \Phi(s_k, t_k) H(t_k) \quad . \tag{5.57}$$

The goal is to find $C(s_k, t_k)$ and $\Phi(s_k, t_k)$ under the following conditions:

$$\begin{aligned}\textbf{minimize}: &\quad E[\{\Delta W(t_k, t_{k+1}) - E[\Delta W(t_k, t_{k+1})]\}^2] \\ \textbf{constraint}: &\quad E[\Delta W(t_k, t_{k+1})] = 0\end{aligned} \tag{5.58}$$

Using the finite dimensional representation (5.56) and the wealth change (5.57) in the above optimization equations leads to

$$E[\Delta W(t_k, t_{k+1})] = \sum_{j=0}^{M_C-1} a_j^k E[A_j(s_k)] - E[G(t_k)] + \sum_{j=0}^{M_\Phi-1} b_j^k E[B_j(s_k) H(t_k)] \tag{5.59}$$

and

$$E[\Delta W(t_k, t_{k+1})^2] = E\left[\left\{\sum_{j=0}^{M_C-1} a_j^k A_j(s_k) - G(t_k) + \sum_{j=0}^{M_\Phi-1} b_j^k B_j(s_k) H(t_k)\right\}^2\right] \quad . \tag{5.60}$$

To solve for the unknown coefficients a_j^k and b_j^k one employs a Lagrange multiplier technique to solve the constraint optimization problem using the following Lagrange function,

$$\begin{aligned} F_k &= E[\Delta W(t_k, t_{k+1})^2] + 2\gamma E[\Delta W(t_k, t_{k+1})] \\ \frac{dF_k}{da_i^k} &= 0 \quad 0 \le i \le M_C - 1 \\ \frac{dF_k}{db_i^k} &= 0 \quad 0 \le i \le M_\Phi - 1 \\ \frac{dF_k}{d\gamma} &= 0 \end{aligned} \tag{5.61}$$

The above lead to a system of linear equations for the unknown coefficients a_j^k and b_j^k and the Lagrange multiplier γ,

$$\begin{aligned} G_{ij} h_j &= q_i \quad 0 \le i, j \le M_C + M_\Phi \\ h_j &= a_j^k \quad 0 \le j \le M_C - 1 \\ h_j &= b_{j-M_C}^k \quad M_C \le j \le M_C + M_\Phi - 1 \\ h_{M_C + M_\Phi} &= \gamma \end{aligned} \tag{5.62}$$

CHAPTER 5 ■ OPTIMAL HEDGING MONTE CARLO METHODS

The first Lagrange condition in (5.61) leads to the following (Monte Carlo dependent) vector and matrix elements,

$$
\begin{aligned}
& 0 \leq i \leq M_C - 1 \\
& q_i = E[A_i(s_k)G_k] \\
& G_{ij} = E[A_i(s_k)A_j(s_k)] \quad && 0 \leq j \leq M_C - 1 \\
& G_{ij} = E[A_i(s_k)B_{j-M_C}(s_k)H_k] \quad && M_C \leq j \leq M_C + M_\Phi - 1 \\
& G_{ij} = E[A_i(s_k)] \quad && j = M_C + M_\Phi
\end{aligned}
\qquad (5.63)
$$

The second Lagrange condition in (5.61) gives

$$
\begin{aligned}
& M_C \leq i \leq M_C + M_\Phi - 1 \\
& q_i = E[B_{i-M_C}(s_k)G_k H_k] \\
& G_{ij} = E[B_{i-M_C}(s_k)A_j(s_k)H_k] \quad && 0 \leq j \leq M_C - 1 \\
& G_{ij} = E[B_{i-M_C}(s_k)B_{j-M_C}(s_k)H_k^2] \quad && M_C \leq j \leq M_C + M_\Phi - 1 \\
& G_{ij} = E[B_{i-M_C}(s_k)H_k] \quad && j = M_C + M_\Phi
\end{aligned}
\qquad (5.64)
$$

Finally, the Lagrange multiplier condition in (5.61) gives

$$
\begin{aligned}
& i = M_C + M_\Phi \\
& q_i = E[G_k] \\
& G_{ij} = E[A_j(s_k)] \quad && 0 \leq j \leq M_C - 1 \\
& G_{ij} = E[B_{j-M_C}(s_k)H_k] \quad && M_C \leq j \leq M_C + M_\Phi - 1 \\
& G_{ij} = 0 \quad && j = M_C + M_\Phi
\end{aligned}
\qquad (5.65)
$$

The above equations must be solved for each time step moving backwards in time from the maturity except for the first time step,

$$\Delta W(t_0, t_1) = C(s_0, t_0) - G(t_0) + \Phi(s_0, t_0) H(t_0) \quad . \qquad (5.66)$$

As all the MC paths start at s_0, the required optimization for the first time step has a solution given by

$$\Phi(s_0, t_0) = \frac{E\{(G(t_0) - E[(G(t_0))])(H(t_0) - E[(H(t_0))])\}}{E[(H(t_0) - E[(H(t_0))])^2]} \quad . \qquad (5.67)$$

and

$$C(s_0, t_0) = E[G(t_0)] - \Phi(s_0, t_0) E[H(t_0)] \quad . \qquad (5.68)$$

At the initiation of this option, $\Phi(s_0, t_0)$ is the initial optimal hedge ratio and $C(s_0, t_0)$ is the average cost of hedging this option. Prudent risk managers do not simply charge the average cost of hedging but add some portion of the total hedge slippage from the wealth change distribution. The amount added is calculated from the required return on risk capital needed for this option (see the following section on risk capital).

Note that all expectations can be estimated by summing over the trajectories of the Monte Carlo simulation,

$$E\left[A_i(s_k)A_j(s_k)\right] \approx \frac{1}{n_{MC}} \sum_{m=1}^{n_{MC}} A_i(s_k^m)A_j(s_k^m) \quad ,$$

where the superscripts of the asset price (m) denote a particular MC path as in Figure 5-4.

Risk Capital

The amount of risk capital one needs to hold against a sold option position will be determined by individual risk preferences. For banks, it may also be dependent on various regulatory requirements, such as the CVA or Basel III charge that goes along with holding such a risky position (see Chapter 7). Whatever the conditions are, they all come down to charging a specific rate on a specific risk capital amount. Here, this specific rate is called the *return on risk capital* or *hurdle rate*, and the specific risk capital amount will be based on an annualized target risk–capital confidence level of 99.9% over one year. This choice is made because of the one-year AA risk rating given by S&P to this confidence interval in their ratings methodology. One is free to choose other levels as they see fit as individual investors' risk-return preferences can differ from one another. As this level is valid for a one-year period, one can calculate a T period *equivalent* confidence level as follows,

$$\Psi = \exp\left[\ln[0.999] \times T\right] \quad . \tag{5.69}$$

Ψ reduces to 99.9% when $T=1$. Let $F(\Delta W(0,T))$ be the deal tenor OHMC P&L cumulative wealth change distribution (the distribution of (5.46). The *total hedge slippage* at a T period *equivalent* confidence level Ψ is given by a VaR-type formula,

$$\Delta W^* = F^{-1}(1-\Psi) \quad . \tag{5.70}$$

Therefore, $\Delta W*$ is the *specific risk capital amount* chosen here. Similar to VAR, it is a loss number at a prespecified confidence interval. The final step is to choose a specific *return on risk capital*. Here a continuously compounded rate of 20% is chosen. (It could have just as well been 15%. The 20% return number comes from Warren Buffett. This is the type of minimum return he demands on his investments. He is requiring a minimal *hurdle* return for an investment to be called successful, so this rate is also referred to as a hurdle rate.) Finally, one must combine the average cost of hedging with the risk capital charge. Letting the required return on risk capital be $h=20\%$, the OHMC sellers price is given by

$$P_{OHMC} = C(s_0,t_0) + |\Delta W*| \times \left[\exp(hT) - 1\right] \quad . \tag{5.71}$$

The absolute value is being used as $\Delta W*$ is almost surely a negative number (the loss amount at a specific confidence interval). This formula charges the average cost of hedging $C(s_0, t_0)$ and adds the required return on the required risk capital amount. Here, the return on risk capital was based solely on the tail of the loss distribution of hedging the option (hedge slippage). Banks may add other threshold numbers that come from differing regulatory requirements. Simply earning a positive P&L for an investment or trading strategy doesn't suffice. One must earn a certain minimum amount that is required for taking on a certain amount of risk. The riskier the trade, the larger the required return.

OHMC Examples

This section provides several examples of the OHMC procedure using graphical depictions of simulated asset prices, hedges, option values, and wealth changes. These examples will be based upon a GARCH(1,1) simulation of the underlying assets and the OHMC wealth change procedure described above. Each example begins with the GARCH(1,1) calibration parameters and the corresponding autocorrelation of squared returns empirical to theoretical fit.

Hedge Fund Index: GARCH Calibration to Daily Returns

The first example deals with a hedge fund index (a proprietary index from a large Wall Street firm) that provides daily end-of-day NAVs. Figures 5-8 and 5-9 display the corresponding GARCH(1,1) calibration parameters and the autocorrelation of squared returns fit. The good autocorrelation fit is not surprising as hedge funds tend to "smooth" their P&L over time to give the appearance of consistent returns.

Portfolio's modeled characteristics						
mu	Long Term Vol	Kurtosis	Vol-cluster time (time-step units)	alpha	beta	Initial Vol
4.79%	7.56%	13.69	16.048	13.33%	84.37%	7.56%

Figure 5-8. *GARCH(1,1) calibration parameters for a hedge fund index*

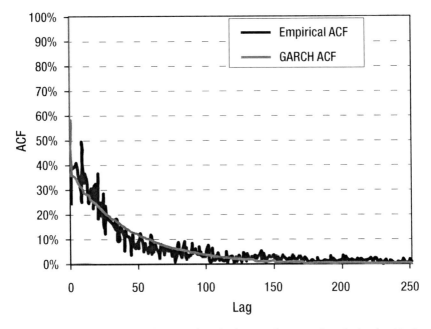

Figure 5-9. *Autocorrelation function (ACF) of squared returns for a hedge fund index*

Option Pricing: Hedge Fund Index: 1.20Yr 110% Strike Call, 2 Day Liquidity

One of the main advantages of the OHMC methodology is that it can price options where the hedging frequency is lower than the asset price frequency. This is a real issue for illiquid assets where one cannot hedge continuously with unlimited volume. In this example, the *discrete hedging frequency* is two days. If the underlying asset moves dramatically between these two days, one cannot rehedge their position until the following day, therefore leading to a potential loss due to hedge slippage. Discrete hedging is in fact the rule rather than the exception. Even hedging an S&P 500 option intraday can lead to hedge slippage during very volatile markets times such as the one depicted in Figure 5-2. Trying to continually hedge during that time was very difficult and those who attempted to rehedge on every move actually lost more money than if they had tried to keep their hedging discrete. The OHMC method attempts to estimate this hedge slippage and take it into account when pricing the option.

CHAPTER 5 ■ OPTIMAL HEDGING MONTE CARLO METHODS

The option that is priced here is a 1.20 yr 110% strike call with 2 day liquidity on the hedge fund index of the previous section. The spot value of all assets has been scaled to 100 for all the examples that follow. The main results are given in Figure 5-10. These results decompose (5.71) $P_{OHMC} = C(s_0, t_0) + |\Delta W*| \times [\exp(hT) - 1]$ as follows:

$$s_0 = 100$$
$$h = 20\%$$
$$T = 1.20 (300 \text{ days})$$
$$\exp(hT) - 1 = 26.88\%$$
$$C(s_0, t_0) = \text{avg heging cost} = 0.53 \quad (5.72)$$
$$|\Delta W*| = 7.9$$
$$|\Delta W*| \times [\exp(hT) - 1] = \text{liquidity \& tail risk cost} = 2.12$$
$$P_{OHMC} = \text{seller's axe} = 2.65$$

$\Phi(s_0, t_0) = $ P&L vol minimizing hedge amount as a percent of spot $s_0 = 0.15$

Deal Tenor Risk Capital Return	
Return	26.88%

OHMC summary output	
seller's axe	2.65
avg hedging cost	0.53
liquidity & tail risk cost	2.12
P&L vol minimizing hedge amount	0.15

Figure 5-10. *OHMC price and optimal hedge*

All the following examples will be in this format. From the cumulative wealth change distribution $F(\Delta W(0, T))$ in Figure 5-11, one can read off the 99.9% confidence level from where the dark line crosses the distribution (-7.9).

CHAPTER 5 ■ OPTIMAL HEDGING MONTE CARLO METHODS

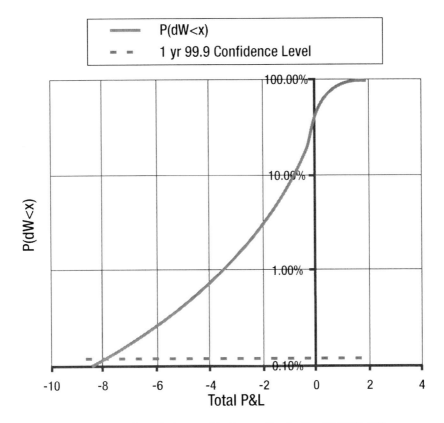

Figure 5-11. *Cumulative wealth change distribution $F(\Delta W(0, T))$*

Figure 5-12 depicts a particular loss contributing asset path from the MC simulation along with the hedge ratio. Since the liquidity is 2 and the term is 300 days, the x-axis depicts 150 hedging intervals. The initial hedge starts at the optimal hedge 0.15% (see axis on the right). This path was chosen because it leads to a loss amount due to a net hedge slippage during the term of the option. This hedge slippage occurred after the 80th hedging interval when the asset dropped dramatically. In Figure 5-13, one can see that the option- ΔW (dW) and the hedge-dW essentially cancel each other before the 80th hedging interval as indicated by the cumulative total wealth change being close to zero. After the assets' large drop (when the call option values drops) and subsequent rapid rise (where the call rises in value along with the appropriate hedge amount), the hedge no longer cancels out the sold option position and one experiences hedge slippage, resulting in a negative cumulative total wealth change. In the risk-neutral framework, this total wealth change is always zero due to the miraculous risk-neutral measure and its oversimplified assumptions. In reality, this is never the case, and the OHMC methodology addresses these issues directly.

CHAPTER 5 ■ OPTIMAL HEDGING MONTE CARLO METHODS

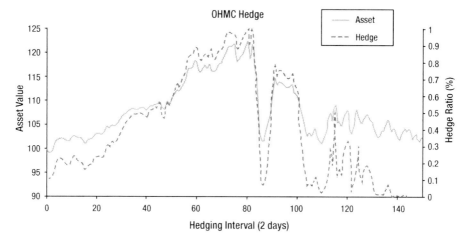

Figure 5-12. *A loss contributing asset path along with its hedge ratio*

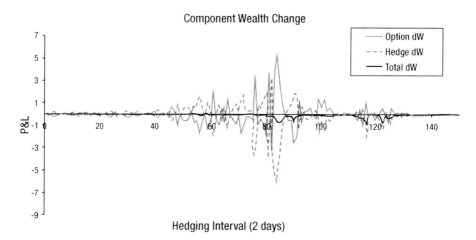

Figure 5-13. *Component wealth changes for the loss path in Figure 5-12*

219

Option Pricing: Hedge Fund Index: 1.20Yr 99% Strike Put, 2 Day Liquidity

Once again, Figure 5-14 displays the decomposition of (5.70) $P_{OHMC} = P(s_0, t_0) + |\Delta W^*| \times [\exp(h\ T) - 1]$ as follows ($P(s_0, t_0)$ is used for puts) where once again $|\Delta W^*|$ is taken from the cumulative wealth change distribution (Figure 5-15):

$$s_0 = 100$$
$$h = 20\%$$
$$T = 1.20 (300\ \text{days})$$
$$\exp(hT) - 1 = 26.88\%$$
$$P(s_0, t_0) = \text{avg heging cost} = 2.50 \quad (5.73)$$
$$|\Delta W^*| = 7.6$$
$$|\Delta W^*| \times [\exp(hT) - 1] = \text{liquidity \& tail risk cost} = 2.03$$
$$P_{OHMC} = \text{seller's axe} = 4.53$$
$$\Phi(s_0, t_0) = \text{P\&L vol minimizing hedge amount as a percent of spot } s_0 = -0.43$$

Deal Tenor Risk Capital Return	
Return	26.88%

OHMC summary output	
seller's axe	4.53
avg hedging cost	2.50
liquidity & tail risk cost	2.03
P&L vol minimizing hedge amount	-0.43

Figure 5-14. OHMC price and optimal hedge

Comparing Figures 5-16 and 5-17, sudden changes in the asset price around the 30th hedging interval begin to cause hedge slippage and losses to the option seller. The hedge ratio in Figure 5-16 should be seen as a negative number (see Figure 5-14) because the option seller must short the underlying to hedge his short put position. Both Figures 5-16 and 5-17 could depict 150 hedging intervals, but the option stays way out of the money after the 100th hedge interval and therefore this later region is not depicted.

CHAPTER 5 ■ OPTIMAL HEDGING MONTE CARLO METHODS

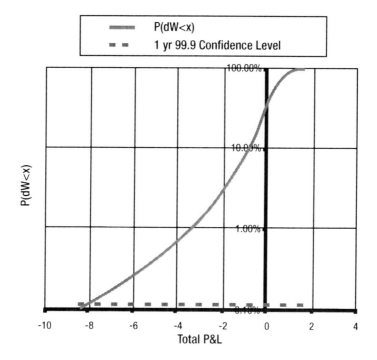

Figure 5-15. Cumulative wealth change distribution $F(\Delta W(0, T))$

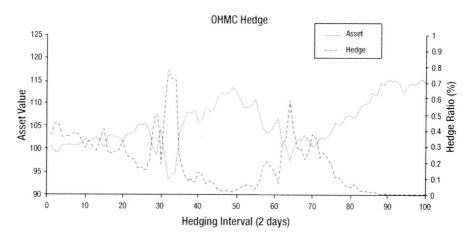

Figure 5-16. A loss contributing asset path along with its hedge ratio

CHAPTER 5 ■ OPTIMAL HEDGING MONTE CARLO METHODS

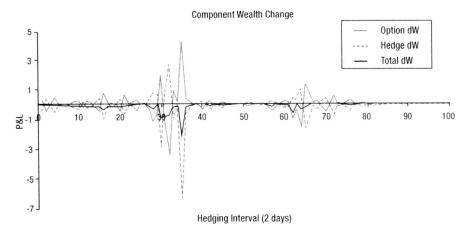

Figure 5-17. Component wealth changes for the loss path in Figure 5-16

Dynamic Portfolio Allocation Index: GARCH Calibration to Daily Returns

This example deals with a proprietary multi-asset index based upon the dynamic allocation rules described in Chapter 4. This index provides daily end-of-day NAVs, but because of the nature of its construction and hedge, it can only be traded every five days (5-day liquidity). Figures 5-18 and 5-19 display the corresponding GARCH(1,1) calibration parameters and the autocorrelation of squared returns fit.

Portfolio's modeled characteristics					
mu	Long Term Vol	Kurtosis	alpha	beta	Initial Vol
13.91%	11.44%	6.44	42.78%	13.32%	13.89%

Figure 5-18. GARCH(1,1) calibration parameters for a dynamic portfolio allocation index

CHAPTER 5 ■ OPTIMAL HEDGING MONTE CARLO METHODS

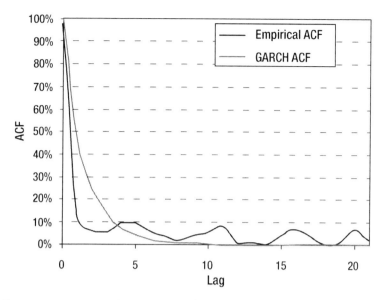

Figure 5-19. Autocorrelation function (ACF) of squared returns for a dynamic portfolio allocation index

Option Pricing: Dynamic Portfolio Allocation: 2.00Yr 110% Strike Call, 5 Day Liquidity

As stated above, this index provides 5 day liquidity. The two year period allows for only 100 hedging intervals. The pricing in Figure 5-20 follows the above pattern.

Deal Tenor Risk Capital Return	
Return	49.18%

OHMC summary output	
seller's axe	5.39
avg hedging cost	2.95
liquidity & tail risk cost	2.44
P&L vol minimizing hedge amount	0.34

Figure 5-20. OHMC price and optimal hedge

223

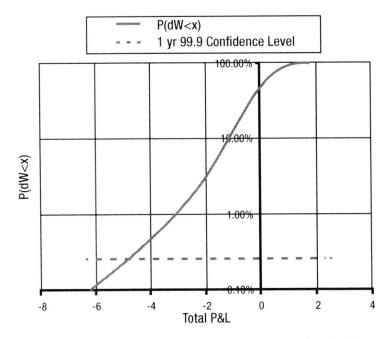

Figure 5-21. Cumulative wealth change distribution $F(\Delta W(0, T))$

Once again, the liquidity and tail cost is derived from 1Yr 99.9% confidence level seen in Figure 5-21. Comparing Figures 5-22 and 5-23 reveals that a substantial loss is experienced near the very end of this option when the option appears to be OTM but the asset price suddenly jumps past the 110% strike.

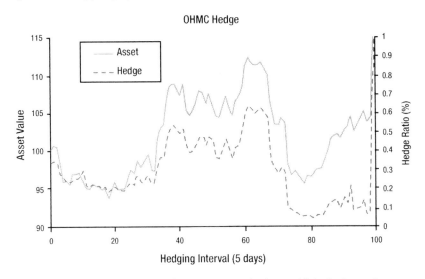

Figure 5-22. A loss contributing asset path along with its hedge ratio

CHAPTER 5 ■ OPTIMAL HEDGING MONTE CARLO METHODS

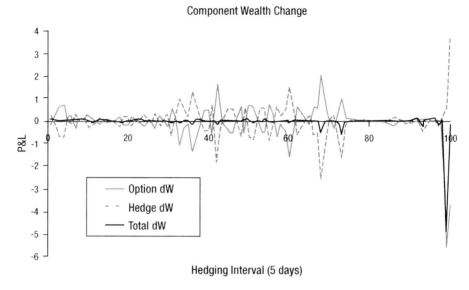

Figure 5-23. *Component wealth changes for the loss path in Figure 5-22*

Option Pricing: Dynamic Portfolio Allocation: 2.00Yr 95% Strike Put, 5 Day Liquidity

Deal Tenor Risk Capital Return	
Return	49.18%

OHMC summary output	
seller's axe	7.82
avg hedging cost	5.80
liquidity & tail risk cost	2.01
P&L vol minimizing hedge amount	-0.43

Figure 5-24. *OHMC price and optimal hedge*

225

CHAPTER 5 ■ OPTIMAL HEDGING MONTE CARLO METHODS

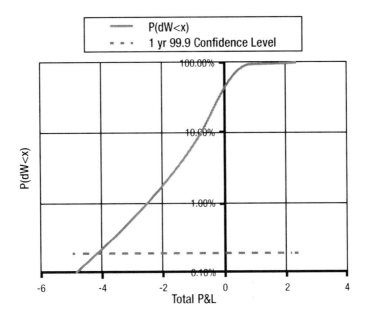

Figure 5-25. *Cumulative wealth change distribution* $F(\Delta W(0, T))$

Figures 5-24 and 5-25 give the OHMC results for this option. Just before the 80th hedge interval in Figure 5-26, a black swan-type event occurs in which the asset suddenly takes a large sudden loss, which is a put option seller's nightmare, especially when the hedge amount at that time was near zero. The option ends OTM with the hedge falling rapidly to zero near the 100th hedge interval.

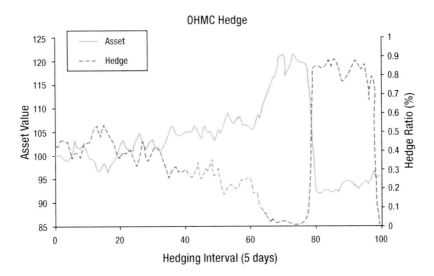

Figure 5-26. *A loss-contributing asset path along with its hedge ratio*

CHAPTER 5 ■ OPTIMAL HEDGING MONTE CARLO METHODS

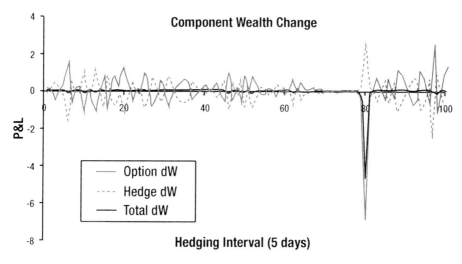

Figure 5-27. Component wealth changes for the loss path in Figure 5-26

Hedge Fund Index: GARCH Calibration to Monthly Returns

This example deals with a well-known hedge fund index. This index provides only reliable monthly NAVs, but because of the nature of its construction and hedge, it can only be traded every three months. Figures 5-28 and 5-29 display the corresponding GARCH(1,1) calibration parameters and the autocorrelation of squared returns fit for monthly returns. Once again, the autocorrelation fit is very good due to the smoothing nature of hedge fund NAVs. The lag time in Figure 5-29 is in months.

Portfolio's modeled characteristics						
mu	Long Term Vol	Kurtosis	Vol-cluster time (time-step units)	alpha	beta	Initial Vol
4.18%	5.30%	15.00	2.700	41.53%	33.89%	10.00%

Figure 5-28. GARCH(1,1) calibration parameters for a monthly hedge fund index

227

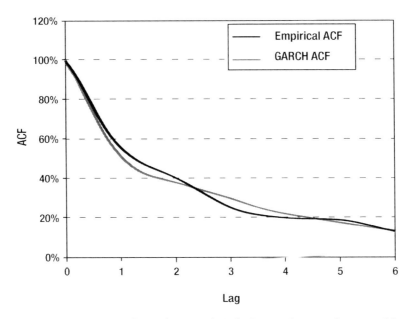

Figure 5-29. Autocorrelation function (ACF) of squared returns for a monthly hedge fund index

Option Pricing: Hedge Fund Index: 3.00Yr 100% Strike Put, 3-Month Liquidity

Note that the tail cost is more than three times the average cost of hedging due to the large amount of hedge slippage coming from the very discrete nature of hedging allowed by this index (Figures 5-30 and 5-31).

Deal Tenor Risk Capital Return	
Return	82.21%

OHMC summary output	
seller's axe	9.78
avg hedging cost	2.16
liquidity & tail risk cost	7.62
P&L vol minimizing hedge amount	-0.28

Figure 5-30. OHMC price and optimal hedge

CHAPTER 5 ■ OPTIMAL HEDGING MONTE CARLO METHODS

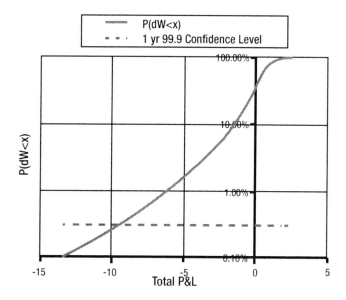

Figure 5-31. *Cumulative wealth change distribution $F(\Delta W(0, T))$*

The hedging intervals in Figures 5-32 and 5-33 are in units of three months.

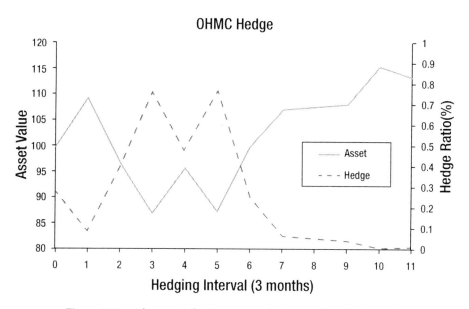

Figure 5-32. *A loss-contributing asset path along with its hedge ratio*

229

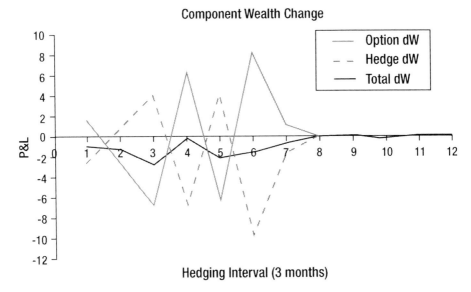

Figure 5-33. *Component wealth changes for the loss path in Figure 5-32*

Option Pricing: Hedge Fund Index: 3.00-Yr 110% Strike Call, 3-Month Liquidity

Once again, the tail cost (Figures 5-34 and 5-35) is multiples of the average cost of hedging due to the large amount of hedge slippage coming from the very discrete nature of hedging allowed by this index.

Deal Tenor Risk Capital Return	
Return	82.21%

OHMC summary output	
seller's axe	10.32
avg hedging cost	1.60
liquidity & tail risk cost	9.01
P&L vol minimizing hedge amount	0.39

Figure 5-34. *OHMC price and optimal hedge*

CHAPTER 5 ■ OPTIMAL HEDGING MONTE CARLO METHODS

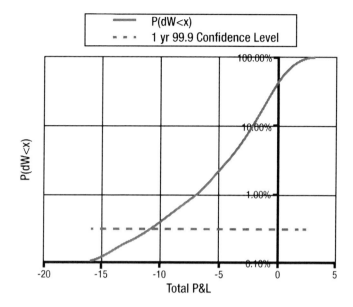

Figure 5-35. Cumulative wealth change distribution $F(\Delta W(0, T))$

The hedging intervals in Figures 5-36 and 5-37 are in units of three months.

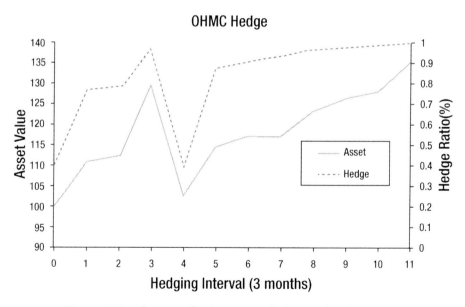

Figure 5-36. A loss-contributing asset path along with its hedge ratio

231

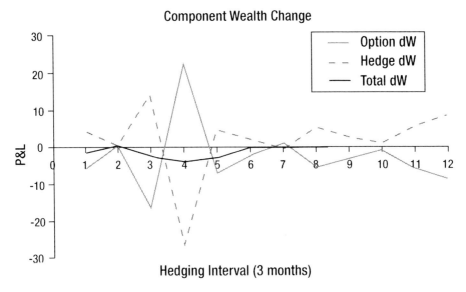

Figure 5-37. Component wealth changes for the loss path in Figure 5-36

Cliquet Contracts

This section describes the OMHC pricing of a knockout cliquet option. More details can be found in Petrelli et al. (2008). A *cliquet option* is a series of call or put options. With the exception of the first option, every option in the series is *forward starting*. For instance, one can have a series of three four-month European-style call options. The first option is a simple three-month call option. The next option starts in three months and ends at the six-month point. The third option starts at the six-month point and ends at the nine-month point. The complexity of cliquets arises from the nature of the *relative strike* of all the options. The strike for cliquets is quoted as a percentage of spot value of the underlying at the start time of the option, such as 105%. This relative strike is used for every option in the cliquet. The difficulty arises because the absolute value of the strikes for the forward starting options is unknown because their "spot" values have yet to be set as they all have starting points in the future. Only when one actually arrives at the starting point of one of these options does the precise value of the strike become known. Therefore, valuation becomes complex because the strikes of these options must also be treated as random variables. This option is clearly *path-dependent* as the actual historical price path taken by the underlying determines the strike of the options. Monte Carlo methods are well suited for path-dependent options. Many cliquets contracts also have one more wrinkle: The strike can be set before the forwarding starting date of an option in the series. For instance, one can have a two-year cliquet composed of a series of 24 one-month options (often called the *roll* interval). The strikes of these options can be set using the value of the underlying three months before the maturity date. This three-month period is called the look-back interval. Finally, these cliquets can be of the *knockout* fashion where if one option in the series is exercised, all remaining options are canceled.

Many of these features come from a popular equity derivative used in the market: *a deep out-of-the-money knockout cliquet put option*. Such options protect investors from sudden downside moves in the underlying asset (a "black swan" event). They are the equity version of a credit default swap that will be discussed in Chapter 6. Such cliquets are often quoted on the S&P 500 and the SX5E. They became even more popular (and more expensive) after the subprime crisis of 2008. Risk-neutral methods often underpriced these options before 2008. The OHMC methodology is well suited to price these knockout cliquets. Because of their similarity to credit default swaps, the price of these knockout cliquet put options are quoted as a running premium that has to be paid during the lifetime of the cliquet option, much a like an insurance premium. If the cliquet knocks out, the premium stops. This running premium has to be introduced into the OHMC wealth change equation.

There are several time scales at play for such an option as depicted in Figure 5-38. The option tenor is denoted by T. The most granular time interval over which asset value observations are available is denoted by τ_{obs}. The hedging interval is denoted by τ_{hedge}. The look-back interval over which a decline in asset value triggers a payoff (for a put cliquet) and a termination of the contract is denoted by $\tau_{look-back}$. The time interval over which the options mature and restart is denoted by τ_{roll}. Note that this time is equivalent to how often a drop in the asset value is checked for the put option exercise condition.

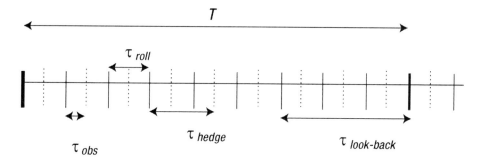

Figure 5-38. *A depiction of the various time scales pertinent to the cliquet contract*

Knockout Cliquet Sellers Wealth Change Equation

A few new definitions are needed in order to write down the wealth change equation for a knockout cliquet put option struck at K [Petrelli et al., 2008].

CHAPTER 5 ■ OPTIMAL HEDGING MONTE CARLO METHODS

Observation Days: $\{t_0, t_1, t_2, ..., t_N = T\}$

Hedging Interval: $(t_k, t_{k+1}]$

Running Premium Rate: η

Payout Trigger Time: $t_d = \min t_i \in \dfrac{s(t_i)}{s(t_{i-lookback})} < K$

Reference Notional: Ψ

Payout Amount: $P(t_d) = \Psi \left[K - \dfrac{s(t_i)}{s(t_{i-lookback})} \right]$

Payoff Trigger Indicator: $I(t_k, t_{k+1}) = \begin{cases} 1 & t_d \in (t_k, t_{k+1}] \\ 0 & t_d > t_{k+1} \end{cases}$ (5.74)

Discounted Payoff: $\omega(t_k, t_{k+1}) = I(t_k, t_{k+1}) P(t_d) df(t_k, t_d)$

Premium Accrual Time: $\chi(t_k, t_{k+1}) = \sum_{t_k}^{t^*} df(t_k, \tau) \Delta(t_k, t^*);\ t^* = \begin{cases} t_d & \text{if } I(t_k, t_{k+1}) = 1 \\ t_{k+1} & \text{otherwise} \end{cases}$

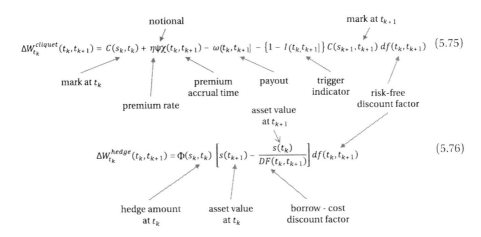

$$\Delta W_{t_k}^{cliquet}(t_k, t_{k+1}) = C(s_k, t_k) + \eta \Psi \chi(t_k, t_{k+1}) - \omega(t_k, t_{k+1}) - \{1 - I(t_k, t_{k+1})\} C(s_{k+1}, t_{k+1}) df(t_k, t_{k+1})$$ (5.75)

mark at t_k / premium rate / premium accrual time / payout / trigger indicator / asset value at t_{k+1} / risk-free discount factor / mark at t_{k+1} / notional

$$\Delta W_{t_k}^{hedge}(t_k, t_{k+1}) = \Phi(s_k, t_k) \left[s(t_{k+1}) - \dfrac{s(t_k)}{DF(t_k, t_{k+1})} \right] df(t_k, t_{k+1})$$ (5.76)

hedge amount at t_k / asset value at t_k / borrow-cost discount factor

Once again, the wealth change equation can be translated into G, H, and F functions as follows,

$$I(t_k,t_{k+1}) = \begin{cases} 1 & t_d \in (t_k,t_{k+1}] \\ 0 & t_d > t_{k+1} \end{cases}$$

$$\Delta W_{t_k}(t_k,t_{k+1}) = C(s_k,t_k) - G(t_k) + \Phi(s_k,t_k)H(t_k) \qquad (5.77)$$

$$G_k = \left(1 - I(t_k,t_{k+1})\right) C(s_{k+1},t_{k+1}) \, df(t_k,t_{k+1}) + \omega(t_k,t_{k+1}) - \eta \Psi \, \chi(t_k,t_{k+1})$$

$$H_k = \left(s_{k+1} - \frac{s_k}{DF(t_k,t_{k+1})}\right) df(t_k,t_{k+1})$$

The OHMC optimization problem is identical to equation (5.45).

As the wealth change equation has been written in terms of G, H, and Φ functions, all the previous matrix equations based upon basis function expansions and Lagrange multipliers are still valid. One need only update the G and H functions when dealing with new payoff types for differing derivative structures. This demonstrates the great flexibility of the OHMC methodology. It can be used as a consistent pricing, hedging, and risk management tool for a wide range of derivative structures. One simply needs to be able to write down the wealth change equation of the derivative structure in question.

Problems

Problem 5-1. *Linear Basis Function Expansion*

Use the linear basis functions (5.4) to approximate the function $s^2 \exp[s^{-2}]$ in the domain $[-3,3]$. Begin with nodes at $(-3,-2,-1,0,1,2,3)$. Discretize the s-space with intervals of length 0.1 —i.e., $(-3.0,-2.9,-2.8,\ldots)$ —and approximate the function at these points. Choose more nodes at more discrete points and see how the fit improves. Provide graphs similar to those in Figures 5-4 and 5-5.

Problem 5-2. *Hermite Cubic Basis Function Expansion*

Use the Hermite cubic basis functions (5.51) and (5.52) to approximate the function $s^2 \exp[s^{-2}]$ in the domain $[-3,3]$. Begin with nodes at $(-3,-2,-1,0,1,2,3)$. Discretize the s-space with intervals of length 0.1, i.e. $(-3.0,-2.9,-2.8,\ldots)$, and approximate the function at these points. Choose more nodes at more discrete points and see how the fit improves. Provide graphs similar to those in Figures 5-6 and 5-7.

Problem 5-3. *One-Time-Step OHMC Problem*

Perform a one-time-step MC simulation of 1,000,000 paths (use Brownian motion or GARCH(1,1) or any model of your choice). Consider either a call or put payoff at this time. Use (5.67) and (5.68) to solve for the average cost of hedging and the optimal hedge ratio for the option.

References and Further Reading

Bouchaud, J.-P., and M. Potters. Theory of Financial Risk and Derivative Pricing: From *Statistical Physics to Risk Management.* Cambridge: Cambridge University Press, 2003.

Kapoor, V., L. Cheung, and C. Howley. *Equity Securitization, Risk and Value, Special Report.* Structured Finance, Standard & Poors, 2003.

Petrelli, A., O. Siu, J. Zhang, and V. Kapoor. *Optimal Static Hedging of Defaults in CDOs.* DefaultRisk.com, April (2006).

Petrelli, A., O. Siu, J. Zhang, R. Chatterjee, and V. Kapoor. *Optimal Dynamic Hedging of Cliquets.* DefaultRisk.com, May (2008).

Petrelli, A., R. Balachandran, J. Zhang, O. Siu, R. Chatterjee, and V. Kapoor. *Optimal Dynamic Hedging of Multi-Asset Options.* SSRN abstract 1358667, January (2009).

Petrelli, A., R. Balachandran, O. Siu, J. Zhang, R. Chatterjee, and V. Kapoor. *Optimal Dynamic Hedging of Equity Options.* SSRN abstract 1530046, January (2010).

Potters, M., J.-P. Bouchaud, and D. Sestovic. "Hedged Monte Carlo: Low Variance Derivative Pricing with Objective Probabilities," *Physica A*, 289 (2001a), 517.

Schweizer, M. "Variance-Optimal Hedging in Discrete Time," *Mathematics of Operations Research*, 20 (1995), 1-32.

Wang, J. A., A. Petrelli, R. Balachandran, O. Siu, J. Zhang, R. Chatterjee, and V. Kapoor. *General Auto-Regressive Asset Model.* SSRN abstract 1428555, July (2009).

CHAPTER 6

Introduction to Credit Derivatives

The risk of a counterparty of a financial contract failing to live up to their obligations is real and can have far-reaching consequences. The financial system is predicated on the fact that when one buys an option or bond or enters into a swap with a counterparty, the expectation is that they will honor all contingent or promised cash flows from the financial instruments in question. The failure to meet a payment of any sort is considered a credit event and is called a *default*. Defaults may occur when companies declare bankruptcy and can no longer meet their debt obligations in terms of interest and principal payments. Government entities—such as countries, states, and municipalities—all can issue debt and therefore can default on this debt. Individuals default when they cannot make their mortgage or credit card payments. The risk of large counterparties such as Lehman Brothers and Bear Stearns defaulting (during the 2008 subprime crisis) can have potentially devastating effects on the financial system as a whole. Large banks such as Citi and Bank of America defaulting can lead to a "run on cash" from their ordinary depositors and potential riots in the streets. The risk of the whole financial system collapsing due to a few events such as the 2008 subprime crisis is known as *systemic risk*. Therefore, the US government along with the Fed bailed out the big banks during the 2008 subprime crisis. Some have argued that this bailout has created an environment of *moral hazard*. If banks know that they will get bailed out, they will take large risks without facing the downside consequences of taking those risks. There is always a counterplay between systemic risk and moral hazard. For instance, individuals defaulting on their mortgages does not create systemic risk; therefore, they are rarely bailed out, leading to no moral hazard issues. Airlines, on the other hand, are crucial for a country such as the United States and therefore will be bailed out, potentially leading to a moral hazard outcome. Most governments will accept the moral hazard risk over the systemic risk. The last time a US president chose not to bail out the financial system was after the stock market crash of October 29, 1929 (Black Tuesday). This led to the Great Depression, which affected the whole world and lasted almost ten years.

How does one hedge the credit risk of a bond? Before the mid-1990s, the only way to achieve this was to go short the bond in the same manner as one shorts a stock. Shorting corporate bonds is difficult inasmuch as corporations issue many bonds, not just one bond (as opposed to stocks). Repoing these bonds is also difficult because many repo counterparties do not feel that risky corporate debt is sufficient collateral for their loans.

With both the issues of hedging credit risk and difficulty of shorting bonds affecting the market, the *credit default swap* was born.

The CDS Contract: Overview

A **credit default swap (CDS)** is a bilateral derivative contract in which two counterparties agree to exchange a regular fixed coupon for a one-time contingent payment on the occurrence of a credit event on a prespecified corporate or government entity. A CDS transfers the risk of the loss of the face value of the reference corporate or government debt instrument from one counterparty to another. It is akin to an insurance contract where the buyer of protection pays a premium (or coupon) to the seller of the CDS in order to receive protection against a credit event of the underlying debt issuer. After a credit event, the premium payments stop. The protection seller thereupon makes a payment of the par value of the contract minus the recovery value of the defaulted bond (which may be zero)—("par - recovery")—as depicted in Figure 6-1. The basic CDS contract is largely a *pure* credit risk transfer mechanism that isolates credit risk from interest rate risk, foreign exchange risk, prepayment risk, and so on.

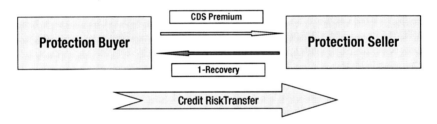

Figure 6-1. Mechanism of a credit default swap

A standard *CDS confirm* specifies the following key terms:

- Underlying reference asset
- Transaction notional
- Trade tenor
- The fixed coupon
- Valid deliverable obligations
- Valid credit events

In 2009, two major standardized contracts for a large majority of CDS transactions were introduced: the *Standard North American Corporate* (SNAC) contract and the *Standard European Corporate* (STEC) contract. Shortly afterward, a standardized CDS for Latin America, Eastern Europe, the Middle East, and Africa was created: the *Standard Emerging Market* (STEM) contract. Previous to the 2009 agreements, the CDS market traded on a par basis, whereby at trade inception the counterparties would agree upon a fixed coupon level which made the net present value of the contract zero, much like a standard USD interest rate swap. Furthermore, the maturity dates of these contracts were chosen by the counterparties themselves. This was a fully OTC market until the introduction of SNAC and STEC. One of the main drivers of this standardization was to eventually move CDS contracts to exchanges. All financial contracts on exchanges are standardized, so SNAC was the first step in this direction. Counterparty credit risk is a key risk in a CDS contract. When Lehman Brothers declared bankruptcy in September 2008, the majority of Wall Street firms had CDS contracts with Lehman. Most of these swaps were either sold to other firms or taken over by Barclays Capital in the US and Nomura in London. If these contracts had been traded on an exchange, the exchange's clearing house would have become the counterparty taking over for Lehman Brothers, thereby dramatically reducing the counterparty credit risk of these transactions.

Both SNAC and STEC have standardized CDS terms, such as fixed coupons and fixed maturity and coupon payment dates. The North American coupons are, depending on the underlying, either 100 bps or 500 bps. The European coupons are 25 bps, 100 bps, 500 bps, or 1,000 bps. Therefore, most CDSs do not have a *present value* (PV) of zero at inception, because the market spread of the underlying does not match the contract coupon spread. Therefore, at the inception of most contracts, an *upfront payment* is made by one counterparty to the other to compensate for a nonzero PV. To calculate this upfront payment, the concept of a *Risky PV01* (present value of a basis point) has to be introduced.

Typical key standardized terms are:

Contract Maturities: Contracts are always traded with the maturity date falling on one of the four roll/coupon payment dates (or following business day): 20 March, 20 June, 20 September, or 20 December. The maturity date is rounded up to the next roll date (i.e., a 5yr contract is almost always a little longer than 5yrs).

Coupons: The coupon basis is Act/360. The first coupon payment is paid in full (like the bond market). Recall that the coupon dates are fixed (Mar, Jun, Sept, or Dec). If a contract is traded between these dates, a full premium is still paid by the protection buyer at the following coupon date. The protection seller "pays back" the accrued interest from the previous coupon date to the date of the transaction. This is similar to paying accrued interest in the bond market.

Protection Period: The *credit event backstop* date is the beginning date from which protection is valid. It is rolling and has a look-back nature. It is equal to the trade date minus 60 days (i.e., it is retroactive and changes for each deal as time moves forward). The reason for this is that it may take time to determine if a credit event has happened, and therefore a credit event may be declared to have occurred in the past. This date rolls forward in time as the seller of protection is liable for a any credit event that occurred in the last 60 days at any point in time during the life of the contract.

Standardized Credit Events: These are defined on the reference entity or the reference obligation, as listed in Table 6-1.

Table 6-1. Standardized Credit Events

Credit Event	Defined on Reference	Comments
Bankruptcy	Entity	Entity is dissolved or becomes insolvent
Failure to pay	Obligation	Fails to make payments when they are due
Restructuring	Obligation	Changes the terms of the debt
Obligation acceleration	Obligation	An obligation becomes due before its original maturity (to avoid default)
Obligation default	Obligation	An obligation becomes *capable* of being declared due before its original maturity
Repudiation/moratorium	Entity	Reference Entity repudiates its obligation or declares a moratorium on payments

Any credit event other than *restructuring* triggers the CDS contract once the *determinations committee* (see below) declares a credit event. The credit trigger is automatic: no credit event notice is needed between counterparties. On the credit trigger day, all premium payments stop (except accrued coupon payments), and the protection leg must be settled by one of the two following ways:

> *Physical settlement:* The protection buyer delivers a valid reference obligation (which is considered to be defaulted or cross defaulted) and receives par.
>
> *Cash settlement:* The protection buyer receives (par − recovery) from the protection seller. The recovery value is the average market value of the defaulted bond (see Auction Settlement below).

Clearly, both these types of settlement procedures have the economic transfer of par − recovery.

Restructuring: The terms of this event could not be agreed on internationally. In North America, it is not a credit event. In Europe, restructuring is a credit event only if the buyer or seller of a CDS wishes to trigger a CDS contract with a restructuring event. They also have conditions on what type of obligations can be delivered if restructuring becomes a credit event. Note that if neither party triggers a restructuring event, the CDS continues. To trigger a restructuring event, one party must serve a *credit event notice* to the other party. The other party may not agree to an event being classified as a restructuring event, which may then lead to a legal battle.

Restructuring Types: These are differentiated by their characteristic clauses in Table 6-2.

Table 6-2. *Restructuring Types*

Value to Protection Buyer	Clause	Comments
Least valuable	No restructuring	Debt restructuring is not a credit event.
	Modified restructuring	Puts a cap on the maturity of a deliverable obligation at the earlier of 2.5 years from the restructuring date or the longest maturity of a restructured bond.
	Modified modified restructuring	Puts a cap on the maturity of a deliverable obligation at the later of the CDS maturity and 5 years after the restructuring date.
Most valuable	Full restructuring	No restrictions on deliverable obligations.

SNAC, STEC, and STEM have different standardized restructuring conventions:

- *North America:* No restructuring
- *Europe:* Modified modified restructuring
- *Emerging Markets*: Full restructuring

Determinations Committee: The new standardization procedures included the creation of regional committees, consisting of 10 dealer banks and 5 nondealers with the responsibility to

- determine if a credit event has taken place
- determine if auction settlement is required
- specify valid deliverable obligations
- determine whether a succession event has occurred (such as merger)

The regions include North and South America, Japan, Asia–ex Japan, Australia–New Zealand, and EMEA (Europe, Middle East, Africa). Each regional committee has different members. Their primary role is to standardize the determination and settlement of credit events.

Auction Settlement: Since the development of the CDS, its popularity has grown to the point that the volume of outstanding notional in the CDS contract has grown larger than the notional of the underlying bonds for many popular CDS names. This is possible because a CDS is a *synthetic instrument*, much like a futures or derivatives contract and can be bought and sold without holding the actual underlying bond. After a credit event, physical settlement meant that protection buyers who did not own the underlying bonds had to go looking for deliverable obligations, which had the unintended effect of bidding up the prices of these defaulted bonds. Therefore, the concept of cash settlement was created. The *credit event auction* was developed to provide a transparent price discovery mechanism for cash-settled CDS. The first stage of the auction is when dealers make a two-way market for the cheapest to deliver bonds. After that, limit orders are taken and matched to open interest in price order until the last order is filled. This last price becomes the cash-settled recovery rate.

Though the CDS contract is essentially an insurance contract on a bond, one of its primary uses is as a synthetic way to go short a corporate or government name. Going short equities is relatively easy to do because stocks are widely held and can be repoed in a straightforward manner (see Chapter 1 for repo contracts). Corporate bonds are much harder to repo because they are not widely held. Furthermore, several different bonds with differing maturities and coupon rates exist for every corporate name. Which one should one go short? The CDS contract provides a straightforward way to go short a corporate name without repoing and selling bonds. Buying a *naked* (unhedged) CDS is equivalent to going short the underlying name. Say one *buys* a 5yr CDS on Corp X at a market spread of 165 bps, and say the SNAC coupon is 100 bps, so there will be an upfront payment by the buyer. This 165 bps is the market's view of the credit risk of Corp X. This same view is also reflected in the price of Corp X's bonds. The effective spread over LIBOR of a 5yr Corp X bond will be close to 165 bps (see the Par Asset Swap section below). When one shorts a bond, one is expecting the price to go down, which is equivalent to the yield going up. The yield going up means the spread over LIBOR will go up (assuming LIBOR stays relatively constant). As this bond spread goes up (because the market believes the credit risk of Corp X is increasing), the CDS market spreads goes up, say, to 175 bps. Now, the naked owner of the original CDS contract can *sell* CDS protection at 175 bps (this is equivalent to closing out a short position). This person is paying 165 bps on the CDS she bought, and making 175 bps on the one just sold for a profit of 10 bps per annum. The buying and selling of CDS protection in this manner is far more common than buying a CDS to actually protect a physical bond. This is one of the reasons why the outstanding dollar notional of a many CDS contracts can be greater than the outstanding notional of the underlying bonds.

The CDS Contract: Pricing

A CDS is very much like a regular interest rate swap. The value of a CDS contract is the difference between the two swap legs, just like a regular interest rate swap is the difference between the fixed leg and the floating leg,

$$PV(CDS) = PV(\text{premium leg}) - PV(\text{default leg}) \quad . \tag{6.1}$$

The value of the premium leg is the present value of future premium payments that must be adjusted for the probability of default, whereupon the premium payments end. Denoting $S(t)$ as the *survival probability* until time t, the PV for a $t_n = T$ maturity CDS premium leg is

$$PV(\text{premium leg}) = C(t) \sum_{i=1}^{n} df(t_i) \Delta(t_i) S(t_i)$$

$C(t) = C(t_i) = $ CDS premium payment at time t (an annualized "coupon") paid at times t_i
paid at times t_i
$df(t_i) = $ discount factor at time t_i
$\Delta(t_i) = $ daycount between t_{i-1} and t_i
$S(t_i) = $ survival probability at time t_i

(6.2)

CHAPTER 6 ■ INTRODUCTION TO CREDIT DERIVATIVES

If $S(t) = 1$, this equation reduces to the PV of the fixed leg on an interest rate swap. Here, the CDS premium $C(t)$ has an explicit time component as it changes continually in the market (though it is fixed once a contract is executed). For the USD interest rate swap rates discussed in Chapter 1, this time component was not made explicit, although it obviously exists. Similar to an interest rate swap DV01, it is very useful to define a time-dependent *default-adjusted present value of a basis point* written as *PV01*. This is like a "credit-risky" version of an interest rate swap DV01 where the default risk is captured by the survival probability factor $S(t)$.

$$PV01(T) = \sum_{i=1}^{n} df(t_i) \Delta(t_i) S(t_i)$$
$$PV(\text{premium leg}) = C(t) PV01(T) \quad . \tag{6.3}$$

The value of the default leg is the present value of a possible future payment by the protection seller. As described above this payment is equivalent to (par − recovery) = 1 − R. Note that default can happen at anytime between premium payments so that the PV of the default leg can be theoretically valued over a continuous time framework. Denoting $Q(t)$ as the default probability at time t and $dQ(t)$ as its differential element (note df is *not* a differential element but the discount factor),

$$PV(\text{default leg}) = (1-R) \int_0^T [df(t)] \, dQ(t)$$
$$R = \text{Recovery Rate of the defaulted bond} \tag{6.4}$$
$$df(t) = \text{discount factor at time } t \text{ (seen from time } 0)$$
$$Q(t) = \text{probability at time } t \text{ of a credit event} = 1 - S(t) \quad .$$

In reality, default events are declared at end of day. As an approximation one can discretize the integral into monthly steps as follows:

$$PV(\text{default leg}) = (1-R) \int_0^T [df(t)] \, dQ(t) = -(1-R) \int_0^T [df(t)] \, dS(t) \tag{6.5}$$

$$PV(\text{default leg}) \cong -(1-R) \sum_{j=1}^{n} df(t_j)[S(t_j) - S(t_{j-1})] = (1-R) \sum_{j=1}^{n} df(t_j)[S(t_{j-1}) - S(t_j)] \tag{6.6}$$

The discretization choice of monthly is arbitrary (but common). One could have just as well have used weekly or daily. Previous to early 2009, the premium $C(0)$ at initiation $t = 0$ would be calculated so that both premium and default legs have the same value (a par swap),

$$PV(CDS) = 0 = PV(\text{premium leg}) - PV(\text{default leg})$$
$$= C(0) \sum_{i=1}^{n} df(t_i) \Delta(t_i) S(t_i) - (1-R) \int_0^T [df(t)] dQ(t) \tag{6.7}$$
$$= C(0) \sum_{i=1}^{n} df(t_i) \Delta(t_i) S(t_i) - (1-R) \sum_{j=1}^{n} df(t_j)[S(t_{j-1}) - S(t_j)] \quad .$$

CHAPTER 6 ■ INTRODUCTION TO CREDIT DERIVATIVES

Solving for the premium gives (in both the continuous and discrete settings)

$$C(0) = \frac{(1-R)\int_0^T [df(t)]\, dQ(t)}{PV01(T)}$$

$$C(0) = \frac{(1-R)\sum_{j=1}^n df(t_j)[S(t_{j-1})-S(t_j)]}{PV01(T)} = \frac{(1-R)\sum_{j=1}^n df(t_j)[S(t_{j-1})-S(t_j)]}{\sum_{i=1}^n df(t_i)\Delta(t_i)S(t_i)} \quad . \tag{6.8}$$

It is important to note that the two sums over the indices i and j in the above equation are over different time intervals. The numerator may be weekly or monthly, whereas the denominator will be either quarterly or semiannually depending on the CDS contract.

When dealing with standard contracts with standard coupons (100 bps, 500 bps, etc.), one can think of them as *off-par* swaps with a premium of $\tilde{C}$. The present value of a standard contract is given by how "off" it is with respect to the par rate. Since the default leg is independent of the premium, one needs to calculate the PV of the off-par premium leg as follows:

$$PV(\text{premium leg}) = \tilde{C} \cdot PV01(T)$$

$$PV(CDS) = \tilde{C} \cdot PV01(T) - PV(\text{default leg})$$

$$= [\tilde{C} - C(0)]PV01(T) + C(0)PV01(T) - PV(\text{default leg}) \tag{6.9}$$

The last two terms cancel as $C(0)$ is a par rate and one is left with

$$PV(CDS) = [\tilde{C} - C(0)]\, PV01(T) \quad . \tag{6.10}$$

Using the market convention, the *upfront payment* made from the protection buyer to the seller is

$$\text{Upfront Payment} = [C(0) - \tilde{C}]\, PV01(T) \quad . \tag{6.11}$$

If the par rate $C(0)$ is higher than the standardized coupon $\tilde{C}$, a positive payment goes from the buyer to the seller. If the par rate $C(0)$ is lower than the standardized coupon $\tilde{C}$, a positive payment goes from the seller to the buyer.

One point to note is that the protection buyer must pay the accrued premium payment up to default from the last coupon payment day. Adjusting for accrued interest at default, the premium leg becomes

$$PV(\text{premium leg}) = C(t)\sum_{i=1}^{n}\left[df(t_i)\Delta(t_i)S(t_i) - \int_{t_{i-1}}^{t_i} df(t_i)\Delta(t_i)\frac{t_i - \tau}{t_i - t_{i-1}} dQ(\tau)\right]$$

$\tau = $ default time between t_{i-1} and t_i

$$PV01^{Adj}(T) = \sum_{i=1}^{n}\left[df(t_i)\Delta(t_i)S(t_i) - \int_{t_{i-1}}^{t_i} df(t_i)\Delta(t_i)\frac{t_i - \tau}{t_i - t_{i-1}} dQ(\tau)\right]$$

$$= \sum_{i=1}^{n}\left[df(t_i)\Delta(t_i)S(t_i) + df(t_i)\frac{\Delta(t_i)}{2}(S(t_{i-1}) - S(t_i))\right] \qquad (6.12)$$

(assuming default τ occurs uniformly over $(t_{i-1}, t_i]$)

$$= \sum_{i=1}^{n}\left[df(t_i)\frac{\Delta(t_i)}{2}(S(t_{i-1}) + S(t_i))\right]$$

$$C(0)^{Adj} = \frac{(1-R)\sum_{j=1}^{n} df(t_j)[S(t_{j-1}) - S(t_j)]}{PV01^{Adj}(T)}$$

The final step is to have a model for the survival probability $S(t)$. This is the topic of the following section.

Intensity-Based Reduced-Form Default Models

To price a CDS contract, one must first model the probability of default of the underlying name. The probability of default always comes down to determining a *default time* Γ. One needs a distribution $F(t)$ of the default times Γ, along with a density function $f(t)$,

$\Gamma = $ **Default Time**

$$S(t) = P(\Gamma > t) = 1 - P(\Gamma < t) = 1 - F(t) \qquad (6.13)$$

$$F(t) = \int_0^t f(s) ds$$

One very commonly used model for defaults is to *reduce* all default conditions down to one variable: the *hazard rate*. The hazard rate is the conditional density function of the default time Γ conditional on no defaults occurring before time t. It can also be seen as the instantaneous forward default probability conditional on prior survival. It is given by

$$h_t \Delta t = P[t < \Gamma < t + \Delta t \mid \Gamma > t] \quad . \qquad (6.14)$$

The probability that default will occur in a very small interval Δt is approximately given by

$$f(t)\Delta t \approx P[t < \Gamma < t + \Delta t]$$

$$h_t \Delta t = P[t < \Gamma < t + \Delta t \mid \Gamma > t] = \frac{f(t)\Delta t}{1 - F(t)} \qquad (6.15)$$

$$h_t = \frac{f(t)}{1 - F(t)}$$

CHAPTER 6 ■ INTRODUCTION TO CREDIT DERIVATIVES

Using the definition of the cumulative probability density,

$$\frac{dF(t)}{dt} = f(t) \quad , \tag{6.16}$$

one finds

$$\frac{1}{1-F(t)} \frac{dF(t)}{dt} = h_t$$
$$\frac{dF(t)}{1-F(t)} = h_t dt \quad . \tag{6.17}$$

Integrating both sides, one finds

$$\int \frac{dF(t)}{1-F(t)} = \int_0^t h_u \, du \tag{6.18}$$

or

$$-\ln[1-F(t)] = \int_0^t h_u \, du \quad . \tag{6.19}$$

Finally, the *survival probability distribution function* $S(t)$ in terms of the hazard rate is given by the exponential of the above relation,

$$S(t) = P(\Gamma > t) = 1 - F(t) = \exp\left(-\int_0^t h_u \, du\right) \quad . \tag{6.20}$$

This distribution is similar to a Poisson distribution. A Poisson distribution counting the number of "jumps" $N(t)$ with a constant *intensity* λ is given by

$$P[\{N(T) - N(t)\} = n] = \frac{(T-t)^n \lambda^n \exp[-(T-t)\lambda]}{n!} \quad . \tag{6.21}$$

In the hazard rate formulation, a default can be seen as one jump, so that survival means no jumps, that is, $n = 0$. Comparing the previous two formulas with $n = 0$,

$$S(t) = P(\Gamma > t) = \exp\left(-\int_0^t h_u \, du\right) = \exp(-\lambda t) \tag{6.22}$$

indicates that the hazard rate model reduces to a Poisson distribution for a constant hazard rate (i.e., no term structure of defaults),

$$h_t = \lambda, \rightarrow \text{flat term structure} \quad . \tag{6.23}$$

CHAPTER 6 ■ INTRODUCTION TO CREDIT DERIVATIVES

A more realistic model, the nonhomogeneous Poisson distribution, has a time-dependent intensity function $\lambda(s)$ and is given by

$$P[\{N(T)-N(t)\}=n] = \frac{\left(\int_t^T \lambda(s)\,ds\right)^n \exp\left[\int_t^T -\lambda(s)\,ds\right]}{n!} \quad (6.24)$$

For $n = 0$, one has

$$P[\{N(T)-N(t)\}=0] = \exp\left[\int_t^T -\lambda(s)\,ds\right] , \quad (6.25)$$

which is precisely the hazard rate model with $h_t = \lambda(t)$ (hence the name "intensity based").

Bootstrapping a Survival Curve with Piecewise Constant Hazard Rates

The CDS market does not directly provide survival probabilities for issuers of debt. Rather, one assumes a functional form for the survival function, such as the hazard rate formulation above, and calibrates it to the market such that it re-prices all CDS quotes on a specific issuer. Essentially, one creates a *term structure curve of hazard rates* for each issuer as follows. Let the survival function be based on a time-dependent hazard rate,

$$S(t) = \exp\left[\int_0^t -h(s)\,ds\right] . \quad (6.26)$$

To calibrate to market CDS spreads, one assumes that the hazard rate is piecewise constant in time,

$$h(t) = h_i, \quad t \in [T_{i-1}, T_i) , \quad (6.27)$$

where the T_i are the maturities of the CDS quotes spreads. These maturities tend to be [6M, 1Y, 2Y, 3Y, 4Y, 5Y, 7Y, 10Y]. The resultant survival function at an arbitrary time t will be given by

$$S(t) = \exp\left(-\sum_{i=1}^{n(t)} [h_i(T_i - T_{i-1})] - h_{n(t)+1}(t - T_{n(t)})\right) , \quad (6.28)$$

where $n(t) := \max i \leq n : T_i \leq t$. The reason for this general expression is that one will need to use survival probabilities with three different partitions of time, namely:

- Monthly times for the default leg.
- Quarterly or semi-annual times for the premium leg.
- Common maturities of [6M, 1Y, 2Y, 3Y, 4Y, 5Y, 7Y, 10Y] for the hazard rates calibrated from CDS quotes.

247

Assume one has par market CDS spreads for various maturities such as $[T_1 = 6M, T_2 = 1Y, \ldots]$. One needs to bootstrap all the hazard rates starting with the first CDS spread. This is in the same spirit as the bootstrapping methodology of the LIBOR yield curve as described in Chapter 2. There, one had to first start with cash LIBOR rates and move on to futures and finally swaps. Here, one needs to calibrate the market CDS spreads in temporal order. The first step is to solve for h_1 using the T_1 CDS spread. Denoting C_{T_1} as the first par rate, the following relation holds,

$$U(T_1) = 0(\text{par spread}) = PV^{prem}(T_1) - PV^{def}(T_1) \quad . \quad (6.29)$$

The premium leg will be given by (i is a quarterly or semiannual index)

$$PV^{prem}(T_1) = C_{T_1} \sum_{i=1}^{T_1} df(t_i)\Delta(t_i)S(t_i) \quad . \quad (6.30)$$

The default leg will be given by (j is monthly index)

$$PV^{def}(T_1) = (1-R)\sum_{j=1}^{T_1} df(t_j)[S(t_{j-1}) - S(t_j)] \quad . \quad (6.31)$$

Using

$$S(t) = \exp[-h_1 \, t], \quad t < T_1 \quad , \quad (6.32)$$

which is the simplest version of (6.28), one must solve for h_1 using the par relationship

$$C_{T_1} \sum_{i=1}^{T_1} df(t_i)\Delta(t_i)S(t_i) = (1-R)\sum_{j=1}^{T_1} df(t_j)[S(t_{j-1}) - S(t_j)]$$

$$C_{T_1} \sum_{i=1}^{T_1} df(t_i)\Delta(t_i)\exp[-h_1 \, t_i] \quad (6.33)$$

$$= (1-R)\sum_{j=1}^{T_1} df(t_j)\left\{\exp[-h_1 \, t_{j-1}] - \exp[-h_1 \, t_j]\right\} \quad .$$

It is important to note that $\Delta(t_j)$ usually uses an Act/360 daycount basis, whereas the time components t_j multiplying the h_1 factors are based on an Act/365 daycount basis. Bootstrapping up, one next solves for h_2 using (6.28) to incorporate the h_1 solution,

$$C_{T_2}\left[\sum_{i=1}^{T_1} df(t_i)\Delta(t_i)\exp[-h_1 t_i] + \sum_{i>T_1}^{T_2} df(t_i)\Delta(t_i)\exp[-h_1 T_1 - h_2(t_i - T_1)]\right]$$

$$= (1-R)\sum_{j=1}^{T_1} df(t_j)\left\{\exp[-h_1 \, t_{j-1}] - \exp[-h_1 \, t_j]\right\} \quad (6.34)$$

$$+ (1-R)\sum_{j>T_1}^{T_2} df(t_j)\exp[-h_1 T_1]\left\{\exp[-h_2(t_{j-1} - T_1)] - \exp[-h_2(t_j - T_1)]\right\} \quad .$$

This expression has been split into two parts: one part up to the first quote ($T_1 = 6M$) and the second part for the second quote ($T_2 = 1Y$). The first part uses the 6M hazard rate and the second part uses the 1Y hazard rate. This process is continued until all par CDS rates have been calibrated.

For standardized contracts with fixed dates, the tenors of the CDSs are not precisely integer years and all CDSs may have already started. Therefore, one must adjust the above formulas for the premium leg using the adjusted PV01 of (6.12), which incorporates the accrued interest.

Credit Triangle

Traders often use a rule of thumb in the credit markets that relates the three key variables: *hazard rates*, *CDS spreads*, and *recovery rates*. This rule can be "derived" using several approximations, as follow. Begin with a basic expression for a par spread,

$$C\sum_{i=1}^{T_1} df(t_i)\Lambda(t_i)\exp[-h_1\, t_i] = (1-R)\sum_{j=1}^{T_1} df(t_j)\left\{\exp\left[-h_1\, t_{j-1}\right] - \exp\left[-h_1\, t_j\right]\right\} \quad . \tag{6.35}$$

Use the following approximations:

- The time partitions are the same (e.g., everything is quarterly).
- The daycounts are all the same (e.g., act/360).

This means that $\Delta T = t_i - t_{i-1} = \Lambda_i = \Lambda$.
The par spread expression reduces to

$$\sum_{i=1}^{T_1} df(t_i)\left\{C\Lambda\exp(-h\, t_i) - (1-R)\exp[-h\, t_{i-1}] + (1-R)\exp[-h\, t_i]\right\} = 0 \quad . \tag{6.36}$$

Pulling out a factor of $\exp(-h\, t_{i-1})$ gives

$$\sum_{i=1}^{T_1} df(t_i)\exp(-h\, t_{i-1})\left\{C\Lambda\exp(-h\Lambda) - (1-R) + (1-R)\exp[-h\Lambda]\right\} = 0 \tag{6.37}$$

$$\sum_{i=1}^{T_1} df(t_i)\exp(-h\, t_{i-1})\left\{(1-R+C\Lambda)\exp(-h\Lambda) - (1-R)\right\} = 0 \quad . \tag{6.38}$$

The solution to the above equation is

$$(1-R+C\Lambda)\exp(-h\Lambda) = (1-R) \tag{6.39}$$

$$\exp(-h\Lambda) = \frac{(1-R)}{(1-R+C\Lambda)} \quad . \tag{6.40}$$

Solving for the hazard rate produces the following expression,

$$h = \frac{-1}{\Delta}\ln\left[\frac{(1-R)}{(1-R+C\Delta)}\right] = \frac{-1}{\Delta}\ln\left[1 - \frac{C\Delta}{(1-R+C\Delta)}\right] \quad . \quad (6.41)$$

Using the approximation $\ln[1-x] \approx -x$, $x \ll 1$, one has

$$h = \frac{-1}{\Delta}\frac{-C\Delta}{(1-R+C\Delta)} \quad (6.42)$$

or

$$h = \frac{C}{(1-R+C\Delta)} \quad . \quad (6.43)$$

Assuming that $C\Delta \ll R$, which is true for most CDS spreads, one is left with the following simple *credit triangle* relationship:

$$h = \frac{C}{(1-R)} \quad . \quad (6.44)$$

This expression will appear in the counterparty credit risk component of Basel III discussed in Chapter 7.

Quotation Conventions for Standard Contracts

Quotations for standard contracts come in two formats: *quoted spreads* for underlyings with relatively low spreads (usually *investment grade*) and points paid upfront for high spread underlyings (*high yield* or distressed names). As mentioned above, even for quoted spreads, there is an upfront payment made as the actual running premium paid is a standardized fixed amount (such as 100 bps or 500 bps). To calculate the upfront payment, one needs a *PV*01. Yet the *PV*01 assumes a model for survival probabilities. Market participants need to agree on a simple model that can be implemented by all such that everyone agrees on the *PV*01 calculation and all upfront payments. The market standard convention for calculating the upfront payment for quoted spreads is to assume that the quoted spread is in fact a par spread and construct a *flat hazard rate curve* (one hazard rate for all times) with a 40% recovery assumption for senior corporate debt and Western sovereigns, and 20% recovery rates for all other names. Using the above hazard rate model with these inputs will give one the *PV*01 needed to calculate upfront payments. The reason this is not the exact par spread is because hazard rates have a term structure and recovery rates vary name by name. The quoted spread can be seen as an implied volatility, whereas the simplified hazard rate model can be seen as the Black-Scholes model. Both the simplified model based on quoted spreads and the full model based on par spreads give the same upfront payment:

(Quoted Spread − Fixed Coupon) · PV01(Quoted Spread Flat Hazard Rates)
= (6.45)
(Par Spread − Fixed Coupon) · PV01(Par Spread Term Hazard Rates)

For instance, assume one has a quoted 5yr CDS spread of C_{quoted} with a standard coupon of 100 bps. One must find (using a root finder) a *constant* hazard rate h_c such that (with a fixed recovery of 40%),

$$C_{quoted}\sum_{i=1}^{5yrs} df(t_i)\Delta(t_i)\exp[-h_c\ t_i] = (1-0.4)\sum_{j=1}^{5yrs} df(t_j)\{\exp[-h_c\ t_{j-1}] - \exp[-h_c\ t_j]\} \quad (6.46)$$

Note that unlike the bootstrapping procedure for par spreads, the above calculated hazard rate has been used for all temporal points. The upfront payment from the protection buyer to the seller for this contract would be

$$\text{Upfront} = [C_{quoted} - 100bps]\sum_{i=1}^{5yrs} df(t_i)\Delta(t_i)\exp[-h_c\ t_i] \quad . \quad (6.47)$$

The coupon payment for this contract would be 100 bps. Once the upfront payment has been calculated, the quoted spread plays no role. One can use the CDSW screen in Bloomberg shown in Figure 6-2 to calculate the upfront payments for standardized CDS contracts. (See also http://www.markit.com/ for a list of standard market quotations of 5YR CDS for various corporate and sovereign names.)

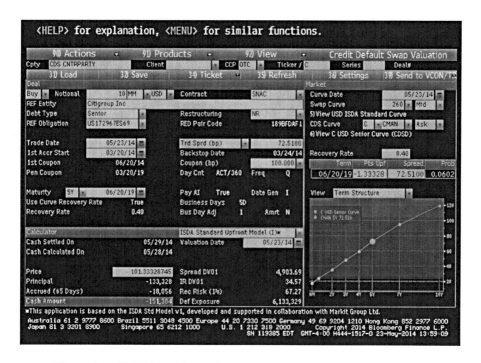

Figure 6-2. *CDSW Bloomberg pricing screen.* Used with permission of Bloomberg L.P. Copyright © 2014. All rights reserved.

Par Asset Swaps

A derivative that is very similar to a CDS is a *par asset swap*. In Chapter 1, the standard USD fixed-floating swap was introduced. For fixed coupon corporate bonds, a similar derivative exists where one can exchange the fixed coupon of the corporate bond for equivalent floating-rate payment of LIBOR + spread. The fixed rate bond—the "asset"—is thereby "swapped" into a floating rate bond. The spread over LIBOR is the *asset swap spread* that makes the present value of both legs of the swap equal at the initiation of the deal. The main point to realize here is that the asset swap continues even if the underlying bond defaults. The fixed coupon payer has to keep paying the coupon and receive LIBOR + spread until the maturity of the swap because an asset swap is a purely synthetic instrument. The payer of the floating leg has effectively bought default insurance against the underlying bond. The asset swap spread he pays is based on the creditworthiness of the underlying bond and, even if the bond defaults, he continues to receive the fixed coupon payments of the underlying bond. In this manner, the floating rate payer is protected from default similar to a CDS contract. The main difference is that a CDS contract pays the holder (par - recovery) under default, whereas the asset swap continues until the original maturity of the underlying bond.

The mechanics are illustrated in Figure 6-3. In the first step, the asset swap seller gives the underlying fixed coupon bond to the asset swap buyer and receives par even though the bond has a market value P^{MKT} that may be away from par (this why it is called a par asset swap rather than the far less common market asset swap). The asset swap spread takes into account the difference between par and the market value P^{MKT} of the bond. In the second step, the two counterparties exchange fixed for floating cash flows. The fixed payments are often due semiannually, while the floating payments are linked to 3M LIBOR and therefore quarterly. Under a default scenario, the asset swap continues as depicted in the "Default" scenario of Figure 6-3. This is why the asset swap spread is close to an equivalent CDS premium for the underlying name.

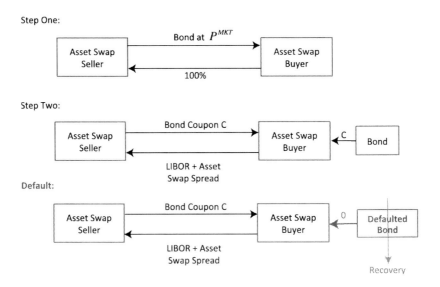

Figure 6-3. Par asset swap

CHAPTER 6 ■ INTRODUCTION TO CREDIT DERIVATIVES

The present value of both legs is straightforward because they do not explicitly depend on the default probability of the underlying bond. Denoting the asset swap spread as A (in bps), one has

$$PV_{fixed} = \sum_{j=1}^{n_{fxd}} c\Delta_j \, df_j \qquad (6.48)$$

$$PV_{float} = \sum_{i=1}^{n_{flt}} (L_i + A)\delta_i \, df_i \quad . \qquad (6.49)$$

The fair value spread is found by equating the seller's and buyer's total return and then solving for the asset swap spread A. One top of the coupon payments, the asset swap seller gets par (100%). The asset swap buyer gets LIBOR plus the asset swap spread A and a bond worth its market price P^{MKT}. Equating these two total return cashflow streams gives

$$1 + \sum_{j=1}^{n_{fxd}} c\Delta_j \, df_j = P^{MKT} + \sum_{i=1}^{n_{flt}} (L_i + A)\delta_i \, df_i \quad . \qquad (6.50)$$

Rearrange the terms and introduce two types of DV01: one for bonds, which are semiannual, and one for 3M LIBOR, which is quarterly,

$$1 - P^{MKT} + c \cdot DV01_{semi-ann} = A \cdot DV01_{quarterly} + \sum_{i=1}^{n_{flt}} L_i \delta_i \, df_i \quad . \qquad (6.51)$$

Recall that LIBOR is related to the LIBOR-discount factors as

$$df(0, t_i) = \frac{df(0, t_{i-1})}{1 + \delta_i L_i} \qquad (6.52)$$

or

$$L_i = \left[\frac{df(0, t_{i-1})}{df(0, t_i)} - 1 \right] \frac{1}{\delta_i} \quad . \qquad (6.53)$$

Substituting this into the floating rate sum term above leaves one at $t_0 = 0$ with

$$\sum_{i=1}^{n_{flt}} [df_{i-1} - df_i] = df(0, t_0) - df(0, T) = 1 - df(0, T) \quad . \qquad (6.54)$$

Therefore, the par spread formula reduces to

$$1 - P^{Mkt} + c \cdot DV01_{semi-ann} = A \cdot DV01_{quarterly} + 1 - df(0, T) \quad . \qquad (6.55)$$

Solving for the par asset swap spread A gives

$$A = \frac{c \cdot DV01_{semi-ann} + df(0, T) - P^{MKT}}{DV01_{quarterly}} \quad . \qquad (6.56)$$

The asset swap spread may also be calculated on Bloomberg as depicted in Figure 6-4.

CHAPTER 6 ■ INTRODUCTION TO CREDIT DERIVATIVES

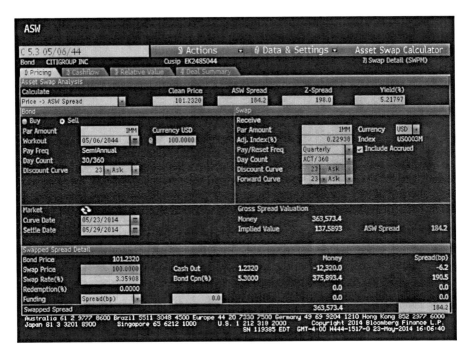

Figure 6-4. Asset Swap Calculator on Bloomberg. Used with permission of Bloomberg L.P. Copyright © 2014. All rights reserved.

One can further define a LIBOR discounted bond price as

$$P^{LD} = c \cdot DV01_{semi-ann} + df(0,T) \quad . \tag{6.57}$$

The final expression for a *par asset swap spread* is therefore given by the difference between two bonds prices divided by a DV01,

$$A = \frac{P^{LD} - P^{MKT}}{DV01_{quarterly}} \quad . \tag{6.58}$$

Note that if the coupon equals LIBOR $c = L_i$ (and pays quarterly), then $P^{LD} = P^{MKT}$ and therefore $A = 0$, as expected. As mentioned above, CDS spreads for bonds are generally close to the equivalent asset swap spread market. In the asset swap market, the bond price along with its coupon is assumed to imply all the credit risk of the name. By swapping this bond through an asset swap, the credit risk component is isolated in the asset swap spread. Asset swap traders always watch the CDS market whereas CDS traders watch the asset swap market for new issue bonds and their asset swap spreads.

CHAPTER 6 ■ INTRODUCTION TO CREDIT DERIVATIVES

Collateralization

Securitization is the general practice of *pooling* various debt instruments—such as bonds, CDSs, mortgages, loans, credit card receivables, and hedge funds—and changing the cashflow characteristics in order to create a new security such as a *collateralized debt obligation* (CDO), MBS, or *asset-backed security* (ABS) that is *collateralized* by the original debt instruments. When the original cash flows are changed, the risk is also altered. The three main types of risks that are altered are

1. **Credit risk**
2. **Prepayment risk**
3. **Interest risk**

Risk 2 is mostly involved in mortgage securitization. In the following, credit risk will be the main issue at hand. Consider the generic CDO structure depicted in Figure 6-5.

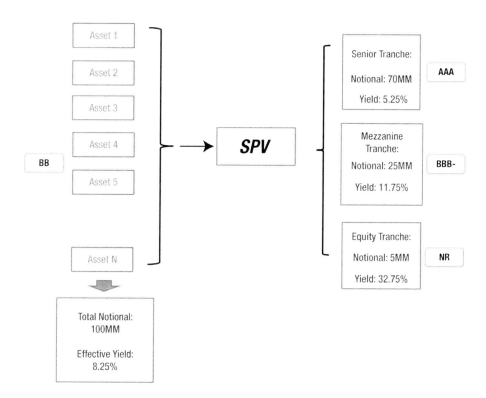

Figure 6-5. Generic CDO tranche structure

255

The underlying assets to the left side of Figure 6-5 could either be corporate bonds, asset-backed securities, emerging market securities, or synthetic instruments like CDSs. This pool of a 100MM of assets is placed in a *special-purpose vehicle* (SPV) to protect the assets from the potential bankruptcy of the issuing firm. These assets collateralize the CDO structure to the right. The original 100MM of assets (say, 100 bonds) has been made into three new tranches. A *tranche* is basically a bond that has a certain credit quality with a given credit rating, as indicated in Figure 6-5. The total notional of these three new tranches is 100MM (in this simplified example). The biggest tranche is the *senior tranche* rated AAA. The middle tranche (*mezzanine*, "mezz") is the next tranche with a rating of BBB-. The bottom tranche has no rating and is called the *equity tranche*. All three tranches have coupons that are dependent on their rating and what cash flow is available from the original pool of BB-rated assets. The main accomplishment for the issuing firm is that they have transformed 100MM of BB-rated bonds, which are hard to sell, into 70MM of AAA-rated bonds, which are easier to sell. The original pool gives off 8.25% annually on 100MM. That's all the money the structure has. Naively put, cash in must equal cash out (whereas in reality, the issuing bank takes a fee). Therefore, the following equality holds,

$$8.25\% \cdot 100mm = 5.25\% \cdot 70mm + 11.75\% \cdot 25mm + 32.75\% \cdot 5mm \quad . \quad (6.59)$$

This is a statement of the *conservation of cash*.

The tranches are created by allocation of default risk (losses after default) and interest rate cashflow priorities. This is allocation procedure is called the *waterfall* structure of the CDO. Losses from defaulting assets in the SPV are absorbed by the equity tranche first. If and when the equity tranche notional has been exhausted, further losses are taken by the mezz tranche. Finally, the senior tranche must absorb any further losses once the mezz tranche disappears. Interest rate payments are made in the reverse order of defaults. The senior tranche receives its full coupon payment first. The mezz tranche receives its coupon payment next, with any remaining cash flows from the SPV going to the equity tranche. This whole structure is very similar to the corporate structure of a firm. Consider a bankruptcy scenario for a firm. All the firm's remaining assets are sold off to raise cash. Thereafter, any owed taxes of the firm and short-term wages of the employees are paid. Then, the senior loans are paid off. Any remaining cash is used to pay the senior secured bonds of the bankrupt company. This cashflow waterfall is continued through sub-debt, preferred shares, and finally the firm's equity holders, who get paid last if any cash remains (hence the name "equity tranche"). Being paid last is equivalent to taking default losses first. Interest rate payments are also similar between a CDO and a firm as senior loans and bonds get paid first with the final remaining amount of cash from earnings going to the equity holders as dividends.

For simplicity, imagine the expected annual default probability of each bond in the SPV is 1.00%. Assume the recovery rate is zero. On average, 1 bond out of 100 defaults every year with a notional of 1MM. This 1MM loss is taken by the equity tranche, which after the first default has a remaining notional of 4MM. This range of a 20% loss is similar to that of a single stock position (hence the name "equity"). The equity tranche is at the bottom of the capital structure, much like the equity in a corporation. Therefore, in return for this high risk, the equity tranche has a coupon of 32.75%. If five bonds default, the equity tranche will vanish and the CDO structure is left with the remaining lowest tranche being the mezzanine. As the equity tranche has no default protection underneath it, it has no credit rating. The mezzanine tranche has the equity tranche below it to absorb losses before it does, but only up to 5MM. Therefore, it has a credit rating but not a very high one,

CHAPTER 6 ■ INTRODUCTION TO CREDIT DERIVATIVES

usually just barely investment grade (BBB- or higher). The senior tranche has 30MM of protection below it. Therefore, 30% of the bonds in this example must default for the senior tranche to start absorbing losses. This leads it to have a very high rating. Even if one bond defaults every year, it will take 30 years to eat into the senior tranche. The underlying bond maturities are around 10-15 years and so the whole structure will, on average, mature before the senior tranche gets hit (within the framework of this simple example). The *real risk* to the senior tranche is if many bonds default at the same time, which comes from the phenomena of *correlated defaults*. The whole game in the valuation of CDO structures comes down to modeling correlated default probabilities. Trading desks that deal in such structures are often called the *correlation desk* with members called *correlation traders*.

With respect to terminology, the *equity tranche* has an attachment point of 0% and a detachment point of 5%. The *mezzanine tranche* has an attachment point of 5% and a detachment point of 30%. The *senior tranche* has an attachment point of 30% and a detachment point of 100%.

CDO^2

Hundreds of CDO structures similar to the one shown in Figure 6-5 were created by Wall Street firms starting from the mid-1990s. One of the main difficulties for these firms was the selling of the lower tranches. In the above example, a 100MM of not-so-desirable BB-rated bonds was transformed into a desirable AAA-rated senior tranche and two other tranches. Often, the two lower tranches could not be sold. The unsold equity tranche notionals may not have been that large, but the unsold mezz tranche notionals began to grow. The mezz tranche is often considered very risky because once the equity piece disappears, the mezz tranche becomes the equity tranche. The equity holder usually got some big payments before disappearing, but the mezz coupon was usually relatively modest for the perceived risk and therefore, many mezz pieces remained unsold. What could one do with so many unsold BBB mezz tranches? One could create another CDO using these mezz tranches. That is, the assets of the left side of Figure 6-5 are now CDO tranches themselves. The resulting structure on the right of Figure 6-5 was then called a *CDO^2* (CDO-squared). Relative to the original structure, the CDO^2 had a bigger senior tranche as the assets that made up the CDO^2 were rated BBB versus the original CDO that was made of BB assets. The senior tranche of the CDO^2 was often called the *super senior tranche* because of its perceived lack of risk. CDO^2's were made from several different types of CDOs, such as corporate bonds CDOs and synthetic CDOs. It all crashed during the subprime crisis of 2008 when CDO^2's made from CDOs with subprime mortgages as their underlying assets began to experience huge losses. The original BBB tranche of the subprime mortgage–backed CDO became the equity tranche as the subprime mortgage market collapsed. The CDO^2 structure based on these subprime mezz tranches suddenly had their pool of assets go from BBB to not rated. The so-called super senior tranches of these CDO^2's took a massive hit. It was like having a AAA+-rated bond that one bought at 100% suddenly being valued at 25%. This is the effect of correlated defaults and naive conception that all AAAs are created equal (which is what the rating agencies tell you).

Standard CDS Indices and Tranches

One of the first structured products in the equity markets was the creation of a basket of well-known single stock names, such as the Dow 30 or the S&P 500. These indices gave a flavor of where the market was trading as a whole. Similarly, the CDS market has created several baskets of CDS names. A pool of CDSs, known as a *CDS index*, is a group of predetermined CDS names, just like the S&P 500 is a well-known group of equity names. There currently two main families of CDS indices: *CDX* and *iTraxx*. The CDX indices contain North American and emerging market companies, and the iTraxx indices contain companies from the rest of the world. They are owned by Markit (see www.markit.com), just like the S&P 500 is owned by Standard and Poor's. These two are the most liquid standardized synthetic credit CDO structures in the market. These structures are called "synthetic" as opposed to "cash" CDOs because the underlying pool is made of CDSs and not physical corporate bonds. Every CDS index has a spread (the *index level*), which is the premium one must pay to buy protection on the whole basket of underlying names in a pro rata format. See Figure 6-6 for various types of CDS indices. Note that every index has a different number of underlying names within their respective baskets.

The S&P 500 occasionally changes its constituent stocks, but the index name stays the same (there is only one S&P 500 index). The credit market, however, issues a new series of CDS indices every six months whereby defaulted bonds or bonds no longer fulfilling certain requirements are taken out. For instance, *CDX.NA.IG.12* is a CDX index of North American (NA) investment-grade (IG) names and is the 12th issue of the series. It is composed of 125 high-quality names. If an underlying security either gets downgraded to high yield or defaults, it gets removed in the 13th series. CDX.NA.HY.BB.21 is a CDX index of North American BB-rated high-yield (HY) names and is the 21st issue of the series. It is composed of 37 BB names. If an underlying security either gets downgraded below BB or defaults, it gets removed in the 22nd series. The main reason to keep all the series alive is because the CDS index level is the premium needed to buy protection on the exact basket of assets in a particular index, and many such contracts are still in existence even after the issuance of a new series. One could argue that a similar thing could have been done with the S&P 500 or the Dow Jones 30. If one buys a deep OTM put option on the Dow Jones 30, they are buying "protection" against a crash of a basket of 30 assets. If an asset is replaced in the Dow Jones during the lifetime of the option, the put buyer loses the crash protection against that asset. For instance, from Figure 1-8, it can be seen that Citigroup was removed from the Dow Jones on June 8, 2009. This was precisely the time (the 2008 subprime crisis) that one would have wanted a put option on the Dow Jones with Citigroup in it. Unfortunately, after this date, one had to find other means to protect oneself against a downward spiral in Citigroup stock.

CDX Indices

Index Name	Number of entities	Description
CDX.NA.IG	125	Investment grade CDSs
CDX.NA.IG.HVOL	30	High Volatility investment grade CDSs
CDX.NA.HY	100	High Yield CDSs
CDX.NA.HY.BB	37	Index of high yield CDSs with a BB rating
CDX.NA.HY.B	46	Index of high yield CDSs with a B rating
CDX.NA.XO	35	CDSs that are at the crossover point between investment grade and junk
CDX.EM	14	Emerging market CDSs
CDX.EM Diversified	40	Emerging market CDSs
LCDX	100	NA First Lien Leverage Loans CDSs

iTraxx Indices

Family	Type	Index Name	Number of entities	Description
Europe	Benchmark Indices	iTraxx Europe	125	Most actively traded names in the six months prior to the index roll
		iTraxx Europe HiVol	30	Highest spread (riskiest) non-financial names from iTraxx Europe index
		iTraxx Europe Crossover	40	Sub-investment grade names
		iTraxx LEVX	40	European 1st Lien Loan CDS
	Sector Indices	iTraxx Non-Financials	100	Non-financial names
		iTraxx Financials Senior	25	Senior subordination financial names
		iTraxx Financials Sub	25	Junior subordination financial names
		iTraxx TMT	20	Telecommunications media and technology
		iTraxx Industrials	20	Industrial names
		iTraxx Energy	20	Energy industrial names

Figure 6-6. Various CDX and iTraxx indices

CHAPTER 6 ■ INTRODUCTION TO CREDIT DERIVATIVES

From these two popular CDS indices, standardized tranches have also been created. Figure 6-7 shows CDX tranches by attachment and detachment points and pre-SNAC quotes along with base and implied correlations (described below). Pre-SNAC and STEC quotes are par spreads in basis points per year except for the 0–3% tranche, where the quote equals the upfront payment of the tranche principal that must be paid in addition to 500 bps per year. CDX SNAC- and iTraxx STEC-style quotes in Figure 6-8 are upfront payments with standard coupons as indicated in the figure. More information can be found on www.markit.com, www.creditfixings.com, and Bloomberg.

CDX.NA.IG.4	Index Level	49 bps				
Tranche	0-3%	3%-7%	7%-10%	10%-15%	15%-30%	30%-100%
Quote	33.5%	199 bps	64 bps	25 bps	10 bps	4 bps
Compound Correlation	19%	5%	16%	21%	32%	

CDX.NA.IG.9						
Tranche	0-3%	3%-7%	7%-10%	10%-15%	15%-30%	30%-100%
Quote	56.0%	353 bps	137 bps	84 bps	47 bps	17 bps
Base Correlation	25%	48%	59%	71%	91%	

Figure 6-7. CDX tranches and pre-SNAC-style 5YR and 7YR quotes

CDX.NA.IG.9	Index Level	73 bps	10YR			
Tranche	0-3%	3%-7%	7%-10%	10%-15%	15%-30%	30%-100%
Quote	36.88%	-3.63%	-13.38%	-1.13%	-2.65%	-3.45%

iTraxx Europe.9	Index Level	32 bps	6/15			
Tranche	0-3%	3%-6%	6%-9%	9%-12%	12%-22%	22%-100%
Quote	4.13%	-6.75%	-4.37%	23.00%	10.50%	4.50%

Tranche Rules

Tranches 0-3 & 3-6 are upfront quotes with a fixed 500bps spread.
Tranches 6-9 has a 300bps fixed spread.
All other Tranches are upfront quotes with a fixed 100bps spread.

Figure 6-8. SNAC and STEC quotes for CDX and iTraxx

Correlation and Copulas
Density Method

In the previous section, CDS indices and their tranches were described as being highly sensitive to correlated defaults among the basket constituents. How does one create correlated random variables? In Chapter 3, the standard definition of correlation was introduced:

$$\rho(X,Y) = \frac{\text{cov}(X,Y)}{\sigma(X)\sigma(Y)} \qquad (6.60)$$

It is important to understand that this is a measure of *linear dependence*. For example, in Chapter 3, it was shown that for the bivariate normal distribution,

$$f(x,y) = \frac{1}{2\pi\sqrt{1-\rho^2}} \exp\left(-\frac{1}{2(1-\rho^2)}(x^2 - 2\rho xy + y^2)\right) , \qquad (6.61)$$

$E[Y|X] = \rho X$. Y is linearly dependent on X. This perfect linear dependence is only true for multivariate normal distributions. That is, the dependence structure between variables is completely determined by the correlation matrix (which reduces to one number for two variables). It is sometimes approximately true for empirical data. Recall the warning that uncorrelated variables are not necessarily independent. If $X \sim N(m, \sigma^2)$ and $Y = X^2$, then $\rho(X, Y) = 0$ but X and Y are not independent. Therefore, dependence can be created through various methods. One can create multivariate normal distributions using the density approach in a similar way. Let

$$\vec{x} = [X_1, X_2, ..., X_N] \rightarrow \text{N dimensional random vector}$$
$$\vec{\mu} = [E[X_1], E[X_2], ..., E[X_N]] \rightarrow \text{N dimensional mean vector} \qquad (6.62)$$
$$\Sigma = [\text{cov}\{X_i, X_j\}], i, j = 1, ..., N \rightarrow \text{N by N covariance matrix}$$

The multivariate normal distribution function is given by

$$f(x_1, x_2, ..., x_N) = \frac{1}{(2\pi)^N |\Sigma|} \exp\left(-\frac{1}{2}(\vec{x} - \vec{\mu})^T \Sigma (\vec{x} - \vec{\mu})\right) , \qquad (6.63)$$

where $|\Sigma|$ is the determinant of Σ. In the two-dimensional case $N = 2$, this reduces to:

$$f(x,y) = \frac{1}{2\pi\sigma_x\sigma_y\sqrt{1-\rho^2}} \exp\left(-\frac{1}{2(1-\rho^2)}\left[\frac{(x-\mu_x)^2}{\sigma_x^2} - 2\rho\frac{(x-\mu_x)(y-\mu_y)}{\sigma_x\sigma_y} + \frac{(y-\mu_y)^2}{\sigma_y^2}\right]\right) \qquad (6.64)$$

where

$$\Sigma = \begin{pmatrix} \sigma_x^2 & 2\rho\sigma_x\sigma_y \\ 2\rho\sigma_x\sigma_y & \sigma_y^2 \end{pmatrix} \qquad (6.65)$$

$$\mu = \begin{pmatrix} \mu_x \\ \mu_y \end{pmatrix} . \qquad (6.66)$$

Variable Method

An alternative way to create correlated normal random variables is to deal with the variables themselves rather than their joint density function. Every variable will have a correlation coefficient with every other variable denoted as ρ_{ij}. If z_i, $1 \le i \le n$, are independent standard normal variables $N(0, 1)$, one can create correlated bivariate normal variables with the following *transformation*,

CHAPTER 6 ■ INTRODUCTION TO CREDIT DERIVATIVES

$$\epsilon_i = \sum_{k=1}^{n} \alpha_{ik} z_k, \, i=1,..,n$$
$$\sum_{k=1}^{n} \alpha_{ik}^2 = 1, \, i=1,...,n \qquad (6.67)$$
$$\sum_{k=1}^{n} \alpha_{ik} \alpha_{jk} = \rho_{ij}, \, 1 \le j < i \le n$$

where ρ_{ij} is the pairwise correlation. For n variables, one will need $n(n-1)/2$ correlation elements because $\rho_{ij} = \rho_{ji}$. This means that if ρ_{ij} is represented as a matrix, the matrix is symmetric. The two conditions above on the α's come from the fact that one requires that

$$E[\epsilon_i^2] = 1 \text{ and } E[\epsilon_i \epsilon_j] = \rho_{ij} \qquad . \qquad (6.68)$$

Consider, for example, the bivariate case of n=2. For $1 \le i \le 2$,

$$\begin{aligned}
\epsilon_1 &= \alpha_{11} z_1 + \alpha_{12} z_2 \\
\epsilon_2 &= \alpha_{21} z_1 + \alpha_{22} z_2 \\
\alpha_{11}^2 + \alpha_{12}^2 &= 1 \\
\alpha_{21}^2 + \alpha_{22}^2 &= 1 \\
\alpha_{21} \alpha_{11} + \alpha_{22} \alpha_{12} &= \rho_{21} = \rho, \, [j < i \to j=1, i=2]
\end{aligned} \qquad (6.69)$$

The solution to the above equations for the α's is ($\rho = \rho_{21} = \rho_{12}$),

$$\begin{aligned}
\alpha_{11} &= 1, \, \alpha_{12} = 0 \\
\alpha_{21} &= \rho, \, \alpha_{22} = \sqrt{1-\rho^2}
\end{aligned} \qquad , \qquad (6.70)$$

which results in

$$\begin{aligned}
\epsilon_1 &= z_1 \\
\epsilon_2 &= \rho z_1 + \sqrt{1-\rho^2} \, z_2
\end{aligned} \qquad , \qquad (6.71)$$

where again z_1 and z_2 are independent standard normal variables $N(0, 1)$. The solution methodology to these equations for the more general case is known as the *Cholesky decomposition* method for matrices (see [Glasserman, 2008]).

Factor Models

For a large number of variables, such as $N > 30$, the above methodology tends to be computationally inefficient. For instance, if one is modeling a portfolio of 125 defaultable bonds, such as CDX.NA.IG, one would need to estimate 7,750 correlation elements. One way around this is to use *factor models*. A one-factor model basically says that all the bonds are correlated to one common factor F (which could be related to a measure of the economy or unemployment, etc.) but otherwise uncorrelated with each other,

$$\epsilon_i = a_i F + \sqrt{1-a_i^2}\, z_i \quad . \tag{6.72}$$

The variables F and z_i are uncorrelated standard $N(0, 1)$ variables and the a_i are called *factor weightings* or *factor loadings*. Each factor loading is assumed to lie in the interval $[0,1]$. The correlation between ϵ_i and ϵ_j is clearly $a_i a_j$. Therefore, the factor weighting coefficients a_i to the factor F implies a correlation between the different ϵ_i variables. Thus, the number of correlations has been reduced from $N(N-1)/2$ to N (i.e., from 7,750 to 125). Each random variable has been decomposed into one systematic component F (the one factor) and an idiosyncratic independent component z_i. For two variables, one has

$$\begin{aligned}\epsilon_1 &= a_1 F + \sqrt{1-a_1^2}\, z_1 \\ \epsilon_2 &= a_2 F + \sqrt{1-a_2^2}\, z_2 \\ E[\epsilon_1 \epsilon_2] &= E[a_1 a_2 F^2] = a_1 a_2 = \rho \quad .\end{aligned} \tag{6.73}$$

Note that if one sets $a_1 = 1$, the above equations reduce to equation (6.71). By adding extra F_i-factors, one can extend this to two- and multifactor models. Finally, F is not restricted to be a standard normal. It could have been drawn from a Student's t- distribution. This will give the ϵ_i's a different correlation structure—such as one incorporating nonlinear and greater tail dependence.

Copulas

Suppose one has several different distribution functions for several variables,

$$[P(X_1 \leq x_1), P(X_2 \leq x_2), P(X_3 \leq x_4), \ldots] \quad . \tag{6.74}$$

Is there a way to correlate these directly at a distribution level rather than at the variable level as explained above? That is, one is looking for a methodology to *couple* the *marginal* distributions $P(X_i \leq x_i)$ into a *joint* distribution. Does there exist a function C such that for all individual distribution function $F(x_i) = P(X_i \leq x_i)$, one has

$$P(X_1 \leq x_1, \ldots, X_d \leq x_d) = C(F(x_1), \ldots, F(x_d)) \quad , \tag{6.75}$$

where the marginal distributions $F(x_i)$ are preserved? Such a function C is known as a *copula*. This is the essence of *Sklar's theorem*.

Sklar's Theorem. *Let F be a joint distribution function with marginals F_1, F_2, F_d. There exists a **copula** $C: [0, 1]^d \to [0, 1]$ such that for all $x_1, x_2, \ldots, x_d$ in $[-\infty, \infty]$*

$$F(x_1, \ldots, x_d) = C(F(x_1), \ldots, F(x_d)) \quad . \tag{6.76}$$

A simple Gaussian copula example should illustrate how this works. Suppose one has two correlated Gaussian variables X and Y with a joint distribution given by the bivariate normal distribution,

CHAPTER 6 ■ INTRODUCTION TO CREDIT DERIVATIVES

$$f(x,y) = \frac{1}{2\pi\sqrt{1-\rho^2}} \exp\left(-\frac{1}{2(1-\rho^2)}(x^2 - 2\rho xy + y^2)\right) \quad . \tag{6.77}$$

Each of these variables has marginal distributions that are also Gaussian (see the appendix of Chapter 3). Further, suppose one has two default times Γ_1 and Γ_2 with marginal distributions $F_1(\tau_1)$ and $F_2(\tau_2)$. Because all (cumulative) distribution functions have a range between [0, 1], we can equate the above marginals as follows

$$F_1(\tau_1) = N(x) \tag{6.78}$$
$$F_2(\tau_2) = N(y) \quad .$$

This is essentially a percentile-to-percentile mapping. The one-percentile of the $N(x)$ distribution has been mapped to the one-percentile of the $F_1(\tau_1)$ distribution, etc. The main point to note is that since X and Y are correlated, the above equations have given Γ_1 and Γ_2 a correlation structure as well. The correlated default times are given by

$$\tau_1 = F_1^{-1}[N(x)] \tag{6.79}$$
$$\tau_2 = F_2^{-1}[N(y)] \quad .$$

One is not restricted to using a Gaussian copula model. One could have chosen to use a bivariate Student's t copula model for X and Y. This would give the default times Γ_1 and Γ_2 a different type of correlation structure. Models must be checked against empirical data to test which correlation structure is appropriate to the data at hand. Finally, the factor model described above can be used within the copula framework where

$$x = \epsilon_1 = a_1 F + \sqrt{1-a_1^2}\, z_1$$
$$y = \epsilon_2 = a_2 F + \sqrt{1-a_2^2}\, z_2 \tag{6.80}$$
$$\rho = a_1 a_2$$

and the percentiles of the distribution of the default times, τ_1 and τ_2, are mapped into the marginal distribution of x and y, respectively. The following example will illustrate this further.

Large Homogeneous Portfolio Approximation

The following example illustrates the use of a one-factor model within the copula framework. Suppose that one has a large portfolio of defaultable bonds. The first simplifying assumption made is that all the bonds have the same cumulative probability distribution for default times $Q(T)$. Second, assume that the correlation of defaults between different bonds within the portfolio are all the same. Begin with a one-factor model of correlated standard Gaussians,

$$\epsilon_i = \sqrt{\rho}\, F + \sqrt{1-\rho}\, z_i \quad . \tag{6.81}$$

CHAPTER 6 ■ INTRODUCTION TO CREDIT DERIVATIVES

Define Γ_i as the time when bond i defaults. One is interested in the probability of default by time T—i.e., $P(\Gamma_i < T)$. Using the Gaussian copula model,

$$Q(T) = N(\epsilon) \quad , \tag{6.82}$$

and therefore

$$P[\Gamma_i < T] = P[\epsilon_i < \epsilon] \quad . \tag{6.83}$$

As mentioned, the factor F could be related to a measure of the state of the economy or the strength of Wall Street (e.g., fed funds being high or low). Therefore, the conditional probability of default, conditional on F should be calculated. From (6.81),

$$z_i = \frac{\epsilon_i - \sqrt{\rho}F}{\sqrt{1-\rho}} \tag{6.84}$$

and

$$P(\epsilon_i < \epsilon \mid F) = P\left(z_i < \frac{\epsilon - \sqrt{\rho}F}{\sqrt{1-\rho}}\right) \quad . \tag{6.85}$$

By the Gaussian copula assumption,

$$P(\Gamma_i < T \mid F) = N\left(\frac{\epsilon - \sqrt{\rho}F}{\sqrt{1-\rho}}\right) \quad . \tag{6.86}$$

Defining D = *probability of default*, one has $\epsilon = N^{-1}[Q(T)] = N^{-1}(D)$ and

$$P(\Gamma_i < T \mid F) = N\left(\frac{N^{-1}(D) - \sqrt{\rho}F}{\sqrt{1-\rho}}\right) \quad . \tag{6.87}$$

This equation gives the percentage of bonds defaulting conditional on F before time T within the *large homogeneous portfolio approximation*. Equation (6.87) is effectively a default rate which increases as F decreases. What does one do with F? In the factor model, it was assumed to be Gaussian (it could have been chosen to be something else). By definition, the probability that this systematic factor F will be less than $N^{-1}(Y)$ is Y. If one chooses a VaR-type level for this factor such as 99%, then $Y = 1 - 0.99$ (the left tail as a low F indicates a higher default rate). Since $N^{-1}(1 - X) = -N^{-1}(X)$, an $X = 99\%$ confidence level of default rates within time T is given by

$$P(T \mid X\% \text{ Confidence Level}) = N\left(\frac{N^{-1}(D) + \sqrt{\rho}N^{-1}(X)}{\sqrt{1-\rho}}\right) \quad . \tag{6.88}$$

This provides a worst-case default rate in the sense that one is $X\%$ confident that it won't be exceeded in time T [Vasicek, 2002].

265

CHAPTER 6 ■ INTRODUCTION TO CREDIT DERIVATIVES

The $X\%$ VaR for the portfolio is given by

$$\text{VaR}(X) = \text{Portfolio Notional} \bullet (1-R) \bullet N\left(\frac{N^{-1}(D)+\sqrt{\rho}N^{-1}(X)}{\sqrt{1-\rho}}\right) \quad . \quad (6.89)$$

Note that in the limit of $\rho \to 0$, this formula reduces to Portfolio Notional $\bullet (1 - R) \bullet D$ as expected. Equation (6.89) is a fundamental formula that is used within the Basel II and III regulatory frameworks discussed in Chapter 7.

Example: Bank Loan Portfolio

Suppose a bank has a $300 million pool of prime client retail loans. All the individual loans are small compared to the total pool. The bank will be interested in the 99.9% VaR over one year. The bank estimates the one-year probability of default to be $D = 2.0\%$. The correlation between different assets will be set to $\rho = 15.5\%$. The recovery of these loans is assumed to be $R = 60.0\%$. This results in a VaR of

$$\text{VaR}(99.9\%) = 300 \bullet 0.40 \bullet N\left(\frac{N^{-1}(0.02)+\sqrt{0.155}N^{-1}(0.999)}{\sqrt{1-0.155}}\right) \quad (6.90)$$

$$= 120 \bullet (0.18123) = \$21.74 \text{million} \quad .$$

An extension of this model is to assume every loan has a different default probability, different recovery, and different notional. If each loan is still small compared to the pool, the total VaR of the pool is *approximately* given by [Gordy, 2003]

$$\text{VaR}(X) \approx \sum_{i=1}^{N} \text{Loan Notional}_i \bullet (1-R_i) \bullet N\left(\frac{N^{-1}(D_i)+\sqrt{\rho}N^{-1}(X)}{\sqrt{1-\rho}}\right) \quad . \quad (6.91)$$

On can easily use a hazard rate formulation for the probability of default D—i.e., $Q[T] = 1 - \exp(-hT)$.

One-Factor Gaussian Model

This has become the standard quotation model for synthetic CDO tranches. Much like the Black-Scholes model, it is almost *completely incorrect* in its assumptions. The naive belief in this model led to massive mishedges during the 2008-2009 financial crisis. Nonetheless, one must understand it to interpret the market quotes for these instruments. Suppose one has a pool of n defaultable instruments. Let Γ_i be the time to default of the ith name. Each name has an unconditional cumulative individual probability distribution for Γ_i given by $P[\Gamma_i < T] = Q_i(T)$. Once again, begin with a one-factor model of correlated standard normals,

$$\epsilon_i = \sqrt{\rho_i}F + \sqrt{1-\rho_i}z_i \quad . \quad (6.92)$$

CHAPTER 6 ■ INTRODUCTION TO CREDIT DERIVATIVES

As before, using the Gaussian copula model,

$$Q(T) = N(\epsilon) \quad , \tag{6.93}$$

and therefore

$$P[\Gamma_i < T] = P[\epsilon_i < \epsilon] \quad , \tag{6.94}$$

and finally, the effective default rate is given by

$$P(\Gamma_i < T \mid F) = N\left(\frac{N^{-1}(Q_i(T)) - \sqrt{\rho_i} F}{\sqrt{1-\rho_i}}\right) \quad . \tag{6.95}$$

This formula has linked the individual default probabilities $Q_i(T)$ using the Gaussian copula model and correlation ρ_i to create a *conditional* (on F) probability distribution for the default time Γ_i (conditioning on F has created the correlation between default times). Now come several simplifying assumptions that are basically the large homogeneous pool assumption used above:

1. $Q_i(T)$ is the same for all names in the portfolio.
2. ρ_i is the same for all names in the portfolio.
3. All the names in the portfolio have the same size.
4. All the names in the portfolio have the same recovery rate R.

One typically uses a hazard rate model for $Q[T] = 1 - \exp(-hT)$ where h is calibrated to the index spread (such CDX or Itraxx). Thus, one is left with

$$P(\Gamma < T \mid F) = N\left(\frac{N^{-1}(1 - \exp(-hT)) - \sqrt{\rho} F}{\sqrt{1-\rho}}\right) \quad , \tag{6.96}$$

which has reduced the problem to calibrating two parameters: the total pool hazard rate h and the effective pool correlation ρ. Now comes the real question for tranche pricing: What is the probability of k-defaults out of n names happening before time T? The market convention here is to use the binomial model along with (6.96)

$$P(k, T \mid F) = \binom{n}{k} P(\Gamma < T \mid F)^k [1 - P(\Gamma < T \mid F)]^{n-k}, \quad k = 0, 1, \ldots, n \tag{6.97}$$

where the binomial coefficient is given by

$$\binom{n}{k} = \frac{n!}{k!(n-k)!} \quad . \tag{6.98}$$

CHAPTER 6 ■ INTRODUCTION TO CREDIT DERIVATIVES

If simplifying assumptions 1 and 2 are relaxed, the $P(k,T|F)$ can be calculated using a simple iterative procedure such as the one given in Andersen et al. (2003) or Hull and White (2004).

One can use this formula in cashflow expectations by integrating over the standard normal variable F. The key measure here is what is the expected tranche notional at time T (conditional on F) $E[\text{tranche}, T|F]$. Consider a tranche with an attachment point a_L (L: lower attachment) and a detachment point a_H (H: higher attachment)—for example, a 3-6% tranche. Say the initial tranche notional is 1 and $R = 0$. With the pool names all having the same size, $k > 3$ will hit the tranche while $k > 6$ will *kill* (defaults will eliminate) the tranche. If $R = 50\%$, $k > 6$ will begin to affect the tranche, whereas $k > 12$ will eliminate it. Define $\text{Int}(x)$ as the closest integer greater than x. For a generic tranche, it feels the effects of defaults in the pool if

$$k \geq \text{Int}[n_L] \qquad (6.99)$$
$$n_L = \frac{\alpha_L n}{1-R} \quad .$$

The tranche will be eliminated if

$$k \geq \text{Int}[n_H] \qquad (6.100)$$
$$n_H = \frac{\alpha_H n}{1-R} \quad .$$

For instance say $n = 125$, $R = 40\%$, and the tranche is 3-7%:

$$k \geq \text{Int}[n_L] = 7 \qquad (6.101)$$
$$n_L = \frac{0.03 \cdot 125}{1 - 0.40} = 6.25$$

and

$$k \geq \text{Int}[n_H] = 15 \qquad (6.102)$$
$$n_H = \frac{0.07 \cdot 125}{1 - 0.40} = 14.58 \quad .$$

From this example, it is clear why one rounds up to the nearest integer. There is no such thing as 6.25 bonds defaulting.

For an evenly distributed portfolio, the size of the underlying bonds (CDS) are $1/n$. The loss coming from one default is

$$(1-R) \cdot \frac{1}{n} \quad . \qquad (6.103)$$

and from k defaults is

$$\frac{k(1-R)}{n} \quad . \qquad (6.104)$$

CHAPTER 6 ■ INTRODUCTION TO CREDIT DERIVATIVES

For $\text{Int}[n_L] \le k \le \text{Int}[n_H]$, the remaining tranche principal is

$$\frac{\alpha_H - \dfrac{k(1-R)}{n}}{\alpha_H - \alpha_L} . \qquad (6.105)$$

Finally, one can write the expression for the conditional expected i^{th} tranche notional at time T $E[\text{tranche}_i, T|F]$ and the unconditional one $E[\text{tranche}_i, T]$ as follows:

$$E[\text{tranche}_i, T|F] = \sum_{k=1}^{\text{Int}[n_L(i)]-1} P(k,T|F) \bullet 1 + \sum_{k=\text{Int}[n_L(i)]}^{\text{Int}[n_H(i)]-1} P(k,T|F) \bullet \frac{\alpha_H(i) - \dfrac{k(1-R)}{n}}{\alpha_H(i) - \alpha_L(i)}$$

$$E[\text{tranche}_i, T] = \sum_{k=1}^{\text{Int}[n_L(i)]-1} P(k,T) \bullet 1 + \sum_{k=\text{Int}[n_L(i)]}^{\text{Int}[n_H(i)]-1} P(k,T) \bullet \frac{\alpha_H(i) - \dfrac{k(1-R)}{n}}{\alpha_H(i) - \alpha_L(i)} \qquad (6.106)$$

where

$$P(k,T) = \int_{-\infty}^{\infty} P(k,T|F)\phi(F)dF \text{ and } \phi \text{ is the standard normal pdf} .$$

$P(k,T|F)$ is calculated as in (6.97) for the simplifying assumptions 1 and 2 above. If simplifying assumptions 1 and 2 are relaxed, then $P(k,T|F)$ can again be calculated using a simple iterative procedure such as the one given in Andersen et al. (2003) or Hull and White (2004).

Now one can price a tranche (assume no accrued interest). Similar to a single-name CDS, one has for the ith tranche

$$PV(\text{tranche}_i) = PV(\text{premium leg}_i) - PV(\text{default leg}_i) . \qquad (6.107)$$

For a tranche, the premium is paid on the remaining notional:

$$PV(\text{premium leg}_i) = C(t) \sum_{j=1}^{N} df(t_j) \Delta(t_j) E[\text{tranche}_i, t_j | F]$$

$C(t) = $ CDS *premium payment at time t (annualized "coupon") paid at times* t_i $\qquad (6.108)$
$df(t_j) = $ *discount factor at time* t_j
$\Delta(t_j) = $ *daycount between* t_{j-1} *and* t_j
$E[\text{tranche}_i, t_j | F] = $ *expected tranche notional at time* t_j .

This equation is analogous to (6.2) where the single name survival probability has been replaced by the expected tranche notional.

The default leg is simply the sum of reductions in tranche notional. Here, it is assumed that default happens midway between time steps:

$$PV(\text{default leg}_i) = \sum_{j=1}^{N} \left(E[\text{tranche}_i, t_{j-1} | F] - E[\text{tranche}_i, t_j | F] \right) df(0.5t_{j-1} + 0.5t_j) \qquad (6.109)$$

CHAPTER 6 ■ INTRODUCTION TO CREDIT DERIVATIVES

At initiation when $t = 0$, the fair value spread $C(0)$ is found by setting

$$PV(\text{tranche}_i) = 0 = PV(\text{premium leg}_i) - PV(\text{default leg}_i) \qquad (6.110)$$

and solving for $C(0)$,

$$C(0) = \frac{\sum_{j=1}^{N} \left(E[\text{tranche}_i, t_{j-1} | F] - E[\text{tranche}_i, t_j | F] \right) df(0.5 t_{j-1} + 0.5 t_j)}{\sum_{j=1}^{N} df(t_j) \Delta(t_j) E[\text{tranche}_i, t_j | F]} \qquad (6.111)$$

This is not quite the final formula. One still needs to integrate out the factor F. Since F is assumed to be a standard normal variable, one has its density function is given by

$$\phi(F) = \frac{1}{\sqrt{(2\pi)}} \exp\left(\frac{-F^2}{2} \right) \qquad (6.112)$$

Finally,

$$C(0) = \frac{\sum_{j=1}^{N} \left[\int \left(E[\text{tranche}_i, t_{j-1} | F] \phi(F) dF \right) - \int \left(E[\text{tranche}_i, t_j | F] \phi(F) dF \right) \right] df(0.5 t_{j-1} + 0.5 t_j)}{\sum_{j=1}^{N} df(t_j) \Delta(t_j) \int \left(E[\text{tranche}_i, t_j | F] \phi(F) dF \right)}$$

(6.113)

One could have started with the unconditional expression given in (6.106) and arrived at the same result.

The main problem with this model is that there is no volatility of credit spreads (or hazard rates). Correlation and the volatility of credit spreads are the main drivers in CDO pricing. This is one of the main reasons the Gaussian copula model completely failed during the 2008 crisis. One such OTC instrument that is highly dependent on credit spread volatility is the CDS swaption, discussed in the final section of this chapter.

Implied Compound and Base Correlations

As already explained, the correlation among defaults is one of the key driving forces in tranche valuation. The tranches have different directional exposures to the default correlation of the pool of underlying assets. The junior tranches are long correlation. The reason for this is that as default correlation increases, the probability of one or two defaults goes down, whereas the probability of several defaults goes up. The junior (equity) tranches absorb losses after one or two defaults. They can disappear completely with several defaults. On the other hand, the senior tranche is unaffected by one or two defaults. They are only affected by multiple defaults. Therefore, senior tranches are short correlation. Correlation and volatility of credit spreads are the main drivers in CDO pricing. The standard model does not have a volatility input, but it does have a (simplified) correlation input. Much like the implied Black-Scholes volatility in the equity option markets, there is an implied correlation for the standard CDX and iTraxx tranche markets (these being the most liquid tranches). If one assumes a recovery rate of $R = 0.40$, the only unknown parameter in the standard one-factor Gaussian copula model is the correlation ρ. For a tranche with points (a_L, a_H), the *implied compound correlation* is the one value of ρ that reproduces the market spread quote for that tranche (similar to the implied vol in the options markets). In general, every tranche has a different correlation (base or implied) as shown in Figure 6-7. Much like an implied volatility smile, one has a *correlation skew* in the CDO market. If the one-factor Gaussian copula model was a real representation of the market, there would be no correlation skew.

The *implied base correlation* is calculated for a hypothetical tranche that starts from the base (0) up to the various attachment points—i.e. (0, α)—such that it is consistent with the market. For example, one would hope the pricing of a (0,6%) base tranche would be consistent with the (0,3%) and (3%,6%) tranches. The consistency steps are as follows:

1. Obtain the implied compound correlation for each tranche.

2. Use the compound correlation to calculate the expected loss of each tranche as a percentage of the initial tranche principal:

$$PV(\text{default leg}|\text{tranche}_i) \quad . \tag{6.114}$$

3. Calculate the expected loss of each base tranche $(0, a_n)$ as

$$\sum_{i=1}^{n} PV(\text{default leg}|\text{tranche}_i)[\alpha_i - \alpha_{i-1}] \quad . \tag{6.115}$$

4. Find the base correlation for the base tranche that is consistent with the number found in step 3.

Stochastic Hazard Rates

This section gives a brief introduction to stochastic hazard rates. Details may be found in [Douglass, 2007] and [Schonbucher, 2003]. Let $P(t, T)$ be the survival probability in the interval $[t, T]$. The probability of default in this interval is $1 - P(t, T)$. The conditional survival probability in the interval $[T, T + \Delta t]$ where Γ is the default time is given by

$$P[\Gamma > T + \Delta t \mid \Gamma > T] = \frac{P(t, T + \Delta t)}{P(t, T)} \quad . \tag{6.116}$$

A discrete time hazard rate defined as the conditional density function of the default time Γ conditional on no defaults occurring before time T as seen from time t is given by

$$H(t,T,T+\Delta t)\Delta t = P[T < \Gamma < T + \Delta t \mid \Gamma > T] = 1 - P[\Gamma > T + \Delta t \mid \Gamma > T]$$

$$H(t,T,T+\Delta t) = \frac{1}{P(t,T)} \frac{P(t,T) - P(t,T+\Delta t)}{\Delta t} \quad . \tag{6.117}$$

Let $h(t, T)$ denote the continuous time hazard rate,

$$h(t,T) = \lim_{\Delta t \to 0} H(t,T,T+\Delta t) = \frac{1}{P(t,T)} \lim_{\Delta t \to 0} \frac{P(t,T) - P(t,T+\Delta t)}{\Delta t}$$

$$h(t,T) = \frac{-1}{P(t,T)} \frac{\partial}{\partial T} P(t,T) \quad . \tag{6.118}$$

CHAPTER 6 ■ INTRODUCTION TO CREDIT DERIVATIVES

Modifying this equation to the present time $t=0$ and changing the notation such that T goes to t, one has

$$h(0,t) = h_t = \frac{-1}{P(0,t)} \frac{\partial}{\partial t} P(0,t) \quad . \tag{6.119}$$

One possible solution to this equation is

$$P[\Gamma > t] = P(0,t) = \exp\left[-\int_0^t h_\mu d\mu\right] \quad . \tag{6.120}$$

It immediately follows that

$$P[\Gamma > t \mid \Gamma > s] = \frac{P[\Gamma > t]}{P[\Gamma > s]} = \exp\left[-\int_s^t h_\mu d\mu\right] \quad . \tag{6.121}$$

By definition,

$$h_t dt = P[t < \Gamma < t + dt \mid \Gamma > t] = \frac{P[t < \Gamma < t + dt]}{P[\Gamma > t]} \quad . \tag{6.122}$$

Therefore,

$$P[t < \Gamma < t + dt] = P[\Gamma > t] h_t dt = h_t \exp\left[-\int_0^t h_\mu d\mu\right] dt \quad . \tag{6.123}$$

Clearly,

$$P[t < \Gamma < t + dt \mid \Gamma > s] = h_t \exp\left[-\int_s^t h_\mu d\mu\right] dt \quad . \tag{6.124}$$

The following is a list of useful hazard rate relationships:

$$\begin{aligned} P[\Gamma > t] &= \exp\left[-\int_0^t h_\mu d\mu\right] \\ P[\Gamma > t \mid \Gamma > s] &= \exp\left[-\int_s^t h_\mu d\mu\right] \\ P[t < \Gamma < t + dt] &= h_t \exp\left[-\int_0^t h_\mu d\mu\right] dt \\ P[t < \Gamma < t + dt \mid \Gamma > s] &= h_t \exp\left[-\int_s^t h_\mu d\mu\right] dt \end{aligned} \tag{6.125}$$

These appear to be similar to the non-homogeneous Poisson process of equation 6.25. This is only true if h_t is non-stochastic (i.e., only a function of time). When it is stochastic, it is called a *Cox process*. One can derive general relationships for idealized financial assets assuming stochastic hazard rates as exemplified in the following three cases.

CHAPTER 6 ■ INTRODUCTION TO CREDIT DERIVATIVES

Case 1: Risky Zero Coupon Discount Bond $B(t)$ Maturing at T with No Recovery

Let I denote the indicator function and r_μ a continuously compounded stochastic interest rate that will be used for discounting. The bond price is the discounted expectation of a par payment at maturity T assuming that the bond has not defaulted, such that $I(\Gamma > T)$,

$$\frac{B(t)}{\exp\left(\int_0^t r_\mu d\mu\right)} = E_t\left[\frac{I(\Gamma > T)}{\exp\left(\int_0^T r_\mu d\mu\right)}\right]$$

$$B(t) = E_t\left[I(\Gamma > T)\exp\left(-\int_t^T r_\mu d\mu\right) | F_t\right] \quad (6.126)$$

$$B(t) = E_t\left[P[\Gamma > T | \Gamma > t]\exp\left(-\int_t^T r_\mu d\mu\right)\right]$$

$$B(t) = E_t\left[\exp\left(-\int_t^T (r_\mu + h_\mu) d\mu\right)\right]$$

The first conditional probability of default relationship from (6.125) was used as the expectation was conditioned upon the information (no default) up to time t (i.e., via the filtration F_t as described in Schonbucher (2003). Filtrations are outside the scope of this book.)

Case 2: Continuous Coupon Payment C_t until Default

Another example is that of a continuously compounded coupon payment C_t until a default event. This could be seen as the continuously compounded coupon payment of a CDS (i.e., the premium leg). Once must calculate the expectation of the integral over time of the discounted coupon payments until a default event,

$$B(t) = E_t\left[\int_t^T C_s P[\Gamma > s | \Gamma > t]\exp\left(-\int_t^s r_\mu d\mu\right) ds\right]$$
$$B(t) = E_t\left[\int_t^T C_s \exp\left(-\int_t^s (r_\mu + h_\mu) d\mu\right) ds\right] \quad (6.127)$$

Case 3: Recovery Payment R_t at Default

Finally, consider the case of a stochastic recovery payment R_t upon a default event. This could be seen as the default leg of a CDS. This is the expectation of a stochastic recovery rate occurring at a default event,

$$B(t) = E_t\left[\int_t^T R_s P[s < \Gamma < s + ds | \Gamma > t]\exp\left(-\int_t^s r_\mu d\mu\right) ds\right]$$
$$B(t) = E_t\left[\int_t^T R_s h_s \exp\left(-\int_t^s (r_\mu + h_\mu) d\mu\right) ds\right] \quad (6.128)$$

273

OHMC and the Static Hedging of a Risky Bond with a CDS

The OHMC methodology of Chapter 5 can be applied to credit derivatives. Recall that the OHMC methodology is interested not only in valuation but also in hedging. Here, one hedges a CDS with an appropriate risky bond as depicted in Figure 6-9 (from [Petrelli et al., 2006]).

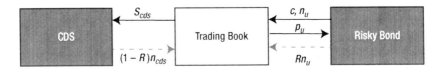

Figure 6-9. *Risky bond hedged with a CDS*

A risky bond with par value of n_u pays a continuously compounded coupon of c per unit time until maturity T. The cost of this bond upfront (current market value) is p_u. One can buy a CDS with notional n_{cds} and a continuously compounded premium spread of s_{cds}. The CDS pays $(1-R)n_r$ in the event of default. Both the recovery rate R and the time to default Γ can be seen as random parameters. If this is a static hedge (i.e., the CDS is not rebalanced during the life of the bond) there are two possible changes of wealth during the lifetime of the bond $\Delta W[0, T]$:

$$\Delta W_{\text{no-default}}(0,T) = -p_u + n_u e^{-rT} + \int_0^T cn_u e^{-r\tau}d\tau - \int_0^T s_{cds}n_{cds}e^{-r\tau}d\tau \quad (6.129)$$

$$\Delta W_{\text{default}}(0,T) = -p_u + [Rn_u + (1-R)n_{cds}]e^{-r\Gamma} + \int_0^\Gamma cn_u e^{-r\tau}d\tau - \int_0^\Gamma s_{cds}n_{cds}e^{-r\tau}d\tau$$

The expected change in wealth is given by

$$E[\Delta W(0,T)] = E[\Delta W_{\text{no-default}}(0,T)] + E[\Delta W_{\text{default}}(0,T)] \quad . \quad (6.130)$$

This expectation is under two distributions: one for the time to default Γ, and the other for the unknown recovery rate R. Assuming these two distributions to be independent, and the time to default to be distributed by a constant hazard rate λ, one can calculate the expectation term by term.

Step 1: p_u

$$E[-p_u] = E[-p_u P[\Gamma > T]] + E[-p_u P[t < \Gamma < t + dt]] \quad (6.131)$$

$$E[-p_u] = -p_u e^{-\lambda T} - p_u \int_0^T \lambda e^{-\lambda t}dt$$
$$E[-p_u] = -p_u e^{-\lambda T} + p_u e^{-\lambda t}\big|_0^T \quad (6.132)$$
$$E[-p_u] = -p_u e^{-\lambda T} + p_u e^{-\lambda T} - p_u = -p_u \quad .$$

CHAPTER 6 ■ INTRODUCTION TO CREDIT DERIVATIVES

This is not a surprise as one pays the bond price regardless of a default event in the future.

Step 2: $n_u e^{-rT}$

$$E[n_u e^{-rT} P[\Gamma > T]] = n_u e^{-(\lambda+r)T} \quad . \tag{6.133}$$

Step 3: $[Rn_u + (1-R)n_{cds}]e^{-r\Gamma}$

$$E[[Rn_u + (1-R)n_{cds}]e^{-r\Gamma}]$$
$$= \iint_0^T [Rn_u + (1-R)n_{cds}]e^{-r\Gamma} P[t < \Gamma < t+dt]f(R)dR \quad . \tag{6.134}$$

Since the distributions of R and Γ were assumed to be independent, one has $[\bar{R} = \int Rf(R)dR]$

$$\int_0^T [\bar{R}n_u + (1-\bar{R})n_{cds}]e^{-(\lambda+r)t} \lambda dt$$
$$= [\bar{R}n_u + (1-\bar{R})n_{cds}] \frac{-\lambda}{(\lambda+r)} e^{-(\lambda+r)t} \Big|_0^T$$
$$= [\lambda \bar{R}n_u + \lambda(1-\bar{R})n_{cds}] \left[\frac{1}{\lambda+r} - \frac{e^{-(\lambda+r)T}}{\lambda+r} \right] \tag{6.135}$$
$$= \frac{e^{-(\lambda+r)T}}{\lambda+r} [\lambda \bar{R}n_u + \lambda(1-\bar{R})n_{cds}] \left[e^{(\lambda+r)T} - 1 \right] \quad .$$

Step 4: $\int_0^T cn_u e^{-r\tau} d\tau - \int_0^T s_{cds} n_{cds} e^{-r\tau} d\tau$

For the coupon and spread payments, the calculation is similar to Case 2 in the section on stochastic hazard rates.

$$E\left[\int_0^T (cn_u - s_{cds}n_{cds})P[\Gamma > t | \Gamma > 0]e^{-rt} dt \right]$$
$$= \int_0^T (cn_u - s_{cds}n_{cds}) e^{-(\lambda+r)t} dt$$
$$= (cn_u - s_{cds}n_{cds}) \left[\frac{1}{\lambda+r} - \frac{e^{-(\lambda+r)T}}{\lambda+r} \right] \tag{6.136}$$
$$= \frac{e^{-(\lambda+r)T}}{\lambda+r} (cn_u - s_{cds}n_{cds}) \left[e^{(\lambda+r)T} - 1 \right] \quad .$$

Adding these steps up produces

$$E[\Delta W(0,T)] = \frac{e^{-(\lambda+r)T}}{(\lambda+r)} \tag{6.137}$$
$$\bullet\, n_u \left[(c+\lambda\bar{R})(e^{(\lambda+r)T}-1) + (\lambda+r) \right] - p_u e^{(\lambda+r)T}(\lambda+r) + n_{cds}\left[[\lambda(1-\bar{R}) - s_{cds}](e^{(\lambda+r)T}-1) \right] \quad .$$

275

As before in the OHMC methodology, for the mean wealth change to be set to zero, the CDS spread must follow,

$$E[\Delta W(0,T)] = 0 \rightarrow$$

$$s_{cds} = \frac{n_u \left[(c + \lambda \bar{R})(e^{(\lambda+r)T} - 1) + (\lambda + r) \right] - p_u e^{(\lambda+r)T}(\lambda + r)}{n_{cds}[e^{(\lambda+r)T} - 1]} + \lambda(1 - \bar{R}) \quad . \tag{6.138}$$

Similar to the OHMC forward calculation, one can solve this by guessing a simple solution. Consider the case of a bond priced at par—i.e. $p_u = n_u$. It then makes sense to have the CDS notional match the bond notional, $n_{cds} = n_u$. Substituting these conditions into the above result gives

$$s_{cds} = (c + \lambda \bar{R}) + \frac{(\lambda + r)}{e^{(\lambda+r)T} - 1} - \frac{(\lambda + r)e^{(\lambda+r)T}}{e^{(\lambda+r)T} - 1} + \lambda(1 - \bar{R}) \tag{6.139}$$

$$s_{cds} = c + \lambda + (\lambda + r)\frac{1 - e^{(\lambda+r)T}}{e^{(\lambda+r)T} - 1} = c - r \quad . \tag{6.140}$$

This result makes perfect sense. The spread of the CDS equals the coupon of the bond minus the risk-free rate, because the CDS takes on pure credit risk and has no funding requirements inasmuch as it is a pure synthetic contract. For bonds priced near par, this is always a good estimate of the "credit spread" of the underlying. Note that in this simple case, the distribution of recovery rates was irrelevant.

The second part of the OHMC methodology is to minimize the wealth change variance,

minimize : $\quad E[\{\Delta W(0,T) - \overline{\Delta W(0,T)}\}^2]$
constraint : $\quad E[\Delta W(0,T)] = 0$ $\quad$. $\tag{6.141}$

For the simple case of a *par bond*, the variance is zero. In the general case, it must be calculated subject to the constraint (6.138). The result can be found in [Petrelli et al., 2006], but it is important to understand that a perfect hedge is not possible under stochastic recovery rates and when a bond is not trading at par. Unfortunately, the standard risk-neutral methodology for pricing credit derivatives assumes the perfect hedge.

OHMC and CDS Swaptions

One of the main inputs that is completely missing from the copula models of the previous section is the volatility of CDS spreads. This is one of the main reasons why the Gaussian copula model completely failed during the 2008 crisis: the future volatility of credit spreads was not taken into account. One such OTC instrument that is highly dependent on credit spread volatility is the *CDS swaption*. Much like the interest rate swaptions of Chapter 1, CDS swaptions come in different flavors, including the following:

CHAPTER 6 ■ INTRODUCTION TO CREDIT DERIVATIVES

- **Payer CDS swaption**: This is a European-style option to purchase a CDS on a prespecified name with maturity T at a prespecified premium (strike) at the option maturity t_e. For instance, a "2yr into 5yr Payer" is a payer swaption, which gives the buyer the option to purchase a 5yr CDS in 2 years at a prespecified premium. Similar to their interest rate cousins, payer swaptions are like call options.

- **Receiver CDS swaption**: This is a European-style option to sell a CDS with maturity T at a prespecified premium (strike) at the option maturity t_e. For instance, a "1yr into 3yr Receiver" is a receiver swaption, which gives the buyer the option to sell a 3yr CDS in 1 year at a prespecified premium. Similar to their interest rate cousins, receiver swaptions are like put options.

- **Knockout swaption**: Because defaults can happen at any time, a CDS contract may not exist for a swaption if the underlying has defaulted *before* the swaption exercise date. Therefore, certain swaptions are knocked out (cease to be valid) if default occurs before the option maturity. Receiver swaptions are all knockouts. Payer swaptions can be of either type.

The OHMC equations are similar to ones for the knock-out cliquet of Chapter 5. The CDS swaption seller's wealth change equation is given by

$$\Delta W(t_k, t_{k+1}) = \Delta W^{swaption}(t_k, t_{k+1}) + \Delta W^{CDS\,hedge}(t_k, t_{k+1}) \quad . \quad (6.142)$$

As usual, one splits up the option and the hedge wealth change components. There are three different cash flows to consider:

- the swaption premium at inception
- default prior to expiry for no-knockout options where (par − recovery) is paid
- at expiry where a settlement of the underlying CDS position is made if the option is exercised

One hedges a CDS swaption with a par CDS of identical maturity as the CDS underlying the swaption contract. As usual, the efficacy of the attempted replication will come down to the fat tail and volatility of CDS spreads, jumps to default, recovery uncertainty, and the discrete hedging time interval available to the seller-hedger. The MC simulation should involve a stochastic model of CDS spreads that are coupled with the default probabilities of the underlying name. Separate correlated stochastic models for interest rates and recovery rates can also be used. The OHMC method is very flexible in this way.

The swaption wealth change equation is given by the following (cf the similar knockout cliquet contract of Chapter 5):

CHAPTER 6 ■ INTRODUCTION TO CREDIT DERIVATIVES

$$\Delta W_{t_k}^{swaption}(t_k, t_{k+1}) = C(t_k) - G(t_k)$$

CDS Swaption value

(6.143)

$$G(t_k) = (1 - I(t_k, t_{k+1}))C(t_{k+1})df(t_k, t_{k+1}) + \omega^G(t_k, t_{k+1})$$

Notional

$$\omega^G(t_k, t_{k+1}) = \begin{cases} I(t_k, t_{k+1})N(1-R)df(t_k, t_d) & \text{no knockout} \\ 0 & \text{knockout} \end{cases}$$

$$I(t_k, t_{k+1}) = \begin{cases} 1 & t_{default} \in (t_k, t_{k+1}) \\ 0 & t_{default} > t_{k+1} \end{cases}$$

Note that the notation above has been made so that it is consistent with the OHMC method introduced in Chapter 5. Therefore, $C(t)$ is **not** the CDS spread as has been the case in this chapter but the value of the CDS swaption. The CDS premium at time t with maturity T will be represented by $s(t, T)$.

The CDS hedge wealth change equation is given by

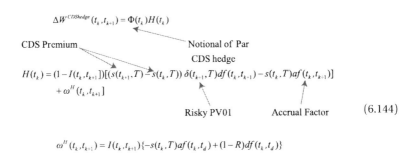

$$\Delta W^{CDShedge}(t_k, t_{k+1}) = \Phi(t_k)H(t_k)$$

CDS Premium   Notional of Par CDS hedge

$$H(t_k) = (1 - I(t_k, t_{k+1}))[(s(t_{k+1}, T) - s(t_k, T))\delta(t_{k+1}, T)df(t_k, t_{k+1}) - s(t_k, T)af(t_k, t_{k+1})]$$
$$+ \omega^H(t_k, t_{k+1})$$

Risky PV01   Accrual Factor

(6.144)

$$\omega^H(t_k, t_{k+1}) = I(t_k, t_{k+1})\{-s(t_k, T)af(t_k, t_d) + (1-R)df(t_k, t_d)\}$$

The accrual factors are like the ones found in equation (5.74) of the cliquet contract of Chapter 5. Table 6-3 shows the three possible payoffs that the CDS swaption seller is hedging.

Table 6-3. *CDS Swaption Seller's Payoff Cash Flows*

CONTRACT	Default before Maturity	Payoff at Maturity t_e $C(t_e)$
Payer Knock-Out	0	$-Max[s(t_e, T) - s_{strike}, 0]\delta(t_e, T)N$
Payer No Knock Out	$-N(1-R)$	$-Max[s(t_e, T) - s_{strike}, 0]\delta(t_e, T)N$
Receiver	0	$-Max[s_{strike} - s(t_e, T), 0]\delta(t_e, T)N$

This brief section is meant to spur the reader onto further research in this crucial area of credit derivative valuation.

Appendix. Bloomberg Functionality

- CDSD ➤ Indices and Tranches ➤ CDS Monitor and Cross Asset View (ratings versus spreads) ➤ Can change Series of tranche (go to CDX series 10 and see that Radian was investment grade versus series 20)
- GCDS: Sector comparison
- WCDS: World CDS
- C Equity Go ➤ CDSV - Credit Monitor ➤ Term structure of Credit Spreads ➤ CDSW (credit model) ➤ view ➤ cashflows or ISDA (shows credit events)
- CDX.NA.IG.20 (Index, North America, Investment Grade, Series 20)
- C Equity Go ➤ CRPR: company credit ratings
- C 5 08/02/2019 Corp (bond) ➤ ASW (asset swap model)
- BANK (financial credit spreads, created during the 2008 crash) ➤ Cross Asset View (ratings versus spreads)
- NI CDRV: credit news
- REDL: reference entity list

Problems
Problem 6-1. Calculate Hazard Rates from Par CDS Spreads

In Figure 6-10, par CDS spreads, a continuously compounded interest rate, a recovery rate, and daycount conventions are given. Calculate the hazard rates using the inputs in Figure 6-10 and complete the output table for at least the first four maturities.

CHAPTER 6 ■ INTRODUCTION TO CREDIT DERIVATIVES

Inputs	
Interest Rate	1%
Recovery	40%
Coupon Daycount	360
Default Daycount	365
Coupon Delta	0.25

MarketQuotes	
ParSpread	
6M	100
1y	110
2y	120
3y	140
4y	140
5y	150
7y	160
10y	165

Output			
Term	Hazard Rates	PV(Def Leg)	Risky PV01
6M			
1y			
2y			
3y			
4y			
5y			
7y			
10y			

Figure 6-10. *Par credit default swap spreads*

Problem 6-2. Standard Convention Upfront Payment

Assume one enters into the 1YR CDS quoted in Figure 6-10. Suppose this CDS follows the SNAC convention of 100bps. What is the upfront payment? How does the standard 1YR hazard rate differ from the 1YR par hazard rate of Problem 6-1?

Problem 6-3. Generating Correlated Bivariate Normal Variables

If z_1 and z_2 are independent standard normal variables $N(0, 1)$, one can create correlated bivariate normal variables with the following transformation,

$$\epsilon_1 = z_1$$
$$\epsilon_2 = \rho z_1 + \sqrt{1-\rho^2} z_2 \quad . \tag{6.145}$$

Step 1: Calculate $E[\epsilon_1^2]$, $E[\epsilon_2^2]$, $E[\epsilon_1 \epsilon_2]$.

Step 2: Generate 10000 bivariate normal random variables using Excel and the above transformation [recall the use of NORMSINV(Rand())].

Step 3: Calculate $E[\epsilon_1 \epsilon_2]$ for your generated 10000 variables. Does the answer make sense?

References

Andersen, L., J. Sidenius, and S. Basu, "All Your Hedges in One Basket," *Risk* (November 2003).

Douglas, R., *Credit Derivative Strategies: New Thinking on Managing Risk and Return* (New York: Bloomberg Financial, 2007).

Glasserman, P., *Monte Carlo Methods in Financial Engineering* (New York: Springer, 2003).

Gordy, M. B., "A Risk-Factor Model Foundation for Ratings-Based Bank Capital Ratios," *Journal of Financial Intermediation*, 12 (2003), 199–232.

Hull, J. C., *Risk Management and Financial Institutions*, 3rd ed. (Hoboken, NJ: Wiley, 2012).

Hull, J. C., and A. White, "Valuation of a CDO and nth-to-Default Swap without Monte Carlo Simulation," *Journal of Derivatives*, 12 (2004), 2.

Petrelli, A., O. Siu, J. Zhang, and V. Kapoor, "Optimal Static Hedging of Defaults in CDOs," DefaultRisk.com, April 2006.

Rajan, A., G. McDermott, and R. Roy, *The Structured Credit Handbook*, 3rd ed. (Hoboken, NJ: Wiley Finance, 2007).

Schonbucher, P., *Credit Derivatives Pricing* (New York: Wiley, 2003).

Vasicek, O., "Loan Portfolio Value," *Risk*, 15, no. 12 (2002), 160–62.

CHAPTER 7

Risk Types, CVA, Basel III, and OIS Discounting

The foregoing chapters described various financial contracts along with their valuation and risk on an instrument by instrument basis. In reality, internal heads of risk management and government regulators must look at the overall risk of the firm across all trading activities and asset classes.

Risk Types

To make firm-wide risk management tractable, the following general categories of risk must be considered.

Market Risk

Chapters 1–5 all dealt with market risk. This is the risk of losses coming from the market change of asset prices that negatively affect the mark-to-market positions of the bank. The change of asset prices can come from various factors, such as stock prices, volatility, and correlation. Market risk factors include the following:

> *Interest rate risk*: Changes in interest rates such as fed funds and LIBOR affects eurodollar futures, swaps, and options such as caps, floors, and swaptions. It also affects all bond-type instruments and loans.
>
> *Equity price risk*: This includes price fluctuations of all indices and single stocks, along with their futures and options.
>
> *Prepayment risk*: For MBS-type instruments, along with interest rate risk, changing prepayment speeds is a major risk factor, especially in decreasing interest rate environments.
>
> *Commodity price risk*: This includes price fluctuations such as in the gold and natural gas futures described in Chapter 1.

Foreign exchange risk: This risk is largely driven by the spot exchange rates and the interest rate differential between the two underlying currencies. FX rates can also be influenced by political events or governmental defaults, such as the Russian local bond defaults of 1998.

Spread risk: Changing asset swap spreads and CDS spreads are included in this market risk category.

Volatility risk: All option positions have this form of risk.

Correlation risk: The tranched CDO contracts of Chapter 6 are exposed to default correlation risk. Multi-asset products such as a basket of equities, commodities, and fixed income instruments are exposed to changing asset–asset correlations.

Credit Risk

Chapter 6 introduced the concept of credit risk beginning with the CDS contract. *Counterparty credit risk* (CCR) and default have such large implications that credit risk is separated from market risk even though the spread changes of credit instruments such as high-yield bonds, assets swaps, and CDSs are market-driven. All OTC contracts are exposed to CCR risk. The collapse of a major counterparty such as Lehman Brothers can have a ripple effect on all market participants, leading to a potential collapse of the whole financial system. The risk of a system-wide collapse is called *systemic risk*, discussed below. The creation of exchanges has mitigated CCR risk for exchange-traded products but has not eliminated it, because counterparties can still default on their obligations on an exchange-traded contract. The exchanges' clearing house simply becomes the new counterparty of the contract. If a large number of counterparties default, even an exchange can collapse. The US government has encouraged the use of exchanges through new regulations and punitive capital requirements for OTC contracts via Basel II and III, respectively treated in their own sections of this chapter.

Operational Risk

Operational risk is a large risk category that deals with such events as computer failures; model failures; internal fraud; large legal settlements; catastrophes such as fires, earthquakes, and terrorist attacks; and inadequate internal processes, such as poor compliance and risk management procedures. Rogue traders who have caused large losses—such as Joseph Jett (Kidder Peabody), Nick Leeson (ING-Barings), Jerome Kerviel (Société Générale), Bruno "The London Whale" Iksil (JPMorgan), and Kareem Serageldin (Credit Suisse)—all fall under the category of operational risk and the subcategory of failed internal risk management processes.

Firms have addressed these issues in various ways. All major Wall Street firms have disaster recovery sites that can replicate large parts of the firm's trading and risk management systems at a physical location that is separate from the main headquarters. Model validation groups within banks, which typically validate all the quantitative models within a firm, have been given more rigorous responsibilities, such as independently creating models used by traders to test for accuracy and stability. Internal audit, product control, and compliance have strengthened their processes and daily mark-to-market price verification of traders' positions. Ultimately, it is the duty of the head of the desk to make sure each trading book is properly marked and hedged.

Liquidity Risk

Asset-specific liquidity risk arises when a financial asset cannot be traded or must be traded at very wide bid-offer spreads. This is called *market liquidity risk*. During the subprime crisis of 2008, the super senior tranches of many CDOs that were traditionally quite liquid because of their AAA ratings suddenly became very illiquid and had to be drastically marked down. Firm-specific liquidity risk arises when a firm can no longer meet its payment obligations and cannot borrow more funds from external sources and becomes *illiquid*. This is associated with *funding liquidity risk*. One can argue that all firms that have defaulted eventually fell because of illiquidity. The bailout of Long Term Capital Management (LTCM) in 1998 by a consortium of its creditors was an example of both market and funding risk. LTCM held highly levered positions in worldwide government and corporate bonds. They also had large positions in equity pairs trading strategies. As with all levered positions such as futures, one must pay a certain amount of cash margin against the levered position. When the mark of the position moves negatively, one must post more margin. Owing to the 1998 Russia financial crisis, the bond positions of LTCM took large losses, and margin calls increased. LTCM had to sell many positions at a loss to meet margin calls. They could not sell enough of certain corporate bond positions because the market became temporarily illiquid in this asset class. Eventually, their funding sources dried up and they were recapitalized by $3.6 billion by fourteen financial institutions under the supervision of the Federal Reserve. In 2008, by contrast, Lehman Brothers also experienced losses and funding illiquidity but was not recapitalized by other financial firms or the Fed and therefore defaulted, precipitating the worldwide financial systemic risk scenario in the latter part of 2008.

Systemic Risk

Regulators fear systemic risk. This is the risk that the default of one or many financial institutions will create a domino default effect throughout the global banking community, leading to a collapse of the financial system as a whole. Regulators are also attempting to protect the deposit base of banks. In the United States, the Fed provides deposit insurance to all depositors through the FDIC. In return for providing this default insurance, the Fed has created certain regulatory requirements for all FDIC-insured banks. International agreements, such as the ones coming under the ever-changing Basel accord, are similar in their fundamental requirements. The basic preventive mechanism of most banking regulations is to ensure that financial institutes keep enough liquid capital to absorb any unforeseen losses that occur when taking risk. The key risk consideration here is to determine the risky assets of the bank according to the above risk categorizations and compare them to the total capital of the bank. Almost all regulatory rules come down to calculating the amount of these risky assets and determining what valid capital is. Thereafter, the regulations require a certain minimum percentage of capital versus risky assets.

It is very important not to confuse *systemic risk* with *systematic risk*. Systematic risk is a part of market risk that affects the market as a whole, as opposed to *idiosyncratic risk* to one specific aspect of the market. The S&P 500 represents systematic risk, whereas the risk in holding a position in Microsoft is idiosyncratic. Idiosyncratic risk can be diversified away, whereas systematic risk cannot be eliminated and therefore commands a certain level of return.

Coherent Risk Measures

The risk measures discussed up to this point have been VaR, CVaR, the term structure of statistics, autocorrelation of squared returns, volatility-return convexity (Chapter 3), and the complete distribution of hedging losses for derivatives through the OHMC method (Chapter 5). Artzner et al. (1999) have proposed certain mathematical properties that any risk measure should satisfy to be considered *coherent*. These coherent risk measures have become popular in the academic literature, so they are briefly introduced here.

Let ρ denote a risk measure and Π a risk position composed of cash, futures and swaps, options, etc. Under a certain predefined time scale τ, $\rho(\Pi)$ is a *coherent risk measure* if the following four axioms are satisfied:

> **Monotonicity:** If $\Pi_1 < \Pi_2$ (in a positive return distribution sense), then $\rho(\Pi_1) > \rho(\Pi_2)$. If the returns of Portfolio 1 Π_1 are almost surely worse than Portfolio 2 Π_2 in the probabilistic sense, the risk of Π_1 is greater than the risk of Π_2. Mathematically, this means that for any alpha, $P(\Pi_1 < \alpha) > P(\Pi_2 < \alpha)$.
>
> **Homogeneity or scale invariance:** For any scalar λ, $\rho(\lambda \Pi) = \lambda \rho(\Pi)$. For example, if you double the size of a portfolio, you double its risk.
>
> **Subadditivity:** $\rho(\Pi_1 + \Pi_2) \leq \rho(\Pi_1) + \rho(\Pi_2)$. This axiom says that the risk of two combined portfolios should be less than or equal to the total risk of the of the two portfolios as seen separately from each other. This is the basic condition of diversification.
>
> **Translation invariance:** If C is a risk-free asset such as cash earning a continuously compounded risk-free rate r, $\rho[\Pi + C\exp(rt)] = \rho(\Pi) - C$.

This states that the risk of the aggregate portfolio is reduced by the risk-free capital amount of C. This leads to the concept of setting aside risk capital as a cushion to protect against unexpected losses and is the driving force behind many regulatory capital requirements. For instance, if one takes $C = \rho(\Pi)$,

$$\rho(\Pi + \rho(\Pi)\exp(rt)) = \rho(\Pi) - \rho(\Pi) = 0$$

and therefore, $C = \rho(\Pi)$ is the right amount of capital reserves to cover the portfolio Π.

VaR is not a coherent risk measure because it fails the subadditivity condition for general distributions. For elliptical distributions, such as the Gaussian distribution, VaR becomes coherent. CVaR, however, is a coherent risk measure for general distributions.

Regulation and Its Effects

Regulators fear systemic risk and thereafter create regulations that require financial institutions to hold a certain minimum percentage of capital versus their risky assets, such that

$$\text{Capital Ratio} = \frac{\text{Eligible Capital}}{\text{RiskWeighted Assets}}. \quad (7.1)$$

While the concept of requiring minimum capital ratios is theoretically a sound idea, regulations must answer the following three crucial questions:

- What assets constitute eligible or core capital?
- What is a sufficient minimum percentage of capital?
- How does one measure the risk of assets?

Core capital is the leading indicator of a financial firm's strength from a regulatory viewpoint. Liquid equity capital is one of the largest components of a bank's *Tier 1* capital. Retained earnings are also a part of Tier 1 capital. Other assets that can be used as capital are not so straightforward and fall under *Tier 2* capital. The exact definitions of Tier 1 and Tier 2 capital have evolved under Basel I, II, and III and may again change in the future. The minimum percentage of capital is usually broken up into a Tier 1 capital ratio and a Tier 1 plus 2 capital ratio with respect to the total risk-weighted assets (see below) of the bank. These ratios are all under 10%, but it is completely unclear how the regulators justified their choice of these numbers. Before the introduction of Basel II, these numbers were small enough that the banking community didn't care how the regulators choose the minimum capital ratios.

The final question is the hardest to answer and is where 99% of the effort of calculating regulatory capital lies. As explained in the beginning of this chapter, different asset classes have different types of risk. A US Treasury bond is less risky than a high-yield corporate bond, but how does one quantify this difference? The total measurement of risk of an asset is called its *risk weight*, and asset exposures weighted according to risk are called *risk-weighted assets* (RWA). These risks need to be calculated at an expected level (the mean of the distribution) and at unexpected levels (the tail of the distribution). Many of these calculations involve sophisticated derivative models, and one needs to understand their limitations when calculating tail risk. Most traders do not have models that calculate tail risk, and therefore these calculations are often left to risk management (though many traders do get involved if the capital numbers are so high that they negate the profit of the trading desk). If the majority of models used by traders were based on the OHMC method of Chapter 5, many of the typical problems of calculating RWA would disappear or at least become more straightforward and natural with respect to the day-to-day activities of the trading desk.

The McKinsey Annual Review [Visalli et al., 2011] on the banking industry report argues that US and European banks "need to grapple with a set of fundamental long-term trends that are increasingly shaping the operating environment." The report makes the following four comments based on the new aggressive regulatory environment:

- *The impact of regulation on profitability*: "The coming regulatory changes will be costly for banks, resulting in increases in bank equity, increased funding costs, and a tightening of consumer protection."
- *A squeeze on capital and funding*: "Growing demand for credit, together with increasing investment in infrastructure, will put a strain on the supply of capital and funding—and thereby increase its cost."
- *A widening gap between growing and nongrowing markets*: "Emerging markets represent a promising opportunity for banks that can access them—but the prospects for those that cannot do so are more challenging. It is likely that the 'growth gap' between the 'haves' and 'have-nots' will increase."
- *Changing consumer behavior*: "Banks face several concurrent changes in consumer behavior, including a shift from borrowing to saving, and an inexorable migration to online channels."

As of 2014, all these predictions have been borne out.

Accounting Credit Valuation Adjustment (CVA)

According to the Financial Accounting Standards Board (FASB 157) and the International Financial Reporting Standards (IFRS 13), fair-value accounting is required for many assets on the balance sheet of a financial institution, including all OTC derivative positions—though not all balance sheet assets outside the trading book have to be accounted for at fair value. As OTC contracts are exposed to CCR, price adjustments that include default risk must be made to such contracts over an above-the-usual market risk pricing. This adjustment is called the *credit valuation adjustment* (CVA). CVA is the difference between the hypothetical value of an OTC derivatives portfolio with no counterparty credit risk and the true portfolio value that takes into account the possibility of the counterparty's default (that is, the expected counterparty risk).

$$\mathbf{CVA}_T = PV_T^{CCR\,free} - PV_T^{CCR\,risky} \qquad (7.2)$$

In *accounting CVA*, these calculations are performed in a risk-neutral framework similar to the one used in pricing the derivative itself. Accounting CVA exists independently of the Basel regulations. Accounting CVA is calculated by all banks on their derivative positions and can become a capital charge on the books of the bank. It can reduce the value of a bank's derivative position by billions of dollars. Most large financial institutions have CVA desks that attempt to reduce these numbers by purchasing CDSs on their more risky counterparties in order to reduce the accounting CVA charge of the bank. In the

CHAPTER 7 ■ RISK TYPES, CVA, BASEL III, AND OIS DISCOUNTING

Basel III calculations below, the accounting CVA charge is subtracted from the CCR RWA calculated in Basel to avoid double-counting the CCR risk for OTC derivatives. The CCR risk calculations in Basel are called *regulatory CVA* calculations to distinguish them from accounting CVA.

The standard methodology to calculate the CVA charge is essentially to use the default leg of a single name CDS given by (6.31) in the hazard rate formulation,

$$LGD * N * \sum_{j=1}^{T} df(t_j)\left(\exp\left[-h(t_{j-1})t_{j-1}\right] - \exp\left[-h(t_j)t_j\right]\right) \quad . \tag{7.3}$$

For a CDS, the notional N is known beforehand and is used with the above equation. For an OTC derivative, the notional is the *exposure* of the derivative at all future times. Because this is a stochastic variable, one needs the *expected exposure at time* t_j, EE_j. As should be clear by now, CCR only exists when one has a *positive* exposure to a counterparty—that is, a positive *mark-to-market* (MtM) on a particular instrument. Therefore, these exposures are calculated only for positive valuations of the underlying instrument or portfolio. For instance, a USD interest rate swap may have a positive MtM to either the fixed or floating side, depending on interest rate movements. On the other hand, simple European call and put options are always positive to the owner. Therefore, in terms of stochastic MtM at a future time t_j, one has $EE_j = E[\text{Max}(\text{MtM}_j, 0)]$.

Because (7.3) calculates defaults between times t_{j-1} and t_j, one uses the average exposure during this period to replace the notional, N, in (7.3) to get the CVA charge,

$$CVA(T) = LGD \sum_{j=1}^{T} \frac{EE_{j-1} df(t_{j-1}) + EE_j df(t_j)}{2} \left(\exp\left[-h(t_{j-1})t_{j-1}\right] - \exp\left[-h(t_j)t_j\right]\right)$$

$$EE_j = E[\text{Max}(\text{MtM}_j, 0)] \tag{7.4}$$

How does one calculate the term structure of hazard rates $h(t)$? In general, a stochastic model for the hazard rates may be used. Yet, for simplicity, regulators allow the use of the *credit triangle* for the hazard rates $h(t)$, as discussed in Chapter 6:

$$CVA(T) = LGD \sum_{j=1}^{T} \frac{EE_{j-1} df(t_{j-1}) + df(t_j) EE_j(t_j)}{2} \left(\exp\left[\frac{-s(t_{j-1})t_{j-1}}{LGD}\right] - \exp\left[\frac{-s(t_j)t_j}{LGD}\right]\right)$$

$$= LGD \sum_{j=1}^{T} v_i \left(\exp\left[\frac{-s(t_{j-1})t_{j-1}}{LGD}\right] - \exp\left[\frac{-s(t_j)t_j}{LGD}\right]\right) \tag{7.5}$$

where

$$v_i = \frac{EE_{j-1} df(t_{j-1}) + df(t_j) EE_j(t_j)}{2} \quad . \tag{7.6}$$

All the expected exposures EE_j must be calculated by MC methods. This is the main task of calculating CVA. Further details of calculating expected exposures are given at the end of this chapter.

While the changes in CVA due to changes in the exposures v_i are complicated to calculate, a counterparty *Credit Spread 01* (CS01) to estimate the change in the CVA resulting from a change in the credit spread term structure of the counterparty (which will be needed for Basel III) can be calculated by reordering the preceding expression as follows,

$$CVA(T) = LGD \sum_{j=1}^{T-1} \left(\exp\left[\frac{-s(t_j)t_j}{LGD}\right] \frac{EE_{j+1}(t_{j+1}) - EE_{j-1}(t_{j-1})}{2} \right)$$
$$+ \exp\left[\frac{-s(t_0)t_0}{LGD}\right] \frac{EE_0 df(t_0) + EE_1 df(t_1)}{2}$$
$$- \exp\left[\frac{-s(T)T}{LGD}\right] \frac{EE_{T-1} df(T-1) + EE_T(T)}{2} \quad . \tag{7.7}$$

Therefore, the CS01 is

$$CS01_i = \frac{\partial CVA(T)}{\partial s(t_i)} = \left(t_i \cdot \exp\left[\frac{-s(t_i)t_i}{LGD}\right] \cdot \frac{EE_{i-1} df(t_{i-1}) - EE_{i+1} df(t_{i+1})}{2} \right) \quad . \tag{7.8}$$

To estimate the change in the CVA resulting from a *parallel* shift in the credit spread term structure of the counterparty, one must calculate $CVA(s + \Delta s)$ as follows:

$$CVA(s + \Delta s) = LGD \sum_{j=1}^{T} v_j \left(\exp\left[\frac{-[s(t_{j-1}) + \Delta s]t_{j-1}}{LGD}\right] - \exp\left[\frac{-[s(t_j) + \Delta s]t_j}{LGD}\right] \right)$$

where

$$v_j = \frac{EE_{j-1} df(t_{j-1}) + EE_j(t_j) df(t_j)}{2} \quad . \tag{7.9}$$

Simplifying the above gives

$$CVA(s + \Delta s) \approx LGD \sum_{j=1}^{T} v_j \left(\exp\left[\frac{-s(t_{j-1})t_{j-1}}{LGD}\right] \left[1 - \frac{(\Delta s)t_{j-1}}{LGD}\right] - \exp\left[\frac{-s(t_j)t_j}{LGD}\right] \left[1 - \frac{(\Delta s)t_j}{LGD}\right] \right) \cdot \tag{7.10}$$

Therefore, to first order ("delta"),

$$\Delta CVA = CVA(s) - CVA(s + \Delta s) \approx \sum_{j=1}^{T} v_j \left(t_{j-1} \exp\left[\frac{-s(t_{j-1})t_{j-1}}{LGD}\right] - t_j \exp\left[\frac{-s(t_j)t_j}{LGD}\right] \right)(\Delta s) \quad . \tag{7.11}$$

This should be compared to the single point bump expression

$$\Delta CVA[s(t_i)] = (\Delta s_i) \cdot CS01_i \tag{7.12}$$

using (7.8). Including a second-order correction ("gamma") would result in the following,

$$\Delta CVA \approx \sum_{j=1}^{T} v_j \left(t_{j-1} \exp\left[\frac{-s(t_{j-1})t_{j-1}}{LGD}\right] - t_j \exp\left[\frac{-s(t_j)t_j}{LGD}\right] \right)(\Delta s)$$
$$- \left[\frac{1}{2LGD}\right] \sum_{j=1}^{T} v_j \left(t^2_{j-1} \exp\left[\frac{-s(t_{j-1})t_{j-1}}{LGD}\right] - t^2_j \exp\left[\frac{-s(t_j)t_j}{LGD}\right] \right)(\Delta s)^2 \quad . \tag{7.13}$$

Accounting CVA looks at the expected counterparty risk of a position, whereas the Basel regulations described below try to determine unexpected (tail) risk coming from various risk categories such as market risk, credit risk, and operational risk.

Wrong-Way Risk

A major assumption was made in arriving at the CVA expression given in (7.4). To see this, first rewrite the general CDS default leg equation (6.4) for the current CVA problem,

$$CVA(T) = LGD \int_0^T df(t) E[\text{Max}(\text{MtM}(t),0)|t=\tau] dQ(t)$$

$\tau = $ default time of counterparty (7.14)
$Q(t) = $ probability at time t of a credit event

Here, the expected exposure of the underlying position $E[\text{Max}(\text{MtM}(t),0)|t=\tau]$ is conditional on the counterparty default time τ, such that there is an explicit dependence on the exposure and the counterparty's credit quality. The situation when the counterparty's credit quality decreases as the bank's positive exposure to that counterparty increases is called *wrong-way risk*. That is, the more exposure one takes to a counterparty, the worse the counterparty gets. In arriving at (7.4), it was assumed that the underlying position and the counterparty are independent, and therefore the expected exposure calculation used an unconditional expectation. There is no standard model for the estimating the impact of wrong-way risk on the CVA capital charge. Basel III, to be discussed below, introduces an explicit capital charge for specific wrong-way risk. According to Basel (2011A), banks must

> have procedures in place to identify, monitor and control cases of specific wrong-way risk, beginning at the inception of a trade and continuing through the life of the trade. To calculate the CCR capital charge, the instruments for which there exists a legal connection between the counterparty and the underlying issuer, and for which specific wrong-way risk has been identified, are not considered to be in the same netting set as other transactions with the counterparty. Furthermore, for single-name credit default swaps where a legal connection exists between the counterparty and the underlying issuer, and where specific wrong-way risk has been identified, EAD counterparty exposure equals the full expected loss in the remaining fair value of the underlying instruments assuming the underlying issuer is in liquidation.

Wrong-way risk is the focus of much current research, such as Rosen and Saunders (2012).

Basel I

In 1988, the Basel Accord (Basel I) began the era of international banking regulations and the global hedging of systemic risk. The Basel Committee regularly met in Basel, Switzerland, under the auspices of the Bank for International Settlements (BIS). The basic mechanism of the Basel regulations was to ensure that financial institutions keep enough liquid capital to absorb any unforeseen losses that occur when taking risk. This, in turn, would provide confidence in the ever expanding global banking system. Nonetheless, it has had many unnecessary side effects that are contrary to a free enterprise-style economic system. The main mechanism in the BIS accords is to determine the risky assets of a bank and compare them to the capital of the bank. Almost all the rules come down to calculating the amount of these risky assets and determining what valid capital is. Thereafter, the regulations require a certain minimum percentage of capital versus risky assets. These rules have evolved in their definition and categorization of risk from Basel I, to II, to II.5, and, as of 2014, Basel III. Under the original 1988 accord and the 1996 amendment, the RWA of a bank were determined by two different risk categories:

- *CCR RWA*: As mentioned above, CCR is the risk of a bank's counterparty defaulting and not being able to either repay a loan or fulfill the payoff of an OTC derivative contract. For OTC derivatives, one must calculate the *positive exposure* to the bank of the derivative contract. A positive exposure for the counterparty (a negative MtM to the bank) is not a credit risk for the bank.

- *Market-risk RWA*: This involves keeping enough capital for the market risks associated with the bank's trading activities. It is generally based on a 10-day 99% VaR number.

In these early times, credit risk was not well understood, and therefore the measurement of credit risk was based on a relatively primitive method to calculate the CCR RWA. On-balance sheet items were simply given a risk weight according to four very broad categories as shown in Figure 7-1. The acronym shown in Figure 7-1, OECD, stands for the Organisation for Economic Co-operation and Development. Currently, 34 countries are included in this organization. (Note that the BRIC countries are not within the OECD framework.) For all these products, the credit risk RWA is calculated by multiplying the appropriate weight w from this table with the product notional N.

Risk Weight	Asset Class
0%	Cash and gold. Obligations from OECD governments and U.S. Treasuries
20%	Claims on OECD banks. Securities from U.S. agencies or municipalities.
50%	Residential Mortgages
100%	All other debt such as corporate bonds, EM bonds, equities, etc.

Figure 7-1. Basel I CCR RWA

The total CCR RWA is given by

$$\text{CCR RWA (Basel I)} = \sum_{i=1} w_i N_i \quad . \tag{7.15}$$

Note that neither the MtM nor explicit credit ratings of products are taken into consideration. This methodology was wholly inappropriate for off-balance-sheet OTC derivatives of that era, and therefore an alternate approach was used. Let V_0 be the current value of the OTC derivative in question (forward, swap, option, etc.) and N be its notional amount. Its *credit equivalent amount CE* is calculated as

$$CE = \text{MAX}(V_0, 0) + aN \quad , \tag{7.16}$$

where a is an add-on factor that arbitrarily takes into account the possibility of the exposure V_0 increasing in the future. The total CCR RWA for OTC derivatives is given by

$$\text{OTC Derivative CCR RWA (Basel I)} = \sum_{i=1} w_i \, CE_i \quad , \tag{7.17}$$

where the risk weight w_i is determined by the risk weight of the counterparty from Figure 7-1.

Clearly, the derivative formula based on V_0 is not forward-looking in any real sense. This problem is partially addressed in Basel II.

The Basel I market risk RWA is based on a 10-day 99% VaR moving average prescription,

$$\text{Market Risk RWA}_t = 12.5 \cdot \text{MAX}\left(k \frac{1}{60} \sum_{i=1}^{60} VAR(0.99)_{t-i}, VAR(0.99)_{t-1} \right) + SRC_t$$

k = magic factor determined by regulators (7.18)

SRC_t = Specific Risk Charge

CHAPTER 7 ■ RISK TYPES, CVA, BASEL III, AND OIS DISCOUNTING

The value of k is often 3. This can be increased, depending upon the quality of the banks VaR models. This formula takes the higher of the 60-day moving average VaR (99.9%) versus the current VaR. The specific risk charge is used for things not considered, such as a company's credit spread, stock price movements, or missing risk factors such as basis risk. Finally, the total capital under Basel I must be at least 8% of the sum of the above two RWAs:

$$\text{Minimum Total Capital} = 0.08 \cdot [\text{CCR RWA} + \text{Market Risk RWA}] \quad . \quad (7.19)$$

The types of capital that may be used by a financial institution are discussed in the Basel III section because the Basel I definitions are now obsolete.

Basel II

A "revised framework" known as *Basel II* was released in June 2004 after Basel I was beset with many issues—most notably that of regulatory arbitrage, which was rampant throughout the financial sector. Basel I gave banks the ability to control the amount of capital they required by shifting between on-balance-sheet assets with different weights and by securitizing assets and shifting them off balance sheet—a form of *disintermediation*. Banks quickly accumulated capital well in excess of the regulatory minimum and capital requirements, which in effect had no constraining impact on the amount of risk a bank could take.

Basel II introduced the concept of *three pillars*:

- **Pillar 1**, *Regulatory capital*: This deals with maintenance of regulatory capital calculated for three major components of risk that a bank faces: credit, market, and operational.

- **Pillar 2**, *Supervisory review*: Supervisors will evaluate the activities and risk profiles of individual banks to determine whether those organizations should hold higher levels of capital than the minimum requirements in Pillar 1 would specify and to see whether there is any need for remedial actions.

- **Pillar 3**, *Market disclosure*: This feature will leverage the ability to create greater market discipline and motivate prudent risk management by enhancing the degree of transparency in the banks' public reporting to shareholders and customers.

Concerning Pillar 1 of Basel II, RWAs are determined by three different risk categories:

- CCR RWA
- Market risk RWA
- Operational risk RWA

According to the Basel Committee on Banking Supervision in 2001 (Basel Committee, 2003), operational risk is defined as: "The risk of loss resulting from inadequate or failed internal processes, people, and systems or from external events." This concerns things like fraud (mismarking positions), legal settlements (discrimination lawsuits), business disruption (computer failures), and so on. It is a very hard thing to measure accurately.

The total capital under Basel II must be at least 8% of the sum of the above RWAs—that is,

$$\text{Minimum Total Capital} = 0.08 \cdot [\text{CCR RWA} + \text{Market Risk RWA} + \text{Operational Risk RWA}] \quad (7.20)$$

CCR RWA

The CCR calculation in Basel—namely, regulatory CVA—is not quite the same as the fair-value accounting CVA methodology described above. The accounting CVA methodology was based on the expected default probabilities of the OTC counterparty using a risk-neutral valuation framework. Basel looks at CCR more from a systemic risk and tail-probability viewpoint. The systemic risk viewpoint manifests itself through the correlated probability of several counterparties defaulting at once. The tail-probability viewpoint manifests itself in a 99.9% confidence interval calculation described below. Consider an obligor of a bank that has a one-year probability of default of D (derived from a hazard rate model or some other model). The method for calculating the probability of default from a systemic viewpoint uses the *one-factor Gaussian copula model* as described in Chapter 6. One considers a universe of counterparties all correlated to each other through the one factor which may represent the general health of the economy. By giving each obligor a copula correlation ρ to this one factor, one is considering the risk of many counterparties defaulting at once, which may in turn cause a major shock to the system as a whole. By considering a worst case 99.9% confidence interval for this one factor, one is taking a risk management viewpoint rather than a valuation viewpoint. With a copula correlation of ρ, the one-year *worst-case* probability of default at the 99.9% confidence interval is given by (6.88),

$$P(99.9\% \text{ Confidence Level}) = N\left(\frac{N^{-1}(D) + \sqrt{\rho} N^{-1}(0.999)}{\sqrt{1-\rho}}\right) \quad (7.21)$$

Using a formula similar to (6.89), the one-year CCR 99.9% VaR for this obligor is

$$EAD \cdot LGD \cdot P(99.9\%)$$
$$EAD = \textbf{Exposure at Default} \quad (7.22)$$
$$LGD = \textbf{Loss Given Default}$$

The one-year expected loss (as opposed to the 99.9% tail loss) is

$$EAD \cdot LGD \cdot D \quad (7.23)$$

which is very similar in nature to the accounting CVA calculation. The capital needed for the counterparty under Basel is the 99.9% VaR over and *above* the expected loss,

$$EAD \cdot LGD \cdot [P(99.9\%) - D] \quad (7.24)$$

The Basel Committee does not allow firms to estimate both D and ρ. Instead, they insist on using a rough empirical formula that gives the copula correlation ρ, given an estimate of D. This formula is

$$\rho(D) = 0.12 \frac{1-\exp(-50 \cdot D)}{1-\exp(-50)} + 0.24 \left[1 - \frac{1-\exp(-50 \cdot D)}{1-\exp(-50)} \right] \quad . \quad (7.25)$$

Because $\exp(-50)$ is a very small number, this formula reduces to

$$\rho(D) = 0.12(1+\exp(-50 \cdot D)) \quad . \quad (7.26)$$

The only insight to take away from this somewhat naive formula is that as D increases, ρ decreases. It appears to say that as the default probability of a company grows, it is more idiosyncratic and less correlated to others in the market, and therefore less correlated to the one factor driving the whole one-factor Gaussian copula model.

Finally, one needs to make a *maturity adjustment* (MA), because the VaR formulas above were based on a term of one year. Again, the Basel Committee has a magic formula given by

$$MA(D,T) = \frac{1+(T-2.5) \cdot b(D)}{1-1.5 \cdot b(D)}$$

$$b(D) = [0.11852 - 0.05478 \cdot \ln(D)]^2 \quad . \quad (7.27)$$

Using the MA, the capital required for the counterparty is

$$EAD \cdot LGD \cdot \left[N\left(\frac{N^{-1}(D) + \sqrt{\rho(D)} N^{-1}(0.999)}{\sqrt{1-\rho(D)}} \right) - D \right] \cdot MA(D,T) \quad . \quad (7.28)$$

To change this into an RWA, one must multiply by 12.5, as it will be again be multiplied by 8% in the final capital calculation. Explicitly pulling out the risk weight RW, one is finally left with

$$\text{CCR RWA} = EAD \cdot RW(D,LGD,T)$$

$$RW(D,LGD,T) = 12.5 \cdot LGD \cdot \left[N\left(\frac{N^{-1}(D) + \sqrt{\rho(D)} N^{-1}(0.999)}{\sqrt{1-\rho(D)}} \right) - D \right] \cdot MA(D,T) \quad . \quad (7.29)$$

All the EADs are generally calculated by MC methods, because one needs exposures to the counterparty at all times in the future until the maturity of the underlying obligor contract. This is the main difficulty in calculating the CCR RWA. The valuation of the EAD is dependent on the future (stochastic) mark-to-market of the position in question at time t_j, MtM_j and is calculated by the following step-by-step process:

$$\text{Expected Exposure}: EE_j = E[\text{Max}(MtM_j, 0)]$$

$$\text{Effective Expected Exposure}: EEE_j = \text{Max}(EE_j, EEE_{j-1})$$

$$\text{Effective Expected Positive Exposure}: EEPE = \sum_{j=1}^{1Y} EEE_j \cdot \Delta t_j \quad (7.30)$$

$$\text{Exposure at Default}: EAD = \alpha \cdot EEPE$$

$$\text{Regulatory Scaling Factor}: \alpha = 1.4$$

The *EEPE* is a time-weighted average of the effective expected exposure EEE_j, which is simply a running maximum. Do not misunderstand the "*P*" in *EEPE*. It is a somewhat unfortunate convention, because in reality all the above exposures are positive. One may even argue that exposures by definition are positive. Note that in certain places in the literature, the expected exposure EE_j is referred to as the expected positive exposure EPE_j. Finally, the magic regulatory scaling factor α is apparently meant to accommodate potential simulation errors, but its quantification as 1.4 is murky.

Figure 7-2 is a schematic of the Basel II CCR RWA calculations.

$$RWA = EAD \times RW$$

Risk Weight Formula

$$RW(D, LGD, T, \rho) = 12.5 \cdot LGD \cdot \left[N\left(\frac{N^{-1}(D) + \sqrt{\rho}N^{-1}(0.999)}{\sqrt{1-\rho}} \right) - D \right] \cdot MA(D,T)$$

Asset Correlation Formula

$$\rho = 0.12 \times \frac{1-\exp(-50 \times D)}{1-\exp(-50)} + 0.24 \times \left(1 - \frac{1-\exp(-50 \times D)}{1-\exp(-50)}\right)$$

Maturity Factor Formula

$$MA(D, T) = \frac{1+(T-2.5) \times b(D)}{1-1.5 \times b(D)}$$

$$b(D) = [0.11852 - 0.05478 \ln(D)]^2$$

Figure 7-2. Basel II CCR RWA

Market Risk RWA

This is similar to the Basel I (7.18) and is based on the 10-day 99% VaR 60-day moving average prescription,

$$\textbf{Market Risk RWA}_t = 12.5 \cdot MAX\left(k \frac{1}{60} \sum_{i=1}^{60} VAR(0.99)_{t-i}, VAR(0.99)_{t-1} \right) + SRC_t$$

k = magic factor determined by regulators

SRC_t = Specific Risk Charge (7.31)

Operational Risk RWA

According to the Basel Committee on Bank Supervision (see References), there are seven categories of operational risk:

1. *Internal fraud*: This includes acts such as insider trading, circumventing regulations, and mismarking positions. Most of the rogue traders mentioned above, such as Joseph Jett and Kareem Serageldin, hid losses by mismarking positions.

2. *External fraud*: This includes acts committed by a third party, such as robbery, forgery, and computer hacking. The expansion of the cybersecurity divisions in all major banks attempts to address computer hacking.

3. *Employment practices and workplace safety*: Violations of standard government employment, health, and safety acts can lead to employee lawsuits, such as discrimination claims and personal injury claims. Large monetary awards paid by banks for such claims damage the banks' capital base and lead to reputational risk and the potential loss of clients.

4. *Clients, products, and business practices*: The fiduciary responsibilities of a bank are very large and wide-ranging. Misuses include the improper use of confidential customer information, improper trading activities on the bank's account, money laundering, and the sale of unauthorized products to unsophisticated clients (such as derivatives). The illegal use of almost $900 million of customers' funds by MF Global in 2011 to cover trading losses by the broker-dealer is an example of the misappropriation of customers' funds. MF Global declared bankruptcy on October 31, 2011.

5. *Damage to physical assets*: The disruption of business due to natural disasters or terrorism are included here. Since the 9/11 terror attacks, all the major Wall Street firms have disaster recovery sites with trading and risk management capabilities that mirror those of the firms' main offices. Many of these disaster recovery sites are in nearby New Jersey.

6. *Business disruption and system failures:*: These include electrical failures, hardware, and software failures, communication problems, and so on. The New York City blackout of 2003 is an example of this. At the time, many large trading floors, such as the one the author was on, had their own generators that automatically came on when the power was lost. The computers simply flickered for a second or so.

7. *Execution, delivery, and process management*: Any failures in processing transactions, such as failing to execute trades that have been initiated by traders or failing to have the proper legal documentation in place to trade various structured financial products, fall under this category.

Somehow, banks must estimate a one-year 99.9% VaR for every one of these operational risk types and determine a single operational risk RWA! As this is a very difficult task (choosing a realistic model is difficult and calibration data is practically nonexistent), the regulators have suggested the following three approaches to determine the regulatory capital charge related to operational risk:

1. *Basic indicator approach*: This is the easiest approach and involves taking 15% of the firms average positive gross income (GI) over the last three years as the regulatory capital for operational risk,

$$\text{Operational Risk Capital Charge} = \alpha \cdot \frac{\sum_{i=1}^{n} GI(t_i) I[GI(t_i) > 0]}{n} . \quad (7.32)$$

The annual $GI(t)$s for each year t include net interest income plus all noninterest income. It is determined by standard accounting practices. The function I is the indicator function used to get only positive annual incomes. Usually, $\alpha = 15\%$ and $n = 3$. Note that in this simple method, an operational risk RWA is *not* explicitly calculated. Unfortunately, this simple approach gives a large charge for many banks and is not the preferred methodology. The 15% is one of those regulatory magic numbers. It is not known to be based on any historical data of operational losses though some studies are under way.

2. *Standardized approach*: This is the second easiest approach and is essentially a more granular than the basic indicator approach. Rather than use one GI and one α, eight common business lines of the bank are separated and assigned their own GIs and α factors. Here the α factors are referred to as β factors. The eight business lines and their β factors are given in Figure 7-3. The regulatory capital for operational risk using this method is

$$\text{Operational Risk Capital Charge} = \sum_{j=1}^{8} \beta_j \frac{\sum_{i=1}^{n} GI_j(t_i) I[GI_j(t_i) > 0]}{n} , \quad (7.33)$$

where $GI_j(t_i)$ is the annual time t_i gross income for a business line indexed by j. Once again, n is often chosen to be 3.

Business Line	Beta Factor
Corporate finance	18%
Trading and sales	18%
Retail banking	12%
Commercial banking	15%
Payment and settlement	18%
Agency services	15%
Asset Management	12%
Retail Brokerage	12%

Figure 7-3. Business lines and beta factors in the standardized approach to operational risk

3. *Advanced measurement approach*: This approach is more along the lines of the RWA approaches for credit and market risk. One must be able to estimate unexpected losses at a 99.9% confidence interval for all seven operational risk categories within each of the eight business lines. Therefore, one needs seven different simulation models to run against each of the eight different businesses to give 56 different 99.9% VaR type RWAs. Good luck with that.

Basel III

Basel III is an outgrowth of what many were calling a hastily-put-together improvement of Basel II, which is now referred to as Basel II.5 (*c.* 2010). One of the largest changes in Basel II.5 was the introduction of a new stressed VaR that must be introduced in the market risk RWA component. The usual VaR is based on the previous four years of historical market data. The *stressed VaR* is based on a specific stressed period of 252 days. The formula for the capital charge is (all 10-day VaRs)

$$\text{Market Risk RWA}_t = 12.5 \cdot \text{MAX}\left(k \frac{1}{60}\sum_{i=1}^{60} VAR(0.99)_{t-i}, VAR(0.99)_{t-1}\right) + SRC_t$$
$$+ 12.5 \cdot \text{MAX}\left(k \frac{1}{60}\sum_{i=1}^{60} \text{Stressed}\,VAR(0.99)_{t-i}, \text{Stressed}\,VAR(0.99)_{t-1}\right) \quad (7.34)$$

Because the stressed VaR is higher than regular VaR, this prescription more than doubles the market risk capital charge compared with Basel II. The stressed VaR should incorporate model parameters calibrated to historical data from a continuous 12-month period of significant financial stress relevant to the bank's portfolio. The stressed time period should adequately reflect a continuous period of financial stress such as the 2008–9 financial crisis. Once again, the stressed VaR capital charge is calculated as the maximum of either the average of the preceding 60-day stressed VaR times a regulatory multiplier, or the most recently calculated stressed VaR. The regulatory multiplier k is set at a minimum of 3, but could rise to 4 or larger if the back-testing performance of the VaR model is deemed of insufficient quality.

Many banks complained to the Basel Committee that the CCR capital charge they were taking was being double-counted inasmuch as they added both the Basel numbers with the accounting CVA numbers. Basel III took this into account by subtracting the accounting CVA number from the Basel II CCR RWA of (7.29). The resulting difference must then multiplied by a magic regulatory factor of 1.6 and is generally referred to as the *jump-to-default* part of Basel III CCR RWA. But Basel III added a CCR spread VaR and stressed CCR spread VaR of the regulatory CVA calculation, much like the stressed market risk RWA calculation above. They also added a stress component to the EAD calculation of (7.30). The basic Basel III CCR RWA is given by

$$\textbf{Basel III CCR RWA} = \textbf{Jump To Default (JTD)} + \textbf{CVA Add-On} \quad , \quad (7.35)$$

where RW is given in (7.29) and the Basel III jump to default is given by

$$\textbf{JTD} = (EAD - \text{Accounting} CVA) \cdot \textbf{RW} \cdot 1.06 \quad (7.36)$$

where

$$\textbf{CVA Add-On} = (12.5)(3)(\textbf{Base CCR } VAR + \textbf{Stressed CCR } VAR) \quad (7.37)$$

and the new Basel III EAD is given by

$$\text{Exposure at Default: } EAD = \alpha \cdot \text{Max}(EEPE, \textbf{Stressed } EEPE)$$
$$\text{Regulatory Scaling Factor: } \alpha = 1.4 \quad . \quad (7.38)$$

Figure 7-4 is a schematic of these complex Basel III CCR RWA calculations. The CCR VaRs are usually calculated using the $CS01$ formula in (7.8). The CVA add-on is also called the CVA *volatility charge*, because it tries to capture the volatility of the counterparty's credit spread—explicitly,

$$\textbf{CVA Add-On} = (12.5)(3)(\textbf{10-day 99\% VAR of CVA}$$
$$+ \textbf{10-day 99\% Stressed VAR of CVA}) \quad \cdot \quad (7.39)$$

The VaR of the CVA measures the credit spread sensitivity of regulatory CVA. The 10-day 99% VaR of CVA can be approximated by taking a 99% 10-day worst case historical spread move of the counterparty and multiplying it by the appropriate CS01 formula given by (7.8). The stressed VaR of CVA component is a *stress on the exposure calculation* needed for the CS01. One must use model inputs calibrated to historical data from a continuous 12-month period of significant stress for the financial instruments at hand to calculate stressed expected exposures. These include stressed volatilities, interest rates, and default probabilities. The stressed *EEPE* is calculated in a similar manner using a stressed expected exposure calculation.

$$RWA = JTD + CVA\ Add\ On$$

$$JTD = (EAD - Accounting\ CVA) \times RW \times 1.06$$

$$CVA\ Add\ On = (12.5)(3)(Base\ CCR\ VAR + Stressed\ CCR\ VAR)$$

VAR of Regulatory CVA

$$CVA = LGD \sum \frac{EE_{j-1}\,df_{j-1} + EE_j\,df_j}{2} \cdot \left[\exp\left(-\frac{s_{j-1}t_{j-1}}{LGD}\right) - \exp\left(-\frac{s_j t_j}{LGD}\right)\right]$$

$$CS01_i = t_i \cdot \exp\left(-\frac{s_i t_i}{LGD}\right) \cdot \frac{EE_{i-1}\,df_{i-1} - EE_{i+1}\,df_{i+1}}{2}$$

$$RW(D, LGD, T, \rho) = 12.5 \cdot LGD \cdot \left[N\left(\frac{N^{-1}(D) + \sqrt{\rho}\,N^{-1}(0.999)}{\sqrt{1-\rho}}\right) - D\right] \cdot MA(D,T)$$

$$\rho = 0.12 \times \frac{1-\exp(-50 \times D)}{1-\exp(-50)} + 0.24 \times \left(1 - \frac{1-\exp(-50 \times D)}{1-\exp(-50)}\right)$$

$$MA(D,T) = \frac{1 + (T-2.5) \times b(D)}{1 - 1.5 \times b(D)}$$

$$b(D) = [0.11852 - 0.05478\ln(D)]^2$$

Figure 7-4. *Basel III CCR RWA*

Capital Requirements under Basel III

Basel III recognizes only two types of capital:

Tier 1: This capital is considered the highest quality buffer against losses. It includes *equity capital* or shareholders' funds consisting of issued and fully paid common stock and nonredeemable preferred stock and *disclosed reserves* consisting of retained profits and general reserves.

Tier 2: This capital includes balance sheet items that ultimately must be redeemed such as subordinated debt (subordinated to all other types of debt that must be repaid first) and undisclosed reserves.

The capital requirements are:

- Tier 1 equity capital must be at least 4.5% of total RWA.
- All Tier 1 capital must be at least 6.0% of total RWA.
- Tier 1 plus Tier 2 capital must be at least 8.0% of total RWA.

Basel III also enhanced the three pillars already introduced in Basel II [Basel, 2011A]:

- **Pillar 1**
    a. *Higher capital*: The minimum of Tier 1 equity capital was raised to 4.5% of total RWA, creating a greater focus on common equity. Also, a capital conservation buffer of 2.5% of common equity was encouraged. Falling below the suggested 7% total of common equity may constrain the bank from discretionary distributions such as dividends.
    b. *Enhanced risk coverage*: The capital treatment of complex securitizations such as tranched CDOs were enhanced, and banks are required to conduct rigorous credit analyses of externally rated securitization exposures. Significantly higher capital requirements now exist for both *trading book and derivative activities*, such as the stressed VaR calculations described above. Furthermore, there are reduced RWAs for trade exposures cleared through *central counterparties (CCPs)*. The regulatory measures are trying to encourage the use of exchanges and *swap execution facilities* (SEFs) to reduce counterparty credit risk throughout the banking community.
    c. *Leverage ratio*: Banks must begin to report a leverage ratio including off-balance-sheet exposures. Too much leverage within the financial system can greatly increase its systemic risk, leading to a collapse. The 1998 LTCM crisis described earlier was an example of too much leverage.
- **Pillar 2**, *Supervisory review*: Regulatory supervisors can now evaluate firm-wide governance and risk management across a bank. They can also further address compensation practices, valuation procedures, accounting standards, risk concentrations, and stress testing abilities.
- **Pillar 3**, *Market disclosure*: This enhances the disclosure requirements to include details of the components of regulatory capital and their reconciliation with reported accounts. Furthermore, the banks must include a comprehensive explanation of how they calculate their various regulatory capital ratios.

Basel III has also proposed the following two risk measures with respect to *liquidity standards* and enhanced regulations for firms it believes to be *systemically important financial institutions* (SIFIs)—i.e., "too big to fail":

- *Liquidity coverage ratio (LCR)*: The LCR is a short-term liquidity risk measure that requires banks to have a sufficient amount of high-quality liquid assets to withstand a 30-day stressed funding scenario.

- *Net stable funding ratio (NSFR)*: The NSFR is the longer-term liquidity risk measure that is designed to address liquidity mismatches across the entire balance sheet of the bank. It compares funding sources to funding needs and introduces risk measures to assess the stability of the funding sources. It incentivizes banks to reduce their reliance on short-term funding and find sources of funds with maturities greater than one year. This will almost surely lead to higher funding costs.

Global SIFIs must have higher loss absorbency capacity to reflect the greater systemic risk they pose to the financial system as a whole. This additional capital requirement will be met with an increase in Tier 1 equity capital in the range of 1% to 2.5%, depending on the bank's systemic risk.

EAD and EPE Profiles

With all the different rules and calculations, one can get lost in the actual problems that arise in calculating Basel III numbers. For most banks, the bottleneck is in calculating the EAD. Specifically for derivatives, the EAD is derived from the *expected positive exposure* (EPE) to the bank at all times in the future until the maturity of the contract. The reason for positive exposures is the simple fact that the bank is interested in CCR only when the counterparty owes the bank money, not the other way around. Furthermore, simply calculating the value of a contract today and seeing whether it is positive or negative is not sufficient. Theoretically, one needs to calculate the value of the contract for every day in the future until maturity because the counterparty can default at any time. Calculating the EPE for complex derivatives is a difficult procedure. Almost everything here uses historical MC simulations. If the time zero present value of the derivative also has to be calculated using MC methods, it becomes even harder to valuate such a structure in the future.

When dealing with a specific counterparty, banks do not calculate Basel III numbers security by security. Rather they calculate EPEs for a portfolio of transactions with that counterparty. Each valid portfolio is called a *netting set*. A netting set could have various instruments in it, such as swaps and options. The positive and negative exposures to the bank are offset with each other to give a net EPE of the netting set to a specific counterparty. There are various complicated rules to what constitutes a netting set and what exposures can be netted [Basel, 2011A]. If the netting set consists of different asset classes, a multi-asset correlated MC simulation is needed. Furthermore, any collateral agreements, margin calls, etc. must be included in this simulation (to be discussed below).

EPE is the average expected positive exposure of a position or portfolio to a counterparty over a period of time, weighted by the simulation time step Δt. Basel III mirrors the concept of stressed VaR, discussed earlier in relation to market risk, in its treatment of CCR. Banks that use the internal model method (IMM) [Basel, 2011A] must calculate the potential exposure amount of a derivative, the EPE, using models that have been calibrated to historical data that includes a period of stressed market conditions. For convenience, the main equations already introduced are given again, where MtM_j is the mark-to-market value of the position in question at time t_j:

$$\text{Expected Exposure}: EE_j = E[\text{Max}(MtM_j, 0)]$$
$$\text{Effective Expected Exposure}: EEE_j = \text{Max}(EE_j, EEE_{j-1})$$
$$\text{Effective Expected Positive Exposure}: EEPE = \sum_{j=1}^{1Y} EEE_j \cdot \Delta t_j \quad (7.40)$$
$$\text{Exposure at Default}: EAD = \alpha \cdot EEPE$$
$$\text{Regulatory Scaling Factor}: \alpha = 1.4$$

Figure 7-5 shows a hypothetical EPE profile based on a MC simulation for a 5yr vanilla par interest rate swap from the viewpoint of the counterparty paying fixed and receiving float. Clearly, the exposure is zero on day one of the swap as the swap rate is set to a par value to make the present value of both legs equal to one another (see Chapter 1). As time goes by, swap rates change and therefore the value of the fixed leg changes. The exact position of the expected peak exposure depends on the level of the future simulated yield curves and their shape (flat, inverted, and so on) but generally appears before the halfway mark of the swap. The reason for this is that as more cash flows are paid and received as time goes by, the exposure naturally decreases, especially for vanilla swaps with no notional exchange. The expected exposure from the peak point simply decreases to the final coupon exchange. The peak occurs at a relative point of interest rate uncertainty weighted by the amount of remaining cash flows. The uncertainty of rates at the maturity point is the greatest. Yet this point has the least amount of remaining coupons, and therefore the exposure is small. The initial day has the most amount of remaining coupons, but the interest rate uncertainty has been included with the choice of the par swap rate, and therefore the exposure at the initial time step is also small.

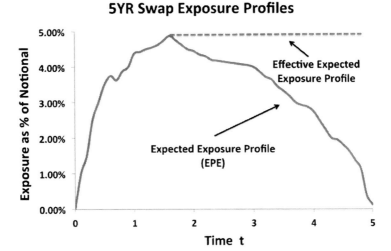

Figure 7-5. EPE profile for a 5yr vanilla par interest rate swap

As has been stressed throughout this book, the expected value as a statistic often plays little role in real risk management. The expected positive exposure may be good enough for regulatory purposes, but one would like to see different confidence intervals of *potential future exposures* (PFE). The EPE profile is simply an average of the positive part of several simulated PFEs. Figure 7-6 shows different hypothetical PFE paths for the 5yr interest rate swap paying fixed with their associated confidence intervals.

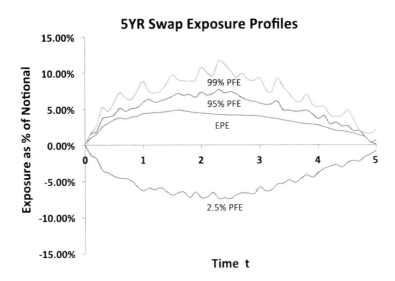

Figure 7-6. PFE profiles for a 5yr vanilla par interest rate swap

Portfolio CCR Aggregation, Netting Sets, and Collateral Margin

When dealing with a specific counterparty, banks do not calculate credit exposures security by security. For a financial institution, credit exposure is a risk at a counterparty level. Therefore, all trades with a specific counterparty have to be considered when calculating CCR for both CVA and Basel. When a bank attempts to aggregate the trades of a counterparty into a portfolio, they usually take into account two legal counterparty agreements: *netting* and *collateral*. Netting agreements are built into many common OTC derivative contracts, such as a swap, where in the event of default, the MtM values of all the derivative positions between the two parties that have netting agreements in place are aggregated. That is, derivative positions with positive value can be used to offset other derivative positions with negative value. If this were not the case, a liquidator in bankruptcy court would chose only positive MtM positions to enforce for his or her client. Therefore, banks will form *netting sets* of various positions with a specific counterparty. With netting agreements, only the *net positive value* of a netting set is considered for counterparty credit exposures. This in turn reduces the overall credit exposure of the netting portfolio, leading to lower capital requirements from both the CVA and Basel rules. For instance, consider a simple portfolio of a long call option and put option on the same underlying. Individually, the EPE profiles for both options occur at opposite underlying values: high levels for the call and low levels for the put. Considered as individual trades, both options could provide substantial exposure. But if one considers both options in a netting set, one MC simulation is used simultaneously for both options, and therefore the high and low underlying levels cannot occur simultaneously, leading to a lower aggregate EPE versus viewing the trades in isolation.

The other legal aspect to consider in CCR trade aggregation is the concept of posting margin similar to the margin collateral mechanism of financial exchanges. Banks tend to monitor their trade exposures with counterparties. For lower-rated counterparties, they either have a maximum dollar amount exposure for a counterparty or require the counterparty to post margin in terms of cash or cash like collateral. As with exchanges, these margin agreements have various definitions.

Initial Margin

Initial margin is the minimum amount of cash-like collateral that must be posted to open a trading line with an OTC counterparty. It is independent of any exposure amounts. Lower-rated counterparties, such as hedge funds, may have to post larger initial margins than their higher-rated competitors.

Variation Margin

Similar to trading futures on an exchange, all positions with a counterparty are marked to market daily. Unlike an exchange, the daily P&L gains and losses are not transferred between counterparties. Rather, a *margin call* is made such that extra collateral needs to be posted for an increase in exposure due to an MtM move (but is rarely equal to the full P&L amount).

Margin Period of Risk

During the 2008 financial crisis, very large margin calls were made, leading to all sorts of disputes between banks. In many cases margin was not posted and counterparties defaulted. In such a circumstance, there is a *close-out* period whereby trades within a netting set of a defaulting counterparty must be replaced or rehedged and any collateral from the counterparty must be sold. These close-out period trades do not happen instantaneously, and the time it takes to execute the appropriate trades can be several days depending on the complexity of trades in a netting set and the liquidity of the assets. During this time, the value of margin collateral may go down and rehedging may become more expensive; therefore it is known as the margin period of risk. According to the Basel rules [Basel, 2006].

> *The margin period of risk is the time period overseeing the last exchange of collateral used to cover netting transactions with a defaulting counterpart and the closing out of the counterparty and the resulting market risk is re-hedged.*

In contrast, the margin period of risk is much shorter for trades on an exchange as the complete P&L of gains and losses are posted daily, the exchange-traded assets are liquid and standardized, and the cure period to post margin is usually one day. This is another reason the regulators prefer exchanges and require very little capital to be held against exchange-traded assets.

Therefore, when calculating EADs on netting sets, one must consider both the margin agreements with the counterparty and the margin period of risk. Basel III rules dictate that for OTC derivatives, this period should be at least 10 days where potential losses in the margin collateral may occur along with losses due to rehedging defaulted positions.

Margin Threshold

This is the minimum positive exposure of a netting set that must occur before a margin call is made. Higher-rated counterparties are allowed certain minimum exposures before banks begin to mitigate the counterparty risk.

Minimum Transfer Amount

This is the minimum amount of excess exposure over the margin threshold that must occur for a margin call to avoid relatively small payments of collateral. Essentially, a margin call is made when the positive exposure is above the sum of the margin threshold and the minimum transfer amount.

All the above aspects must be taken into account when performing an MC simulation on a netting set for the purposes of calculating EADs. Clearly, the information needed to calculate Basel III or CVA numbers for even the most basic instrument has substantially increased. Furthermore, many financial trading and risk systems do not keep all the above information together along with the traded derivative, thereby creating an IT nightmare for the capital optimization efforts of banks.

OIS Discounting

The Dodd-Frank Wall Street Reform and Consumer Protection Act (Dodd-Frank), signed into law by President Barack Obama in July 2010, created the largest ever overhaul of financial regulations in the United States since the regulatory reform that followed the Great Depression. It made massive changes to the US financial regulatory environment. It put large burdens on all federal financial regulatory agencies, and its consequences have reverberated throughout the financial services industry. Even to attempt to provide a brief summary of all aspects of this law would be a nightmare (and require several lawyers). Among the plethora of wide-ranging rules and recommendations, Dodd-Frank created the Office of Financial Research (OFR), and required the "risk retention" of a certain amount of notional value of CDOs and other structured collateralized products by the originators. They also prohibited banks and certain non-bank financial institutions from "proprietary trading" (non-client-based risk taking) and investing in hedge funds and private equity firms. The act also sets out that certain derivatives contracts must be cleared through central counterparty clearinghouses (CCPs). Specifically, it mandates that interest rate swaps must be either cleared through CCPs or for OTC swaps, they must be collateralized through the use of credit support annexes (CSAs) between counterparties. Even though collateralization sounds simple enough, it has created extra difficulties in valuation and risk. For instance, it creates the introduction of margin periods of risk in the EAD calculation of netting sets, as described above. It also has changed the face of discounting and caused the creation of various new types of discount curves.

As discussed in Chapters 1 and 2, LIBOR-based discounting was largely valid before the 2008 financial crisis. LIBOR is effectively a rate used for unsecured short-term borrowing for AA-rated financial institutions. Prior to 2008, the majority of large financial firms were rated around AA. Post 2008, the landscape has changed substantially. For instance, as of early 2014, Citi was rated Baa (BBB) by Moody's. Such a low rating for a major US bank would have been unthinkable before 2008. Baa is only two notches away from non-investment grade (sometimes called "junk" in the 1980s and '90s). Citi clearly does not borrow at LIBOR flat anymore. Furthermore, because LIBOR has always been related to the credit rating of AA, it is not a true risk-free rate. In the United States, the only true risk-free rate is *overnight fed funds*, as described in Chapter 1. Pre-2008, the spread between fed funds and LIBOR was around 10 bps, meaning that the differential was small enough not to cause any undue valuation errors. Post 2008, this spread reached levels greater than 300 bps, indicating a severe credit crunch because banks were unwilling to lend to each other in the broker-dealer money market space. To switch to the true risk-free rate, the fed funds overnight rate must be turned into a more suitable term rate that is linked to fed funds. Such a rate is called the *overnight index rate* (OIR), and in the United States it is the *geometric average of overnight fed funds* over a prespecified period, such as three months. It is clearly a floating rate index. An *overnight index swap* (OIS) is a fixed-for-floating rate swap where the floating rate index is the OIR. The OIS rate is the rate swapped for the floating geometric average of the effective fed funds rate. The floating leg essentially replicates the accrued interest on a notional amount that is rolled over daily at overnight fed funds. Similar to the US OIR, other countries have floating-rate overnight indices, such as EONIA (EUR), SONIA (GBP), CHOIS (CHF), and TONAR (JPY). The OIS rates in these currencies are linked to the local central bank rates of the country in question. The *fixed-versus-compounded-floating rates* are swapped at the maturity date for swaps less than one year. For OIS with maturities longer than one year, payments are swapped annually.

How does collateralization affect the valuation of an interest rate swap? Suppose a bank has an interest rate swap with a lower-rated counterparty. According to the banks CSA with this counterparty, the swap must be collateralized by the MtM of the swap. Say that the bank is paying a swap rate of 3% and receiving 3M LIBOR. Furthermore, assume there is only 6 months left in the swap and the current market swap rate is 4%. Clearly the bank has a positive MtM for this swap. In the pre-2008 world the MTM would simply be $1\% \cdot \Delta \cdot df_{Libor}(0, 6m)$ where a LIBOR discount factor was used. The bank could get this much of cash collateral from the counterparty, invest it in LIBOR, and be credit risk neutral for that day. If the counterparty defaults, the cash collateral grows at LIBOR until the maturity, when it becomes equal to the positive MtM of the swap, that is, $1\% \cdot \Delta$. This is the purpose of MtM and collateralization. In the case of counterparty default, the collateral plus the interest earned on the collateral must cover the cash payment of the swap at maturity. The problem with this argument is that US banks do not earn LIBOR on their cash accounts, they earn overnight fed funds. Pre-2008, the fed funds–versus–LIBOR spread was relatively small. After the crisis, the LIBOR–OIS spread exploded, reaching a maximum level of 364 basis points in October 2008. In general, LIBOR is a higher rate than fed funds because LIBOR is an AA-rated interest rate, whereas fed funds is risk-free. Therefore, the correct amount of cash collateral should be $1\% \cdot \Delta \cdot df_{OIS}(0, 6m)$, which uses an *OIS discount factor*. This amount of collateral, which is greater than the LIBOR-discounted collateral, will grow (compounded) at the overnight fed funds rate until maturity when it reaches the correct cash payment amount. The LIBOR-discounted amount would have left the bank under-collateralized. Therefore, collateralized swaps need to be discounted at OIS rates and not LIBOR.

The most straightforward way to build an OIS curve is to use market OIS par rates that one can find on Bloomberg. These exist for tenors starting at one week and going out to 5 years. For tenors less than 1 year, the par OIS rates are zero coupon rates to maturity. For maturities greater than 1 year, the swap pays annually. The bootstrapping of discount factors is similar to that of Chapter 2. These OIS tend to be liquid only to the 5 year point. Thereafter, *LIBOR–OIS basis swaps*, which extend out to 30 years and imply the spread between the *basis of LIBOR* and the *basis of OIS*, can be used in conjunction with standard 3M LIBOR swaps. Basis swaps tend to be swaps of two floating legs, such as floating-LIBOR–versus–floating-fed funds OIR plus a *basis swap spread*. The basis swap spread is tenor dependent and reflects the difference in the two floating interest rates [Tuckman, 2012]. The basis swap spread between LIBOR and the fed funds–based OIR is a measure of financial stress and reached a peak during the 2008 crisis.

The role of credit risk has now fully entered into the world of interest rates and their associated derivatives leading to the use of various different discounting curves, such as the following:

- *Collateralized trades need to be discounted using an OIS curve.* As described above, these trade types need to be discounted at the effective rate earned on cash by the bank, which in the US is fed funds. The correct rate index is therefore the OIS rate (<< LIBOR).

- *Uncollateralized trades need to be discounted using a unsecured funding curve.* For uncollateralized OTC swaps, the bank's unsecured funding rate for the specific credit rating of the counterparty must be used. The correct rate is the risky unsecured funding rate, which is much greater than LIBOR.

- *LIBOR tenor basis risk grows.* Pre-2008 one could get relatively good estimates of 6M LIBOR L_{6M} from a 3M LIBOR L_{3M} curve such as the one built in Chapter 2 using simple compounding,

$$[1+\delta(0,3M)L_{3M}(0,3M)][1+\delta(3M,6M)L_{3M}(3M,6M)] = \\ [1+\delta(0,6M)L_{6M}(0,6M)]. \quad (7.41)$$

Even at that time, there was a 3M-6M LIBOR basis swap, which implied the spread between the basis of 3M LIBOR and that of the basis of 6M LIBOR. The 3M-6M LIBOR basis was never too large, but it has now become significant because of the greater awareness of the credit and liquidity risk of LIBOR. LIBOR contains both counterparty and liquidity risk and therefore, longer tenors are more risky just like CDS spreads tend to grow with maturities (see Chapter 6). Therefore 6M LIBOR rates will be higher than their 3M counterparts and this spread is traded using 3M-6M LIBOR basis swaps where one floating leg pays 6M LIBOR and the other floating leg pays 3M LIBOR plus a basis swap spread that is tenor dependent.

Therefore, post-2008,

$$[1+\delta(0,3M)L_{3M}(0,3M)][1+\delta(3M,6M)L_{3M}(3M,6M)] \neq \\ [1+\delta(0,6M)L_{6M}(0,6M)]. \quad (7.42)$$

Effectively, this means that banks must also create 6M LIBOR-based discounting curves, along with the standard 3M LIBOR curve and the OIS curve. There are a plethora of curves that are needed now that credit risk has entered (or been recognized in) the interest rate world.

- *Collateral and Cheapest to Deliver.* Under various CSAs, cash collateral may be posted in various currencies, such as EUR or GBP. This collateral currency choice gives the posting party a *cheapest-to-deliver* option that is driven by cross-currency basis swaps. A cross-currency swap is swap between two parties to exchange interest payments and principals denominated in two different currencies. The posting party will deliver the currency that is cheapest to obtain, similar to the cheapest-to-deliver option of Treasury bond futures (see Chapter 1).

Because of all these issues, curve-building requires many more instruments than the ones described in Chapter 2. For instance, a minimum set of market inputs may include the following:

- OIS and OIS–LIBOR basis swaps
- LIBOR futures

CHAPTER 7 ■ RISK TYPES, CVA, BASEL III, AND OIS DISCOUNTING

- LIBOR swaps of different tenors such as 6M LIBOR and LIBOR basis swaps such as 3M versus 6M LIBOR.
- Various cross-currency swaps

Therefore, the risk management of a single currency swap book is no longer just restricted to just 3M LIBOR cash, futures and swaps but must take into account the various risks associated with the instruments described above.

Calculating "Adjusted" Forward LIBOR Rates from OIS Curves and Basis Swaps

In the pure LIBOR-discounting framework of Chapters 1 and 2, forward LIBOR rates and par swap rates had simple formulas based on LIBOR discount factors df^L created from pure LIBOR instruments, such as

$$L_j = \left[\frac{df^L(0,t_{j-1})}{df^L(0,t_j)} - 1\right]\frac{1}{\delta^j}$$

(7.43)

L_j = 3M foward LIBOR set at t_{j-1}

δ_j = Act/360 daycount fraction from t_{j-1} to t_j

and the term T par swap rate $S(T)$,

$$S(T) = \frac{1 - df^L(0,T)}{Dv01^L(T)}$$

$$DV01^L(T) = \sum_{i=1}^{T}\Delta_i df^L(0,t_i)$$

Δ_i = 30/360 daycount fraction from t_{i-1} to t_i . (7.44)

Now assume one has OIS discount factors df^{FF} created from fed funds OIS-based par swap rates. How does one calculated so-called *adjusted forward* LIBOR rates? Because there exists a basis between LIBOR (L_i) and fed funds OIR (OIR$_i$), reflecting the lower credit rating of LIBOR, one must first start with the par tenor-dependent basis swap spreads $b(T)$ and the LIBOR–OIS basis swap equation, which equates the PV of both floating legs using OIS discount factors df^{FF},

$$\sum_{j=1}^{T} L_j \delta_j df^{FF}(0,t_j) = \sum_{i=1}^{T}[\text{OIR}_i + b(T)]\Delta_i df^{FF}(0,t_i)$$. (7.45)

One can also write a similar formula for a $T-1$ basis swap,

$$\sum_{j=1}^{T-1} L_j \delta_j df^{FF}(0,t_j) = \sum_{i=1}^{T-1}[\text{OIR}_i + b(T-1)]\Delta_i df^{FF}(0,t_i)$$. (7.46)

CHAPTER 7 ■ RISK TYPES, CVA, BASEL III, AND OIS DISCOUNTING

Separating out the last LIBOR payment in (7.45) gives

$$L_T \delta_T df^{FF}(0,T) + \sum_{j=1}^{T-1} L_j \delta_j df^{FF}(0,t_j) = \sum_{i=1}^{T}[\text{OIR}_i + b(T)]\Delta_i df^{FF}(0,t_i) \quad . \quad (7.47)$$

Substituting the right-hand side of (7.46) into the above gives

$$L_T \delta_T df^{FF}(0,T) + \sum_{i=1}^{T-1}[\text{OIR}_i + b(T-1)]\Delta_i df^{FF}(0,t_i) = \sum_{i=1}^{T}[\text{OIR}_i + b(T)]\Delta_i df^{FF}(0,t_i) \quad , \quad (7.48)$$

which reduces to

$$L_T \delta_T df^{FF}(0,T) = b(T)DV01^{FF}(T) - b(T-1)DV01^{FF}(T-1) + \text{OIR}_T \Delta_T df^{FF}(0,T) \quad , \quad (7.49)$$

where a fed funds $DV01$ has been introduced, similar to the familiar LIBOR $DV01$ of Chapter 1.

Since the fed funds-based OIS discount factors df^{FF} are derived from par OIS swap rates, one can use a formula similar to the forward LIBOR rate formula (7.43) for forward OIR,

$$\text{OIR}_T = \left[\frac{df^{FF}(0,T-1)}{df^{FF}(0,T)} - 1\right]\frac{1}{\Delta_T} \quad , \quad (7.50)$$

which is derived from the basic relationship

$$df^{FF}(0,T) = \frac{df^{FF}(0,T-1)}{1 + \text{OIR}_T \Delta_T} \quad . \quad (7.51)$$

Using (7.50) in (7.49) produces the desired result,

$$L_T \delta_T df^{FF}(0,T) = b(T)DV01^{FF}(T) - b(T-1)DV01^{FF}(T-1) \\ + df^{FF}(0,T-1) - df^{FF}(0,T) \quad , \quad (7.52)$$

or finally

$$L_T = \frac{b(T)DV01^{FF}(T) - b(T-1)DV01^{FF}(T-1) + df^{FF}(0,T-1) - df^{FF}(0,T)}{\delta_T df^{FF}(0,T)} \quad . \quad (7.53)$$

These are called *adjusted forward* LIBOR rates because they are derived from true risk-free fed funds discount factors. Note that when the basis swap spreads are zero, $b(t) = 0$, the above formula reduces to (7.43).

References

Artzner, Phillipe, F. Delbaen, J. M. Eber, and D. Heath, "Coherent Measures of Risk," *Mathematical Finance*, 9 (1999), 203.

Basel Committee on Bank Supervision, *Sound Practices for the Management and Supervision of Operational Risk*. Bank for International Settlements, Basel, Switzerland (revised February 2003).

Basel Committee on Bank Supervision, *International Convergence of Capital Measurement and Capital Standards*. Bank for International Settlements, Basel, Switzerland (revised June 2006).

Basel Committee on Bank Supervision, *Basel III: A Global Regulatory Framework for More Resilient Banks and Banking Systems*. Bank for International Settlements, Basel, Switzerland (revised June 2011A).

Basel Committee on Bank Supervision, *Operational Risk: Supervisory Guidelines for the Advanced Measurement Approaches*. Bank for International Settlements, Basel, Switzerland (revised June 2011B).

Rosen, Dan, and David Saunders, "CVA the Wrong Way," *Journal of Risk Management in Financial Institutions*, 5, no. 3 (2012), 252.

Tuckman, B., and A. Serrat, *Fixed Income Securities*, 3rd ed. Hoboken, NJ: John Wiley & Sons (2012).

Visalli, Stefano, Charles Roxburgh, Toos Daruvala, Miklos Dietz, Susan Lund, and Anna Marrs, *The State of Global Banking: In Search of a Sustainable Model*. McKinsey Annual Review on the Banking Industry, September 2011.

CHAPTER 8

Power Laws and Extreme Value Theory

The commonly used risk measures of VaR and CVaR almost always deal with the tails of a distribution. A risk manager often needs to report the 99% and 99.9% VaR and CVaR. He or she rarely needs to find the 60% VaR or CVaR. This indicates that much of the full distribution is ignored for risk purposes, even though a lot of effort may have gone into creating the whole distribution of future gains and losses of some asset. This prompts the question, "Why not simply have a methodology to create only the tail of a distribution and ignore everything else?" *Extreme value theory* (EVT) is a field of probability that studies the distribution of extreme realizations of a given distribution function. The fundamental result of EVT is that the distribution of extreme values of *independent and identically distributed* (IID) random samples from a given distribution essentially converges to one out of three EVT-type distributions. This means that the asymptotic nature of extreme values does not depend on the exact nature of the parent distribution. This is particularly useful for risk purposes, as there is no general agreement on which fat-tailed distribution is the ideal one to use for an asset class. EVT tells you that the precise type of distribution may not matter for risk purposes. Throughout this chapter, losses will be seen as positive numbers—e.g., a loss of $100MM. Using this nomenclature, the right side of the tail will be of interest to risk management.

Power Laws and Scaling

Before discussing EVT, I introduce the relatively straightforward power-law distribution, which shares some features with EVT. If the probability of a continuous variable is inversely related with that variable to a certain power, the distribution is said to follow a power law given by

$$f(x) = \frac{C}{x^{\alpha+1}} \tag{8.1}$$

with $\alpha > 0$. This power-law distribution is a fat-tailed distribution used primarily for applications that need extreme moves in the underlying variables. It is almost always used to fit asymptotic data—that is, only the tails of empirical distributions. The reason for this

CHAPTER 8 ■ POWER LAWS AND EXTREME VALUE THEORY

is that the power-law distribution does not always have finite moments (that is, the mean, variance, and so on may be infinite) and therefore is used to model only the extreme part of an empirical distribution. More precisely, a *Type I Pareto distribution* is a two-parameter distribution given by

$$P(X > x) = \begin{cases} \left(\dfrac{x_m}{x}\right)^{\alpha} & x \geq x_m \\ 1 & x < x_m \end{cases}, \qquad (8.2)$$

where the minimum value of the random variable is x_m (the *scale parameter*) and the power-law parameter is $\alpha > 0$ (the *shape parameter*). The cumulative distribution function is given by

$$F(x) = P(X \leq x) = \begin{cases} 1 - \left(\dfrac{x_m}{x}\right)^{\alpha} & x \geq x_m \\ 0 & x < x_m \end{cases}, \qquad (8.3)$$

which can be differentiated to produce the density function

$$f(x) = \begin{cases} \alpha \left(\dfrac{x_m^{\alpha}}{x^{\alpha+1}}\right) & x \geq x_m \\ 0 & x < x_m \end{cases}. \qquad (8.4)$$

Figure 8-1 illustrates several of these Pareto distributions. Note that a smaller α leads to a fatter tail.

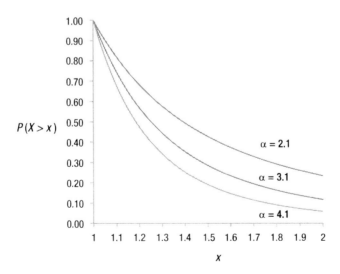

Figure 8-1. *Pareto distributions with different shape parameters ($x_m = 1$)*

CHAPTER 8 ■ POWER LAWS AND EXTREME VALUE THEORY

Figure 8-2 represents Figure 8-1 as a log-log (base e) graph—i.e., $\ln[P(X>x)] = -\alpha \ln(x), x_m = 1$. The linearity indicates several things such as method of calibration and a (potentially hazardous) method of extrapolation. It also indicates scale invariance.

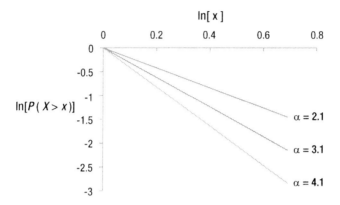

Figure 8-2. *A log-log plot of Pareto distributions with different shape parameters ($x_m = 1$)*

Scale invariance means that as one changes the scale of the problem from x to cx, the densities $f(x)$ and $f(cx)$ are proportional, showing that the relative probabilities between rare and not-so-rare events stays the same regardless of scale. Explicitly,

$$f(cx) = \alpha \left(\frac{x_m^\alpha}{(cx)^{\alpha+1}} \right) = c^{-\alpha-1} f(x) \quad . \tag{8.5}$$

Furthermore, the rescaled equation of the log plot in Figure 8-2,

$$\ln[P(X > cx)] = \ln[c^{-\alpha} P(X>x)] = -\alpha \ln[c] - \alpha \ln[x] = -\alpha \ln[cx] \quad , \tag{8.6}$$

($x_m = 1$), indicates that rescaling from x to cx moves the power law up and down the log scale. In fact, it has been shown [Embrechts et al., 1997] that a general distribution function is scale-invariant if and only if it has a power-law tail, such that the tails match a Pareto distribution up to a multiplicative constant.

How does the power law expression react to a shift such as x to $x + c$? Substituting $x + c$ into the density function equation (8.4) gives

$$\begin{aligned} f(x+c) &= \alpha \left(\frac{x_m^\alpha}{(x+c)^{\alpha+1}} \right) \\ &= \alpha x_m^\alpha (x+c)^{-\alpha-1} \frac{x^{-\alpha-1}}{x^{-\alpha-1}} \\ &= \alpha x_m^\alpha \left[1 + \frac{c}{x} \right]^{-\alpha-1} x^{-\alpha-1} \\ &= L(x) x^{-\alpha-1} \end{aligned} \tag{8.7}$$

Since $L(x)$ is a slowly varying function, such that

$$\lim_{x\to\infty} L(x) = \lim_{x\to\infty} \alpha x_m^\alpha \left[1+\frac{c}{x}\right]^{-\alpha-1} \to \alpha x_m^\alpha \quad , \tag{8.8}$$

one has

$$\lim_{x\to\infty} f(x+c) \to f(x) \quad , \tag{8.9}$$

and therefore the tail of the *shifted power law* $f(x+c)$ still has a power-law-style distribution.

Moments

As mentioned in the preceding section, the power-law distribution may be an appropriate representation of the tail of a fat-tailed distribution. But how does it perform over the full range of the random variable it describes? To investigate this, one needs to calculate its moments, and here the power law reveals its weakness as a complete all-in-one distribution. Assuming $\alpha > n$, the *raw moments* for the distribution in (8.4) are given by

$$E[X^n] = \alpha x_m^\alpha \int_{x_m}^\infty \frac{x^n}{x^{\alpha+1}} dx = \alpha x_m^\alpha \int_{x_m}^\infty \frac{1}{x^{\alpha-n+1}} dx$$

$$= -\alpha \frac{x_m^\alpha}{\alpha-n} \left[\frac{1}{x^{\alpha-n}}\right]_{x_m}^\infty = \frac{\alpha}{\alpha-n} \frac{x_m^\alpha}{x_m^{\alpha-n}} = \frac{\alpha x_m^n}{x-n} \tag{8.10}$$

Below are the first four standardized moments. Note that they exist only for values of $\alpha > n$.

- Mean

$$\mu = \frac{\alpha x_m}{\alpha-1}, \ \alpha > 1 \tag{8.11}$$

- Variance

$$\sigma^2 = E[(X-\mu)^2] = \frac{x_m^2 \alpha}{(\alpha-1)^2(\alpha-2)}, \ \alpha > 2 \tag{8.12}$$

- Skewness

$$\frac{E[(X-\mu)^3]}{\sigma^3} = \frac{2(1+\alpha)}{\alpha-3}\sqrt{\frac{\alpha-2}{\alpha}}, \ \alpha > 3 \tag{8.13}$$

- Excess kurtosis

$$\frac{E[(X-\mu)^4]}{\sigma^4} - 3 = \frac{6(\alpha^3+\alpha^2-6\alpha-2)}{\alpha(\alpha-3)(\alpha-4)}, \ \alpha > 4 \tag{8.14}$$

Extrapolation

As mentioned in the Power Laws and Scaling section, one of consequences of the power law's scaling properties is that it can be used for extrapolation. The power-law distribution may be used to calculate the odds of an extreme move even if these extreme moves were not used in the calibration of α and x_m. Let us say one has 1,000 P&L scenarios (either real or Monte Carlo) for an equity position. Furthermore, say that the 99% VaR is $75.40MM. Other scenario results are shown in Table 8-1. These are the large moves (losses) for the position over a certain period of time. One may now ask the question, "What is the probability of loss of $150.00MM?"

Table 8-1. Large P&L Losses and Their Probabilities

Loss	Empirical Probability
$75.40MM	1/100
$87.96MM	1/230
$100.53MM	1/350
$113.10MM	1/675
$125.66MM	1/998

One can calibrate a power law to these results. The first thing one must decide is what will be the minimum loss amount x_m where the power law is valid? Often, the 99% VaR is chosen—i.e., x_m = $75.40MM in Table 8-1. One simple (but often misleading) way to calibrate the P&L scenarios is to use the scaling properties of the power law and perform a least-squares fit of a line through the log-log equation

$$\ln[P(X > x)] = -\alpha[\ln(x)] + \ln(x_m^\alpha) \quad (8.15)$$

The corresponding linear regression equation (see Chapter 4) is

$$\ln[P(X > x)] = a[\ln(x)] + b + \varepsilon \quad , \quad (8.16)$$

with the power-law shape parameter given by

$$\alpha = |a| \quad . \quad (8.17)$$

For the values in Table 8-1, one finds using the LINEST() function in Excel that $\alpha = 4.468$ (see Figure 8-3).

CHAPTER 8 ■ POWER LAWS AND EXTREME VALUE THEORY

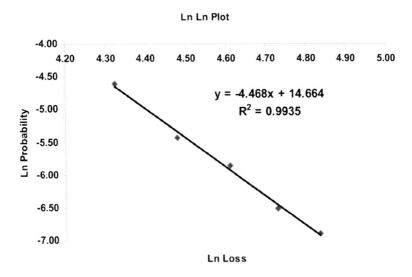

Figure 8-3. *Linear regression of power law applied to the values in Table 8-1*

Therefore, our power-law distribution fit is

$$P(X > x) = \frac{1}{100}\left(\frac{75.40}{x}\right)^{4.468}. \tag{8.18}$$

The factor in front is to make sure that the 99% VaR comes out correctly, such that $P(X > x_m) = 1\%$. Now, one may answer the question, "What is the probability of loss of $150.00MM?" It is given by (and this is the extrapolation part)

$$P(X > 150) = \frac{1}{100}\left(\frac{75.40}{150}\right)^{4.468} = 1/2161. \tag{8.19}$$

Basically, the power law has been used to extrapolate deep into the tail. The confidence in this extrapolation is that it is a heavy-tailed distribution that has been calibrated specifically to the empirical tail rather than the whole distribution itself. Further extrapolated results are given in Table 8-2. A more accurate calibration method is discussed in the "Maximum Likelihood Calibration" section.

CHAPTER 8 ■ POWER LAWS AND EXTREME VALUE THEORY

Table 8-2. *Extrapolated P&L Losses and Their Power Law Probabilities*

Loss	Pareto Probability
$150MM	1/2,161
$175MM	1/4,303
$200MM	1/7,815
$250MM	1/21,181
$300MM	1/47,834

One must always beware of putting too much faith in extrapolated results, for one is assuming a specific behavior past the point of available data. Unfortunately, extrapolation is occasionally the only methodology available when data points are rare.

Power-Law Monte Carlo Simulation

To create a Monte Carlo simulation that follows a Pareto distribution, one needs to generate random numbers that follow such a distribution. In Chapter 3, MC simulation was achieved through the inverse transform method. One can use a similar technique for power-law-type distributions. As with all normalized distributions, the power-law cumulative distribution has a range between 0 and 1,

$$P(X \le x) = 1 - \left(\frac{x_m}{x}\right)^\alpha \to [0,1] \text{ for } x \ge x_m \quad . \tag{8.20}$$

Therefore, one can generate a uniform random number between 0 and 1 and take the inverse transformation,

$$U \sim Unif[0,1]$$
$$X = P^{-1}(U) \quad . \tag{8.21}$$

For Gaussian variables, the inverse transformation is well known (the function exists in Excel). For the power-law distribution, the inverse transformation is derived as follows. Recall the definition of an inverse function. If one has a function

$$f(x) = y \quad , \tag{8.22}$$

then its inverse (if it exists) is given by

$$g(y) = x \quad , \tag{8.23}$$

or more explicitly

$$g(f(x)) = x \quad . \tag{8.24}$$

CHAPTER 8 ■ POWER LAWS AND EXTREME VALUE THEORY

The inverse of (8.3) is

$$g(y) = x_m[1-y]^{-1/\alpha} \qquad (8.25)$$

since

$$g\left[1-\left(\frac{x_m}{x}\right)^\alpha\right] = x_m\left[1-\left(1-\left(\frac{x_m}{x}\right)^\alpha\right)\right]^{-1/\alpha} = x_m\left[\left(\left(\frac{x_m}{x}\right)^\alpha\right)\right]^{-1/\alpha} = x_m\frac{x}{x_m} = x \qquad (8.26)$$

Therefore, the steps needed for a power-law MC simulation are as follows:

Step 1: Choose the input parameters α and x_m.

Step 2: Generate uniform random numbers.

Step 3: Use the inverse transform (8.25) to get a power-law-like variables.

Step 4: Calculate the empirical moments of the MC variables.

Step 5: Compare these to the theoretical moments of the power law variables. Use equations (8.11)-(8.14). Note that depending on the choice of α, these moments may not exist.

Step 6: Estimate a "calibrated" α and x_m for the MC variables.

One may use the simple linear regression technique of (8.16) to achieve step 6. Another method that often leads to better results in parameter estimation is the maximum likelihood method, presented in the next section

Maximum Likelihood Calibration

Identifying power-law behavior and calibrating an appropriate distribution can be complicated procedure. The naive strategy discussed in the "Extrapolation" section of using a logarithmic plot to fit a least squares straight line can often lead to misleading results for more realistic data sets or MC simulations. For example, let us assume a power-law MC simulation has been performed using $x_m = \$75.40$MM, as in the "Extrapolation" section, but with $\alpha = 6.50$. In this case, the precise α is known. Using the simulation results, one can use an appropriate binning methodology and create a histogram of the results (that is, a probability density as described in Chapter 3). Using the simple strategy of creating a log plot and using linear regression provides a calibration of $\alpha = 6.05$, as indicated in Figure 8-4.

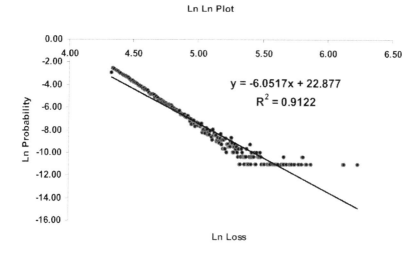

Figure 8-4. *Linear regression of power-law MC simulation*

Clearly, one would like an approach that provides a calibration closer to the input α of 6.50. One such approach is the *maximum likelihood method* of estimating exponents. This method does not take into account the explicit empirical probabilities but uses the empirical loss values in the joint probability distribution to find the "best" exponent that maximizes the probability with respect to the empirical results. Let $x = [x_1, x_2, ..., x_n]$ be a set of n IID data points (market or MC) that will be used to fit a power-law distribution. The probability that these values will be generated from our a power-law distribution is proportional to a joint distribution given by

$$L(\alpha, x_m) = \prod_{i=1}^{n} f(x_i) = \prod_{i=1}^{n} \alpha \frac{x_m^{\alpha}}{x_i^{\alpha+1}} \quad . \tag{8.27}$$

This is called the *likelihood function* of the given data set. One needs to maximize this function with respect to both α and x_m to best fit the given data set. One typically works with the logarithm of this function,

$$l(\alpha, x_m) = n\ln(\alpha) + n\alpha \ln(x_m) - (\alpha+1)\sum_{i=1}^{n} \ln(x_i) \quad . \tag{8.28}$$

This is clearly a monotonically increasing function of x_m. Since the distribution is nonzero for $x \geq x_m$, it makes sense to set the estimate of x_m to

$$\bar{x}_m = \min_i [x_i] \quad . \tag{8.29}$$

To find the best estimate for α, one needs to solve

$$\frac{\partial l}{\partial \alpha} = \frac{n}{\alpha} + n\ln(\hat{x}_m) - \sum_{i=1}^{n}\ln(x_i) = 0 \quad , \tag{8.30}$$

which has a solution of

$$\hat{\alpha} = n\left[\sum_{i=1}^{n}\ln\left(\frac{x_i}{\hat{x}_m}\right)\right]^{-1} . \tag{8.31}$$

Using this formula for the results from Figure 8-4, one gets a calibrated shape parameter of $\alpha = 6.53$, which is much closer to the input of $\alpha = 6.50$ used to generate the power-law distribution. This formula is a statistical estimate and has an expected error given by

$$\hat{\sigma}_\alpha = \frac{\hat{\alpha}}{\sqrt{n}} . \tag{8.32}$$

Extreme Value Theory

Many different types of methods have been studied to describe the tails of a distribution. Such mathematical techniques are critical for risk management purposes. Another such method is to use limit laws to derive limiting tail distributions of a set of random variables. As noted at the opening of this chapter, the fundamental result of EVT is that the distribution of extreme values of IID random variables essentially converges to one of three EVT-type distributions. This means that the asymptotic nature of extreme values does not depend on the exact nature of the parent distribution. That is, the qualitative behavior seen in the limit is not unique. The most familiar limit law in probability theory, the *central limit theorem*, also possesses this nature. That is, suppose $X_1, X_2, ..., X_n$ are independent random variables with a common distribution function $F(x) = P(X \le x)$. Denote as S_n, the nth sum of these variables: $S_n = X_1 + X_2 + ... + X_n$. The central limit theorem states that this sum has a limiting distribution that is Gaussian. For suitable mean and variance parameters $a_n = nE[X]$ and $b_n = \sqrt{n\text{Var}(X)}$, the central limit theorem states that

$$\lim_{n\to\infty} P\left(\frac{S_n - a_n}{b_n} \le x\right) = N(x) \quad . \tag{8.33}$$

Given an unknown distribution $F(x)$, EVT would like to model the extreme values of $F(x)$ (the tail) without concerning itself with the center of the distribution $F(x)$. The question now arises: "How does one define *extreme*?" There exist two common parametric approaches to EVT that essentially differ in their definition of extreme. The first approach is called the *block maxima method*. Consider M IID random variables $(X_1, X_2, ..., X_M)$ of positive losses (recall the nomenclature in use). Divide the given M observations into n blocks of k observations each. For instance, if one has $M = 1,000$ observations, one may create $n = 10$ blocks each having $k = 100$ sample observations. From each block, pick the maximum loss of each block: $M_n = \max(X_1, X_2, ..., X_k)$. One clearly will have a set of n maxima. Figure 8-5 illustrates the block maximum principle.

CHAPTER 8 ■ POWER LAWS AND EXTREME VALUE THEORY

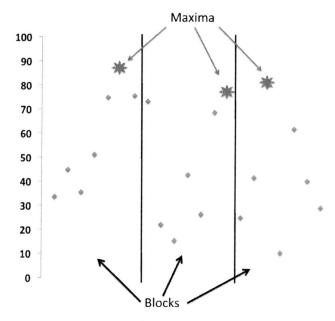

Figure 8-5. The block maxima method

EVT deals with the normalized maxima M_n. A theorem of Gnedenko (1943) says that **if**, for suitable location parameters a_n and scaling parameters b_n, one has

$$\lim_{n \to \infty} P\left(\frac{M_n - a_n}{b_n} \leq x \right) = H_\xi(x) \qquad (8.34)$$

where $H_\xi(x)$ is a nondegenerate distribution, **then** $H_\xi(x)$ has to be one of the following three types of nondegenerate EVT distributions, namely:

Frechet: $\xi > 0$

$$H_\xi(x) = \begin{cases} 0, & \text{if } x \leq 0 \\ \exp[-x^{-1/\xi}] & \text{if } x > 0 \end{cases} \qquad (8.35)$$

Gumbel: $\xi = 0$

$$H_0(x) = \exp[-\exp(-x)], \ x \in \Re \qquad (8.36)$$

Weibull: $\xi > 0$

$$H_\xi(x) = \begin{cases} \exp[-(-x)^{-1/\xi}], & \text{if } x \leq 0 \\ 1 & \text{if } x > 0 \end{cases} \qquad (8.37)$$

where ξ is the shape parameter. The convergence to one of these three EVT distributions depends upon the tail characteristics of the original distribution $F(x)$. If $F(x)$ has a power-law-type fat-tailed distribution, such as the Student's-t or Pareto distributions,

325

CHAPTER 8 ■ POWER LAWS AND EXTREME VALUE THEORY

its asymptotic distribution of extreme values is that of the *Frechet* type. If $F(x)$ has an exponentially decaying tail (no fat tails)—such as the Gaussian, lognormal, or chi-squared distributions—its extreme values behave like a *Gumbel* distribution. Finally, the *Weibull* distribution appears in the asymptotic behavior of short-tailed distributions, such as the beta distribution. Clearly, the Frechet type is the EVT distribution of interest to risk management.

Jenkinson (1955) introduced a unified framework for the three EVT distributions above. The following representation is now referred to as the *generalized extreme value* (GEV) distribution:

$$H_\xi(x) = \begin{cases} \exp[-(1+\xi x)^{-1/\xi}] & \xi \neq 0, 1+\xi x > 0 \\ \exp[-\exp^{-x}] & \xi = 0 \end{cases} \quad (8.38)$$

For $\xi > 0$, one finds the Frechet type. For $\xi = 0$, one finds the Gumbel type. For $\xi < 0$, one finds the Weibull type. A three-parameter scale and location family of distributions can also be obtained from the above by defining

$$H_{\xi,\mu,\sigma}(x) = H_\xi\left[\frac{x-\mu}{\sigma}\right], \quad (8.39)$$

where μ is the location parameter and σ is the scale parameter.

As was discussed earlier, there are two parametric approaches to EVT. The second approach is similar to the way one moves from VaR to CVaR. In this second approach to EVT, one would like to understand conditional expectations—specifically, *exceedances over thresholds* as illustrated in Figure 8-6. The points shown are identical to Figure 8-5, but the maxima methodology is different.

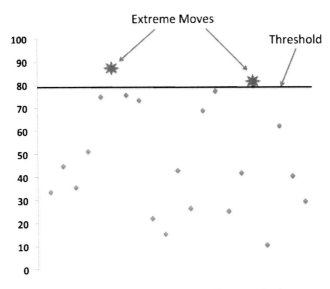

Figure 8-6. *The threshold exceedance method*

CHAPTER 8 ■ POWER LAWS AND EXTREME VALUE THEORY

Note how the extreme moves picked up by the two differing methods in Figures 8-5 and 8-6 choose a slightly different set of extreme points. If $F(x)$ is the cumulative distribution function of the losses of some portfolio (as positive values), the probability that x lies between u and $u + y$ is $F(u+y) - F(u)$ (see Chapter 3). The probability that x is greater than u, the threshold, is $1 - F(u)$. The distribution of *threshold exceedances*, $Y = X - u > 0$, is given by

$$F_u(y) = P[X \leq u + y \mid X > u] = \frac{F(u+y) - F(u)}{1 - F(u)} \quad . \tag{8.40}$$

The asymptotic distribution of $F_u(y)$ as $u \to \sup\{x : F(x) < 1\}$ (the conditional tail) for a wide class of distributions is given by

$$G_{\xi,\mu,\sigma}(x) = \begin{cases} 1 - \left[1 + \xi\left(\frac{x-u}{\sigma}\right)\right]^{-1/\xi} & \xi \neq 0 \\ 1 - e^{-\left(\frac{x-u}{\sigma}\right)} & \xi = 0 \end{cases} \tag{8.41}$$

where

$$\begin{cases} (x - u) \geq 0 & \text{if } \xi \geq 0 \\ 0 \leq (x - u) \leq -\sigma/\xi, & \text{if } \xi < 0 \end{cases} \tag{8.42}$$

and $\sigma > 0$, $-\infty < x < \infty$. This is known as the *generalized Pareto distribution* (GPD) [Embrechts et al, 1997].

It is worth noting that a GDP approximation of (8.41) exists if and only if the GEV limit, $H_\xi(x)$, exists in (8.34); in that case, if $H_\xi(x)$ is written in the GEV form in (8.38), then the shape parameter ξ in (8.38) is the same as the corresponding parameter in (8.41).

Maximum Likelihood Calibration for the GPD

The two parametric approaches to EVT—the GEV distribution and the block maxima method—and the GPD along with the threshold exceedances method all share the same issue: how to estimate either the number of blocks and block sizes or how to set the threshold amount u. In the simple power law example of Table 8-1, a 99% VaR was used as a minimum for extreme moves. But other percentiles may be chosen, as there is no precise range for u.

Let $x = [x_1, x_2, \ldots, x_n]$ be a set of IID data points (market or MC) that will be used to fit a GPD distribution with $\xi \neq 0$. The parameters ξ and σ are often estimated using a maximum likelihood method similar to the one described for the power laws above. One can choose u to be a value such as the 95% or 99% VaR of the loss distribution. First, rank all the x's greater than u in order from highest to lowest. The probability density function associated with (8.41) is given by differentiating it with respect to x, leading to

$$g_{\xi,\mu,\sigma}(x) = \frac{1}{\sigma}\left[1 + \xi\left(\frac{x-u}{\sigma}\right)\right]^{-1/\xi - 1} \quad . \tag{8.43}$$

If there are n_u losses greater than u, the likelihood function ($\xi \neq 0$) is given by

$$\prod_{i=1}^{n_u} \frac{1}{\sigma}\left[1+\xi\left(\frac{x_i-u}{\sigma}\right)\right]^{-1/\xi-1} \quad . \tag{8.44}$$

As before, it is preferable to maximize the log of this function, such that

$$\sum_{i=1}^{n_u} \ln\left(\frac{1}{\sigma}\left[1+\xi\left(\frac{x_i-u}{\sigma}\right)\right]^{-1/\xi-1}\right) \quad . \tag{8.45}$$

The Power-Law Equivalence of the GPD

One can show that the GPD with $\xi > 0$ has a power-law tail. From (8.40), it is known that in the asymptotic limit, $P[X > u + y \mid X > u] = 1 - G_{\xi,\mu,\sigma}(x)$. The unconditional probability $P[X > u]$ is given by $1 - F(u)$. The unconditional probability $P[X > x = u + y]$ implied from the conditional results above is

$$[1-F(u)][1-G_{\xi,\mu,\sigma}(x)] \quad . \tag{8.46}$$

Since the probability that x is greater than u is $1 - F(u)$, if n was the total number of observations and n_u the number of losses greater than u, than $[1 - F(u)]$ can be estimated by n_u/n. This implies that

$$P[X > x] \approx \frac{n_u}{n}\left[1+\xi\left(\frac{x-u}{\sigma}\right)\right]^{-1/\xi} \quad . \tag{8.47}$$

If one sets the threshold level u as

$$u = \frac{\sigma}{\xi} \quad , \tag{8.48}$$

and defines the inverse of the exponent ξ

$$\alpha = \frac{1}{\xi} \quad , \tag{8.49}$$

and finally lets

$$C = \frac{n_u}{n}\left[\frac{\xi}{\sigma}\right]^{-1/\xi} \quad , \tag{8.50}$$

then (8.47) reduces to a power law form similar to (8.1),

$$P[X > x] \approx \frac{C}{x^{\alpha}} \quad . \tag{8.51}$$

With respect to (8.47), when the number of exceedances n_u in, say, a year is asymptotically Poisson with mean λ and, conditionally on $n_u > 0$, the threshold exceedances are IID from the GDP, the joint process of exceedance times and excesses over threshold is called the *Poisson-GDP model*.

VaR and CVaR

As has been demonstrated, EVT is a methodology for fitting the tails of a distribution and can be used, with care, to extrapolate details of the tail when sufficient data may not be available. For instance, if one has 900 data points of losses and needs to estimate a 99.9% VaR number, it is not possible simply by using the data at hand. One may instead fit either a GEV distribution or GPD and then estimate the VaR from the EVT formula. A simple example using the GPD method follows. First, the definition of VaR given in (3.92) must be replaced as follows when considering a time series of positive losses:

$$\text{VaR}_\alpha = \inf\{r_\alpha \in \Re : P(r > r_\alpha) \leq 1-\alpha\} = \inf\{r_\alpha \in \Re : F(r_\alpha) \geq \alpha\} \quad (8.52)$$

Essentially, one is looking for the point such that

$$F(\text{VaR}_\alpha) = \alpha = 1 - P(X > \text{VaR}_\alpha) \quad (8.53)$$

Using the unconditional probability (8.47) derived above, one can find expressions for VaR and CVaR under the GPD model. Substituting (8.47) into (8.53) gives

$$\alpha = 1 - \frac{n_u}{n}\left[1 + \xi\left(\frac{\text{VaR}_\alpha - u}{\sigma}\right)\right]^{-1/\xi} \quad (8.54)$$

Solving for VaR_α gives the GPD VaR formula

$$\text{VaR}_\alpha = u + \frac{\sigma}{\xi}\left(\left[\frac{n}{n_u}(1-\alpha)\right]^{-\xi} - 1\right) \quad (8.55)$$

By calibrating u, ξ, and σ, one may use this formula to estimate various levels of VaR beyond that directly accessible from the initial data. For instance, maybe a 95% VaR is used to get the threshold u to calibrate ξ and σ, and then the above formula is used to get a 99.9% VaR. CVaR_α, given by (3.97), is basically the average of VaRs beyond the α point normalized by the area of the resulting region. For positive losses (the right tail), CVaR_α is derived from VaR as follows:

$$\text{CVaR}_\alpha = \frac{1}{1-\alpha}\int_\alpha^1 \text{VaR}_z\, dz. \quad (8.56)$$

CHAPTER 8 ■ POWER LAWS AND EXTREME VALUE THEORY

Substituting the VaR formula (8.55) into the integral above and performing the integral leads to

$$CVaR_\alpha = \frac{1}{1-\alpha} \int_\alpha^1 \left[u - \frac{\sigma}{\xi} + \frac{\sigma}{\xi}\left(\frac{n}{n_u}\right)^{-\xi}(1-z)^{-\xi} \right] dz \qquad (8.57)$$

$$CVaR_\alpha = u - \frac{\sigma}{\xi} + \frac{1}{1-\alpha}\frac{\sigma}{\xi}\left(\frac{n}{n_u}\right)^{-\xi}\frac{(1-\alpha)^{-\xi+1}}{1-\xi} \ . \qquad (8.58)$$

Using the VaR_α formula of (8.55), one has

$$CVaR_\alpha = u - \frac{\sigma}{\xi} + \frac{VaR_\alpha}{1-\xi} - \left(\frac{u-\frac{\sigma}{\xi}}{1-\xi}\right) \ . \qquad (8.59)$$

By simplifying the above expression, one is left with the GPD CVaR formula

$$CVaR_\alpha = \frac{VaR_\alpha + \sigma - \xi u}{1-\xi} \qquad (8.60)$$

By calibrating u, ξ, and σ, one may use this formula to *estimate* various levels of CVaR beyond what is directly accessible from the initial data. Once again, care must be taken when using these formulas to extrapolate risk numbers deep into the loss tail.

Problems
Problem 8-1. Power-Law MC Simulation in Excel

Use the following steps to create a power-law MC simulation in Excel.

Step 1: Choose the input parameters α and x_m.

Step 2: Generate 65,000 uniform random numbers using the RAND() function in Excel.

Step 3: Use the inverse transform (8.25) to get a power-law-like variables.

Step 4: Calculate the empirical moments of the 65,000 MC-generated variables.

Step 5: Compare these to the theoretical moments of the power law variables. Use equations (8.11)–(8.14). Note that depending on the choice of α, these moments may not exist.

Step 6: Estimate a "calibrated" α and x_m for the 65,000 MC variables.

Use both the simple linear regression technique of (8.16) and the maximum likelihood calibration (8.31) with its error term given by (8.32). Which method gives the more accurate estimate of the input α?

Problem 8-2. The Power-Law Nature of the GPD

Use the parameters given in equations (8.48)–(8.50) to show that the GPD distribution of (8.47) reduces to the power-law distribution (8.51).

References

Embrechts, P., C. Kluppelberg, and T. Mikosch, *Modelling Extremal Events for Insurance and Finance* (Berlin: Springer, 1997).

Fisher, R. A., and L. H. C. Tippet, "Limiting Forms of the Frequency Distribution of the Largest or Smallest Member of a Sample," *Proceedings of the Cambridge Philosophical Society*, 24 (1928), 180-190.

Gnedenko, B. V., "Sur la distribution limite du terme maximum d'une serie aleatoire," *Annals of Mathematics*, 44 (1943), 423-453.

Jenkinson, A. F., "The Frequency Distribution of the Annual Maximum (or Minimum) Values of Meteorological Elements," *Quarterly Journal of the Royal Meteorology Society*, 87 (1955), 145-158.

CHAPTER 9

Hedge Fund Replication

Asset replication, in general, deals with the concept of replicating the returns of one asset with the returns of several other assets. The term does not refer to *derivatives replication*, in which one uses linear instruments to replicate nonlinear ones, as described in Chapters 1 and 5. The simplest example of asset replication is a mutual fund or exchange-traded fund (ETF) on the S&P 500 index. An ETF is similar to a mutual fund (which can be bought or sold at the end of each trading day for its net asset value) except that it can be traded throughout the trading day. The S&P 500 index owner, Standard and Poor's Financial Services LLC, does not provide investments into the index inasmuch as it is largely a ratings agency and financial research company. Mutual fund providers such as the Vanguard Group must replicate the returns of the official index S&P 500 index in order to provide a *tracking* or *replicating* mutual fund. The replication is fairly straightforward, because Standard and Poor's provides the names of all 500 underlying stocks as well as its market capitalization weighting methodology. An exact replication strategy would require one to hold all 500 stocks at all times in exact proportion to their weights in the index. Vanguard's main concern is *tracking error*, a measure of how closely a replicating fund follows the index to which it is benchmarked. The most common measure of tracking error is the root-mean-square of the difference between the mutual fund returns and the index returns. For a mutual fund, the tracking error is based on closing day prices, whereas for an ETF such as the SPDR S&P 500 ETF—the "spiders" of State Street Global Advisors (SSgA)—the tracking error uses intraday prices. Because of transaction costs and fees, both tracking mutual funds and ETFs slightly underperform the reference index. Replicating or tracking funds and ETFs are available for a wide range of popular equity and bond indices such as the Russell 3000, FTSE 100, CAC 40, SX5E, and Barclays Aggregate Bond Index (formerly the Lehman Brothers Aggregate Bond index).

Replicating an index where the underlying components are known, as in the examples in the preceding paragraph, is a relatively straightforward task. Replicating an asset where its underlying components are not completely revealed is a much harder task. For the majority of mutual funds that do not track a well-known index but are based on actively managed portfolios, this is the case. These types of mutual funds provide some transparency into their holdings, but they do not reveal the details of their particular trading strategy. Therefore, replicating such a fund is far more difficult than replicating a well-known index such as the S&P 500. One may ask the purpose of replicating a non-index-style mutual fund when one can purchase the mutual fund directly. This question leads directly to a discussion of the three main drivers for attempting fund replication: the perceived superior performance of the fund relative to the market (*alpha*, defined more precisely below); a fund's high commission fees; and its restrictions on access or participation.

If a particular mutual fund has low fees and is easily accessible, there is no reason to create a replicating or tracking fund. On the other hand, if the fees are relatively high or the access is limited, one may try to build a tracker fund that has lower fees and is easily accessible. Many actively traded mutual funds do not have excessive fees or highly limited access such as large minimum investment amounts. An investment class that does in fact have such issues is hedge funds.

Overview of Hedge Fund Styles

A *hedge fund* is a limited partnership or limited liability company that pools monies of certain sophisticated or qualified investors into an investment vehicle that is administered by the hedge fund management firm. Hedge funds invest in a diverse range of markets and use a wide variety of trading strategies to provide excess returns over the market, described later in this section. The name "hedge fund" is a complete misnomer, for there is no requirement for hedge funds to actually hedge their investments. In fact, hedge funds often take relatively risky positions with substantial leverage. As such, they may not be offered or sold to the general public, and they escape a substantial amount of the regulatory oversight and accounting rules, such as Basel III and CVA, that are required of more traditional finance companies. Furthermore, they provide limited liquidity, because a hedge fund's net asset value (NAV) is often quoted no more than monthly, and purchases and withdrawals are limited to quarterly or worse. Hedge funds have traditionally charged "2 and 20"—meaning a 2% annual fee plus 20% of any positive returns of the hedge fund. Minimum investment amounts are often in the millions of dollars with lockup periods of one to two years, which "lock up" the investment by restricting the withdrawal of the investment for the prespecified time period. How can hedge funds get away with all these fees and restrictions? It comes down to the hotly debated topic of *alpha* (excess return).

The terms *alpha* (α) and *beta* (β) are often used in finance with respect to the *capital asset pricing model* (CAPM). The CAPM model implies that investors are only compensated for beta—i.e., for the exposure of their portfolio to the systematic risk or market risk of the sector in question. For instance, if one has a portfolio of large cap US stocks, one is compensated for the relative exposure of this portfolio to the overall risk of the US equity market or a market benchmark index like the S&P 500 and not to any asset-specific or unrelated market risk factors. According to CAPM, this relation is given by

$$(r_t^P - r_t^{RF}) = \beta(r_t^{S\&P500} - r_t^{RF}) \quad , \tag{9.1}$$

where r_t^P is the return of the portfolio over a time period t, r_t^{RF} is the risk-free interest rate (LIBOR or OIS), and $r_t^{S\&P500}$ is the return on the S&P 500 over the same period. However, if one were to perform a linear regression of the portfolio returns against the S&P 500 returns over an appropriate historical period, one would get a relationship of the form,

$$(r_t^P - r_t^{RF}) = \alpha + \beta(r_t^{S\&P500} - r_t^{RF}) + \varepsilon_t \quad . \tag{9.2}$$

The additional alpha parameter, α, in this linear regression equation can be viewed as the risk-adjusted excess return (if statistically significant and positive) over the systematic risk of the market in question (namely, the S&P 500, in the case of a portfolio of US stocks). It is often argued that alpha is a measure of the portfolio manager's trading skill, because it is the excess return of an actively managed portfolio versus a passive market index. Many hedge funds claim to provide substantial alpha and therefore charge large fees with the highly restrictive requirements mentioned above. The first question that may arise is, "What is the correct systematic risk factor to use in the regression?" For instance, if one traded technology stocks during the dot-com boom of 1997-2000 and performed a regression against the S&P 500, one would get a very large alpha. Yet if one performed a regression against the more appropriate NASDAQ index, the alpha would be substantially less. Therefore, alpha is always relative to the appropriate benchmark index and corresponding beta.

Generically, there are two types of beta: *traditional* and *alternative*. Traditional betas are those related to the systematic risks of investments that the common investor experiences, such as portfolios of stocks and most bonds. These betas are often represented as *long-only* equity indices, such as the NASDAQ or the Barclays Aggregate Bond index. The definition of *alternative beta* requires the consideration of investment techniques such as short selling, derivatives, and leverage, which are the bread-and-butter techniques of hedge funds. These nontraditional investment risks are often more complex than the long-only cash market of the common investor and may involve several systematic risk factors at once. Lars Jaeger, who popularized the term *alternative beta*, observes [Jaeger, 2008]:

> *Since alternative beta is so complex, it's no surprise that much of what is now understood to be alternative beta was once thought to be alpha. This hidden beta was disguised as manager alpha simply because earlier models were not sophisticated enough to account for it.*

The heart of hedge fund replication is to create a replicating portfolio tracking certain types of alternative beta (sometimes called *hedge fund beta*) in a more liquid and transparent manner and with far lower fees than a traditional hedge fund. The different types of alternative beta are related to the specific investment styles of hedge funds. Some of the main hedge fund styles are the following. The first three strategies fall into the equity hedge bucket because they largely use equity securities, keeping some amount of partial hedges in place.

- *Equity hedged—long short*: A strategy that maintains long and short positions primarily in the equity markets through cash, futures, and occasionally derivative securities. The short position may serve as a partial hedge, but these strategies tend to a have a long sector bias.

- *Equity hedged—market neutral*: The most common strategy in this style is the statistical arbitrage pairs trading strategy, discussed in Chapter 4.

- *Equity hedged—short bias*: A strategy that employs analytical techniques to short companies deemed to be overvalued. Pure naked shorts are not often used, and so some long hedge positions may be in place. The overall strategy, of course, has a short bias.

- *Relative value—convertible arbitrage*: Convertible bonds are fixed-income instruments with an embedded option to purchase the stock of the underlying company. These strategies often come down to a relative value play on the embedded option of the convertible bond with respect to a generic option on the related underlying stock.

- *Relative value—volatility arbitrage*: In this volatility trading strategy, sophisticated techniques, such as the OHMC method, are used in a relative value play on implied volatility versus realized volatility.

- *Event-driven—merger arbitrage*: This strategy involves investing in securities of companies that may be on the verge of a merger or other significant corporate transaction. Merged companies tend to replace each other's stock with just one stock. A *cash tender offer* is one in which a fixed amount of cash is offered for the acquired company's stock (which is then delisted). A *stock swap* is a transaction in which the stock of the acquiring company is offered at a fixed ratio in exchange for the stock of the acquired company. The value of the acquired companies stock may rise suddenly on the news of a merger, whereas the value of the acquiring company's stock may fall.

- *Event-driven—distressed*: This strategy involves investing in securities of companies in substantial distress or near bankruptcy. The strategy is to take positions in a distressed company's securities and hold them throughout the restructuring or bankruptcy process. The financial goal is that after any restructuring or motion out of bankruptcy, the original distressed securities will have risen substantially in value. These types of strategies may take years to make returns and are often driven by lawyers (so beware!).

- *Macro—active trading:* These strategies utilize active trading methods, typically with high-frequency position turnover. If trading is systematically made at subsecond intervals, this is referred to as *high-frequency trading*. It falls under the macro category because many such strategies focus on fundamental relationships across geographic areas. For instance, trading may happen simultaneously across thirty different futures exchanges worldwide.

- *Macro—currency trading*: These strategies take advantage of discrepancies between various foreign exchange rates or attempt to predict changing global interest rates and their effects on currency valuation.

Replicating Methodologies

There are basically three schools of thought when it comes to hedge fund replication. They are as follows:

- *Mechanical trading strategies*: This form of replication involves actually executing the popular trades of a certain hedge fund strategy. Specific hedge fund trades can either be deduced or become known to the larger financial community and replicated exactly. The problem with this method is that it can only produce alternative beta but rarely alpha, because that depends upon the proprietary trading rules of hedge funds, which are rarely revealed to the general public.

- *Factor-based approach*: The factor-based approach to replication uses a pool of liquid assets to replicate the return stream of a particular hedge. The simplest method is to use multiple linear regression on a set of factors. This method selects the underlying assets (factors) that have the highest explanatory powers for the specific hedge fund returns. For monthly quoting hedge funds, the model performs a new linear regression each month using a rolling time frame of historical data and selecting the best weightings for each of the underlying factors. This method is clearly backward-looking and misses any large events in the market because it relies on a rolling window of historical returns. Improvements to the naive linear regression method use either Kalman filtering [Kalman, 1960] or particle-filtering techniques, which increase the speed at which the replication reacts to sudden market changes. Although the factor-based Kalman filtering method is the only method discussed in detail in this chapter, hedge fund replication is a highly specialized and rapidly evolving field.

- *Distributional approach*: This is a far more modest approach in which one does not try to track point-by-point returns but rather attempts to replicate the statistical properties of the long-term distribution of returns of the hedge fund in question. By *distributional properties* are meant the moments: mean, vol, skew, kurt, and so forth. The mean return is of course the biggest attribute that one would like to replicate, but success in this method is defined over a much longer period (years) because distributional properties take time to play out. This method was made popular by H. Kat and H. Palaro (2005). Kat and Palaro have a method to transform the desired distribution into a derivatives-style payoff function and then replicate the desired payoff function using an option methodology (mostly Black-Scholes). Papageorgiou uses the OHMC method to perform a similar style replication [Papageorgiou et al., 2008].

A Heuristic Example

Before discussing the Kalman filtering method, I adapt a popular heuristic example of the Kalman filter from Maybeck (1979), which provides a more precise mathematical argument using conditional expectations.

Suppose that a sailor is lost in a sailboat on a one-dimensional line as in Figure 9-1. The lost sailor would like to estimate her location. The actual location at time t is denoted x_t. The boat is drifting randomly on the line according to a Gaussian distribution. The location changes with a mean equal to 0 and a variance equal to Q, and therefore the state of the system evolves according to

$$x_t = x_{t-1} + w_{t-1}, w \sim N(0,Q) \quad . \tag{9.3}$$

CHAPTER 9 ■ HEDGE FUND REPLICATION

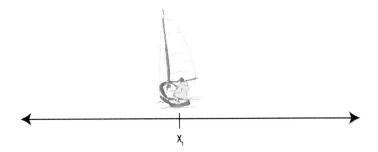

Figure 9-1. *Sailboat moving in one dimension*

The sailor has two measurement instruments to estimate her location: looking at the stars (eyesight) and a GPS device. At time $t-1$, her eyesight will be used to estimate her position and at time t, the GPS device will be used. Each of these devices will make a measurement in which the error of the measurement is assumed to follow a Gaussian distribution with error variances given by

$$\text{Stars}: \hat{x}_{t-1}, \text{Measurement Variance}: P_{t-1}$$
$$\text{GPS}: z_{t-1}, \text{Measurement Variance}: R$$
(9.4)

where the mean is the measurement itself and the notation is chosen to accord with that in the next section, "Replication through Kalman Filtering." First, one makes a measurement looking at the stars, $\hat{x}_{t-1}$. From this, one can make an initial prediction (signified by the superscript -) of where the boat will be at time t—i.e., $\hat{x}_t^-$. Thereafter, one makes another measurement with the GPS device, z_t. The main concept here is how to *combine* this measurement z_t with the initial prediction $\hat{x}_t^-$ to provide an *optimal* estimation of the current location of the sailboat. For clarity, the steps to be followed are the following:

Step 1: Use the stars and make a measurement of the boat's position at time $t-1$. This measurement is $\hat{x}_{t-1}$ with an error variance of P_{t-1}.

Step 2: One can now make an initial prediction of where the boat will be at time t. Given that the boat has a mean drift of zero, the boat is, on average, expected to be at the same location between time steps $t-1$ and t,

$$\hat{x}_t^- = \hat{x}_{t-1}$$
(9.5)

Between times $t-1$ and t, the boat drifts with a variance equal to Q. Therefore, one has two sources of error associated with predicting the location at time t: one from the natural drift of the boat and the other from the measurement from stars. One can simply add these error variances together to produce an *initial* predicted error at time t

$$P_t^- = P_{t-1} + Q$$
(9.6)

Step 3: Use the GPS device at time t to obtain a measurement of z_t. The error associated with this measurement has a variance of R.

Step 4: Combine the above two estimates in an optimal way. Because each of the measurements has a Gaussian distributed error, one can write the probability of a measurement x being the correct measurement according to each instrument as a Gaussian distribution with the appropriate mean and variance given by the following measurement methodology (see Figure 9-2):

$$p_{stars} = \frac{1}{\sqrt{2\pi P_t^-}} \exp\left[\frac{-(x-\hat{x}_t^-)^2}{2P_t^-}\right]$$

$$p_{gps} = \frac{1}{\sqrt{2\pi R}} \exp\left[\frac{-(x-z_t)^2}{2R}\right] \quad (9.7)$$

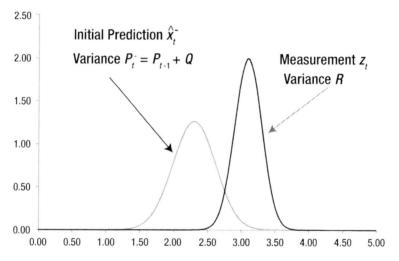

Figure 9-2. Example of the variances of a measurement and an initial prediction to be optimally combined

Given that the measurements are independent, one can combine these probability distributions by simple multiplication,

$$p_{optimal} = p_{gps} \cdot p_{stars} \quad (9.8)$$

For a more mathematically sound method using conditional expectations, see Maybeck (1979).

With some effort, this can be rewritten as

$$p_{optimal} = \frac{1}{\sqrt{2\pi P_t}} \exp\left[\frac{-(x-\hat{x}_t)^2}{2P_t}\right] \cdot \frac{1}{\sqrt{2\pi(P_t^{-2}+R^2)}} \exp\left[\frac{-(z_t-\hat{x}_t^-)^2}{2(P_t^{-2}+R^2)}\right] \quad (9.9)$$

where

$$K_t = \frac{P_t^-}{P_t^- + R}$$

$$\hat{x}_t = \hat{x}_t^- + K_t[z_t - \hat{x}_t^-]$$

$$P_t = \frac{P_t^- R}{P_t^- + R} = (1 - K_t)P_t^- \quad . \tag{9.10}$$

In order to normalize (9.9) to get a density function, the second exponential term—which looks like a Gaussian for z_t but is constant with respect to x—must be dropped, producing a normalized density function for x (see Figure 9-3):

$$p_{optimal} = \frac{1}{\sqrt{2\pi P_t}} \exp\left[\frac{-(x - \hat{x}_t)^2}{2P_t}\right] \quad . \tag{9.11}$$

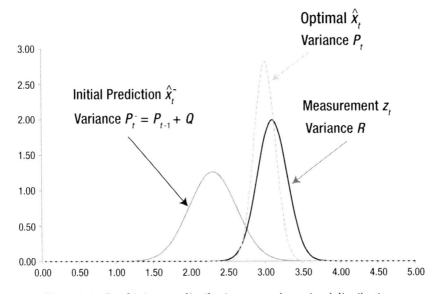

Figure 9-3. *Combining two distributions to get the optimal distribution*

Equations (9.5), (9.6), and (9.10) are the basic Kalman filtering equations for the position of the boat. K_t is the Kalman filter. It is the weight for how much the difference in measurements $z_t - \hat{x}_t^-$ affects the optimal estimation and it is also the weight for the variance P_t of the optimal estimation. Note that if the star measurement variance P_t^- is much larger than R, the Kalman filter K_t is almost 1—meaning that one must weight the difference by 100 percent, leaving one with $\hat{x}_t \approx z_t$ and thereby completely ignoring the star measurement. If R is much greater than P_t^- (which is unrealistic for a GPS device), the Kalman filter K_t is almost zero leaving one with $\hat{x}_t \approx \hat{x}_t^-$ thereby completing ignoring the GPS measurement (indicating a faulty GPS device).

Basically, the Kalman filter is a mathematical method used to estimate the true value of a hidden state, given only a sequence of noisy measurements. It is a recursive algorithm and generates optimal estimates of the state under the conditions that the state transition process and the mapping to observables are linear (in their simplest form) and the state process noise, observation noise, and estimate errors are Gaussian and have known variances. In the next section, the Kalman filter will be applied to the weights of different assets of a replicating portfolio.

Replication through Kalman Filtering

Factor replication, in general, deals with the concept of replicating or tracking the returns of a hedge fund strategy with the returns of several other assets (the factors). The returns of the target asset and the factors can be observed. What is not observed are the portfolio weights of the factors that best track the target asset. These weights have a time evolution similar to the location of the sailboat per (9.3), except that the equation is now multidimensional inasmuch as one generally has more than one factor. Assume that the target asset returns $r_t^{observed}$ can be described as a weighted average of n-factor returns $r_t^i, i=1,..,n$ with n-factor weights $\beta_t^i, i=1,..,n$ and an error term ε, such that

$$r_t^{observed} = \sum_i \beta_t^i r_t^i + \varepsilon$$
$$\mathbf{x}_t = (\beta_t^1, \beta_t^2, ..., \beta_t^n) \quad . \tag{9.12}$$

The general linear Kalman filter is comprised of two models: a *process model* and a *measurement model*.

Process Model

The underlying factor weight process $\mathbf{x}_t$ (the vector of β_t^i) evolves linearly according to the evolution equation

$$\mathbf{x}_t = \mathbf{A}_t \mathbf{x}_{t-1} + \mathbf{B}_t \mathbf{u}_{t-1} + \mathbf{w}_t \quad , \tag{9.13}$$

where

$\mathbf{A}_t$: *the weight transition model at time t*
$\mathbf{u}_{t-1}$: *a possible control process*
$\mathbf{B}_t$: *the control input model t*
$\mathbf{w}_t$: *the weight process noise assumed to be a Gaussian vector with mean zero and covariance Q, i.e. $N(0, Q)$* . (9.14)

This equation should be compared to (9.3) by setting $\mathbf{A}_t$ to the identity matrix $\mathbf{A}_t = \mathbf{I}$ and $\mathbf{B}_t = 0$. Note that the *weight process noise* term $\mathbf{w}_t$ is a *Gaussian vector* with the same dimensions as the number of factors n along with a covariance matrix $\mathbf{Q}$.

Measurement Model

The weight process is not directly observable but can be mapped to a measurable value $r_t^{observed}$ (the actual return of the target asset) using the vector of factor returns $\mathbf{H}_t$

$$r_t^{observed} = \mathbf{H}_t \mathbf{x}_t + v_t \quad , \tag{9.15}$$

where

$\mathbf{H}_t$: *the factor returns at time t*
v_t : *the measurement process noise assumed to be Gaussian with mean zero and variance R, i.e. $N(0, R)$* (9.16)

The measurement process noise term v_t is one-dimensional, as the target asset return is a number.

Kalman Filter

The exact derivation of the Kalman filter is not given here, but it has a similar flavor to the sailboat example of the preceding section [Maybeck, 1979]. Nonetheless, the setup of the derivation is useful for a qualitative understanding of what the Kalman filter tries to achieve.

Let $\hat{\mathbf{x}}_t^-$ be an a priori estimate of the weight process at time t given knowledge of the process at time $t-1$ and $\hat{\mathbf{x}}_t$ be an *a posteriori* weight estimate at time t given the measurement $r_t^{observed}$. Basically, $\hat{\mathbf{x}}_t^-$ is ones best guess of the replicating factor weights given all the information up to time $t-1$. $\hat{\mathbf{x}}_t$ are the new adjusted factors weights once the value of the target asset return is known at time t, i.e. $r_t^{observed}$. Note that one will never know the actual weight process $\mathbf{x}_t$ because it is a hidden state process. The best one can do is get the best estimate of it—i.e., $\hat{\mathbf{x}}_t$. The Kalman filter shows how to get the best estimate. One can define *a priori* and *a posteriori* error estimates as

$$\epsilon_t^- = \mathbf{x}_t - \hat{\mathbf{x}}_t^-$$
$$\epsilon_t = \mathbf{x}_t - \hat{\mathbf{x}}_t \quad . \tag{9.17}$$

One can also define *a priori* and *a posteriori* error estimate covariances,

$$\mathbf{P}_t^- = E[\epsilon_t^- \epsilon_t^{-T}]$$
$$\mathbf{P}_t = E[\epsilon_t \epsilon_t^T] \quad . \tag{9.18}$$

The *Kalman Filter* $\mathbf{K}_t$ is chosen to minimize $\mathbf{P}_t$ by adjusting the *a priori* estimate of the weight process as follows

$$\mathbf{K}_t = \mathbf{P}_t^- \mathbf{H}_t^T (\mathbf{H}_t \mathbf{P}_t^- \mathbf{H}_t^T + R)^{-1}$$
$$\hat{\mathbf{x}}_t = \hat{\mathbf{x}}_t^- + \mathbf{K}_t \left(r_t^{observed} - \mathbf{H}_t \hat{\mathbf{x}}_t^- \right)$$
$$\mathbf{P}_t = (I - \mathbf{K}_t \mathbf{H}_t) \mathbf{P}_t^- \tag{9.19}$$

where T stands for vector or matrix transpose. The above series of equations should be compared to equation (9.10) in the sailboat example (let $H = 1$). Once again, the Kalman filter $\mathbf{K}_t$ is the multiplier for how much the difference in observed versus predicted $r_t^{observed} - \mathbf{H}_t \hat{\mathbf{x}}_t^-$ affects the optimal estimation $\hat{\mathbf{x}}_t$. It also affects the variance $\mathbf{P}_t$ of the covariance between the optimal estimation $\hat{\mathbf{x}}_t$ and the actual hidden process $\mathbf{x}_t$. The Kalman filter can be seen as the correction to the original a priori prediction. This prediction-correction process is followed as new target asset returns become known.

The steps for a simple Kalman filter replication strategy with $\mathbf{A}_t$ equal to the identity matrix $\mathbf{A}_t = \mathbf{I}$ and $\mathbf{B}_t = 0$ are detailed in the following three sections.

Inputs

One must first identify a set of factors (assets) that will be used to replicate the target asset. Thereafter, one needs to make estimates of the variance R and covariance $\mathbf{Q}$. Because these parameters are held constant, their estimation is critical for the success of the replication. An initial first step is to use a simple multilinear regression model of the asset factors versus the target asset to estimate the diagonal elements of the covariance matrix $\mathbf{Q}$ using the error variances of the linear regression. Further refinements are more empirical than mathematical and are often based on historical backtesting. Finally, one needs an initial set of weights $\hat{\mathbf{x}}_0$.

Time Update with an Initial Prediction

For any time step t, start with the previous time step's results $\hat{\mathbf{x}}_{t-1}$ and $\mathbf{P}_{t-1}$ to predict the a priori time t states:

Make at initial estimate of the weight vector,

$$\hat{\mathbf{x}}_t^- = \hat{\mathbf{x}}_{t-1} \qquad (9.20)$$

Project the error covariance ahead,

$$\mathbf{P}_t^- = \mathbf{P}_{t-1} + \mathbf{Q} \qquad (9.21)$$

Measurement (Observation) Update with Kalman Filter Correction

At time t, one has the actual observed target asset return $r_t^{observed}$ and the time t factor returns $\mathbf{H}_t$. Using these, construct the Kalman filter to correct the initial a priori predictions in the previous step. Construct the Kalman filter weight,

$$\mathbf{K}_t = \mathbf{P}_t^- \mathbf{H}_t^T (\mathbf{H}_t \mathbf{P}_t^- \mathbf{H}_t^T + R)^{-1} \qquad (9.22)$$

CHAPTER 9 ■ HEDGE FUND REPLICATION

Update the predicted estimate with the actual target asset return measurement using the Kalman filter weight on the difference,

$$\hat{\mathbf{x}}_t = \hat{\mathbf{x}}_t^- + \mathbf{K}_t \left(r_t^{observed} - \mathbf{H}_t \hat{\mathbf{x}}_t^- \right) \quad . \tag{9.23}$$

Update the error covariance for the next time step,

$$\mathbf{P}_t = \left(I - \mathbf{K}_t \mathbf{H}_t \right) \mathbf{P}_t^- \quad . \tag{9.24}$$

This predictor-corrector recursive process is illustrated in Figure 9-4.

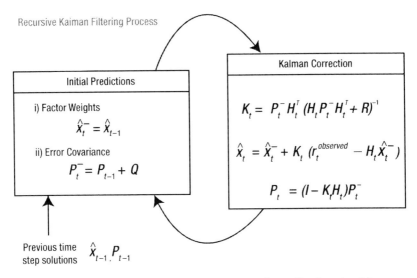

Figure 9-4. The predictor-corrector recursive Kalman filtering algorithm

Figures 9-5 to 9-7 illustrate the application of the linear Kalman filtering to the following three hedge fund strategy indices (from www.hedgefundresearch.com):

- HFRI Equity Hedge Index
- HFRI Quantitative Directional Index
- HFRI Emerging Market Index

Asset Replication: Kalman Filtering

Example: methodology applied to a more concentrated equity long/short portfolio.

Annualized Hypothetical Return Statistics
(January 2003 – February 2011)

Statistics	HFRI Equity Hedge Index	KF Methodology - Equity Hedge Index
Average Tracking Error		-0.38%
Standard Deviation of Tracking Error		3.77%
Monthly Correlation		91.16%
Quarterly Correlation		93.85%
Mean Return	7.81%	7.43%
Volatility	8.67%	9.14%

Component	Market Sector	Bloomberg Ticker
S&P 500 E-mini Index Future	U.S. Equity	ES1 Index
Nasdaq 100 Index Future	Non-financial U.S. Equity	NQ1 Index
Euro Stoxx 50 Index Future	Eurozone Equity	VG1 Index
FTSE 100 Index Future	U.K. Equity	Z 1 Index
Hang Seng Index Future	Hong Kong Equity	HI1 Index
SPI 200 Index Future	Australian Equity	XP1 Index
Nikkei 225 Index Future	Japanese Equity	NX1 Index
S&P/TSE 60 Index Future	Canadian Equity	PT1 Index
USD 3M Eurodollar Future	Short-term Interest Rates	ED1 Comdty
US 2Y Note Future	U.S. Treasury	TU1 Comdty
US 5Y Note Future	U.S. Treasury	FV1 Comdty
US 10Y Note Future	U.S. Treasury	TY1 Comdty
Gold Future	Gold	GC1 Comdty
Oil Future	Oil	CL1 Comdty
Copper Future	Copper	HG2 Comdty
Dollar Index Future	U.S. Dollar	DX1 Curncy
Euro Currency Future	Euro	EC1 Curncy
GBP Currency Future	British Pounds Sterling	BP1 Curncy
JPY Currency Future	Japanese Yen	JY1 Curncy
AUD Currency Future	Australian Dollar	AD1 Curncy
CHF Currency Future	Swiss Franc	SF1 Curncy
CAD Currency Future	Canadian Dollar	CD1 Curncy
Money Market	Risk Free	N/A

Hypothetical Historical Performance

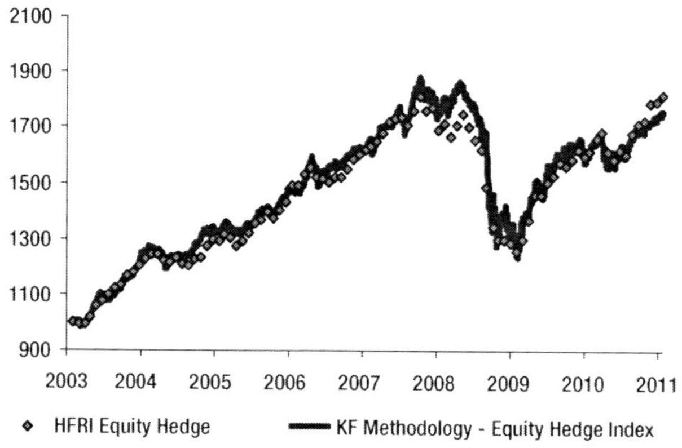

Figure 9-5. Replication of the HFRI Equity Hedge Index

Data Source: Bloomberg

CHAPTER 9 ■ HEDGE FUND REPLICATION

Asset Replication: Kalman Filtering

Example: methodology applied to a more concentrated directional portfolio.

Annualized Hypothetical Return Statistics (January 2003 – February 2011)	HFRI Quantitative Directional Index	KF Methodology - Quantitative Direction Portfolio
Average Tracking Error		0.04%
Standard Deviation of Tracking Error		4.39%
Monthly Correlation		91.81%
Quarterly Correlation		92.15%
Mean Return	10.14%	10.18%
Volatility	10.28%	11.07%

Component	Market Sector	Bloomberg Ticker
S&P 500 E-mini Index Future	U.S. Equity	ES1 Index
Nasdaq 100 Index Future	Non-financial U.S. Equity	NQ1 Index
Euro Stoxx 50 Index Future	Eurozone Equity	VG1 Index
FTSE 100 Index Future	U.K. Equity	Z 1 Index
Hang Seng Index Future	Hong Kong Equity	HI1 Index
SPI 200 Index Future	Australian Equity	XP1 Index
Nikkei 225 Index Future	Japanese Equity	NX1 Index
S&P/TSE 60 Index Future	Canadian Equity	PT1 Index
USD 3M Eurodollar Future	Short-term Interest Rates	ED1 Comdty
US 2Y Note Future	U.S. Treasury	TU1 Comdty
US 5Y Note Future	U.S. Treasury	FV1 Comdty
US 10Y Note Future	U.S. Treasury	TY1 Comdty
Gold Future	Gold	GC1 Comdty
Oil Future	Oil	CL1 Comdty
Copper Future	Copper	HG2 Comdty
Dollar Index Future	U.S. Dollar	DX1 Curncy
Euro Currency Future	Euro	EC1 Curncy
GBP Currency Future	British Pounds Sterling	BP1 Curncy
JPY Currency Future	Japanese Yen	JY1 Curncy
AUD Currency Future	Australian Dollar	AD1 Curncy
CHF Currency Future	Swiss Franc	SF1 Curncy
CAD Currency Future	Canadian Dollar	CD1 Curncy
Money Market	Risk Free	N/A

Hypothetical Historical Performance

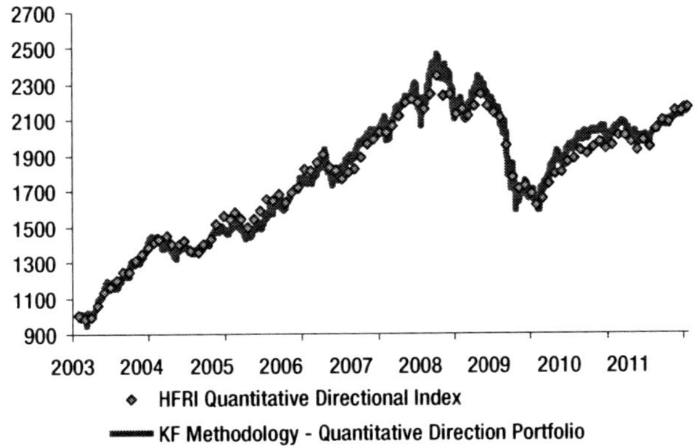

Figure 9-6. Replication of the HFRI Quantitative Directional Index

Data Source: Bloomberg

Asset Replication: Kalman Filtering

Example: methodology applied to a more concentrated emerging markets portfolio.

Annualized Hypothetical Return Statistics (January 2003 – February 2011)	HFRI Emerging Market Index	KF Methodology - EM Portfolio
Average Tracking Error		-0.26%
Standard Deviation of Tracking Error		5.46%
Monthly Correlation		91.74%
Quarterly Correlation		93.60%
Mean Return	14.62%	14.36%
Volatility	12.14%	13.69%

Hypothetical Historical Performance

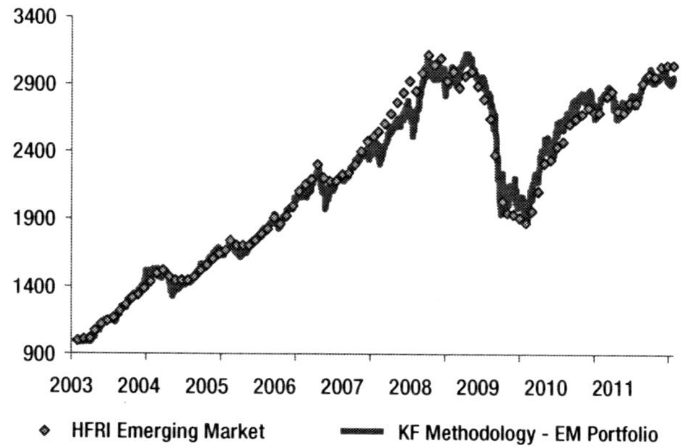

Component	Market Sector	Bloomberg Ticker
S&P 500 E-mini Index Future	U.S. Equity	ES1 Index
Nasdaq 100 Index Future	Non-financial U.S. Equity	NQ1 Index
Hang Seng Index Future	Hong Kong Equity	HI1 Index
Mexican IPC Index Future	Mexican Equity	IS1 Index
Brazil Bovespa Index Future	Brazilian Equity	BZ1 Index
S&P CNX Nifty Index	Indian Equity	NZ1 Index
USD 3M Eurodollar Future	Short-term Interest Rates	ED1 Comdty
US 2Y Note Future	U.S. Treasury	TU1 Comdty
US 5Y Note Future	U.S. Treasury	FV1 Comdty
US 10Y Note Future	U.S. Treasury	TY1 Comdty
Gold Future	Gold	GC1 Comdty
Oil Future	Oil	CL1 Comdty
Copper Future	Copper	HG2 Comdty
Money Market	Risk Free	N/A

◆ HFRI Emerging Market ── KF Methodology - EM Portfolio

Data Source: Bloomberg

Figure 9-7. Replication of the HFRI Emerging Market Index

In these three figures, the replicating index is the solid line of daily NAVs, whereas the monthly quoting HFRI (hedge fund research index) strategy indices are represented as dots. The corresponding underlying factors, along with their Bloomberg tickers, are also shown. The original choice of factors begins with a large pool of diversified assets. The first run of the Kalman filter indicates which assets are important and which ones are superfluous. After a few iterations, the pool of factors is reduced to a meaningful set. For instance, note that the HFRI Emerging Market Index has the fewest factors but clearly has the sensible ones, such as the Brazil Bovespa Index Futures contract and the S&P CNX Nifty Index (Indian equity). The tracking error shown is the root-mean-square of the difference between the monthly replicating portfolio returns and the monthly index returns. It has been calculated annually and has an associated standard deviation. The other statistics such as mean, volatility, and correlation are also based on monthly returns.

References

Jaeger, Lars, *Alternate Beta Strategies and Hedge Fund Replication* (Hoboken, NJ: John Wiley & Sons, 2008).

Kalman, R. E., "A New Approach to Linear Filtering and Prediction Problems," *Journal of Basic Engineering*, 82 (1960), 35–45.

Kat, H., and H. Palaro, *Who Needs Hedge Funds? A Copula-Based Approach to Hedge Fund Return Replication*, Technical Report, Cass Business School, City University, 2005.

Maybeck, P., *Stochastic Models, Estimation, and Control*, vol. 1 (New York: Academic Press, 1979).

Papageorgiou, N., B. Remillard, and A. Hocquard, "Replicating the Properties of Hedge Fund Returns," *Journal of Alternative Investments* (Fall 2008).

Index

A

ABS. *See* Asset-backed securities (ABS)
Adjustable-rate mortgages (ARMs), 14
Alternative beta, 335
Asset-backed securities (ABS), 48
Asset classes
    commodities, 2
    equities, 2
    fixed-income assets, 1
    foreign exchange (FX), 2
    MBS, 1
    products, generic types
        cash instruments, 2–3
        derivatives and structured products, 2
        futures, 2
        swaps, 2
At-the-money (ATM) strike caps/floors, 41
Autocorrelation
    covariance and correlation, 112
    definition, 112
    EEM *vs.* EEM DPA, 125
    in Excel, 113
    returns and squared returns, 114, 125
    theory of joint distributions, 112
    volatility clustering, 113
Auto loan ABS, 48

B

Basel II
    CCR RWA, 295–297
    market disclosure, 294
    market risk RWA, 297
    operational risk RWA.
        See Operational risk
    regulatory capital, 294
    supervisors, 294
Basel III
    capital requirements, 302–304
    CCR RWA, 301–302
    market risk RWA, 300
Basis point (bp), 3
Beta distribution
    defaulted senior secured bonds, 101
    defaulted subordinate bonds, 100
    empirical moments, 99
    moment-matching method, 99
    probability theory, 71
    recovery rates, 98, 100
Binomial distribution, 69
Binomial trees, 188–192
Black-Scholes model
    description, 169
    holes, 186–188
Black's formula
    European call options, 37
    European put options, 38
    market implied volatility
        ATM Strike, 41
        caps and floors, 40
        receiver swaption, 43
Black swan theory, rare events, 76
Bloomberg market data screens
    BTMM. *see* Bloomberg Treasury and Money Markets Monitor (BTMM)
    cash instruments
        commercial paper, 13
        debt instruments, 7
        discount rate, 16
        Dow Jones, 11–12
        equity indices, 10
        Eurodollar deposits, 7
        fed funds, 6
        gold, 16
        LIBOR, 14
        NASDAQ Composite Index, 12–13

349

Bloomberg market data screens (cont.)
    prime rate, 16
    repo and reverse repo, 9–10
    S&P 500, 12
    spot forex, 14–15
    US Treasury bills, notes and bonds, 7
    derivative products, 29
    structured products, 30
    USSW. *see* USSW (US Swap)
Bloomberg Treasury and Money Markets Monitor (BTMM), 3–4
Bootstrapping
    Act/360 daycount basis, 248
    default leg, 248
    first and second quote, 249
    hazard rate formulation, 247
    maturities, 248
    piecewise constant, 247
    premium leg, 248
    survival probabilities, 247
BTMM. *See* Bloomberg Treasury and Money Markets Monitor (BTMM)

C

Capital asset pricing model (CAPM), 334
Cash LIBOR rates, 55
Cash traders, 2
Cauchy-Schwarz Inequality, 129
CCR. *See* Counterparty credit risk (CCR)
Chi-squared fitting, 95
Cliquet contracts, 232–233
Coherent risk measures
    homogeneity/scale invariance, 286
    monotonicity, 286
    subadditivity, 286
    translation invariance, 286
Commercial mortgage-backed securities (CMBS), 47
Commercial paper (CP), 13
Conditional VaR (CVaR), 104
Continuous random variable, 69
Counterparty credit risk (CCR)
    exchange-traded products, 284
    futures exchange, 17
    initial margin, 307
    margin period of risk, 308
    minimum transfer amount, 308
    netting and collateral, 307
    regulatory CVA calculations, 289
    RWA, 292, 295–297
    variation margin, 307
Credit default swap (CDS). *See also* Bootstrapping; Intensity-based reduced-form default models; Par asset swaps; Securitization, CDS
    auction settlement, 241–242
    bank loan portfolio, 266
    Bloomberg functionality, 279
    cash settlement, 240
    CDO^2, 257
    contract maturities, 239
    copulas, 263–264
    coupons, 239
    default swap, 238
    indices and tranches
        CDX and iTraxx indices, 259
        equity markets, 258
        pre-SNAC-style 5YR and 7YR quotes, 260
        SNAC and STEC quotes, 260
        synthetic, 258
    risk, 237
    triangle, 249
    density method, 260–261
    determinations committee, 241
    factor models, 262–263
    financial system, 237
    government entities, 237
    implied compound and base correlations, 270–271
    insurance contract, 238
    portfolio approximation, 264–266
    OHMC methodology
        cash flows, 277
        CDS hedge wealth change equation, 278
        credit spread, 276
        distributions, 274–275
        knockout swaption, 277
        payer swaption, 277
        receiver swaption, 277
        risky bond, 274
        stochastic hazard rates, 275
        swaption wealth change equation, 277
        wealth change variance, 276
    physical settlement, 240
    pricing. *See* Credit default swap (CDS): Pricing, CDS

protection period, 239
quotation conventions, 250–251
restructuring types, 240
run on cash, 237
SNAC, 238–239
standardized credit events, 239
STEC, 238–239
stochastic hazard rates
    continuous coupon payment, 273
    Cox process, 272
    recovery payment, 273
    risky zero coupon discount
        bond, 273
    survival probability, 271
systemic risk and moral hazard, 237
variable method, 261–262
Credit valuation adjustment (CVA)
    accounting, 288
    counterparty Credit Spread 01
        (CS01), 289–290
    expected exposures, 289
    mark-to-market (MtM), 289
    price adjustments, 288
    wrong-way risk, 291
CVaR. *See* Conditional VaR (CVaR)

D

Dealer CP, 13
Deltas, 36
Density approach, 88, 94
Density function
    Excel histogram-creating method
        dynamic data, 82
        static data, 81
    Gaussian densities, 85–86
    Gaussian distribution, high kurtosis, 84
    histogram. *See* Histogram
    mixed Gaussian density function, 86
    normalization of histogram, 82
    solver function, Excel, 95
90D eurodollar futures, 56
Discount rate, 16
Discount Window, 16
Discrete random variable, 69
Distribution function, 68
Distribution moments
    black swan theory, rare events, 76
    expectation operator, 73
    fat-tailed distributions, 76
    Gaussian distribution, 73
    kurtosis, 73, 75, 76
    mean/expected value, 72
    skewness, 73, 75
    standard deviation, 73
    variance, 73
    volatility of returns, 73
Dollar value of a basis point (DV01), 25
Dow Jones Industrial Average (DJIA),
    11, 13–15
Dynamic hedging, 37
Dynamic portfolio allocation (DPA)
    autocorrelation, squared returns, 123
    description, 107
    Emerging Markets Index iShares
        (EEM), 123
    equally weighted portfolio, 116–117
    Markowitz "efficient frontier", 115
    modern portfolio theory, 114
    portfolio variance, 116
    rules, 119
    S&P 500 DPA (SPX DPA), 120
    skewness and kurtosis, 122
    systematic trading strategies, 118
Dynamic portfolio allocation index,
        daily returns
    autocorrelation function, 223
    GARCH(1,1) calibration
        parameters, 222
    option pricing, 223–226

E

Equity hedged
    long short, 335
    market neutral, 335
    short bias, 335
EVT. *See* Extreme value theory (EVT)
Exchange-traded fund (ETF), 333
Extreme value theory (EVT)
    block maxima method, 324–325
    generalized extreme value (GEV)
        distribution, 326
    mathematical techniques, 324
    maximum likelihood calibration,
        GPD, 327
    power-law equivalence, GPD, 328
    threshold exceedance method, 326

INDEX

F

Fannie Mae. *See* Federal National Mortgage Association (FNMA/"Fannie Mae")
Federal Farm Credit Banks (FFCB), 48
Federal funds target rate (FDTR), 6
Federal Home Loan Banks (FHLB), 48
Federal Home Loan Mortgage Corporation (FHLMC/GOLD/"Freddie Mac"), 48
Federal National Mortgage Association (FNMA/"Fannie Mae"), 48
Financial contracts
  Basel I, 292–294
  Basel II, 294–300
  Basel III, 300–304
  CCR aggregation, netting sets and collateral margin, 307–308
  CVA. *See* Credit valuation adjustment (CVA)
  EAD and EPE profiles, 304–306
  OIS discounting, 309–313
  regulation and effects, 287–288
  risk types. *See* Risks
Financial instruments
  American option, 30
  asset classes. *see* Asset classes
  auto loan ABS, 48
  bear put spread, 34
  bear spread calls, 34
  Bloomberg Price Quotes, 49
  Bloomberg screens. *see* Bloomberg Market Data Screens
  bull put spread, 33–34
  bull spread calls, 33
  butterfly put spread, 35–36
  call option, 27, 30
  caps and floors, 39
  characteristics, 30
  combination strategies, 33
  covered (hedged) strategies, 33
  daycount conventions, 6, 49–50
  dynamic hedging and replication, 36
  emerging markets, 1
  futures and swaps, 30
  hedging (replication), 32
  high-yield trading, 1
  implied volatility, 38
  in-the-money (ITM), 31
  investment-grade trading, 1
  nonlinear instruments, 31
  out-of-the-money (OTM), 31
  payoff (or profit) function, 28–29, 31
  positions, 32
  put option, 30–31
  spot instruments, 30
  spread strategies, 33
  straddle, 36
  strike price, 30
  swaption
    ATM strike formula, 44
    payer, 43
    receiver, 43
    swap rate, 43
    VCUB Bloomberg screen, 45–46, 49
  total return index, 10
  VCUB Bloomberg screen, 41–42
Fixed-income assets, 1
Freddie Mac. *See* Federal Home Loan Mortgage Corporation (FHLMC/GOLD or "Freddie Mac")
Frequencies, 79
Futures contract
  characteristics, 18
  crude oil, 18
  90-day eurodollar futures, 20
  fed funds futures, 19
  forward contracts, 18
  futures exchange, 17
  10-year Treasury note futures, 21–22

G

Gamma distribution, 71
GARCH process
  average variance, 170
  Black-Scholes model, 169
  calibration of GARCH (1,1) model, 166–169
  GARCH(1,1) variance, 164–166
  geometric Brownian motion, 164
  instantaneous variance, 170
  leverage effect, 164
  long-term volatility, 170
  preset fixed *vs.* floating volatility, 163
  time-weighted difference, 170
  unconditional variance, 165–166
  Wall Street derivative trader, 163
Generalized Pareto distribution (GPD)
  maximum likelihood calibration, 327
  power-law equivalence, 328–329
Generalized student's-t distribution, 72, 95
Geometric Brownian motion

autocorrelation function, 158
description, 155
Ito's lemma, 193
kurtosis, 158
log-normal process, 156
moments calculation, 156
skewness, 157–158
stationarity condition, Wiener process, 158
substitution, 156
Ginnie Mae. *See* Government National Mortgage Association (GNMA "Ginnie Mae")
Government National Mortgage Association (GNMA "Ginnie Mae"), 48
Government-sponsored enterprises (GSEs), 48
GPD. *See* Generalized Pareto distribution (GPD)

H

Hedge fund index
  daily returns
    autocorrelation function, 216
    GARCH(1,1) calibration parameters, 215
    option pricing, 216–221
  monthly returns
    autocorrelation function, 228
    GARCH(1,1) calibration parameters, 227
    option pricing, 228–232
Hedge fund replication
  alternative beta, 335
  capital asset pricing model (CAPM), 334
  factor-based approach, 337
  hedge fund, 334, 335
  Kalman filtering
    correction, measurement update, 343–344, 348
    HFRI emerging market index, 347
    HFRI equity hedge index, 345
    HFRI quantitative directional index, 346
    inputs, 343
    measurement model, 342
    process model, 341
    time update, initial prediction, 343
  mechanical trading strategies, 336
  net asset value (NAV), 334

risk-free interest rate, 334
sailboat movement, 338–340
tracking error, 333
traditional betas, 335
Hermite cubic basis function, 235
Histogram
  bins, 79
  empirical densities, 83
  Excel histogram
    creating method, 81
    tool inputs, 81
    tool output, 82
  and frequencies, 79
  mixed Gaussian density function, 87
  normalization, 82
  raw, 80

I

Implied volatility, 37
Intensity-based reduced-form default models
  cumulative probability density, 246
  poisson distribution, 246
  probability, 245
  survival probability distribution function, 246
Ito process, 151–153, 163, 188

J

Joint distributions and correlation
  Cauchy-Schwarz inequality, 129
  conditional expectation, 132
  convolution, 133
  and covariance, 129
  density functions, 126, 131
  independence, 128
  marginal function, 127

K

Knockout cliquet, 233, 235

L

Linear basis function, 235
Linear regression, power law, 320, 323
Liquidity risk, 285
Log-normal distribution, 71
London Interbank Offered Rate (LIBOR), 14

353

M

Macro—active trading, 336
Macro—currency trading, 336
Market capitalization weighting methods, 10
Market risk
    commodity price, 283
    correlations, 284
    equity price, 283
    foreign exchange, 284
    interest rate, 283
    prepayment, 283
    RWA, 297, 300-301
    spreads, 284
    volatility, 284
MC simulations. *See* Monte Carlo (MC) simulations
Moment matching, calibrating distribution
    beta distribution to recovery rates, 98
    chi-squared fitting, 95
    fitting by hand, 94
    mixed Gaussian distribution, 92
Monte Carlo (MC) simulations
    description, 159
    discretization method, 162
    financial engineering, 77
    Milstein method, 163
    path, 159-160
    stock returns, 192-193
    SX5E in Excel, 160, 193
    time setting, 159
    VaR and CVaR risk calculation, 161-162
Mortgage-backed securities (MBS)
    ABS, 48
    description, 1
    Fannie Mae and Freddie Mac, 48
    Ginnie Mae, 48
    interest rate risk, 47
    pass-through securities, 47
    prepayment characteristics, 47
    structured products, 47
    US government agency bonds, 48

N

National Association of Securities Dealers Automated Quotations (NASDAQ), 12
NAV. *See* Net asset value (NAV)
Net asset value (NAV), 106
New York Stock Exchange (NYSE), 13
Normal (Gaussian) distribution, 70
Normalized central moments, 73

O

OIS discounting. *See* Overnight index swap (OIS) discounting
One-factor Gaussian model
    binomial, 267
    Black-Scholes, 266
    cashflow expectations, 268
    density function, 270
    hazard rate, 267
    large homogeneous pool assumption, 267
    OTC instrument, 270
    tranche principal, 269
Operational risk
    advanced measurement approach, 300
    basic indicator approach, 299
    business disruption and system failures, 298
    clients, products and business practices, 298
    damage, physical assets, 298
    definition, 294
    employment practices and workplace safety, 298
    events, 284
    execution, delivery and process management, 299
    external and internal fraud, 298
    model validation groups, 284
    standardized approach, 299-300
Optimal hedging Monte Carlo (OHMC) methods
    call and put options, 195
    cliquet contracts, 232-233
    dynamic hedging and replication, 196-199
    dynamic portfolio allocation index, daily returns. *see* Dynamic portfolio allocation index, daily returns
    fund index
        daily returns, 215-221
        monthly returns, 227-229, 231
    Hermite cubic basis function, 235
    investor, 195

knockout cliquet, 233, 235
leverage, 195
linear basis function, 235
marked-to-market value, 195
 and replication, 196–199
 trade derivatives, 195
wealth change equations
 European options, 203–204
 formulation, 200
 forward contracts, 200–203
 maturity and work, 200
 problem and solution, 204–208, 210–213
 risk capital, 214–215
 risk-less bank balance, 199
 self-financing portfolio, 199
 time, t_n and t_{n+1}, 199–200
Ornstein-Uhlenbeck (OU) process, 153–155, 174–175
OU process. *See* Ornstein-Uhlenbeck (OU) process
Overnight index swap (OIS) discounting
 adjusted forward LIBOR rates, 312–313
 collateralization, 310
 curves, 310–311
 floating legs, 310
 floating-rate overnight indices, 309
 risk-free rate, 309
 risk retention, 309
Over-the-counter (OTC) trade, 18

P, Q

Par asset swaps
 cashflow streams, 253
 counterparties exchange, 252
 default probability, 253
 DVO1, 253–254
 fixed rate bond, 252
 LIBOR-discount factors, 253
Pareto distributions, 316–317, 321
Poisson distribution, 70
Poisson-GDP model, 329
Power laws and scaling
 description, 315
 maximum likelihood
  calibration, 322–323
 moments, 318–320
 MC simulation, 321–322
 Pareto distributions, 316
 scale invariance, 317

Price weighting methods, 10
Pricing, CDS
 default leg, 243
 off-par premium leg, 244
 premium leg, 242, 244
 regular interest rate swap, 242
 upfront payment, 244
Probability theory, tools
 σ-Algebra, 66
 beta distribution, 71
 binomial distribution, 69
 continuous random variable, 69
 discrete random variable, 69
 distribution function, 68
 events, 66
 gamma distribution, 71
 generalized student's-t distribution, 72
 log-normal distribution, 71
 normal (Gaussian) distribution, 70
 Poisson distribution, 70
 probability space, 67
 random variables, 67
 sample space, 66
 and set theory, 66

R

Random variables
 description, 67
 Excel functions, 79
 inverse transform method, 77, 87
 MC simulations, 77
Recovery rate, 98
Residential mortgage-backed securities (RMBS), 47
Risk measures
 coherent, 286
 credit, 284
 financial
  credit, 101
  market, 101
  operational, 101
 liquidity, 285
 market, 283
 operational, 284
 probability, extreme losses, 101
 systemic, 285–286
 VaR. *See* Value at risk (VaR)
 wrong-way, 291

355

S

Sample space, 66
Securitization, CDS
  credit risk, CDO structure, 255
  risks, 255
  special-purpose vehicle (SPV), 256
  tranches, 256
Skew normal distribution, 90
Standard & Poor's 500 Index (S&P 500), 12
Standard European Corporate (STEC)
  CDX and iTraxx, 260
  and SNAC, 238
  upfront payment, 260
Standard North American Corporate (SNAC)
  CDX and iTraxx, 260
  and STEC, 238
  upfront payment, 242
State Street Global Advisors (SSgA), 333
Stochastic integrals
  covariance, 149
  description, 148
  Ito's lemma, 149-151
  mean, 148
  quadratic variation, 148
  regular calculus, 148
  Riemann integral, 148
  variance, 148
  Wiener process. *see* Wiener process
Stochastic processes
  calculus
    continuous, 144
    distribution function, 144
    integrals. *see* Stochastic integrals
    parameter, 144
    quadratic variation, 147
    stationary, 145
    Wiener process, 145-147
  description, 143
  distributions, 143
  diversification component, 180
  drift, 178-179
  ETF factor-neutral calibration and trading strategy, 175-178
  filters, 183-185
  GARCH. *see* GARCH process
  geometric Brownian motion. *see* Geometric Brownian motion
  market-neutral portfolios, 179
  MCD *vs.* XLY, 194

MC simulations. *see* Monte Carlo (MC) simulations
pairs trading, 194
statistical arbitrage trading strategy pitch, 180-183
statistical modeling
  automated execution system, 172
  backtesting and risk assessment, 171
  data sets, 171
  equilibrium statistics, 175
  mean reverting OU process, 174-175
  methodology/algorithm, 171
  pairs trading, 172-173, 194
  systematic, 170
Swaps
  description, 2
  fixed swap rate payments (fixed leg), 23
  futures
    description, 27
    5-years, 27
    10-years, 28-29
  LIBOR floating rate payments (floating leg), 23
  spreads, 26
  types, 23
  valuation
    discount factors, LIBOR, 25
    LIBOR floating rate, 26
    present value (PV), future cash flows, 24
    zero coupon bond, 24
  vanilla interest rate swap, 19-21, 23-24
Systemic risk, 285

T

Term structure, statistics
  "down" volatility, 110
  kurtosis, 108
  mean, 106
  net asset value (NAV), 106
  skew, 107
  "Up" volatility, 110
  volatility, 110
Tracking error, 333
Traditional betas, 335

U

USSW (US Swap), 3, 5-9

V

Value at risk (VaR)
  and CVaR, estimation, 104, 329–330
  description, 101
  function of returns, 102
  identical VaR(80), 103
  number, 102
  sorted returns, 105
VaR. *See* Value at risk (VaR)
Variance-gamma model, 71
Volatility clustering, 112–113

W, X

Wiener process
  Ito's lemma, 152
  log normal process, 152–153
  OU process, 153–155
  stochastic calculus, 145
  trivial autocorrelation function, 146

Y, Z

Yield curve
  bootstrapping method, 54
  cash LIBOR rates, 55
  constraints, 53
  construction, 54
  90D eurodollar futures, 56
  generic discount factors, 60
  swaps, 58
  uses, 53

Get the eBook for only $10!

> Now you can take the weightless companion with you anywhere, anytime. Your purchase of this book entitles you to 3 electronic versions for only $10.

This Apress title will prove so indispensible that you'll want to carry it with you everywhere, which is why we are offering the eBook in 3 formats for only $10 if you have already purchased the print book.

Convenient and fully searchable, the PDF version enables you to easily find and copy code—or perform examples by quickly toggling between instructions and applications. The MOBI format is ideal for your Kindle, while the ePUB can be utilized on a variety of mobile devices.

Go to www.apress.com/promo/tendollars to purchase your companion eBook.

All Apress eBooks are subject to copyright. All rights are reserved by the Publisher, whether the whole or part of the material is concerned, specifically the rights of translation, reprinting, reuse of illustrations, recitation, broadcasting, reproduction on microfilms or in any other physical way, and transmission or information storage and retrieval, electronic adaptation, computer software, or by similar or dissimilar methodology now known or hereafter developed. Exempted from this legal reservation are brief excerpts in connection with reviews or scholarly analysis or material supplied specifically for the purpose of being entered and executed on a computer system, for exclusive use by the purchaser of the work. Duplication of this publication or parts thereof is permitted only under the provisions of the Copyright Law of the Publisher's location, in its current version, and permission for use must always be obtained from Springer. Permissions for use may be obtained through RightsLink at the Copyright Clearance Center. Violations are liable to prosecution under the respective Copyright Law.

Lightning Source UK Ltd.
Milton Keynes UK
UKOW02f0840100916

282677UK00001B/4/P